Broadcasting
in the Arab World

International and Comparative Broadcasting
A Series Edited by Sydney W. Head

Broadcasting in the Arab World

A Survey of Radio and
Television in the Middle East

Douglas A. Boyd

Temple University Press
Philadelphia

Temple University Press, Philadelphia 19122

Published 1982
Printed in the United States of America

Research for this project was made possible by a grant from the Ford Foundation.

Library of Congress Cataloging in Publication Data

Boyd, Douglas A.
    Broadcasting in the Arab world.

    (International and comparative broadcasting)
    Bibliography: p.
    Includes index.
    1. Broadcasting—Arab countries. I. Title. II. Series.
PN1990.6.A65B69   384.54′0917′4927   81-23309
ISBN 0-87722-237-1   AACR2

To Carole, George, J. Y. B., and the Arab people

Contents

Part 4. Conclusion

Preface

In a study of this magnitude, one must depend on both official and unofficial contacts to provide information and to give access to facilities and documents. However, radio and television systems in the Arab world are operated directly by the government or indirectly through a government-sanctioned broadcasting organization. In some cases respondents provided information "off the record" because their jobs might be jeopardized by having their names associated with this study. Where possible, I provide references, and it is only in those cases where attribution is missing that I protected the source. I take complete responsibility for all of the information in the publication with the exception of the chapters on the Maghreb—the North African countries of Algeria (Michael Pilsworth), Libya (Drew McDaniel), Morocco (Claude-Jean Bertrand), and Tunisia (Donald Browne).

A large measure of thanks goes to my students of the second-year English class at the University of Riyadh, College of Engineering. It was in November 1963 that I learned from this class that Arab radio broadcasting was a great deal different from the American commercial system in which I had worked for several years. The Egyptian "Voice of the Arabs" was popular during this period and various programs on the Egyptian station were very popular with the Saudi Arabian students. It became obvious to me that what was broadcast was taken as the "truth." During our conversational English exercises, the students expressed some interesting views about the assassination of President Kennedy—as a result of their radio experiences. It was these Saudi students who first inspired me to study Arab broadcasting. Several of the students had been to Cairo and had seen Egyptian television—a medium they were fascinated with because it seemed at the time to be the ultimate symbol of modernization. During that Saudi academic year, the government announced the kingdom had decided to construct a television system, one with which I was later to work.

Thanks go to the Saudi Arabian government, which has been receptive to my research efforts over the years. Dr. Abdulrahman Shobaili, former Director General of Television and presently Deputy Minister of Higher Education, has provided encouragement since he first expedited the granting of permission for a three-month research trip to the kingdom in the spring of 1972. Professor and Mrs. John Y. Benzies have given continued support and helped make my 1972 stay in Saudi Arabia possible.

Without a grant from the Ford Foundation, this work would not have been possible. David Davis, formerly Officer-in-Charge, Office of Communication, and Chuck Robarts, Deputy Regional Representative for the Middle East and North Africa, were kind enough to approve funding. Ford offices in New York and Cairo were helpful with travel arrangements and visas. Additional thanks go to: Mr. Ali Shummo, the Sudan; Salamah Abdul-Kadi, Jordan; Jawad Zada, Jordan; Professor Nabil Dajani, Lebanon; Mr. George Vasilliou, Cyprus; Terry Timmons, Saudi Arabia; Peter Hillger, United Arab Emirates; Anthony Ashworth, Oman; Adly, Mona and Salim Bseiso, Kuwait; Shakib Al-Janabi, First Secretary, Embassy of India, Iraqi Interest Section, Washington, D.C.; Hamdy Kandil, UNESCO-Paris; and J. P. Regnier, Radio Monte Carlo Middle East. The United States International Communication Agency and the Foreign Broadcast Information Service provided various research reports and literature. Finally, thanks go to the British Broadcasting Corporation Monitoring Service and Written Archives in Caversham Park, England, and to Peter Herrmann of the BBC External Broadcasting Research Department, London.

Sydney W. Head, the editor of the Temple University Press International and Comparative Broadcasting series, spent long hours on the initial draft of this manuscript.

Professor John Benzies and Carole Boyd read every word of the manuscript. Their comments and suggestions were invaluable. Mrs. Myrna Hofmann placed all material on a word-processing system and graciously undertook the frequent corrections and changes that were made.

Special thanks go to Carole, Kathie, and John Boyd, who understood the necessity of the lengthy trips to the Middle East and who cooperated during intense periods of writing.

Transliteration. Arabic terms and names have been transliterated in a standardized form throughout this publication. In most instances, the spelling is that preferred by the person or country involved. For example, I took the spelling for a country's major cities and landmarks from official maps rather than from a more scientific transliteration from Arabic used by arabists. The former president of Egypt, Gamal Abdel Nasser, apparently preferred the spelling *Abdel.* However, in a book he wrote and published in the United States, the spelling appears as Abdul. In this manuscript, both spellings are used. For the reader who wishes a more interesting and knowledgeable comment on this subject, I suggest the preface to the Penguin Modern Classics edition of T. E. Lawrence's *Seven Pillars of Wisdom*: in reply to an editor's question as to whether Jedda and Jidda (Saudi Arabia) were spelled with deliberate inconsistency throughout the manuscript, Lawrence replied "Rather!"

Part 1   Introduction

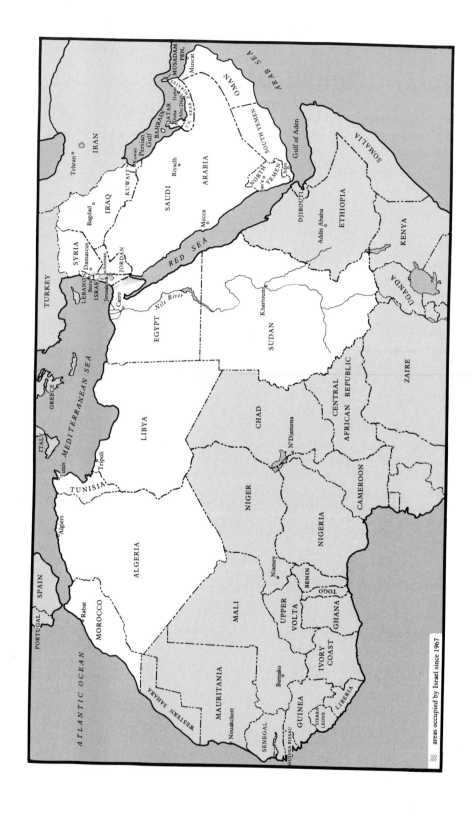

areas occupied by Israel since 1967

1   Arab World Broadcasting: Developments, Trends, Constraints

This study attempts to cover the subject of radio and television broadcasting in the Middle East, specifically the Arab world. The term Middle East is subject to varying geographical interpretation by both scholars and those who have a general idea about the area from newspapers, magazines, and broadcast media news reports. The term Middle East appears to be British in origin (Koppes 1976, pp. 95–98) and describes an area over which the British had considerable influence. For the purposes of this undertaking the term Arab world is more appropriate because it provides some linguistic and ethnic boundaries and excludes such countries as Turkey, Iran, Israel, and Cyprus, which are often classified geographically as part of the Middle East. The study does include countries that are members of the Arab League—an association of Arab countries formed after World War II—with the exception of two countries, Somalia and Mauritania, which, while Islamic states, are not historically part of the Arab world. The countries discussed herein include Egypt, the Sudan, Lebanon, Syria, Jordan, North Yemen, South Yemen, Iraq, Kuwait, Saudi Arabia, Bahrain, Qatar, the United Arab Emirates, Oman, Algeria, Libya, Morocco, and Tunisia. The chapters that follow will discuss these countries as broadcasters, international broadcasting to and within the Arab countries, broadcasting cooperation among Arab countries, and problems of broadcasting in the Arab world. Egypt and Saudi Arabia are covered in more detail than other countries. Egypt is an Arab world leader in the development of broadcasting and has influenced radio and television development in the region. Saudi Arabia is a wealthy and politically important country that has introduced broadcasting with great caution because of the conservative nature of its Islamic culture.

Historical, religious, geographical, climatic, political, economic, and linguistic factors in this region make its broadcast media unique: each will be noted in the subsequent chapters as it impinges on the development of the electronic media. Before each country is discussed in detail, however, several general observations may be helpful.

Radio receivers are abundant in the Arab countries. Even when radio was a young medium there was a strong desire among Arabs to acquire sets. During the late 1950s, the availability of relatively inexpensive transistor sets enabled lower-income people to purchase receivers. The sets, which could be operated on batteries, became popular in villages where electricity had not yet been provided. The "transistor revolution" coincided with political movements in areas such as North Africa, Egypt, and Iraq that overthrew ruling royal families or were successful in gaining independence from colonial powers. The new leaders, such as Gamal Abdel Nasser of Egypt, were interested in rapid social and economic change and saw radio broadcasting as a means of bypassing the print media, which were generally responsive to the literate elite who could both afford publications and read them.

In the Arab countries, a clear distinction between domestic and international radio broadcasting is difficult to make. Back in the 1950s, some Arab countries started building relatively powerful medium-wave (standard AM) transmitters in order to reach as far as possible. The medium-wave band at that time was not as cluttered with high-powered signals as it is today, and these domestically-intended programs could be received in neighboring countries. Even now residents of Khartoum (the Sudan) and Riyadh (Saudi Arabia) can listen regularly to the domestic service of Radio Cairo. The service can be heard with particular clarity at night and in the past was often the only service available, as the countries in which listeners resided did not have a reliable national radio service that was capable of reaching all of the country. The Arab culture is traditionally an oral culture. With few competing forms of information and entertainment, radio listening was, and in some places still is, a major pastime.

Those countries that were slow to develop radio services—Kuwait, Saudi Arabia, Qatar, and the United Arab Emirates—were most vulnerable to radio propaganda from countries such as Syria, Iraq, and Egypt, which had political interests in deposing their ruling families. During the 1960s and, of course, the 1970s, these countries rapidly developed radio broadcasting facilities because they recognized the need for reliable communication with the indigenous population as well as with the Arab expatriates who came to work among them. The oil-rich countries could afford modern high-powered transmitters and impressive radio production studios. When the price of oil quadrupled after the 1973 Middle East War, the petroleum-exporting countries found themselves in potentially influential positions internationally and within the Arab world, and radio broadcasting became increasingly important to governments that attempted to disseminate a specific point of view. Increasingly since that time, then, governments and news-gathering organizations have monitored Middle East radio broadcasts to note both dramatic and subtle shifts in political policy, or to follow developments inside countries not easily covered by foreign journalists, such as the course of the Mosque takeover in Mecca, Saudi Arabia, in November 1979.

The large number of high-power medium-wave transmitters constructed during the 1970s throughout the Arab world has had an adverse effect on reception: the medium-wave band is now extremely congested and reception has deteriorated because of the high level of background noise. But though Arab radio engineers often describe the medium-wave band in the Middle East as a "jungle," generally favorable conditions for reception on both mediumwave and shortwave still exist, and international broadcasts— those from outside of but intended for the Arab world—are numerous. Arabic is now second only to English as an international broadcasting language, forty-six international broadcasting organizations providing Arabic-language programming to the Arab world, many of them broadcasting on mediumwave. Thus people in the Arab world can receive fairly reliably, even on inexpensive transistor radios, programs from the Voice of America, the British Broadcasting Corporation, Deutsche Welle (Germany), and Radio Monte Carlo Middle East (France). Surveys indicate that these and other services are avidly listened to in the Arab world by followers of Arab and international events. One explanation for the general receptivity to such non-Arab international radio broadcasts is the general organizational framework of Arab radio and television: each country included in this study has a broadcasting system that is either directly operated by the government or is run by an organization that is funded and directly influenced by a government agency, generally a ministry of information.[1] Listeners understand that the government has its priorities and its points of view, and those who listen to non-Arab international broadcasts appear to be listening in order to gain another opinion about a local or international event. Listening during times of crisis is an almost standard procedure in the Middle East, particularly among the elite.

The term international broadcasting—or broadcasting across national boundaries—is usually associated with the radio medium. This is due, in part, to the technical limitations of television, a medium that is generally limited to line-of-sight reception: with the exception of FM signals, radio transmissions travel much farther, and short-wave signals can be received very far from the location of the transmitter and antenna. But frequently, in the Arab world, television from one country is viewed in other countries. Cairo television may be seen during the warm summer months in Israel, Lebanon, and even Syria. International television viewing is pervasive in the

---

[1]Several years ago the Arab ministers of information met and decided to standardize the name of their ministries. Prior to this action many were named ministries of national guidance, which, at least in English, had a harsh ring to it.

Arabian Gulf states, where the warm, humid weather during the long summer helps transmission conditions. Indeed, in some areas of the Gulf it is possible to receive as many as nine television signals. Furthermore, some countries have intentionally built transmitters to reach neighboring countries. When Kuwait television was being regularly received in Saudi Arabia's Eastern Province in the late 1960s, Saudi Arabia constructed a powerful station in Dammam with the hope of reaching Kuwait. The station did not perform to expectations but was converted in the mid-1970s to the German Phase Alternate Line (PAL) color system, so that Bahrain and the United Arab Emirates could receive color programming on their own standard. Saudi Arabia constructed a lower-power UHF transmitter to broadcast to its citizens on its own chosen color standard—the French Sequential Color and Memory (SECAM) system.

Television service is a reality in all Arab countries—rich and poor alike, for even the poorer countries such as Egypt, the Sudan, and Syria realize that television can be an important political and developmental tool. Television equipment is expensive and must be paid for with hard currency.[2] Each time that a poor country makes the decision to increase transmission power or to buy a new camera or video tape recorder, money is being diverted from other developmental projects. In the large, less affluent countries such as Oman and the Sudan, where it is necessary to utilize satellite ground stations and leased satellite transponders for internal distribution of television, the expense is often painful; but it is apparently seen by political leaders as necessary. In the more affluent Arab countries in North Africa and the Arabian Gulf, television facilities are modern and extensive: television in the Gulf started slowly in the late 1960s but expanded rapidly in the 1970s.

In the Gulf States, as in other parts of the Arab World, large sums of money are necessary for expensive radio and television broadcasting equipment. However, the Gulf States have the additional expense of importing personnel for operation and maintenance. These countries have a relatively small native-born population, and with numerous business and civil service opportunities available to able citizens, there are not enough people to undertake all the development schemes desirable. The result, for the broadcast media in the Gulf, is that most of the people who work at the stations are Arabs from other countries—often Egypt, Jordan, or Lebanon. In a few countries in the Gulf, nonindigenous Arabs even hold important management positions.

In many Arab countries a radio is a status symbol: the larger and more intricate the set, the higher the status. Expensive all-wave radios (shortwave and FM in addition to the standard broadcast band), with built-in cassette capability, are so popular as to have generated a whole new industry in many

[2]Hard currencies are those that are internationally recognized and traded. Arab currencies such as the Egyptian and Sudanese pound are basically worthless outside of those countries.

Arab countries—the pirate duplication of both western and Middle Eastern music tapes. But because of the availability in Arab countries of low-cost transistor radios from Japan, South Korea, Taiwan, and the People's Republic of China, and because of the low or nonexistent import tax on these radios, people lower on the income scale can also afford to purchase or to have access to a set.

New technologies and better economic conditions have, then, changed listening patterns since Brunner noted in 1953 that a substantial amount of Arab radio listening was done by groups of people—mostly men—in village coffee houses (1953, p. 149). Even so, it is not unusual for people to listen to radio and view television in groups in commercial establishments or in private residences. The explanation for this is, in part, the Arab concept of friendliness and hospitality: when a person is in public, perhaps listening to music or news on a radio in the street, there is an implied invitation for others to join him.

Through individually owned sets or sets within families or clubs or in public places, the availability of television programs in Arab countries is probably much higher than readers not familiar with the Middle East may suspect—though again a distinction must be drawn between the affluent and the poor countries. In the Gulf states of Kuwait, Saudi Arabia, Qatar, and the United Arab Emirates, set ownership is very high for the native-born population. People can quite easily afford imported, mostly Japanese, color sets. In countries such as Syria, Egypt, and the Sudan, it is policy to make televison sets available to as many people as possible. There is very strong motivation among the poor to acquire a television receiver: in Egypt it is not unusual for a television set to be purchased by village leaders before electricity reaches their area. In a poor section of Cairo, an extended family may pool resources to purchase a used black-and-white set from a neighborhood dealer. In that crowded, polluted city it is often necessary and cheaper to be entertained in the home; and parents moreover believe that television is a way in which their children's education, and possibly their view of the world, can be broadened.

In the Arabian Gulf states, television has relatively little competition. Few cinemas and nightclubs exist and, of those, fewer appeal to the home- and family-centered Arab culture. A new and interesting form of television is therefore becoming pervasive there: the Arabian Gulf, specifically Kuwait and Saudi Arabia, may be the largest video cassette market in the world. Tape libraries for the U-Matic as well as VHS and Beta format machines are thriving and the underground market for pirated American and British television programs is now a major business.

To a great extent programming is basically entertainment-oriented on Arab television stations and it is not unfair to say that both radio and television in the Arab world are believed by consumers to be primarily for entertainment. The director of Egyptian television observed during a May

1980 meeting that "a television set is usually bought with the intention of entertainment. Nobody thinks of television as a means of education when they go to buy a television set." (Tawffik 1980a). However, this does not mean that educational programs do not exist. And in some Arab countries a good deal of programming time is concerned with political information—though in general such nonentertainment programming, including news and commentary, merely extols the accomplishments of the political leaders.

Imported entertainment programs from Europe and the United States are used to some extent on all Arab televison systems. The percentage of imported western programs is higher in the Gulf states, where there is a limited artistic tradition and where, during the initial stages of television's development, the emphasis was put on construction of physical facilities rather than on programming. Western programming appears to be quite in keeping with the beliefs of the systems' administrators, whose respective countries look to the west for political support and economic ties; and the elite, who have had the funds to travel to the west, rather expect that western programs will be provided as a matter of course. In states such as Kuwait and Dubai that have two channels, one channel is devoted exclusively, or nearly so, to non-Arab programming. The trend toward permissiveness in western television programs has served, however, to narrow the choice of those available to Arab countries, as programs have to be edited for excessive sex, violence, and, in the case of Saudi Arabia, references to Christianity.

Television stations in the Arab Middle East have always telecast classic Egyptian cinema productions as a main category of Arabic-language programming, but it was not until after the 1967 Middle East War and the termination of the conflict in Yemen that they started importing new Egyptian films and video tapes. By the mid-1970s such productions were an important source of hard currency for the Egyptian Radio-Televison Federation, but their high prices and the move of President Sadat toward the eventual signing of a treaty with Israel caused some states to reduce or altogether to stop Egyptian program purchases. At the same time, the Egyptian political and economic situation caused a new production system to appear: artists preferred to work outside the country to gain more money through payment in hard currency and to avoid some Egyptian personal income tax. Their new productions were essentially Egyptian written, produced, directed, and acted, but were taped in London, Athens, Amman, Bahrain, or Dubai: relatively high-quality Arabic-language programs have proliferated. Many are contemporary in that they deal with the problems of families attempting to cope with the clash of generations. Some are historical in nature and deal with traditional Islamic themes: these latter are particularly appropriate for sale to the Gulf states, which have attempted to make television somewhat more Islamic since events such as the Soviet invasion of Afghanistan, the Mecca Mosque occupation, and the Iranian Revolution.

Television in the Arab Middle East has a predominantly western style: television is itself, after all, a western invention that has been molded by western film and artistic traditions. Creativity in the television medium is moreover tied to electronic requirements and technological innovations: with each new innovation—zoom lens, special effects generator, video tape, chroma key, video tape editing—comes a new creative use for it. Virtually all television stations in the Arab world were purchased from and installed by West European and American equipment manufacturers: usually the installation agreement called for production training of the buyers by western experts, or for their training in the country where the equipment was manufactured. Furthermore, various programs sponsored by both western and Middle Eastern governments as well as by private foundations, have taken experts to the Arab countries to advise, or sent Middle-East nationals to the United States, Great Britain, France, or West Germany to train in television production. The natural result of all this is a western-type television program in Arabic. There is very little that is uniquely Arab in Arab world television.

Three additional aspects of Arab broadcast media need attention. They are related but separate problems. First, almost no serious research has been done in the Arab world on radio and television. The systems in Lebanon and Jordan undertake a continuous marketing study of listeners so that they will have information on which to base commercial rates; some social science research has moreover been done to determine media use in villages. But almost no "effects" research has been done even by those systems, and they have not worked in cooperation with university investigators. The research void is caused by a lack of funds for an activity that is not believed to be a priority, a general misunderstanding of research methodology, and a lack of qualified personnel to undertake and interpret research results. Although not unique to the Arab world, this situation points to a second concern related to Arab broadcasting, a lack of mechanisms or structures for citizen input to the system. This does not mean that phone calls and letters from listeners and viewers are ignored: little effort, however, is made to solicit citizen comment about radio and television programming on a regular basis. Many media managers believe that by themselves they have the ability and knowledge to provide a well-rounded broadcast schedule that includes news, entertainment, and educational programming: for them, the statement by former French broadcast official Arthur Conte— "I am the public"—applies (Thomas 1972, p. 150). There is also an occasional fear voiced that citizen feedback would not be positive, and officials are not sure how to react to negative comments.

Finally, while there are exceptions in the Arab Middle East, broadcast officials do not seem to have a philosophy or goals for radio and television that are tied to the goals of the country and the appropriate central planning organization. This is particularly true with respect to programming policy for both news and entertainment. There is a surprising lack of communication and cooperation between ministries of information and education, for example; and in countries such as the Sudan, where the Ministry of Information is responsible for radio programming and the Ministry of Communication is responsible for studio and transmitter-equipment maintenance and operation, the inevitable interagency conflicts have not worked to the advantage of the consumer.

The preceding overview of broadcasting in the Arab world is not intended to be comprehensive, but rather is provided as a start toward the discussion of individual systems of radio and television in a part of the world that increasingly dominates the political and economic concerns of many nations.

Part 2 National Systems

mod. = 1805 Mohammed Ali ruler + descendants
1952 = revolution, military coup
           Negaib, Nasser (died 70) Anwar Sadat V-P

Nasser

2   Egypt, the Sudan, Lebanon, Syria, Jordan, North Yemen, South Yemen

2.1   Egypt

The Arab Republic of Egypt is located in the northeastern corner of the African continent. An estimated 41 million people live within the country's 386,611 square miles. The majority of the population resides in the Nile Delta, in the Nile Valley, and along the Suez Canal—a relatively small arable area on which the country depends, for it still has essentially an agricultural economy. Migration from rural areas to cities has contributed to Cairo's traffic, pollution, and housing problems.

Egypt has a rich and recently well publicized history. The country's modern historical period dates from 1805, when Mohammed Ali became ruler with Ottoman blessings. Descendants of Ali ruled the country until the revolution of 23 July 1952, which resulted in a military coup that exiled King Farouk and brought to power first Mohammed Neguib and then, very soon, Gamel Abdel Nasser, Egypt's president until his death in 1970. Anwar Sadat, another of the officers involved in the revolution, was vice president when Nasser died and succeeded him and Neguib as president. All three presidents have influenced the electronic media.

It is important to understand the development of radio and television in Egypt before broadcasting in other countries is discussed. Under Nasser's leadership, the country was the first to construct high-powered medium-wave and short-wave transmitters to reach the indigenous population as well as to carry the Nasserite Pan-Arab message to the remainder of the Arab world. Nasser started a foreign-language service that rivaled those of the major international broadcasters. Broadcast facilities were provided from which various African and Middle Eastern revolutionary groups might broadcast to their own countries. When Egypt started a television service, the country was able to undertake a massive artistic effort, its well-developed film industry and tradition of live theater providing what almost all other countries in the Arab world lacked—performers as well as personnel to operate the complicated equipment and to produce programs. Even after the March 1979 Egyptian-Israeli peace treaty, which resulted in agreements by Arab ministers of information to boycott Egyptian media, Egyptian films, video tapes, and artists still, ironically, dominated Arab television.

2.1.1 Radio

Radio broadcasting in Egypt began haphazardly in the 1920s, thereby following the pattern of some European countries as well as that of the United States. Reportedly, over one hundred amateur wireless stations were operating during this period, mostly in the Cairo area (UNESCO 1949, p. 217). Nor were all stations operated by amateurs; merchants ran stations that disseminated commercial messages between songs (Metwally n.d., p. 1), utilizing a format not unlike that of popular commercial stations in other parts of the world. But by 1930 most of these stations had closed because of decreased interest on the part of the operators: stations that operated as businesses had found that too few radio sets existed at the time and that economic conditions in Egypt were not conducive to commercial radio. Recent Egyptian perceptions of the early stations are interesting and have tended to vary with the political climate in the country. In the late 1960s, the pre-1931 stations were said to have had "no national objectives for the public interest. . . . [A]ll they were interested in was material gains" (*Arab Broadcasts* 1970a, p. 63). However, by the late 1970s they were seen as unacceptable because "competition . . . increased and this led to higher advertisement costs, together with a lot of inconvenience" (Metwally n.d., p. 1).

One of the obvious problems that the Egyptians faced was how to organize the regulation of the new medium. The British were quite influential in the administration of the country at the time, but they appear to have been powerless to bring radio under any kind of formal government regulatory structure—or uninterested in doing so. A United States Department of Commerce report of 1930 describes the government's attitude:"[T]he identity of [the two Cairo stations] is known to the public, but officials are careful to avoid 'learning officially' of them since any cognizance would probably necessitate closing the station" (Batson 1930, p. 103). In 1931 the government indeed decreed that all stations be closed, thereby leaving Egypt without a radio service for a time. But radio broadcasting was rapidly developing throughout the world, and sets were becoming more common in the large cities such as Cairo among upper-class families and among the large expatriate community of Britons, Greeks, and Italians. The government, no doubt influenced by British residents and by the British Broadcasting Corporation example, determined that radio broadcasting would be a government-sanctioned activity. A memorandum to this effect was sent to the Council of Ministers by the Ministry of Communications on 15 July 1932.

One week later the Ministry of Communications memorandum was adopted and a ten-year renewable contract was signed with the Marconi Company of the United Kingdom to provide a noncommercial broadcast service for Egypt. The system was financed by a license fee on receivers, 60% of which was paid to Marconi to operate the station and 40% of which was for the government to utilize in connection with actual construction and costs associated with the operation of transmitters (Metwally n.d., p. 1). The official opening date of the Marconi-operated Egyptian radio service was 31 May 1934 (*Arab Broadcasts* 1970a, p. 63).

This service proved to be a professionally operated and popular undertaking. The sale of radio sets and therefore income for both Marconi and the government steadily increased. By late 1939, the number of receivers in Egypt was estimated to be 86,477 at a yearly license fee of about four dollars each (*Arab Broadcasts* 1971, p. 63). While radio ownership was clearly beyond the means of the average Egyptian, radio receivers were acquired by enterprising merchants who understood that a receiver would be a popular attraction at a restaurant or coffee house, which in the Arab world is still a main gathering place for males in late afternoon and evening hours. It is the custom for people to gather, visit, consume coffee, tea, or cold beverages, and gossip and discuss the prevailing political climate. Radio ownership became common in the the the 1960s and 1970s. When television was introduced in Egypt and other Arab countries, merchants and coffee house owners tended to replace radios with television sets.

During the formative years of Egyptian radio, the service attracted many talented announcers, actors, musicians, and journalists from the established theater, film, music, and print media sectors of Cairo. Several of these early employees, most of whom worked at first on a free-lance basis, became influential in future Egyptian broadcasting and information undertakings; many of the more talented have since worked for systems in other Arab countries. The BBC used Egyptian announcers when it started its London-based Arabic service in January 1938.[1]

The physical facilities, if not the entire tone of Egyptian broadcasts under the Marconi contract, were unmistakably British. *Wireless World* described the first studio:

Egyptian broadcasting has gone "all British" in the matter of its new studio in Cairo, the architectural design of which follows the Tudor style. The studio is approached through a small soundproof lobby illuminated by an old English lantern. The specially treated walls of the studio are paneled and at one end is an old English fireplace on which stand three electric candles showing red, green, or white, as desired, for signaling from the control room. [1935, p. 15]

---

[1]For additional information see Part 3.

The Marconi contract was renewed in 1943 with a stipulated expiration date of 31 January 1949. One important provision of the new government-Marconi contract called for more direct Egyptian participation in the management of broadcasting. The new contract even mandated the percentage of Egyptian salaried and hourly paid employees (*Arab Broadcasts* 1970a, p. 63). However, the second contract did not last until 1949; and on 4 March 1947 the government cancelled the Marconi contract and the radio service became Egyptian owned and operated (*Arab Broadcasts* 1971, p. 63). "National considerations" are generally given as the motivation to terminate the contract, but a more specific explanantion was the increasing Egyptian resistance to British policy, particulary in something as sensitive as radio broadcasting, and the general weakness of British influence in the Arab world following World War II.

2.1.2 Government Broadcast Administration

The history of Egypt's government regulation or control of broadcasting is no different from that seen in other developing and some developed countries. One of the main difficulties these governments faced was deciding in whose care they would place the new medium—a problem that they did not completely understand and one whose resolution for political or developmental purposes they could not settle. The Ministry of Communication was responsible for radio until 19 August 1939, when it was moved to the Ministry of Social Affairs; on 18 April 1942, it was placed under the Ministry of Interior, where it remained until the end of World War II. After the termination of the second Marconi contract, and until the 1952 revolution, the broadcast service was moved at various times between Social Affairs and Interior. After the revolution, it was administered by the military officers in control, until a ministry of information was established. Even since the Ministry of Information was started and broadcasting has been given some autonomy by the formation of the Egyptian Radio-Televison Federation, ultimate control over the electronic media has alternated—depending on political circumstances—between the Information Ministry and the Office of the President.

2.1.3 Prerevolutionary Broadcasting—Egyptianization

Between the end of the second Marconi contract and the 1952 revolution, radio broadcasting underwent a period of administrative consolidation during which the government attempted to define the goals and philosophy that the medium should follow. The British Marconi management had established the basis for a well run professional broadcast operation, but the foreign management was perceived by Egyptians to be no longer needed, since a cadre of Egyptian managers had been trained to take responsibility. Continued British management was considered to be particulary inappropriate in view of the anti-British feelings that surfaced after World War II.

In 1949, public law No. 98 was promulgated in an attempt to make radio an independent organization under the Council of Ministers. The law provided another stipulation: it mandated that the language of the radio sevice be Arabic, the national language (*Arab Broadcasts* 1970a, p. 65). The service had never broadcast domestically exclusively in Arabic. The first general program, started in 1934, broadcast in Arabic, French, and English, featuring a mixture of music, news, drama, and informational programs. When a second transmitter was constructed, a four-hour European Program was added, broadcasting French and English to the foreign community and to those Egyptians who had acquired a second language. It would be inaccurate to say that the foreign program was imposed by Marconi management. The Egyptian elite has been relatively western in orientation since the 1800s, and it is not unusual for upper-class Egyptian homes to use French or English as a language of convenience.

2.1.4 Radio Broadcasting after the Revolution

It is beyond the scope of this study to enumerate the motivations for the 1952 revolution. However, factors that contributed to the military takeover by the Free Officers included a general dislike for King Farouk, who was viewed by many leaders as inept and as possessing personal habits inappropriate for the leader of an Islamic society. Egypt also had serious political problems of its own making, and difficult relations with Great Britain, which had stationed troops in the country; important too was the Egyptian Army's basic failure to be an effective fighting force during the 1948 Palestine War.

Axiomatically, revolutionary governments assume control of the mass media. Neguib and then Nasser inherited a radio system that, while modest in size, immediately became the voice of the revolution—though even a revolution could not make Arabic the exclusive language of Egyptian radio. They did not have to nationalize it, as it was already a government-organized activity. Radio service employees were, in fact, government employees who supported the revolution and helped organize a broadcast service that articulated its goals and provided favorable coverage of Nasser's speeches and appearances. The Egyptian print media, on the other hand, had a long history of independence, both financial and editorial. While many journalists supported Nasser, some did not. As a result, Nasser slowly tightened control of the print media until 1960, when they were in effect nationalized.[2]

---

[2]There are several sources that discuss Egyptian print journalism history. Consult, for example, Almaney 1972, pp. 340–48, and Nasser 1979.

It will probably never be known why Nasser devoted Egyptian administrative energy and such extensive economic resources to the establishment
of what is still the Arab world's largest and most influential broadcast
service. However, two observations about this man may help to clarify his
motivation for the expansion of radio and, later, for the construction of a
television service. Nasser was different from most other Arab leaders who
came to power in the 1950s. Like them, because of his Army background, he
was relatively sophisticated; but he also came from a modest rural environment and understood and was able to capitalize on his knowledge of the oral
Arab culture and the power and emotionalism of the Arabic language.
Secondly, Nasser had a wider vision of his leadership than most people
initially thought. In his 1955 monograph, *Egypt's Liberation: The Philosophy of the Revolution*, Nasser notes three areas of influence in which he
envisioned both himself and Egypt working, both militarily and diplomatically, against imperialism and nationalism. He called these areas "circles":
the first, the Arab circle, "the most important, . . . the one with which we are
most closely linked"; the second, the African continent on which Egypt is
located, on which Nasser saw (and attempted to foment) struggle between
whites and blacks; and the third, the Islamic circle, "which circumscribes
continents and oceans and . . . is the domain of our brothers in faith" (1955,
pp. 85-111). It was after this publication was printed that Nasser became
interested in the Third World movement. The three circles became the
target areas for an elaborate radio system.

2.1.5 Radio Studio Facilities and Services

In the introduction to this study it was stated that the distinction between
domestic and international broadcasts in the Arab world is not easily made.
The following discussion of individual Egyptian radio services therefore
does not emphasize where the broadcasts are received, but rather what the
Egyptians intend the audience to be.

Short- and medium-wave transmitters are scattered throughout the country and are provided with programs to broadcast by means of a network of
both cable and microwave links: the only service that does not originate
from the central broadcasting complex in Cairo is a local radio service in
Alexandria. The broadcasting complex, completed in the early 1960s,
houses production, engineering, and administration for both radio and
television. Over forty radio studios operate around the clock there, ranging
in size from news reading rooms to studios that will accommodate symphony
orchestras.

2.1.6 Domestic and Regional Broadcasts

Main Program. The Main Program is a direct outgrowth of the original
broadcast in 1934. In other Arab countries it is known as "Radio Cairo," as
are some of the other Egyptian radio services. One of the problems that

researchers have found in undertaking radio listening survey research in the Arab world is that non-Egyptians cannot always distinguish among the numerous Egyptian radio services that they receive. The stations are clearly identified as distinct services, the confusion as to the name of the specific service appearing to stem in part from the announcers' custom between programs of preceding the name of the service with the statement, "This is Cairo"—stating the location of the broadcast service's origin rather than its specific name. This custom probably comes from the BBC External Services practice in both English and Arabic of saying "This is London."[3] At the time of the revolution, the Main Program broadcast 11 hours per day. The program was expanded, immediately after July 1952; and by 1962 it was on the air for just under 20 hours per week, as it was in 1980 (Metwally n.d., p. 6). Much of the initial increase in transmitting power after the revolution was given to the Main Program; and during the 1950s and 1960s, when Egypt wanted to reach other Arab countries, short-wave transmitters were brought on-line for added coverage. Another reason for adding short-wave transmitters for dissemination of what was essentially a domestic service was to allow the large Egyptian expatriate community in the Gulf to receive this program.

The Main Program has something for everyone: a mixture of regularly scheduled newscasts, music, commentary, and various forms of entertainment, the most dominant of which is drama. Entertainment, not entirely devoid of an educational message, occupies a large portion—probably as much as one-half—of the total daily transmission schedule. The Main Program, along with another service, the "Voice of the Arabs," was the most important means of reaching Egyptian supporters in other Arab countries prior to the 1967 war. As is discussed under the "Voice of the Arabs" (6.2.4), the general tone of Egyptian broadcasts dramatically changed after the Arab defeat in that war. It changed even more dramatically after Anwar Sadat became president in 1970. The following 1970 statement about the goals of the Main Program provides some insight into the importance that Egypt attached to it:

[T]he most important [of the goals] . . . are the supportive maintenance of the morale of the audience to stay ready and alert for the battle [against Israel] and awareness of the facts, dimensions, goals, and means of psychological warfare, and strengthening of the relationship between the masses and the active army on the front. [*Arab Broadcasts* 1971, p. 68]

The service is indeed important, both because it is a continuation of the first identifiably Egyptian program and because many of the other Egyptian services are spin-offs from its broadcasts.

[3]The name of the BBC's Arabic-language magazine is *Huna London*, "here is" or "this is" London.

This study does not include an extensive analysis of estimated audiences for international radio broadcasts. However, even limited information from available surveys can provide a basic idea about audience trends at the time the surveys were done. Provided that respondents did not confuse Radio Cairo (Main Program) with other services—Voice of the Arabs was identified separately—17.9% of respondents in the 1974 survey done in Kuwait listened to Radio Cairo once per week or more often. Among respondents to the same survey, 17.5% said that they listened to the Voice of the Arabs at least once per week; and approximately one-third said that they tuned that often to an Egyptian radio service.[4] A survey done in Jordan in September 1978 revealed that 16.3% and 18.4% of respondents tuned "once a week or more often" to Radio Cairo and the Voice of the Arabs respectively (USICA 1978b, p.11). Regardless of the prevailing political climate in the Middle East, then, residents of other countries appear to be interested in what the Egyptian Main Program is saying.

Sudan Program. Egypt and the Sudan have a continuing close relationship that dates from the time before 1956 when the two countries were administratively linked by the British. The service has its origins in a weekly 30-minute feature, "Sudan Corner," broadcast on the Main Program. The weekly feature was lengthened after the revolution, apparently as a means of strengthening relations between Egypt and its neighbor to the south. In 1953 the program, still on the Main Program wave length, was further expanded to 30 minutes per day. On 27 March 1954 the program became an entirely separate service with its own transmitter and assigned frequency (Metwally n.d., p. 4), and an office was opened in Khartoum, Sudan, to help provide its program material (*Arab Broadcasts* 1971, p. 72). The service has increased since its 1962 four and one-half hour transmission time per day to a daily six and one-half hours.

Second Program. The Second Program was started "on May 5, 1957 to provide the elite with the developments of contemporary intellectual, cultural and artistic trends" (Metwally n.d., p. 4). Similar in format to the BBC's Radio 3, the service is intended to cater to intellectual tastes in the urban areas of Cairo and Alexandria. Its medium-wave transmissions were

---

[4]This study notes results of various research efforts by the United States International Communication Agency to determine radio and other media habits. The Agency does not undertake data collection itself but contracts with survey research organizations to do surveys based on a questionnaire design prepared by USICA. Radio surveys undertaken in the Middle East during the 1970s were often done on a shared-cost basis with the BBC, which in turn had some say in the questionnaire design. Associated Business Consultants of Beirut, Lebanon, did several of the surveys in the early 1970s. There was some concern about the reliability of ABC, and the Lebanese Civil War interrupted its activities. Most of the survey work in the Arab world is now done by Middle East Marketing Research Bureau of Nicosia, Cyprus. It was this organization that did the field work for the multi-country 1977 and 1979 McCann Middle East Media Studies ("VOA-CAAP Audience Estimate for Kuwait 1974" 1975, p. 10).

extended to three and one-half hours per day in 1962 (Shaban 1974), a schedule that still applies.

Alexandria Local Service.   The only Egyptian radio service to originate outside of the broadcasting complex in Cairo, the Alexandria Local Service was started on 26 July 1954[5] and was intended to be the first of a series of local services that officials believed would serve to reflect the character of each major region. "Alex" was the ideal location for such a new service, as the city is Egypt's second largest and is an important Mediterranean port; and its radio service is probably the only one in Egypt to request and later utilize research regarding listener attitudes and preferences (Mahrns 1974). Transmission time has remained relatively constant since the service was started at eight hours per day.

The Alexandria broadcast remains Egypt's only local radio service despite the stated intentions of the broadcast administration in the revolutionary days. Scarce financial resources are an obvious factor. However, another reason local services were not added is that the government wanted to retain administrative control. The concentration of both engineering and production facilities in one building in downtown Cairo makes defense against dissident forces easier.

People's Program.   The People's Program was created on 29 July 1959 in order to combine the various special interest programs formerly included, even prior to the revolution, in the Main Program. These programs, known as "Corners," were targeted to farmers, women, youth, the armed forces, and the police (Metwally n.d., p. 4). The People's Program transmissions are primarily intended for the group of people who make up the majority of Egypt's population—the fellaheen, or illiterate farmers, and those former fellaheen who have migrated to urban centers. The casual visitor to Cairo, who is mainly interested in major tourist attractions, may not realize the extent of subsistence-level living in Egypt: only a few miles from Cairo, people live in a manner not unlike that of their ancestors thousands of years ago. This group is, then, the main target audience for this service and for the special programming—carefully presented in the form of Arabic that is most easily understood by listeners—that it features. The People's Program has used most known forms of radio programming in order to promote national development: to promote farming advances, literacy training, population planning, and the concept of nationhood among a people who have tended to be distrustful of government.[6]

By the mid-1970s, the Program devoted three hours per day to educational programs, one and three-quarters hours to broadcasts tied to the national

---

[5]This date is much celebrated in Egypt because it is the date, three days after the revolution started, that King Farouk was exiled.
[6]A 1958 study suggests that the mass media, particularly radio, had an effect on rural villages. See Hirabayashi and Khatib 1958, pp. 357–63.

school curriculum, and one-half hour per day to literacy training. In 1970 the service embraced the Canadian Farm Forum concept, whereby programs about farming and other development topics are produced and transmitted to groups of listeners who then discuss the program after it is completed. One of the directors of the People's Program had attended a meeting in Europe where an Indian delegate showed a film on the Canadian Forum concept as it operated on Indian radio: impressed, she had decided to try a similar program in Egypt. The program started with six "clubs" in one province and then gradually spread. For a short time, Egypt attempted an unusual twist to the project: on one evening the radio broadcast was followed by a discussion and then a television program on a subject similar to that of the radio broadcast (Al-Mowaled 1974). This format has not been continued due to problems with television receiver maintenance and the fact that Egypt does not generally have the administrative skill or the motivation to coordinate such undertakings.

Daily program time reached a peak of nine hours in 1972 and has dropped slightly to eight and one-half hours per day. Egyptian peasants listen to a variety of Egyptian and foreign radio services, but it is probably the People's Program on transistor radios that Xavier Delcourt referred to as "part of the[ir] minimum daily requirement, beside the 'foul,' the traditional bean puree" (1978, p. 42).

Middle East Program. The Middle East Program traces its beginnings to a 1959 Presidential Decree of Nasser's, establishing the following new goals for Egyptian broadcasting:

1. Elevating the standards of the arts.
2. Strengthening national feeling and social cooperation, spreading solidarity between social groups and supporting accepted traditions.
3. Participating in the spread of culture among the masses.
4. Discussing social problems and strengthening spiritual and moral values.
5. Reviving the Arabic literary, scientific and artistic heritage.
6. Informing the public about the best products of human civilization.
7. Enlightening the public about both internal and international news.
8. Informing foreign countries about the U.A.R. and the Arab world.
9. Encouraging talents in different areas of thought and creativity.
10. Strengthening relations between national residents and expatriates.
11. Providing public entertainment. [*Arab Broadcasts* 1971, p. 64]

The decree also—and most importantly here—gave the broadcasting organization "economic character." It allowed broadcast services to accept commercial advertising and to utilize, within certain limits, the "hard" international currency that might result from such advertising. This initial move on the part of Nasser has been helpful to the electronic media in Egypt because the commercial income can so readily be used for the purchase of spare parts and equipment: the broadcasting organization thus avoids the complex bureaucratic process of obtaining permission to spend hard currency from the government economic and banking establishments. Radio advertising was first allowed on the People's Program and later on the Alexandria Local Service.

The Middle East Program was intended to be a frankly commercial regional service: programming began on 31 May 1964 (*A.R.E. Broadcasting in Brief* n.d., p. 3), from a powerful medium-wave transmitter near Alexandria that helped send the commercial message as far as the Arabian Gulf and throughout North Africa. The service was immediately attractive to marketers of international products in the Middle East (cigarettes, cosmetics, aspirin, food products, automobiles, candy, etc.) who found that many national broadcast systems, particularly in the wealthier states, allowed no advertising at all. In fact, during the 1960s, the Middle East Program had commercial competition only from the Jordanian Radio Service, whose low-powered transmitters covered only a restricted area. Strong competition appeared only in the 1970s when an increasing number of Gulf states allowed local radio advertising.

The Egyptian commercial service quickly became popular. Primarily a nighttime and early morning service, its format was "DJ" Top-40 style, with fast patter on the part of the announcer between commercial messages and popular songs—a format in which Egypt led the Arab world. On an international level, Radio Monte Carlo Middle East (see 5.3) took the basic Middle East Program format and, with the aid of Egyptian announcers, made it more professional (Regnier 1980).

Egyptian broadcasting officials are reluctant to discuss income from commercial advertising. Most sales take place through large Cairo-based advertising agencies, the majority of which are affiliated with the large publishing houses. One of the obvious problems that a potential advertiser on the Middle East Program faces is a lack of research data that provide a basic profile of listeners. The research department of Egyptian broadcast organization restricts itself to program analyses and has not been asked to undertake research that would provide advertisers with an estimate of the number and demographic characteristics of its listeners. By contrast, survey research results are used heavily in the marketing strategy of the services's main competitor, Radio Monte Carlo Middle East.

Holy Koran Broadcast. Egypt's religious service, first transmitted on 29 March 1964 (*A.R.E. Broadcasting in Brief* n.d., p. 3), features Koran readings, religious discussions, and commentary for 18½ hours daily on both short- and medium-wave frequencies. It was started for sincere religious reasons: Egypt has long been an important Islamic nation that has made contributions to religious ethics. But such broadcasts helped Nasser in two respects. First, they provided a kind of continuous evidence that the government realized the importance of the conservative Islamic factions of the Egyptian population, some of whom opposed Nasser. Second, the broadcasts were a reminder to those in Egypt and other countries that Egypt was still a Moslem country despite the close ties that it had at the time with the Soviet Union and the East European countries, which are viewed by many of the more traditional states as having philosophies that are incompatible with Islam.

Youth Broadcast. Started in 1975, the Youth Broadcast is the newest Egyptian radio service. It broadcasts in the afternoon from 1500 to 1700 hours on the same frequency as the People's Program, and is intended to reach a school-age audience with an educational, political, and social message.

European Program. Begun like the Main Program in 1934, the European Program at the time of the revolution did not exceed four hours per day. These hours were rapidly expanded to 15 in 1962, cut back to 14 in 1978 (Metwally n.d., p. 7), and later expanded to 17 hours per day. Although radio and television programming in European languages, primarily English, is done by almost every Arab country, Egypt has been a leader in European-language broadcasting among those states east of the North African countries. It has, as noted earlier, a large European expatriate community who speak English, French, German, Italian, and Greek: in addition there is an Armenian community that retains its culture and language. The European program starts, then, at 0700, with 15-minute broadcasts in Greek, German, Italian, and French. News broadcasts are spread throughout the day at specified intervals: French at 1400 and 2100, English at 1450 and 2000, German at 1800.[7] Programming between the news bulletins is heavily music oriented with specific periods set aside for requests, popular music, etc. Some programming is supplied by embassies and by cultural centers that are supported by foundations or governments. The basic format appears to be quite flexible and depends on the number and sort of qualified people, most of whom work on a part-time basis, who are available to read news and produce programs.

Musical Program. The music service first started in March 1968 (*Arab Broadcasts* 1971, p. 73), during a difficult period of time after the Egyptian defeat in 1967, and it may have been meant to provide a diversion from what observers agree was, prior to June 1967, a steady diet of rather heavy-handed Nasserite rhetoric. There are occasional brief interruptions, but the music is basically continuous and actually constitutes two services on separate medium-wave frequencies—one for Arabic and another for popular European music. Total programming time is nine and one-half hours per day.

Palestine Broadcast. Almost every Arab country provides time for a program that is devoted to discussion of the Palestinian problem. These

---

[7]The daily schedule for Egypt's two television channels and the European Program is published in the daily Egyptian English-language newspaper. See *The Egyptian Gazette* 1980, p. 3.

radio services strive mainly to attract Palestinians who reside in the country where the broadcast originates, but they also seek to attract local non-Palestinian Arabs and Palestinians who reside in Israel, the Occupied West Bank, and other Arab countries. With the possible exception of non-government financed, clandestine PLO broadcasts from Lebanon during and after the 1975 Civil War, those who operate the program production and transmission facilities are dependent on the ever-shifting political climate under the host government. The result everywhere is an erratic transmission schedule and constantly changing program formats.[8]

The Egyptian Palestine Program became an "independent" service on 29 October 1960, with a daily half-hour broadcast. The schedule was expanded gradually until it reached six hours per day in three transmission periods: 0800 to 1000, 1200 to 1300, and 1600 to 1900 (Metwally n.d., p. 7). The programs use designated times on other national radio services: for example, the first two-hour broadcast uses the Voice of the Arabs wave length (see 6.2). But Egypt has also occasionally curtailed its Palestine broadcasts or stopped them altogether. The most serious interruptions appear to have occurred between 1975 and 1979—a period during which Egypt concluded several agreements with Israel, starting with the return of the Sinai and continuing with a formal Egyptian-Israeli peace treaty. After the September 1975 Egyptian-Israeli Sinai agreement, the Egyptian government temporarily stopped all Palestine broadcasts from Egyptian facilities because the broadcasts were criticizing the host government (Tanner 1975, p. 3). Resumed broadcasts were again halted in the late 1970s during the preliminaries to the peace treaty between Egypt and Israel.

Voice of the Arabs. The radio service called "Voice of the Arabs" was officially inaugurated on 4 July 1953 (*A.R.E. Broadcasting in Brief* n.d., p.3), one year after the revolution; it is covered in more detail in Chapter 6. Daniel Lerner was probably the first to examine the service within its Arab media milieu and to suggest some direct effects of the broadcasts (1953, pp. 255, 309, 310). From a 30-minute per day beginning the program expanded rapidly, reaching seven hours per day in 1954; by the 1967 Middle East War, the service stopped just short of 24-hour per day operation. At this writing, the daily transmission time is 18 hours.

The Voice of the Arabs is probably the best known and most widely listened to service in the Arab world. It further provides the best example of how Nasser used radio to promote his own views on Pan-Arabism, which included, for a period of time, calls for assassinations and the overthrow of selected Arab governments. Nasser and his advisors realized that in order to bring the Nasserite message to the rest of the Arab Middle East—the "first circle"—radio was the ideal medium. The channel would be one that could utilize Arabic, a language that lends itself to an emotional rather than a

[8]For a comprehensive discussion of Palestine radio broadcasts, see Browne 1975, pp. 133–50.

logical appeal. Radio further bypassed the problem of illiteracy in the Arab world. Finally, the countries in which the Voice's message would be received were unable to defend themselves against the service because they lacked the facilities. Few Arab countries in the 1950s had a viable domestic broadcasting service to provide an alternative to the Egyptian broadcasts and virtually no jamming transmitters were available to stop them. More important, at the time the service started and experienced its greatest growth, the political leaders in other Arab countries neither understood nor appreciated how potentially disruptive the Voice would be.

Some of the Voice's strong rhetoric was markedly effective in aiding those in other countries, most notably Jordan, Iraq, and North Yemen, who wanted to instigate government change or to influence government policy—especially when a western power such as Great Britain was involved.

Until his dismissal after the 1967 Middle East War, Ahmed Said served as director and chief announcer of the Voice of the Arabs. Under his guidance its basic format was formulated: attacks on those Arab countries that did not agree with Nasser's policies were packaged between music of famous Egyptian singers, drama, "talks," and news. In the late 1950s, special programs were sent out to specific regions, singling out for attack a country such as Saudi Arabia—a favorite target—or in some cases even singling out specific people for vituperation. The 1967 war ended what might be called the "Ahmed Said Era." It had been Said who contributed most to the psychological defeat that Egyptians and other Arabs felt immediately after the war: it had been he, although not he alone, who had provided the prewar confidence in military victory—an optimism that continued into the second day of the Six Day War. When the enormity of the defeat became known to Egyptians, they seemed to know that they had been misled both prior to and during the early stages of the war. It was surely the "Ahmed Said Era" to which Issawi referred in his succinct characterization of the Voice of the Arabs: it "has to be heard to be believed: for sheer venom, vulgarity, and indifference to truth it has few equals in the world" (1963, p. 217).

After 1967 the tone of the service changed dramatically, as though those who were then appointed to administer it were attempting to compensate for past excesses. One of the official Voice goals as of 1971 was to promote "adher[ence] to the scientific interpretation of language [and] purif[ication of] that language [of] repetition, exaggeration, superficiality, and unpreparedness" (*Arab Broadcasts* 1971, p. 69). Senior employees of the Voice state now that the transmissions have become so bland that they are indistinguishable from the Radio Cairo domestic service.

2.1.7 Foreign-Lanuage and Beamed Services

The expansion of foreign-language and special beamed broadcasts depended heavily on studio and transmitter facilities that were built after the 1952 revolution. Before 1952, Egypt did not have any short-wave transmission capability: installation of short-wave transmitters was immediately ordered. Their completion on 3 July 1953 marked the beginning of programs to Southeast Asia, India, and Pakistan. As new transmitters and studios were made available, more services were added, with the ultimte goal of reaching areas of the world that Egypt and Nasser wanted to address. The new services tended to concentrate on those "circles" that Nasser identified in his writings: the Islamic nations, Africa south of the Sahara, and later the Third World. One of the reasons that the numerous language services were possible is the nature of the program that the Egyptians pursued to attract Third World students to Egyptian educational institutions. Students, a few contract employees, and people who had requested residence in Egypt as part of various resistance movements became the backbone of the foreign-language services. The completion of the Cairo broadcasting complex in the early 1960s provided the studio and administrative space to house, coordi-nate, and expand the foreign broadcasts. The political and economic changes that followed the 1967 war have tended to stabilize transmission hours and to eliminate some languages. However, the exposure that the international broadcasts are perceived to bring remains attractive, and some officials speak of expanding English-language broadcasts to a world-wide service similar to the one now operated by Radio Moscow.

Table 1 indicates the chronology of Egyptian international broadcasts in hours and minutes per day, as of 1979.

The Hebrew service, one of the earlier foreign-language programs that Egypt categorized as international broadcasting, deserves special mention before the discussion of Egyptian radio is concluded. The majority of the broadcasts have been on medium-wave, as Israel is the intended target. The broadcast hours in Table 1 are somewhat misleading, since they reflect the post-1979 Egyptian-Israeli peace agreement transmission schedule. During the 1960s and until 1978, the Hebrew program ranged from 12 to 15 hours per day, operating mostly in the afternoon and evening. The format until 1978 was very heavy-handed, with news, commentary, and interview pro-grams designed to promote the Arab cause among Hebrew-speakers; most of the service's announcers are trained at Cairo University, where Hebrew is taught, and some further improved their speaking skills by talking with Israeli prisoners captured and interned in Egypt after the October 1973 War. The service, some of which is broadcast in English, has used western popular music in generous amounts to attract listeners. Those who adminis-ter the Hebrew service point to a 1974 United States Information Agency survey, which indicates that the Hebrew Service did indeed attract listeners, about the same number as Radio Cairo's Main Program (USIA 1975b, pp. 2,5,11). However, Israelis who have listened note that many tune in only because of curiosity and the popular music. And the music featured on the Egyptian Hebrew service has apparently been less of an attraction since the Israeli domestic radio service started playing western popular music. Egypt

Table 1. Egyptian Foreign Language Services

Year Started	Language	Time	Target Area
1953	Indonesian	1:45	Indonesia
	English	1:15	Indian Peninsula
	Urdu	1:50	Pakistan
	Arabic	1:00	South East Asia
1954	Turkish	1:00	Turkey
	Hebrew	5:00	Israel (post peace agreement)
	Persian	–	Iran (discontinued 10 Dec. 1977)
	Swahili	2:00	East Africa
	Malayan	45	Malayasia
1955	Portuguese	1:15	Portugal
	Spanish	1:15	Latin America
	Arabic	1:00	Latin America
	Amharic	1:00	Ethiopia
1956	English	1:30	Europe
	French	1:30	Europe
	Tigrigna	–	Eritrea (discontinued 1956)
1957	Somali	1:00	Somalia
1958	Kurdish	–	Syria, Iraq, Iran, in Surani and Karamanji dialects (operates intermittently)
	Bengali	1:00	Bangladesh and India
	German	1:00	Europe
1959	Italian	1:45	Europe
	Arabic	–	Europe (discontinued 5 July 1969)
	English	1:30	West Africa
	French	2:00	West Africa
	Hausa	2:00	Nigeria, Ghana, Sierra Leone, Niger, Dahomey, Togo, Ivory Coast, Chad, Liberia, Cameroon
1960	Lingala	45	Zaire
1961	Nyanja	–	Zambia and Malawi (discontinued 24 Dec. 1977)
	English	2:00	Central and South Africa
	Foulani	1:00	West Africa
	Siamese	30	Thailand
1962	Lesotho	–	Swaziland and South Africa (operates intermittently)
	Pushtu	1:00	Afghanistan
1963	Portuguese	–	Angola-Mozambique (discontinued 14 Dec. 1977)
1964	Shona	45	Zimbabwe
	Sindebelle	45	Zimbabwe
1965	Zulu	45	Southern Africa
1966	Indian	1:00	India
	Yoruba	1:00	Nigeria, Dahomey
	Ibo	–	West Nigeria (discontinued 5 July 1969)

Table 1. (continued)

Year Started	Language	Time	Target Area
	English	1:30	North America
	Arabic	–	West Africa (discontinued 10 Dec. 1977)
	Arabic	–	East, Central and South Africa (discontinued 11 Jan. 1969)
1967	Afari	1:00	Djibouti
1968	Russian	–	Soviet Union (discontinued 12 Dec. 1977)
	Bambara	1:00	Mali, Guinea, Ivory Coast
	Oulouf	1:00	Senegal and minorities in neighboring countries
	French	–	Canada (discontinued 10 Dec. 1977)
	Arabic	1:00	North America
	Arabic	–	Vietnam (discontinued 1 July 1976)
	Arabic	2:00	North America

SOURCE: Metwally n.d., pp. 9–12; *WRTH* 1980, pp. 164–65; *A.R.E. Broadcasting in Brief* n.d. p. 5.

has decreased the service's hours for two reasons: first, the peace agreement implies a normalizing of relations that almost mandates some changes in the service. Second, since the peace agreement, Egypt has had to strive to explain its actions to the other Arab countries, many of whom have attempted to isolate Sadat as a political leader. Part of the transmission time devoted to Hebrew prior to 1979 was later used to broadcast to the other Arab countries in Arabic (Rushty 1979).

By 1973, 20 years of expansion in international radio broadcasting had made Egypt the sixth largest international broadcaster, in terms of weekly program output. As Table 2 indicates, however, Albania and North Korea have surpassed Egypt, which in 1978 ranked only eighth.

2.1.8 Radio Transmission Facilities

Until 1956 most of Egypt's radio transmitters were located at the Abu Zabal site near Cairo, the location of the original Marconi transmitter. Since that time transmitter sites have been spread throughout the country, with most facilities being located between Cairo and Alexandria in the Nile Delta. During the 1956 British-French-Israeli invasion of Egypt, the Royal Air Force bombed the Abu Zabal transmitter site with the hope of eliminating the transmission capability of both Radio Cairo (Main Program) and the Voice of the Arabs. The attack only temporarily interrupted their services (El-Kashlan 1974), and a British plan to replace Cairo's services with an anti-Nasser station on Cyprus failed. The incident did teach the Egyptians a lesson: diversify transmitter locations and prepare stand-by transmitters and studios for possible future attacks.

Table 2. Weekly Broadcast Hours, 1950 to 1978

Country	1950	1960	1970	1975	1978
Soviet Union	533	1015	1908	2001	2010
United States*	597	1495	1907	2029	1813
Chinese People's Republic	66	687	1267	1423	1436
German Federal Republic	–	315	779	767	789
United Kingdom	643	589	723	719	711
North Korea	–	159	330	455	602
Albania	26	63	487	490	564
Egypt	–	301	540	635	542

SOURCE: *British Broadcasting Corporation, BBC Handbook 1980* 1979, p. 57.
*Includes Voice of America, Radio Liberty Radio Free Europe.

The many aforenamed services required a system of high-powered medium- and short-wave transmitters that could be supplied with a broadcast signal from a master control area. The system could thus feed signals to selected transmitters and extend the reach of a specified service, should the decision be made to do so. The broadcasting complex completed in the early 1960s provided the switching capability. Transmitter construction throughout the1950s and 1960s, as Table 3 indicates, provided the power.

Transmitter and antenna construction is a particularly expensive undertaking for a country such as Egypt that not only must import the high technology but has so little money with which to pay for it. Between 1956 and 1974 some transmitters were supplied by the Soviet Union and the East European countries with which Egypt had close ties at the time. Various military, trade, and cultural agreements during this period apparently helped secure loans and credits that were used to purchase transmission equipment. President Sadat later turned to the west—specifically to the United States—for military and economic assistance, and by mid-1970s western countries became transmission equipment suppliers again. Egypt felt that new transmitters were needed in order to defend itself against radio attacks by other Arab countries that objected to the move to normalize relations with Israel. Some of the older medium- and short-wave transmitters needed to be refurbished or replaced. The transmitters the Egyptians believed to be powerful in the 1950s and 1960s—for example, medium-wave transmitters of 500 kilowatts—were no longer very effective or reliable in reaching other parts of the Arab world, where many of the countries had installed transmitters of 1000 kilowatts. In 1978, then, the Egyptian Radio-Television Federation embarked on a transmitter expansion program that will effectively double its short-wave and triple its medium-wave transmission capablity. This program is designed to provide additional high-powered transmitters for the Voice of the Arabs and the Koran Program and to place lower-powered transmitters in the Egyptian provinces in order to rebroadcast the already established national services.

Table 3. Egyptian Medium- and Short-Wave
Transmission Power, 1952 to 1970

Year	Mediumwave (kW)	Shortwave (kW)	Total
1952	72	–	72
1953	74	140	214
1954	176	270	446
1955	180	380	560
1956	180	380	560
1957	202	380	582
1958	544	530	1074
1959	834	500	1334
1960	834	540	1374
1961	834	740	1574
1962	834	790	1624
1968	2188	1700	3888
1969–1970	2188	1850	4038

SOURCE: *Arab Broadcasts* 1971, p. 76; and El-Kashlan interview.

The new high-powered medium-wave transmitters are being supplied by Continental Electronics of Dallas, Texas. To upgrade the Koran Program, a 500-kilowatt facility was ordered for Tanta, in the Delta. To increase the power of the Voice of the Arabs Program, a 1000-kilowatt medium-wave transmitter was ordered for the Nile Delta area: the Egyptians were later to order another so that the Voice would be broadcast by a 2000-kilowatt facility—two 1000-kilowatt transmitters operating in parallel (Abdu 1979). Eighty low-power transmitters for 20 sites were ordered from the Harris Corporation Broadcast Products Division of Quincy, Illinois, under a 5.8 million dollar contract awarded in March 1979 ("Harris wins $5.2 Million Egyptian Radio Contract"1979). These transmitters have been intended primarily for the rebroadcast of domestic programs.

Modern Egypt has found itself in serious economic straits. With a rapidly expanding population, it has had to import food and market it at subsidized prices in order to feed its people. The large-scale American aid program that followed the Sinai disengagement agreements between Egypt and Israel appeared to be a partial solution to the country's serious economic situation. First negotiated by Kissinger under the Nixon and Ford administrations, the aid program was again expanded under President Carter and provided for assistance in all facets of development. Each ministry or major administrative unit in the Egyptian government could apply for assistance through a central aid-coordinating office that ranked projects in terms of importance and then passed them along to the mission of the Agency for International Development (AID) in Cairo. Under this arrangement, the Egyptian Radio-Television Federation requested loans through the Ministry of Information for both radio and television equipment. It was agreed however, that the purchase of television equipment— possibly because television was perceived by some American officials as a luxury— was not to be given the same priority as the purchase of that for radio. Thus three loans were arranged for the eventual Continental and Harris radio-transmitter contracts.

A possible explanation for the United States government's interest in financing new Egyptian radio transmitters came to light in the summer of 1980. Apparently the Central Intelligence Agency had persuaded Egyptian authorities to use an undetermined number of its transmitters to broadcast an anti-Khomeini radio service known as "The Free Voice of Iran." Before the broadcasts were identified as being broadcast by American intelligence personnel, entertainment programs were interspersed with news and commentary that called for the support of former Iranian Prime Minister Shahpur Bakhtiar. *The New York Times* quoted American officials as saying that "Egypt had been promised additional transmitter facilities by the United States through the Agency for International Development to compensate for the Egyptian facilities used by the C.I.A." (Binder 1980, p. 3).

There apparently was special concern at both the American Embassy in Cairo and the State Department in Washington over the request for funds to order the second 1000-kilowatt transmitter for the new Voice of the Arabs facility. The more seasoned State Department officials may have remembered the strong anti-American propaganda broadcast by the Voice during the 1950s and 1960s. An even more vivid recollection, perhaps, was how the Voice of the Arabs and Cairo Radio's Main Program were used by Nasser during the opening hours of the 1967 war to broadcast to other countries the allegation that American and British planes were flying cover for Israeli fighters that neutralized the Egyptian Air Force. The immediate result of those broadcasts had been violent anti-American demonstrations throughout the Arab world, which led to the severing of diplomatic relations between many Arab countries and the United States. Also, State Department and International Communication Agency officials may have thought that the expenditure would simply be an inappropriate use of economic development funds. These American concerns were allayed and the additional funds for the second transmitter were allocated (Bang 1979). Egypt appears to be willing to invest valuable economic resources—and to invest

Table 4. U.S. AID Loans to Egyptian Radio-Television Federation for Radio Transmitters

Loan Number	Amount
030	$10 million
036	$ 5 million
038	$ 5 million

SOURCE: Loan figures were supplied by the Agency for International Development n.d.

time in complicated negotiations—in order to maintain its stature as the Arab world's most influential broadcaster.

2.1.9 Egyptian Television

By the fourth anniversary of the Egyptian revolution, Nasser and his advisors had reason to believe that their efforts in radio were effective, both internationally and domestically. It appeared only natural to those close to radio that television broadcasting would be the next step. Egypt was not the first country to establish television in the Arab world. In 1956 the Iraqi government purchased a small station that was imported originally as part of a British trade fair, providing the beginnings of Arab world government-controlled television. Prior to the opening of the Baghdad station, the American armed forces had established low-power stations on the American standard for military personnel at Wheelus Air Force Base near Tripoli (Libya) and Dhahran (Saudi Arabia). Moreover, the Arabian American Oil Company (ARAMCO) had begun a similarly low-powered station that still operates for employees in Saudi Arabia's Eastern Province.

Despite Egypt's precarious economic situation during the last part of the 1950s, the decision was made to begin a television service. Studies were undertaken and international corporations submitted bids in 1956, but the joint British-French-Israeli Suez invasion stopped work on television until 1959 (Nassr 1963, p. 86). In late 1959 a contract was signed between the United Arab Republic and the Radio Corporation of America to provide a complete television service for Egypt and the beginnings of a service for Syria.

To digress briefly, the designation United Arab Republic stems from the union between Egypt and Syria from 1958 to 1961: the countries were united under the one name, which symbolized Nasser's Pan-Arab philosophy. The action by the two countries was thought to be a beginning. It was hoped that other countries would follow suit, until the countries of the Arab world were united, and geographical boundaries, most of them arbitrarily imposed by Europeans, were eliminated.[9] Egypt kept U.A.R. as its official name until it was changed to Arab Republic of Egypt after Nasser's death. During the Syrian-Egyptian union, the two broadcasting organizations were merged by public law No. 717, dated 5 May 1959 (*Arab Broadcasts* 1970a, p. 66), and employees were rotated between countries. However, more Egyptians went to Syria than vice versa and some Syrians voiced concern that the exchanges were not equally beneficial.

Little information is available from either the American or the Egyptian government concerning the origins of the RCA television contract. By 1959 the United States had an amiable, although not close, relationship with the

[9]Several other unsuccessful attempts at merger were made or discussed by Arab countries, e.g., Syria-Jordan, Egypt-Libya, and North and South Yemen.

Nasser government. The United States had refused to supply arms and help finance construction of the High Dam in Aswan in the mid-1950s, and Egypt had turned to the Soviet Union and Eastern European countries for military assistance and help with the dam project. It has been alleged that the United States helped financially with the introduction of television by lending money for or subsidizing the RCA contract. This has been denied by both governments, but observers believe that Egypt's hard currency holdings at the time were not sufficient for such an undertaking. If indeed no United States assistance was offered, and Egypt used hard currency from its own small store, its commitment to a television service was serious indeed.

One possible explanation for the selection of RCA for the large Egyptian installation and the more modest Syrian one is that the company was perhaps then the only one that could complete the task by the specified date. At the time, RCA was probably the only company that could supply cameras, antennas, video tape recorders, and audio, switching, and microwave equipment without sub-contracting to other firms. RCA also had the experience and personnel to provide a complete television system.

Immediately after the RCA contract was signed, the government started building the large Cairo broadcasting complex on the Nile; but television, it was decided, would be introduced before the completion of the new building. The first studios were located temporarily in an old building in downtown Cairo because television's initial broadcast was targeted for the eighth anniversary of the revolution. The first pictures appeared on 21 July 1960 (Nassr 1963, p. 86), using the 625-line European standard.

Three separate channels were provided under the RCA contract. The Main Program was transmitted on Channel 5 from a 10-kilowatt transmitter. Channels 9 and 7, each with 2-kilowatt transmitters, were introduced as respectively the Second Program and the Cultural/Foreign Program. The Main Program was the first to be extended throughout the country through links to other transmitters, the first of which was in Egypt's second largest city, Alexandria. After the major population areas were linked, two channels—the Main by 1975 (Tawffik 1980a, p. 1) and the Second by 1979 (Abdu 1979)—were available to most of Egypt's population from a chain of transmitters along the length of the Nile. This coverage was made possible by the fact that Egypt's population is so largely distributed along the narrow agricultural area irrigated by the Nile. Although Egypt is the size of Texas and New Mexico geographically, the country's 41 million people are thus crowded into a relatively small area, the country's arable lands being among the most densely populated in the world. The country did not have to wait, then, to link distant villages by satellite ground stations, as did Saudi Arabia, Oman, and the Sudan, when such facilities became available: the construction of microwave stations along the river was coordinated with the telecommunications authority and the Egyptian railway system.

Nasser and his advisors were unique among Middle Eastern leaders at the time both because of the role they envisioned for both radio and television and because of their commitment of financial resources and personnel to the attainment of that vision. It was generally the practice in other Arab countries to start modest radio and television operations and then to determine whether they should be expanded in terms of programming capability and coverage area. Nasser inherited a limited radio service and rapidly expanded programming and transmission capability; television started as a multi-channel operation and (as we have seen) its extension to the major population centers of the country was begun as soon as microwave links could be created.

2.1.10 Television, 1960 to 1967

Because of its well-financed radio service and film industry, Egypt had the talent to start a multi-channel operation without importing engineering or production staff from other countries. This talent also enabled Egypt to produce a relatively high percentage of its own programs—something no other Arab country was able to do.

The television channels were intended to parallel the spread and success of the three main kinds of program groupings found on radio: a Main Program (Channel 5) would provide a mixture of popular programming, news, and programs with developmental and educational themes; a Second Program (Channel 9), designed initially to be for the urban areas, would feature programs that would appeal to a sophisticated audience; and a Third Program (Channel 7) would cater mostly to the foreign community, featuring Egyptian-made programs in French and English as well as transmitting imported films and tapes. The third channel was closed after the 1967 war for financial reasons, as it was believed to be a luxury. Some of its programs were shifted to the other channels (Rahman 1974).

From the beginning, Egyptian television has featured an abundance of Egyptian feature-length films: they are its most important source of local programs. After the revolution, many films had maintained the traditional formats of Egyptian films—romance, music, and slapstick comedy—but they were now oriented toward the development of a new socialist nation where education, dedication, and hard work were to better the Arab world. The film industry and the television channels did not, even so, turn out mere political pap. The Egyptian character is essentially kind, fun-loving, and possessed of a sophisticated sense of humor: these traits are too engrained in the population for bland programming to conquer.

A great deal of early television programming was done live and some was taped on the RCA machines supplied as part of the television contract. The television portion of the broadcasting complex was designed for 11 large studios plus small ones for interviews and news. Several were constructed so that the television drama could take place on a stage before a live audience of several hundred people. By western television standards these productions, some of which were replayed into the mid-1970s, were not well done. Much of the action was improvisation. Camera shots consistently included hanging microphones and actors waiting offstage. The overall effect was that of a theater performance being recorded by television cameras. It was only when the export market for taped plays became lucrative that dramatic productions became more sophisticated, done without an audience in a large studio with the intention of editing the final product.[10]

Several mobile units were supplied as part of the RCA contract and these were used for sporting events, major public speeches by Nasser and other political leaders, and the often televised airport greetings of visiting heads of state. Film shot for television was, however, the main way of covering events in Egypt. Monochrome film stock was relatively inexpensive and the country had an abundance of people to shoot, process, and edit it. In addition, the edited product could easily be duplicated and sent via air to other television stations.

News was a regular feature and was deemed important enough for more than one channel to show the same newscast in Arabic. Later, regularly scheduled newscasts in both French and English were started. After the revolution, Egypt developed the practice of having the state news agency provide guidance regarding the order of news items on both radio and television, and during periods of political crisis, Egypt's Middle East News Agency would actually supply the material. This practice, generally referred to by Arab journalists as "news protocol," has been adopted by virtually every Arab country. The term refers to a set of guidelines for each country's media which mandates that stories about the head of state and his family come first, generally to be followed by stories on those Arab countries with which the country has close relations. Stories about the rest of the Arab world and other foreign countries follow. The effect has been to give the head of state a great deal of visibility: he is almost always featured, if only in a still picture of his receiving visitors.

Dizard notes that while Nasser and his themes appeared to be omnipresent, those who were controlling the medium used "*relative* restraint . . . in [their] television propaganda" (1966, p. 150). Egypt did not attempt to utilize what was seen as an entertainment medium to show executions, as did Syria, or to show endless televised revolutionary trials, as was done in Iraq. Dizard accurately observes that Nasser was careful to avoid appealing directly to the television audience; rather, his speeches to various groups on selected occasions were televised, thereby leaving the impression "of tele-

---

[10]This writer first observed Egyptian television in 1964, and later observed it during a one-month residence in August 1974 and a nine-month residence from September 1976 to June 1977.

vised coverage of events in which [Nasser was] the leading orator addressing a meeting to which the television audience [was] invited as onlookers (1966, p. 151).

During these early television years, foreign programming was also used. Older movies that had originally been subtitled for cinema were purchased by Egyptian television; American and British programs were televised. However, during this period, the new shows were relatively few, as it was so expensive to dub or to subtitle them. As additional Arab countries started television systems, it became feasible for program distributors to help finance those costly operations. Some of the work was undertaken in Egypt, but increasingly the subtitling and dubbing center of the Arab world became Beirut, Lebanon, where in the 1950s the ARAMCO television station in Saudi Arabia had had its programming subtitled. The programs that were prepared for showing in Egypt tended also to be shown in Lebanon, Saudi Arabia, Kuwait, and other countries because they were basic action/adventure or comedy series acceptable to Moslem culture with only minor editing: "Leave it to Beaver," "I Love Lucy," "Bonanza," "Combat," and "Gunsmoke" were among them.

2.1.11 Television, 1967 to 1974

The June 1967 war resulted in an Egyptian defeat that was militarily, economically, and psychologically devastating. The Israelis captured the Sinai and the Egyptian Air Force was temporarily eliminated. The closing of the Suez Canal destroyed Egypt's main source of hard currency. As previously noted, the pre-war media compaign had implied that Egypt would be militarily successful against Israel, and when the extent of the defeat became known to the population, it was crushing. President Nasser, in a speech broadcast on television and virtually every radio transmitter in Egypt, assumed blame for the defeat and attempted to resign; but the population took to the streets and urged him to stay on as president.

Immediately after the war, there was a decrease in the amount of foreign programming that was shown on television. The third channel, over which much had been telecast, was eliminated, and the British and American programs that constituted the bulk of the imported programs were deemed unacceptable due to the break in diplomatic relations with Great Britain and the United States. Almost all forms of programming on television placed less emphasis on Egypt's military capability, tending instead toward the nationalistic, the educational, and the religious. When Egypt decided to assume a closer relationship with its military supplier, the Soviet Union, and to construct an air defense system against Israeli air attack, military personnel and hardware from the Soviet Union poured into the country—and cultural agreements between Egypt and the Soviet bloc countries brought increased programs from them. The broadcast system being financially hard-pressed, television started showing films about Soviet and East European life: there was no particular liking for such programs among television programmers, but they were either free of charge or inexpensive and pleased those whom Egypt at the time believed to be its friends.

The general technical quality of Egyptian television declined between 1967 and 1974. There was less money for new equipment and the original RCA equipment began to show signs of deterioration because of lack of maintenance and the difficult Egyptian climatic conditions of heat and dust. Also, Egypt needed to purchase its spare parts from a company that had been banned from doing business in the Arab world: certain companies, including Coca-Cola, Ford, and the Radio Corporation of America, had in 1967 been put on the Arab League boycott list[11] for alleged business dealings with Israel. That problem was solved, at least temporarily, by purchasing RCA parts through a supplier rather than directly from RCA.[12] The financial picture for television improved slightly between 1970 and 1974 because of program sales to other Arab countries—some of which, like Saudi Arabia, had refused to purchase Egyptian-made television programs until about 1970 because of the difficult relations between the two countries after Nasser sent troops to fight in North Yemen. The post-1970 program sales produced some hard currency that the Egyptian Radio-Television Federation could use to upgrade equipment, by purchasing such things as Ampex video tape recorders and Marconi cameras. But the change in government after Nasser's death and Sadat's ascendancy to the presidency in 1970 does not appear to have had much effect on television programming or the structure of the Federation. Sadat is extensively covered by television in the same manner Nasser was, but Sadat has never been so commanding an orator. Sadat's television appearances almost always occur on the occasion of his addresses to the National Assembly or during functions such as national celebrations.

Perhaps so few changes took place in television and radio after 1970 because of the manner in which the broadcast media operate as a government bureaucracy. On 13 August 1970 President Nasser signed a presidential decree (*Arab Broadcasts* 1970b, pp. 50–57) annulling the 1966 decrees that had established radio, television, and broadcast engineering as separate departments under the Ministry of Information. The new decree formally established the Egyptian Radio-Television Federation and created four distinct sectors—radio, television, engineering, and finance—each of which had a chairman who reported directly to the Minister of Information. All

[11]The Arab League Boycott Office is located in Damascus, Syria. It attempts to ban foreign companies that either trade with or have a strong presence—such as a manufacturing capability—in Israel.

[12]The ban stopped Arab countries from purchasing new equipment from RCA, although Saudi Arabia did buy an entire television station for the Eastern Province from RCA after the boycott was announced. Arab countries that have operating RCA transmitters must still purchase spare parts from the company. However, most RCA studio equipment in the Arab world has been replaced with non-RCA equipment purchased from the United States, Europe, and Japan.

personnel connected with broadcasting in Egypt, including some Ministry of Information officials, were transferred to serve under the aegis of a section. The exact number of employees now connected with the Federation is not known by the Egyptian government, but estimates range from 12,000 to 15,000. One reason for the wide disparity in the estimates is that many of the employees, including this writer at one time, are temporary and come only to do a specific announcing shift or to take a part in a play. The broadcasting organization in Egypt is indeed large, with too many permanent staff members; the various sectors could function effectively—some say a great deal more efficiently—with one-third to one-half the people.

But this situation is not unique within the Egyptian bureaucracy. A university education in Egypt is much sought after by the people on the lower end of the socio-economic scale as a way of gaining entry into the middle class; those in the middle and upper classes want a university education in order to maintain their places in society. After the revolution, the government expanded opportunities for Egyptians to gain an education: new campuses were built and old ones were enlarged. When the number of graduates increased in the late 1950s, the government realized that few employment opportunities existed for educated men and women, thus rendering them a potentially disgruntled force politically. The solution was to guarantee every university graduate a government job. Graduates are assigned to various departments almost on a random basis, although some attempt is made to utilize training in finance, languages, and the social sciences. The Federation, then, like virtually every other government organization, is flooded with people who have no other place to go. One often sees in government offices large numbers of people with little to do except invent ways to make the bureaucracy more cumbersome. In 1980 the gross monthly pay for a new graduate in his first government job was only 30 Egyptian pounds, or approximately $42.90 at the tourist exchange rate: the salary, low even by Egyptian standards, tends to discourage graduates from seeking government employment and rather functions, in effect, as a kind of unemployment compensation.

Whatever the perceived quality of Egyptian television after its initial stage of development, Egyptians were watching the medium. Lorimor and Dunn found that 73% of respondents in their study watched television; 1% of the sample watched between seven and eight hours, with more women than men viewing more than three hours each day (1968–69, p. 683).

2.1.12 Television, 1974 to 1980

There are those who argue about which country won the October 1973 Egyptian-Israeli War. Egyptians know that they were at least the side that achieved a psychological victory—one that brought them out of a long period of depression and self-examination following the 1967 war. During the brief engagement itself and immediately afterward, the Egyptian media took a very different approach than they had during and after the 1967 war. Radio tended to be more honest about the military situation as it reported it from the front, and to be less boastful about the apparent victory when the Suez Canal was crossed. Television programming, which took a little longer to produce and air and would presumably be seen only within Egypt, was a bit more upbeat, reflecting the confidence Egyptians were recovering as good news came in. The Egyptians also improved their approach to helping the international press by increasing liaison with reporters and facilitating the shooting, processing, editing, and exporting of newsfilm. Plans solidified for construction of a satellite ground station to transmit and to receive television signals.

After the 1973 war, it was not so much program philosophy or formats that changed as subject matter and mood. Nine months after the Egyptian-Israeli engagement, Egyptian television still showed drama that dealt with some aspect of the military victory, dancers in fatigues reenacted the Suez crossing, and interviews with government officials, religious leaders, and university professors examined virtually every aspect of the military action. President Sadat continued to make public appearances and speeches that were covered extensively. News items and special programs about the United Nations, United States, and Israeli agreements regarding military disengagement received a high priority.

More than any other Egyptian mass medium, television has tended to reflect the changing international political orientation of the country. Before the 1973 war, Sadat dismissed his vice president and other officials who were apparently plotting, with Soviet help, against him. This action, known as the "corrective revolution," led to, among other things, Sadat's order for all Soviet military advisors to leave the country. During the Nixon administration, Kissinger promoted the reestablishment of the United States–Egyptian diplomatic relations that had been severed in June 1967. These moves along with the general mood of the Sadat government gradually changed Egypt during the 1970s from a socialist orientation to one that was more hospitable to free enterprise and decidedly pro-west.

After 1974, the year when the door was formally opened to the west, the number of western (mostly British and American) programs on Egyptian television increased. The television sector decided to continue the development of color. The French government had been successful in persuading Egypt to adopt the SECAM system and had installed SECAM color equipment in one of the Egyptian studios before the 1973 war. After the war, the decision was made to convert both production and transmission facilities to color. This action helped the technical quality of television because in 1974 most of the monochrome equipment that had been installed by RCA in 1960, such as switchers and cameras, had been too long in use—and it was, after all, only monochrome. Color television was believed by some to be a luxury that Egypt could not afford, but the attitude among broadcasting officials prevailed: the new equipment was necessary for the production of programs to be sold to other countries that were converting to color and anyway monochrome television equipment was becoming increasingly difficult to purchase. In August 1974 Ahmed Abul-Magd, then Minister of Information, officially opened a new and impressive color television production studio (*Egyptian Gazette* 1974, p. 1). Outfitted with sophisticated audio, lighting, and video equipment from Great Britain, it was used primarily for taping of drama.

After 1974, the revenue that television derived from advertising and from program sales to other Arab countries increased significantly. The aforementioned change in Egypt's political orientation had a great deal to do with the increase in advertising. Sadat's "Open Door Policy" encouraged foreign companies to invest and do business in Egypt and some currency restrictions on the importation of goods were lifted, resulting in a change in the variety and the amount of foreign goods in Egyptian shops. Disposable income among some middle- and upper-middle-class urban Egyptian families increased, due both to the open door policy and the high salaries of family members working in Gulf countries. And, although before 1974 there was little incentive for companies to advertise, and most advertising had been restricted to Egyptian state industries that marketed petroleum products, soap, cigarettes, insect sprays, and electrical appliances such as hot water heaters, advertising had always been permitted on Egyptian television. In 1976 the old products were still advertised: but they were joined by commercials for American and European cigarettes (later banned from broadcasting), American and Japanese automobiles, American air conditioners, food, and imported perfumes, cosmetics, and soft drinks.

Egyptian advertising rates are two-tiered, providing a lower cost in Egyptian pounds for local advertising by businesses and state industry. Commercials for imported products must be paid for in hard currency and are much more expensive than local advertising, often by as much as a factor of four (Egyptian Radio-Television Federation 1979). Separate figures for television advertising income are not available; but Table 5 indicates the amount of yearly income received from advertising on both radio and television. Note the significant increase after 1974.

The changing economic mood in Egypt and the increased economic fortunes of the Arabian Gulf states after the 1973 war combined to make the production of television programs for other countries a profitable business for Egyptian producers. As noted earlier, television organizations in other Arab countries have generally relied on Egypt as a source of Arab-produced material for television when politics would permit it. Egyptian talent (and therefore the Cairene dialect) are well known throughout the Arab world because of Egyptian films, radio, and recorded music. Until the 1970s, tapes of programs made for Egyptian audiences were sold to other countries: during the 1970s, especially the late 1970s, more productions were under-

Table 5. Egyptian Advertising Revenue from
Radio and Television, 1961 to 1978

Fiscal Year	Amount in Dollars
1961–1962 (4–1 to 3–31)	12,484
1962–1963 (4–1 to 3–31)	158,563
1963–1964 (4–1 to 3–31)	171,367
1964–1965 (4–1 to 10–10)	126,970
1965–1966 (4–1 to 10–10)	157,379
1966–1967 (10–11 to 10–23)	174,341
1967–1968 (10–23 to 10–24)	198,091
1968–1969 (10–23 to 10–24)	446,466
1969–1970 (10–23 to 10–24)	474,816
1970–1971 (10–23 to 10–24)	552,088
1971–1972 (10–24 to 12–31)	596,521
1973 (1–1 to 12–31)	709, 932
1974 (1–1 to 12–31)	977,316
1975 (1–1 to 12–31)	1,504,360
1976 (1–1 to 12–31)	2,355,678
1977 (1–1 to 12–31)	3,376,271
1978 (1–1 to 12–31)	5,235,300

SOURCE: The figures were gathered by Karen Dajani in connection with her Temple University dissertation. Amounts in dollars were converted from Egyptian pounds at the official "incentive" or tourist rate of 68 piasters per dollar (K. Dajani 1979, p. 167).

taken with the express idea of marketing them in other countries, particularly those countries in the Gulf that could afford to purchase them at relatively high prices.

The potentially lucrative market in the Gulf provided an opportunity for independent producers, using Egyptian talent, to rent the Egyptian color television studios for the production of drama for export. This practice, of course, led to direct competition for the television operation itself. In 1976, the Egyptian studio rentals were curtailed, and at one point television-sector employees were banned from working in Egypt for private producers (*Egyptian Gazette* 1976, p. 1). This move prompted the producers to rent studios in Great Britain, Germany, Greece, Jordan, Bahrain, and Dubai, to import Egyptian talent, and to tape programs that they then sold directly to Arab world television stations. Once the producers and talent left Egypt for television series production, they were reluctant to return to tape programs in Cairo even when the television organization tried to entice them to do so: the Egyptian television studios and editing facilities were rented for relatively high prices, and producers had learned that they could travel abroad, import Egyptian talent, and produce programs more cheaply elsewhere than in Egypt. In other countries, the producers did not have to pay everyone from janitors to engineers for their "cooperation," and talent liked leaving the country to work because they were paid there in hard currency and could avoid the relatively heavy Egyptian tax. Eventually, the Egyptian Radio-Television Federation created its own production company, the "Voice of Cairo," which used the Cairo television facilities but was organized along private sector lines so as to compete more effectively for material and talent. Competition has only increased—but the "Voice of Cairo" has been actively involved in both production and program sales in the Arab world. Certainly the competition has tended to stabilize rapidly increasing program prices.

Since Egypt's peace treaty with Israel, many Arab countries have joined the call by the more militant countries to isolate Egypt and boycott its exports. Many countries have broken diplomatic relations with Egypt or reduced the size of diplomatic missions in Cairo; Libya, Syria, and Iraq stopped all airline flights to Egypt. Countries that have supported the boycott vowed no longer to purchase Egyptian television programs, adding that they did not need to buy directly from Egypt because so much quality material, produced outside of Egypt, was available from Egyptian artists.[13] However, there has been no evidence to suggest that Egyptian program sales to the Arab world decreased as a result; they may actually have increased (Tawffik 1980b; Abdullah 1979). The post-boycott marketing efforts of the television sales staff in Cairo became more aggressive, and the creation of a program-marketing company structured to give the impression of being independent from the Egyptian government helped those who still wanted to buy from Egypt. Finally, because so much Egyptian talent has been used in both "Voice of Cairo" and independent productions taped outside Egypt, it has been difficult for viewers to tell where programs were made. This situation has worked to the advantage of program purchasers in other countries who have felt that they should at least appear to abide by the boycott—though eventually the Arab political situation might indeed hurt Egyptian program sales, which have been financially very important to Egyptian television. Between 1973 and 1978, the Federation received over $20 million from television program sales to Arab countries, as Table 6 indicates; Table 7 provides the number of hours of television programs that were sold to Arab countries in 1978. A combination of advertising revenue and income from program sales helped Egypt begin to convert to SECAM color transmission in 1977; gradually, local production, including news, became color. All new transmitters, many of which were added between 1977 and 1980, were capable of color transmission: they brought the Second Program to locations previously served by the Main Program (Abdu 1979).

---

[13]The boycott organizers are interested in drawing the distinction between the Egyptian people and the Egyptian government. Those Arab world television officials who do support the boycott do not consider programs produced outside of Egypt with Egyptian talent subject to the boycott.

Table 6. Egyptian Television Program Sales

Year	Amount
1973	$2,154,803
1974	2,342,230
1975	2,724,888
1976	2,916,586
1977	4,804,940
1978	5,692,975
Total	$20,636,422

SOURCE: K. Dajani 1979, p. 181.

In 1979, some countries decreased or stopped altogether the purchase of Egyptian television programs. Lebanon produces most of its own Arabic-language programming, and South Yemen and Libya have not purchased material for several years. Iraq stopped the purchase of programs after the decision to boycott was taken at a Baghdad (Iraq) meeting in 1979. Decreases in program sales may retard the improvement of the technical quality of Egyptian television because of the positive correlation between hard currency income and the amount available for equipment purchases.

Because of the complex nature of the Egyptian Radio-Television Federation budget, the percentage of income from various sources is difficult to determine. Sources of income include advertising revenue, program sales, funds from the state budget, and revenue from a type of license on receivers. During the Nasser years the government attempted to encourage the availability of radio and television receivers: the radio license fee, which was the original means of financing Egyptian radio, was eliminated not only because

Table 7. 1978 Egyptian Arab World Program Sales

Country	Hours Sold
Algeria	50
Bahrain	300
Iraq	200
Jordan	300
Kuwait	400
Morocco	60
Oman	120
Qatar	500
Saudi Arabia	300
Sudan	350
Syria	200
Tunisia	260
United Arab Emirates	500
Yemen	550

SOURCE: Abdullah 1979.

the tax was difficult to collect after transistor radios became common, but because the government did not want to discourage radio ownership among those who could least afford the license fee. It was felt, however, that television would require some kind of contribution from set owners, who would initially be urban citizens able to afford to help finance the medium. The problem that Egypt faced along with many other developing countries was how to verify set ownership and to collect fees. Culturally, both poor and financially well-off Egyptians function outside of government controls and tend to mistrust government officials and institutions. The government believed that cheating would be so widespread as to render ineffective a license fee system similar to that used in Japan and many West European countries. The Egyptian solution was one that guaranteed income for television but was not particularly fair, as it did not necessarily gain income directly from those who used the medium. An amount was added monthly to electricity bills, which were all handled through the national electricity authority: Egyptian homes have few electrical appliances and the belief was that those who were heavy consumers of electricity were heavy television users. Some such surcharge was probably the only way that revenue could be collected systematically, and Egypt was not alone in adopting the system. In the late 1970s Cyprus, following the example of Greece, changed to a television license fee system very similar to Egypt's.

An Egyptian viewer today, having access to electricity and a television receiver and within range of transmitters, is provided with about 30 hours of television programming per week on two national channels. The Main Program generally begins daily between 1500 and 1600 and runs continuously until approximately midnight. The Second Program begins about 1700 and also lasts until around midnight. Transmissions are extended on Friday and Sunday, the Moslem and Christian days of rest respectively; for important sporting events such as soccer matches; and during selected months throughout the school year, when instructional programs are broadcast in the morning. Although factors such as availability of programs, political events, national celebrations, and important religious months such as Ramadan and Hajj all alter the schedule, the basic daily schedule for the two national channels has remained about the same since the 1970s. A schedule of television programs for selected days during the week of 23 January 1980, as it was published in Egyptian daily newspapers, is shown in Figure 1. The broadcasting authority publishes a weekly magazine, *Broadcasting*, which provides a more detailed television and radio schedule; the publication also provides articles about broadcasting personalities and features about various aspects of the broadcast media.

There is something for everyone on Egyptian television. Both channels use the "continuity announcer" format, in which someone—usually an attractive female who is striving to become a television or cinema star—introduces each program. Between programs, slides of Cairo or the Egyp-

Figure 1. Schedules of Egyptian Stations

First Program
Channel 5 (Cairo)

Second Program
Channel 9 (Cairo)

Wednesday, January 23, 1980

First Program	Second Program
1600 Opening and Koran	1700 Opening and Koran
1615 Children's Program	1715 Foreign Serial
1645 English for You	1800 Educational Program
1700 Press Review	1830 Literacy Program
1730 Religious Competition	1900 News in French
1800 News	1930 Competition
1830 Police Magazine	2000 Events of the Last 24 Hours
1900 Educational Program	2030 The Guide
2015 "Lost Love" Arabic Serial	2100 Around the World
2050 Religious Program	2115 Sound of Music
2100 News in Arabic	2145 First Aid Program
2130 Cultural Symposium	2200 News in English
2215 A Choice for You	2214 "Lion of the Nights"
2350 Koran and Close Down	(Arabic Film)
	2345 Religious Program
	2355 Close Down

Thursday, January 24, 1980

First Program	Second Program
1450 Opening and Koran	1700 Opening and Koran
1415 Children's Program	1715 Arabic Film
1445 Football (Soccer) Match	("Nice Mothers-in-Law")
1700 Religious Program	1900 News in French
1730 Man and Civilization	1915 Children of the World
1800 News (in Arabic)	1930 Symposium
1830 Foreign Serial ("Switch")	2000 Events of the Last 24 Hours
1930 My Life	2030 Foreign Serial
2015 Arabic Serial ("Lost Love")	2100 Round the World
2050 Religious Program	2115 Ballet
2100 News in Arabic	2200 News in English
2130 Arabic Comedy ("Original and Copy")	2215 Scenes and Colors
2345 News Summary	2245 Foreign Film
2350 Koran and Close Down	2345 Religious Program
	2355 Close Down

Friday, January 18, 1980

First Program	Second Program
1000 Opening and Koran	1700 Opening and Koran
1015 Children's Cinema	1710 Foreign Serial
1115 Friday's Prayers	1800 Weekly Program Review
1230 Woman's Magazine	1830 Cultural Program
1330 Cultural Program	1900 News in French
1410 News Summary	1930 Religious Program
1415 Light Upon Light	2000 Events of the Last 24 Hours
1500 Football (Soccer) Match	2030 Cinema Magazine
1700 Weekly Program Review	2100 Green Revolution
1730 Health Magazine	2145 Variety
1800 News in Arabic	2200 News in English

Figure 1. (continued)

First Program	*Second Program*
Channel 5 (Cairo)	Channel 9 (Cairo)

Friday, January 18, 1980 (continued)

1830 Foreign Serial	2215 Foreign Film
1930 Arabic Music	2345 Koran and Close Down
2015 Arabic Serial ("I Love Her")	
2100 News in Arabic	
2130 Science and Faith	
2200 Arabic Film ("The Second Wife")	
2345 News Summary	
2350 Koran and Close Down	

SOURCE: Schedules were obtained from the *The Egyptian Gazette* 23 January 1980, p. 3; 24 January 1980, p. 3; 18 January 1980, p. 3.

tian countryside are shown with background music; short taped popular songs and clustered commercials are seen. The transitions between programs are not always according to schedule because program times are by western standards only estimates. Foreign programs with no commercials inserted are considerably shorter than the standard 30 minutes or one hour. Also, there is a shortage of video tape recorders during transmission time because they are heavily utilized for the recording of satellite feeds for news and local production.

The medium is not without critics. *The Egyptian Gazette*, Cairo's daily English-language newspaper, has often led press criticism of various aspects of television. The Bairam Holiday—a feast period at the end of the religious month of Ramadan—brings special programming to television. Mamdough Dakhakhni reviewed three 1976 television plays in these pungent words:

Over the three Bairam days Television's Channel 5 treated peak lunch-hour audiences to three dreadful "comedies" that should have found their way into the dustbin a long time ago. The first play "Intaha el Dars Ya Ghabi" ("Hey Stupid, the Lesson's Over") is a weak and vague attempt to introduce a science fiction theme. . . . [It] is pure unadulterated rubbish, full of "Egyptianisms" and typical of the lowest form of slapstick comedy. A foreign visitor might well think that it was a play written by the mentally retarded . . . or at least with a view to encouraging mental retardation growth rates in the country. . . . In "Music in the Native Quarter," [the writers] turn this adaptation of the film "The Sound of Music" into an improbable and meaningless farce. The military type of gentleman so common in yesterday's Europe cannot be translated into Arabic. . . . It is more than a joke to say that when "School for Delinquents" is on TV the traffic both in Alexandria and Cairo tends to fall off dramatically. One wonders whether this is the reason why it is shown so frequently. [1976, p. 4]

A 1977 editorial attacks television more generally by noting that "television is a LE [Egyptian Pound] 12 million per year liability to the state and poses a mental hazard to 38 million people." It continues:

There are two prominent schools of thought on the quality of TV programmes and both have very sharply defined views. One believes that the programmes are written "by the mentally retarded, for the mentally retarded, and in order to promote mental retardation growth rates" in the country. The other thinks that "taking into consideration the acute shortage of public lavatories in Cairo, the TV building, under the present circumstances, would be put to far better use by being converted into a giant public convenience."
Talented Egyptians are nowhere to be seen. The vast majority have fled to other Arab states where the pay is good and where their talents are appreciated and put to good use. No one should be surprised if films made in the Gulf by Egyptians are sold to Egyptian TV and this will be the rule rather than the exception if TV continues to be run like an agricultural co-op.[*Egyptian Gazette* 1977, p. 2]

In 1980 the criticism turned to popular sporting events—particularly soccer—on television:

Consider the commentator who, while holding an interview, suddenly dashed away from the camera's view leaving the microphone in the hands of the bewildered guest. Only recently the same man left his seat again, this time to take part in a shouting match with spectators. There are commentators who countless numbers of times forget they are on the air and chat away or clear their throats raucously. . . . Last month a booth was installed at Cairo stadium for the commentator, and so sparing him from having literally to fight off spectators who obstruct his view. This may also do away with the taunting of fans who, as TV audiences saw only a few weeks ago, had tug o' war with a commentator, using the microphone cord as rope. [*Egyptian Gazette* 1980, p. 2]

Comments like the above are infrequent but deal perceptively with some of the major flaws both obvious and not so obvious to the viewer. But, in fact, most television viewers are apparently satisfied with what they see; and many feel fortunate to own or to have access to a receiver.

2.1.13 Set Ownership and Viewing Patterns

In 1969 the government claimed that there were 498,000 television sets in Egypt (Arab States Broadcasting Union 1969). Since this estimate was given, the number of sets has probably more than doubled. Among the more affluent, a television set—a color set after 1977—has become a normal part of a household. Increasingly, expatriate Egyptian salaries from employment in the Gulf help low-income families acquire sets; many Egyptians bring them on the plane with them when they return to Egypt on leave, as sets in the Gulf states are easily available and relatively inexpensive because of the absence of import taxes.

Shops in Egypt carry a variety of television receivers. Both Japanese and European sets may be found, in addition to the monochrome receivers that are assembled in Egypt. The Nasser government started a state television receiver manufacturing company in Cairo shortly after television was begun. The first agreement was with RCA; but, with the Arab League boycott, other agreements were made. For a period of time, sets were assembled with parts from a Hungarian electronics firm. The locally made sets have a price advantage but the imported sets have a reputation of being more reliable. All color sets are imported.

Television is an ideal medium for a culture that is family-oriented and tends to center much of its entertainment around the home. Cairo and Alexandria are culturally rich, with live music, theatre, cinemas, and sporting activities—mostly associated with private clubs. However, the majority of Egyptians are not in an economic or social position to take advantage of these opportunities and must stay closer to home. Even for those with the money and motivation to seek enjoyment outside the home, the over-population in Cairo makes it physically difficult:

[T]he streets are crowded to explosion point. It is very hard, sometimes practically impossible to find a parking place for your car. That is why most Cairenes turn to television for their evening entertainment. This also applies to most other cities, not overlooking inflation which does not allow driving out or going to the movie with the economic means of the average Egyptian. [Tawffik 1980a, pp. 5–6]

During the period when television was new, the government subsidized and installed hundreds of sets in rural and urban cultural centers. This worked well until the sets started to deteriorate. Over the years, the number of villages that have been connected to the national electrical grid has increased. As this has happened, the villages—most of which are in proximity to the Nile and therefore in range of a television transmitter—have become television-oriented. The usual pattern of set acquisition starts with a local businessman or political leader who purchases a set. As financial conditions permit, families follow. Sets are usually also available to those who visit the local coffee house, as the owners realize the attraction that a set has for customers. An American volunteer worker near Beni Sueif, a town south of Cairo, noted that as electrical poles that would carry electricity to her village were erected, a local leader and a businessman both purchased sets—prior to electricity's actually reaching the population (Corcoran 1980).

In an urban setting such as Cairo, the problem is more a lack of money than electricity. Often more than one family shares a television set by having several members contribute to the purchase price. In the more crowded, lower-income sections of Cairo, such as Bulaq and Shubra, young couples as well as residents in their forties save for years to get a set. It is the custom for women to sell pieces of gold jewelry, often representing family savings, in order to make the important purchase. Given a choice between a refrigerator and a television set, many lower-income people select the television set (Rugh 1980). Many acquired their sets second hand from dealers who occasionally help finance them: there is a section of Cairo between the Opera Square and the Khan Khalili Suq (market) where used parts for everything from old radios to antique radar sets are sold; and there older sets are returned to working order and sold, in an open market fashion, to those who are about to make a first television set purchase. Among the lower classes, television set ownership is more than a status symbol: it is a means of family entertainment within what is essentially an urban subsistence-level existence and a way of providing what is believed to be a better education for children, if only by giving them a view of the world.

A characteristic of Arab broadcast organizations is that they do not support media research efforts. Egypt's is no exception. The research office of the Egyptian Radio-Television Federation does some content analysis studies, but it mainly counts transmission hours for both radio and television; the Egyptians are ready and able to provide the number of hours per week devoted to a specific type of program such as drama or music, but studies that attempt to assess how and under what conditions citizens utilize the electronic media are almost nonexistent. Even students at Cairo University and the American University have not been encouraged to undertake such studies. A possible explanation of this is the reluctance of a traditional people to respond to official questioning, and the fear among broadcasting officials of negative criticism.

In a 1977 study of the media habits of Egyptian editors, television was mentioned often as a source of entertainment rather than information (Boyd and Kushner 1979, p. 109). This writer found that one grouping of Egyptians, most of them government officials who were entertainment-oriented, liked and trusted television (Boyd 1978, p. 503).

Egypt may have a radio and television system that is too large for a country of its size and financial resources. It employs more people than are necessary for the efficient operation of its two television and numerous radio services. The system is the largest and the most influential in the Arab world and it is likely to remain so no matter what the political environment of the Middle East or the intentions of the political leadership in Egypt. Too much money has been invested in facilities—and too many people depend for a living on the media—to change the system.

2.2 The Sudan

The Democratic Republic of the Sudan is the largest country in Africa, with an area of 967,500 square miles. The country shares frontiers with eight nations: Egypt, Libya, Chad, the Central African Republic, Zaire, Uganda,

Kenya, and Ethiopia. Its estimated population of 16 million live in predominantly rural settings within nine provinces.

The Sudan gained independence from Great Britain in 1956. After independence, the country underwent a period of political adjustment during which military and elected officials alternately administered the country. In a May 1969 military coup, Jaafar Nimeri emerged as a respected leader and was later elected president. Probably the major accomplishment of Nimeri's leadership has been a 1972 treaty with the South Sudan Liberation Front, which had been fighting to separate the southern and northern parts of the country. The Sudan is unlike most other Arab countries in that a sizable number of its citizens in the south are not Moslems and do not speak Arabic. The 1972 agreement recognizes both the English language and Christianity in the south and grants some degree of autonomy to the three southern provinces.

Economic problems have troubled the country since independence. Primarily an agricultural country, the Sudan has hopes of becoming the "breadbasket of the Middle East"; but development has been slow. The fact that the Sudan has no oil to help with development means that its valuable foreign exchange has increasingly had to go for petroleum imports.

The Sudan has had serious problems with the development of a broadcasting system. The country is very large and its population scattered. Unlike Egypt's, its political leadership has not placed a high priority on the electronic media. Even during the intense military operations in the south prior to the 1972 treaty, a time when the government was trying to make the populated areas of the south feel that they were equal members of a united country, no attempt was made, either by enlarging broadcasting facilities or by creating a specifically directed program, to communicate with the "rebels." Several factors have complicated broadcasting development: a lack of hard currency for equipment, a division of administrative responsibility for radio between two ministries, and technical problems with the construction of transmitters that could reach the population with a broadcasting signal. These and other problems have resulted in a situation in the Sudan that does not exist in any other Arab country, and possibly exists in no other developing country: the television service is more effective in reaching the entire population than is radio.

2.2.1 Radio Broadcasting

In Omdurman, just across the Nile from Khartoum, on 1 April 1940, the British started radio transmission from a small studio in the Post Office (Ministry of Information and Culture 1971, p. 105; Salheen 1979)—the institution with which early broadcasting efforts were aligned in many countries with a colonial past, as in some European countries. Apparently, a strong motivation for this service was the need to communicate with the local population in response to Axis activity in Ethiopia and North Africa;

the location of the radio studios in Khartoum's neighboring city, where the White and Blue Niles converge, gave the Sudanese radio services the name Radio Omdurman. The expansion of facilities moved slowly after World War II, but preparations were made for the eventual move of the studios to a one-time girls' school, where all broadcasting facilities are now headquartered. That studio building still functions as the main production and transmission center for Sudanese radio, despite its age and maintenance problems—the governments that were in power after independence, until Nimeri took office, seeming to have had priorities other than broadcasting development.

In the Arab world during the 1950s, most broadcasting production and the associated technical facilities were placed under a ministry of information, while the authority responsible for telecommunications within the country—for cable, microwave, or satellite connections between transmitters and studios or between transmitters in various cities as part of a network interconnection—was often a ministry of communication. In the Sudan, the Ministry of Communication has operated and maintained radio facilities, including studio equipment; and in the Ministry of Information there have been consequent problems in radio production and morale, its staff having to work so closely with others having different loyalties. The various strong personalities that have headed the two ministries have not succeeded in changing this status quo. As late as 1977, it was not unusual for President Nimeri to call the Director General of Radio Broadcasting early in the morning to determine why the main Arabic service was not on the air at the designated sign-on time: the Director General once advised him to call authorities at the Ministry of Communication, as they were responsible for transmitter operation (Salheen 1977). When television was started, the Ministry of Information, which directly operates both of the electronic media, stipulated that television be entirely operated by Ministry of Information engineers.

A great deal of help was offered to the Sudan's infant broadcasting effort by other nations, and many radio employees were sent for training in other countries such as the United States, Great Britain, West Germany, and Australia. For a period of time in the 1960s, the United States Agency for International Development helped with training by contracting with the National Association of Educational Broadcasters to bring American personnel to the Sudan to advise on training. Professor Sydney Head was among several Americans who were in residence in Omdurman helping with this task. Radio officials still consistently state that lack of trained personnel is the biggest problem they face: those who become skilled technicians, producers, and announcers are attracted to high-paying jobs in the Arabian Gulf. After the 1967 Middle East war, during the period that roughly coincided with Egypt's closeness with the communist bloc nations, the Sudan grew more dependent on the Soviet Union and Eastern European countries for economic and military aid: thus, in 1971, it was the Sudan's Russian advisors who suggested the construction of a super-power 1500-kilowatt medium-wave transmitter. They as well as the Sudanese realized that the existing low-power short- and medium-wave transmitters—some of which had been supplied by the United States Agency for International Development (AID) (Head 1974, p. 226)—were inadequate for national coverage even at night, when medium-wave signals travel their longest distances. Czechoslovakia then granted the Ministry of Communication a loan that the two ministries associated with radio broadcasting were "pressed" to use for a powerful transmitter (Shummo 1979), and a contract was signed with the Czechoslovakian Tesla Company for a super-power transmitter and two smaller units. (The Tesla Company has supplied several powerful units to Arab world countries that have or have had close relations with the Soviet Union, among them Egypt, Syria, and Iraq.) But problems developed shortly after the transmitter deal was concluded and the equipment shipped to the Sudan. President Nimeri grew increasingly dissatisfied with what was believed to be Soviet involvement in Sudanese internal affairs: military and trade agreements with the Soviet Union and East European countries were terminated, and relations between the Sudan and those countries grew cool.

The result of the estrangement, for both ministries associated with radio, was a slowdown in work on the vitally important transmitter. First, the supplier said that it was having problems supplying specific parts for the facility; then personnel problems were blamed for the delay in installation. By 1976, the transmitter was tested, but unspecified design flaws emerged that kept it from operating at peak efficiency. An even more serious problem concerned the electrical power to operate the transmitter—actually two 750-kilowatt units designed to work in parallel for a total output of 1500 kilowatts. The transmitter site, near a national hydro-electric project south of Khartoum, had been selected with an eye to power access. However, the powerful transmitter required about five million watts of power to operate at peak power, and only about 9000 kilowatts were available from the hydro-electric generators: therefore, with not enough power available for the local population, agricultural operations, and the transmitters as well, only one of the transmitters has operated—intermittently. These electrical power and design problems have still not been solved (Rahman 1979a) and many Sudanese must still, then, listen to foreign radio stations to receive news and entertainment; but no additional transmission facilities are planned by the Sudanese government. Officials believe that they have no choice but to get the existing powerful transmitters operating.

In the mid-1970s, Ministry of Information and Communication officials realized that studio space was not adequate for program production and transmission. A small studio complex was constructed adjacent to the existing studio building in Omdurman and new Philips audio equipment was installed and tested; but though broadcast installations almost always have strict security systems in developing countries, and in coup-prone Sudan security has been provided by the army, the equipment was destroyed before it had ever been used.[14] When President Nimeri returned from a trip to the United States and Europe on 1 July 1976, he found an attempted coup in progress, apparently backed by Libyan leader Kaddafi.[15] A small army unit guarding the radio studios succeeded in saving the older studios from destruction, but the new building was gutted by fighting. Work immediately commenced on reconstruction of the building, and new equipment was ordered and installed. By 1979, the studio addition was in use. The 1976 coup attempt has had a lasting effect on security around the complex, which also houses the television studios. It is now an army post with permanently stationed troops and each entrance is guarded with combat-ready troops in tanks. Even if a coup is successful in the future, employees who are loyal to the president will not be immediately helpful to those who may want to broadcast, since they have been ordered to return immediately to their native villages should something happen: that will make it difficult for a new government to find them quickly and restore what might amount to normal programming.

2.2.2 Radio Services

National Program.   Intended to reach the entire country with a mixture of news, music, commentary, and educational and cultural programs, the National Program is in Arabic. The ill-fated super-power transmitter was supposed to carry this program, which in 1980 operated for 18 hours per day (0600 to 2400) on mediumwave and shortwave. Several attempts have been made to produce a continuing series of educational programs; and programs about nutrition and medicine have received particular attention from the radio services, in cooperation with the Ministry of Health. Table 8 indicates the average weekly schedule of health and social programs, most of which are broadcast via the National Program.

Those in charge of programs that are intended to promote national development are attempting to carry out the task assigned, and do even more than strictly required, but a shortage of both trained personnel and transmission power to reach a national audience has tended to discourage some officials.

Koranic Station.   Most Arab world countries devote radio transmission time to Koran readings and religious discussions for their predominantly Moslem citizens. Egypt and Saudi Arabia have special services for this purpose; but the Sudan, not having their facilities, limits such programming to a two-hour 1530 to 1730 block on both mediumwave and shortwave.

---

[14]The writer inspected the devastated studio building on 2 February 1977.
[15]For details of the attempted coup see *Newsweek*, 16 August 1976, pp. 36–37.

Table 8. Radio Programs: Health and Social

Program Title	Category	Minutes per Week
Your Health	Health Education	15
Nutrition	Health Education	15
From the Fruits of Religion	Drama	30
The Cooperatives	Social	30
Play of the Week	Social	30
People and Tunes	Social	60
Youth Magazine	Social	30
Family Magazine	Social	30

SOURCE: Shummo 1977.

Voice of the Sudanese Nation. The service called "Voice of the Sudanese Nation" operates from 1730 to 2300 daily on one short-wave transmitter and is apparently receivable throughout the Sudan on shortwave; but the majority of Sudanese citizens lack radios with short-wave capability and short-wave listening is not popular among them. Most of the Voice's programs are in Arabic, but news in French and English is part of the daily schedule and constitutes the only non-Arabic programming that is done.

Juba Local Service. Following the 1972 peace accords with the southern Sudan, the predominantly non-Arabic speaking population in the area was given some degree of autonomy, and part of this restructuring was the appointment of regional ministers based in Juba to parallel ministers who headed the major governmental departments in Khartoum. The Minister of Information for the Southern Region has responsibility for a local broadcast service, which includes local programming in English and Arabic, but the majority of the time the Juba station rebroadcasts one of the Omdurman services. Perhaps the most obvious irony in the gestures that the national government has made to the south is a relative lack of attention to special-

Table 9. Voice of the Sudanese Nation

Time	Program
1730–1745	News in French
1745–1800	News in English
1800–2000	Music and Culture
2000–2015	News
2015–2100	Music, Culture, and Sports
2100–2115	News
2115–2245	Music and Culture
2245–2255	News Summary
2255–2300	Koran
2300	Close Down

SOURCE: *Sudanow* October 1979a, p. 70.

ized broadcast coverage, although both radio and television transmitters have been installed to serve the area. The government insists on broadcasting in the recognized national language, Arabic, which most of the southerners do not speak. English is also used, but the language is not universally spoken. Leaders from the south are making efforts to convince the national government to introduce vernacular languages so that programming in Dinka, Zandi, and Nur can be started (Thiik 1979).

A lack of radio facilities to reach the entire country has serious implications when one considers political events in the Arab world. The Sudan finds itself in a position similar to that of Saudi Arabia during the 1960s, when the kingdom did not have the transmitter power to reach citizens with information that would counter radio attacks by other countries. The Sudan's generally pro-west orientation during the late 1970s, combined with its support of Egypt's President Sadat and its troop withdrawal from the Arab peace-keeping force in Lebanon, has caused it to be the target of radio propaganda from other Arab countries—notably from Libya, Syria, and Iraq. The Sudanese government is too shrewd and forthright to engage in a word-for-word radio battle with other Arab countries, a relative restraint that its lack of transmitters makes almost necessary, but its problem still persists in that the attacks are heard by a Sudanese population who might react as a result of their cumulative effect. Lacking adequate domestic facilities, Sudanese radio and television have used available equipment plus the government-controlled print media to disseminate replies and denials through the Sudan News Agency (SUNA), which supplies almost all national news to the media. In March 1979, both Libyan and Syrian radio services broadcast news about Sudanese strikes and arrests that the government claimed did not occur, the stories having been filed through SUNA facilities by Syrian and Libyan news agency representatives in Khartoum (Ministry of Information and Culture 1979, p. 4); and Iraqi Radio reported, in October 1979, that the Sudanese president was wounded while speaking to a gathering of Sudanese businessmen, his presidential palace having been stormed. A reply to the Iraqi allegations typifies the basic Sudanese reaction to all such attacks:

We have never heard, except from the Tekriti Baath mass media that a coup could be accomplished by simply storming a Presidential Palace. The [Iraqi] News Agency could not tell us about the broadcasting station and other important utilities. Naturally it had nothing to say because on the same day and the following morning the President's voice was being heard on Radio Omdurman to the accompaniment [*sic*] ovation of enthusiastic masses. . . .
Fabricated news about Sudan in the Iraqi mass media would have no effect on the Sudan and its people. The Sudanese President is always among the masses, a thing Iraqi leaders would never venture to do. [*SUNA-Daily Bulletin* 1979, p. 7]

There are now few countries in the Arab world that lack the transmission strength to make a domestic or an international impact on radio-conscious Arabs; but the Sudan is one of the few.

Data are not available on radio station preferences in rural areas of the Sudan. However, a May 1977 survey done for the International Communication Agency in Khartoum and Port Sudan provides information about urban preferences for foreign stations. Most survey respondents listened to foreign stations in Arabic; Radio Cairo was the station most often mentioned, with 20% of the respondents stating that they listened to it at least once per week. Percentages for Radio Voice of the Gospel (RVOG), the British Broadcasting Corporation, the Voice of America, and Radio Monte Carlo were respectively 16, 13, 12, and 9: the survey was taken just after RVOG, a station operated by a religious organization in Ethiopia and respected for its newscasts, was taken over by the Ethiopian government (USICA 1978a, p. 11). These figures are for urban areas where the Sudanese radio signal is strong; and it is quite likely that the incidence of both medium- and short-wave foreign radio listening in rural areas is higher, due to reception problems with the Sudanese radio signal there. But factors of convenience aside, the popularity of foreign radio generally stems from the knowledge among listeners that government media almost always promote news items favorable to the government in power. Foreign radio is seen as a source of another point of view.

2.2.3 Television

Both the British and West Germans demonstrated television in the Sudan in 1962 (Ministry of Information and Culture 1971, p. 106), but the development of the medium has been undertaken almost entirely by the Federal Republic of Germany. The West German government's attempt was to provide a basic system and to train personnel for program production that would be largely development-oriented: but while educational programmng is present on Sudanese television, the medium has become entertainment-oriented, featuring a high percentage of programs from the west and from Egypt.

In 1963 a low-power transmitter was installed in a makeshift studio in an old hostel adjacent to the Radio Omdurman studio complex. For the first eight years of the undertaking, German engineers and production specialists were in residence, installing equipment and training Sudanese in all facets of television. Some personnel were sent to Germany and other countries for training. During the early stages of television, transmission was restricted to a few hours each evening and served only an area around the capital—one that had few television sets, despite government efforts to put some receivers in public places. Sets were installed in clubs, coffee houses, and restaurants in a manner similar to efforts in other Arab countries. Television viewing quickly became a communal activity.

The expansion of television facilities was hampered initially by government disinterest and a lack both of funds and of any means of interconnecting stations outside the capital, no telecommunications system then existing for networking. In the 1960s, the government realized that it must devise a national system for the dissemination of mass communication—for networking, telex, and telephone—in addition to providing reliable communication for the military and government. This was to be an expensive undertaking for a poor country that constitutes over 8% of the African continent. As a first step, microwave stations were built stretching from the Khartoum-Omdurman area to those centers that were most heavily populated; and in 1972 a second television station was opened in Wad Medani, a predominantly agricultural area about 180 kilometers south of the capital in El Gezira Province. A third station was opened about 300 kilometers north of the capital in Atbara in the Nile Province, a center of activity for the Sudanese Workers Trade Union, where the Sudan Railway is headquartered (Sudan Television n.d., "Extension," p. 3). These stations are part of the Sudan Rural Television Project, which is financed by various government departments with large shares both of financial help and inspiration from the West Germans, and they were constructed so that programs to serve the viewers in each area could be produced locally. (Programming includes features about occupational health, literacy, social problems, and agriculture.) These stations being linked by a microwave system to the Omdurman television complex, like the simple relay transmitters surrounding the capital, also rebroadcast from them (Rahman 1979b). Another part of the Project is a kind of Tele-Club system: receivers powered by gasoline generators have been placed in a hundred villages with separate viewing centers for men and women.

As part of the same burst of expansion, after the 1972 peace accord with the Southern Region was reached, plans were finalized with the usual West German assistance for a new, more powerful, PAL color-capable transmitter to be built in Omdurman, and for the construction of a new studio building to house equipment that would replace unreliable older equipment. Administrative offices and a studio complex were completed in 1974 in a building next to the original television facility: two large new studios provided more production space and served as the originating point for the color transmissions that started in 1974; live studio color news and interviews began in 1976 (Rahman 1979a). In 1980 two studios to be used exclusively for news and interviews were completed in another adjoining building, thus allowing local production to take place during the evening transmissions. Most of the new color equipment is German and includes one-inch video tape recorders and a new remote truck with small ENG-type mini-cameras. All video tape equipment, except for the German one-inch Bosch machines, is Ampex and is relatively new. Inadequate video tape recording facilities have hampered the production of local programs, but

Sudanese television greatly benefited from a meeting of the Organization of African Unity in Khartoum in 1978. Television coverage of the gathering was important to the Sudan as well as to those attending the meeting. Each country in attendance wanted a taped daily transmission to be sent via the INTELSAT system to its own television system, showing its involvement in the Pan-African conference; and President Nimeri, wanting the world and his countrymen to see the Sudan in the African spotlight, provided a special allocation of funds so that additional television equipment—specifically five Ampex recorders—could be purchased.

And, in 1978, the Sudan Domestic Satellite System (SUDOSAT) was inaugurated. The system, which also provides telephone and telex service, is operated by the Sudan Telecommunications Public Corporation and provides the national television signal to the provincial capitals of Nyala, El Fasher, Kadugli, El Damazin, Dongola, Karima, Wadi Halfa, Malakal, Bor, Juba, Yambio, and Wau (Sudan Television n.d., "Extension," p. 4). On the whole, the distribution of television by the national microwave and satellite system thus completed has worked quite well. Television service has been interrupted regularly, however, by ground station and transmitter failures caused by lack of spare parts, maintenance personnel, and fuel to power generators—the latter sometimes being created by thefts of fuel from the generator storage tanks.

2.2.4 Television Programming

The one national color channel operates for about 52 hours per week, sending out a daily seven-hour evening transmission and broadcasting additional hours on Friday mornings and afternoons. The national service is a mixture, made up 60% of religious programs, locally produced dramatic shows, educational programs, interviews, news, and sports, and 40% of programs imported from the United States and Great Britain and Egypt and other Arab countries. The Director General of Television has commented on the balance between locally produced and imported programs:

We can't broadcast only local programmes because it would be very expensive. For instance, the price of a 60 minute, hired film is about $100. If we wanted to produce the same programme here, it would cost $700. So we have to keep this ratio.

We are importing material from abroad in order to compensate and to balance, and to save money for local programmes. If we produced only local programmes, we would need three or four times the funds available. We're learning by getting experience from others. [Akol 1979, p. 43]

Officials also give political reasons for importing programs:

If we just broadcast our own programmes, our viewers wouldn't be in a position to see whether we were progressing or not. Take the Egyptian series for example: people look at them from different angles—the subject, the quality and the technique. By showing them, we give our viewers the chance to evaluate our own work. The imported 40 per cent is divided twenty-twenty: half are Arabic series, mostly Egyptian; the best Arabic programmes are made in London or Dubai where they can get the best production facilities.

The other half comes from the West, mostly America. But we don't buy these series—we rent them subtitled. [Akol 1979, p. 43]

Among the American programs televised have been 13-week segments of almost every American popular action/adventure series that has not been completely adult-oriented, since both sex and excessive violence must be edited from the programs. The Director General defends American programs such as "Kojak" because they are easily edited for sex ("we don't show legs—no kissing, no sex") and because "we're teaching our people that crime is advancing and it will reach us one day—if it's not here already." The television authority attempts to be responsive to viewer reactions to the imported western programs. For example, "Six Million Dollar Man" was removed from the air because viewers complained that their children were jumping from roofs like Steve Austin (Akol 1979, p. 43).

An important part of daily programming is the 2100 news. The newscast is in color, usually lasts for 20 to 30 minutes, and closely resembles an American small- to medium-market television newscast utilizing two news readers on camera alternately. Accounts of presidential activities are important in the newscast, but other stories of national origin on tape or film are shown among items on international news and local sports and weather. The Sudan has the capability of receiving the European Broadcasting Union's two daily news summaries by satellite; but for several weeks in late 1979, Sudanese television could not use the material because the Ministry of Communication had not paid the down-leg satellite costs. International news came on a delayed basis via air shipments of news film from Visnews and UPITN from London. Almost all locally done newsfilm in 1980 was black and white because of a lack of raw color film stock and the chemicals to process footage. This situation serves to highlight the financial problems of Sudanese television. Those who are responsible for the overall operation of the television network must constantly watch hard currency expenditures so that, for example, enough lighting instruments and replacement lamps are available.

The Sudanese television viewer receives a varied program diet from the one national channel. Those who receive the signal from the Wad Medani and Atbara stations may additionally see the development-oriented programs designed specifically for their respective areas: occasionally, such locally produced programs are telecast nationally from the Omdurman headquarters. The schedule in Figure 2 reflects national network programming for three typical days in October 1979. During that month, Sudanese

Figure 2. Three-Day Sample Schedules of Sudanese Television

Friday

1000 Program Schedule and Koran
1010 Friday Debate
1030 Children's Program
1230 Women's Program and Religious
      Songs—Closedown until 1330
1330 Islamic Serial
1430 Egyptian Plan
1630 Green Plains
1700 Football
1740 The World in a Week
1830 Your Life
1900 Arabic Serial
2000 Wrestling
2125 World Events
2135 English-Language Serial
2200 Arabic Film, News in Brief, Koran
2400 Close Down

Sunday

1700 Program Schedule and Koran
1710 The Religious Word
1730 Islamic Serial and Cartoon
1830 Parliament Members
1900 Arabic Serial and Cartoon
2000 Judicial Problems
2030 Sudanese Drama
2100 News
2130 Guest of the Week
2140 English-Language Film News in Brief,
      Koran
2400 Close Down

Thursday

1700 Program Schedule and Koran
1710 The Religious Word, Cartoon
1730 Islamic Serial, Cartoon
1830 The Unknown Universe
1900 Arabic Serial
2000 Weekly Discussion
2020 Sports
2100 News
2130 English-Language Serial
2230 Variety Show, News in Brief, Koran
2400 Close Down

SOURCE: *Sudanow* October 1979b, pp. 69–70.

television broadcast what has been termed the most popular imported program ever to be shown, "Roots," subtitled in Arabic.

2.2.5 Broadcast Financing

Financing for Sudanese radio has traditionally been from receiver licenses imposed under British rule. Since independence, military and civilian governments have not enforced the license fee that is supposedly collected by the postal authority. Both problems of collection after the introduction of the small, relatively inexpensive transistor radio and the government's eagerness for the population to acquire radio and television receivers have all but eliminated the license fee. The government has had to assume the responsibility for most broadcast financing, particularly the expense of ground stations and transmitters for the completion of the national television network. Both radio and television are financed partially by advertising; and an organization that is independent of both the radio and the television programming departments is responsible for all aspects of that effort, including the taping of the commercial announcements themselves. Commercials were first allowed on Radio Omdurman in April 1961 (Head 1962, p. 51), and on Sudanese television in June 1965 (*Sudan Echo* 1965).

Products sold in the Middle East are promoted by 30- and 60-second filmed commercials that are usually made in Egypt and Lebanon: advertised products include Aspro (aspirin), Halls Cough Drops, Rothman Cigarettes, Dr. Scholl Shoes, Signal Tooth Paste, and some food products such as processed cheese. Local television advertising includes spots for local stores and cinemas and a few products that are manufactured or assembled by state or local industries; the local commercials generally feature a slide of the product or a poster, giving details of the product or service with a voice-over. Neither the video nor the audio quality of the commercials is very good and the contrast of their faultiness with the high technical quality of Sudanese television in general is stark—due in part to the fact that the audio for commercials is taped on home- rather that broadcast-quality audio tape equipment, in a small studio operated by the radio and television sales office. There is almost no communication between that office and the radio and television administration. While the broadcast administration recognizes that the commercials do produce revenue, it believes that the clustered commercials detract from its programs; and, unfortunately, it realizes no direct advantage from the advertising income, all of which goes directly to the Ministry of Finance. The government estimated that about $600,000 was realized from broadcast advertising in 1979.

2.2.6 Television Viewing Patterns

In 1968, Sudan Television commissioned a survey of viewers in the Khartoum-Omdurman area to determine viewing patterns, program preferences, and attitudes toward news and commercials. The study, "The First Survey of Television: 1968–1969," was done by university and secondary school students; the methodology, data collection, and interpretation must be read with that circumstance in mind. Following are several findings of the study.

1. Of the 1,481 people interviewed only thirty were illiterate (which indicates that the sample was not a cross-section of the Sudanese population).
2. In Khartoum, 94.9 per cent of those questioned said that they owned television sets. (This may be an accurate figure if the word "own" is taken as "have access to.")
3. The most popular local program was "Tahat El Adwa" ("Under the Light"), a program of live Sudanese music.

. 4. About one-third of the sample said that they liked television commercials while the remainder said that they did not.
5. About three-quarters of the respondents said that they liked foreign
films on television (Sudan Television n.d., "First Survey").

As is the case in most other Islamic countries, conditions for television
viewing in the Sudan are favorable: members of its family-centered culture
have neither the general opportunity nor the funds to seek entertainment
outside the home. Several families may contribute money to purchase a set,
or working family members, including children, may all help finance the
important purchase. The communal nature of television is perhaps best
illustrated by an incident that occurred in Khartoum in February 1977. On a
warm evening, an American friend and the writer were walking from the
main downtown shopping area to a house in the suburbs and paused at the
open gate of a home to see what was being televised on the set placed in the
garden. Immediately there was an invitation to watch television with the
family. . . .

Since independence, problems have hindered the development of
Sudanese radio and television. Lack of trained personnel and funds, a
disruptive civil war, destruction of some equipment during an attempted
coup, and poor transmitter design and installation have all affected media
development. During the 1960s, various aid programs helped to establish
radio facilities and to train personnel for what it was hoped would be the
beginning of a well-organized national radio system—yet as outsiders were
puzzled to note, when the federal government was trying to stop the fighting
in the Southern Region, there was almost no media campaign to parallel the
military one. After 1972, both radio and television transmitters were placed
in Juba, but they have tended to be for the rebroadcast of the national
programs, with little attempt to allow local radio programs or local television.

The President is considering a proposal from broadcasting officials that
would create a semiautonomous public corporation for radio and television.
This would function under the Ministry of Information as a similar one does
in Egypt. It would have considerable financial freedom, and it would at last
give Radio Omdurman control over its own transmitters and engineering
personnel—though television appears now to have been categorically successful in becoming the national electronic medium, its signal being so
successfully distributed via satellite ground stations and local transmitters.

Whatever Sudan's eventual solution to the problems of its electronic
media, television will continue to be the most effective means of providing
the citizens of Africa's largest country with information and entertainment.

2.3 Lebanon

The basic geographical boundaries of present-day Lebanon were first defined by the Ottoman Empire, which ruled the area for 400 years prior to World War I. The present boundaries were established in 1920, when France administered both Syria and Lebanon under a League of Nations mandate. Lebanon achieved independence in 1943, but it was not completely free to manage its own affairs until the end of World War II.

The population of Lebanon can only be estimated, as no official census has been done since 1932. At that time, it was found that the population was almost evenly divided between Moslems and Christians. The various ethnic and religious communities have always vied for political power, and when Lebanon became a modern state, these factions tended to fractionalize the population. It is an oversimplification to state that the basic division in the country is between Moslems and non-Moslems. Groups such as Armenians, Greek Orthodox, Palestinians, Nasserites, Communists, and Druz, have made the political history since 1946 colorful and, in 1975, explosive. The Lebanese Civil War of 1975 suggested that the free-wheeling Lebanese economy that had attracted international business concerns in the 1950s and 1960s had neglected some of the basic needs of the population. The fighting did not end until an Arab League peace-keeping force dominated by the Syrian Army occupied parts of the country in 1976. Thousands of people were killed during the fighting and much of Beirut was destroyed. The Syrian Army brought a measure of peace to Lebanon, and by 1979 a facade of normality had returned to sections of the country. However, the army, police, and many government services are either nonexistent or ineffective. There are Christian and Moslem sections of the country, and Beirut remains divided and largely lawless—no longer a tourist center.

The country's 4,015 square miles and estimated population of 2.5 million make it one of the world's smallest nation states. There is an elected parliament and the government leaders include, by unwritten agreement, a Maronite Christian President and a Sunni Moslem Prime Minister.

2.3.1 Radio

The first identifiable radio station in Lebanon was constructed in 1937 by the French government and was operated by France with the help of local employees (UNESCO 1949, p. 225). One motivation for the construction of the early French station was to counter the Arabic-language radio propaganda of the Italians and Germans. In 1941 the transmission facilities of "Radio Levant" were destroyed by the Vichy French government to frustrate the Allies when they occupied the country (N. Dajani 1979, p. 21). The facilities were rebuilt and for a period, until formal independence took place in 1946, both the French and British legations supplied programming for the one short- and one medium-wave transmitter.

The studio and transmitters were formally handed over to the Lebanese government in 1946. An agreement with the French allowing a specified period of use per day was signed and is still in effect. The radio system was renamed the Lebanese Broadcasting Station and put under the Directorate of Propaganda and Publishing, part of the Ministry of the Interior (N. Dajani 1979, p. 21). After this formation of a broadcast operation under the complete control of the Lebanese government, several attempts were made to expand programming and facilities. The government was not convinced that radio was an important part of national development and the low-power service remained essentially unchanged until the 1958 Civil War, which was precipitated by a changing political mood in the Arab world, starting with the Egyptian Revolution in 1952 and continuing through the overthrow of the royal family in Iraq in 1958 and the instability in Jordan during the same year. The Lebanese government asked for and received help from the United States and in 1958 the United States Marines landed in Lebanon.

Prior to 1958 the government had decided to allocate funds for the construction of the building to house the Ministries of Tourism and Information and for new and more powerful medium- and short-wave transmitters. Because of the appearance of several clandestine radio stations during the war, this project moved forward with some speed. It became obvious to the government that the coverage of the mountainous country by the low-powered transmitters was incomplete and that the population was not particularly loyal to the station, which was perceived to be a government-controlled outlet for those in power. By the late 1950s, Lebanese could tune to Israel, Jordan, Syria, and Egypt for news and entertainment. A new Ministry of Information building was completed in 1962 near the Hamra area of Beirut and new transmitters were installed. The Ministry of Information and the broadcasting section underwent several reorganizations, and the government reached agreement with the various clandestine stations to stop operating. The equipment of these illegal stations was stored rather than destroyed or sold as the owners believed that the day would come when the equipment would again be needed. The new building provided ample room for what was thought to be present and future needs of the Lebanese Radio Station, later called Radio Lebanon. Six production and on-air studios in the building utilized German equipment, most of which has been well maintained.

Perhaps the biggest problem between 1962 and 1972 was an increasing awareness among listeners that the radio service reflected the attitude and policies of the government. The station served not so much as a voice for the government's public relations office as a means of denying access by various political groups to the airwaves. There were few frank discussions about the myriad of problems that faced the country. The political leaders believed that discussions might only fan smoldering political beliefs. Access to the radio medium was further restricted by the policy of not allowing advertising on radio. The station has been financed by government funds in a manner consistent with many other radio stations in the Arab world, a policy thought by the Lebanese to be inconsistent with their traditional free-wheeling economy. Some opposition leaders wanted political advertising so that they could purchase airtime for the dissemination of their views.

During the 1960s, Lebanon experienced an unprecedented period of economic growth. Egypt was not a hospitable environment for wealthy Arabs from the Gulf states. Beirut, on the other hand, offered numerous investment opportunities as well as an active night-life and pleasant weather for vacations. These same factors attracted international businesses, which established Middle Eastern headquarters in Beirut. Particularly visible were American and European banks that came to do business in the "Switzerland of the Middle East."

Even up to the 1975 Civil War, when the system fell into chaos, the transmissions of Lebanese radio had not been as highly structured and defined as was the case, for example, in Egypt. Services centered around transmissions, which were predominantly in Arabic. A secondhand FM transmitter was acquired and used for the music program in the late 1960s and the facility was modified in the early 1970s for stereo transmission. Short-wave transmitters were added relatively early in the history of Lebanese broadcasting. It was believed that Lebanon should have a voice that reached other Arab countries as well as countries to which large numbers of Lebanese had emigrated, mainly in Africa, Europe, and North and South America. The schedule of Lebanese transmissions in Table 10 indicates the scope of programming as of 5 March 1972.

Furthermore, there were omnidirectional short-wave broadcasts of programs during specified periods of the day. There is no evidence that these broadcasts were listened to with any degree of regularity or enthusiasm in other countries; the Ministry of Information has not commissioned research that would provide such information.

The criticism that the state radio denied access of political groups to the airwaves came to a head in 1972. Lebanon has always had an active press which has afforded an outlet for all manner of political thought. The printing of numerous daily, weekly, and occasional publications prior to the 1975 Civil War actually constituted a sizable portion of the Lebanese economy and helped the development of Lebanon's once-thriving book publishing industry. In fact there were too many outlets for political thought, and the few respected papers tended to express either the government point of view or the prevailing political philosophy of the major established political parties. The Lebanese political factions did not lack outlets for political expression; they did lack access, however, to the government-controlled radio.

The spring 1972 Lebanese elections brought the radio access problem to the forefront. Kamal Jumblatt, a Socialist Deputy, stated that he would start

Table 10. Radio Lebanon Shortwave Schedule

Target Area	Time (GMT)	Meter Band
Africa		
English	1830–1900	19.53
Arabic	1900–2000	19.53
French	2000–2030	19.53
South America		
Portuguese	2300–2330	19.53
Arabic	2330–0030	19.53
Spanish	0030–0100	19.53
North America, Mexico, and Europe		
French	0130–0200	31.43
Arabic	0200–0230	31.43
English	0230–0300	31.43
Spanish	0330–0400	31.43

SOURCE: "New Hours of Overseas Transmissions on Shortwave by Radio Lebanon," 1 April 1972.

his own radio station to compete with the government operation. The government made it clear that such an act would be illegal despite the stipulation in the Lebanese Constitution that guaranteed freedom of expression. There is no specific law prohibiting the establishment of a private station, but there is a procedure that stipulates how one must go about it. During one of the Radio Lebanon reorganizations, a government decree (No. 3870) issued in 1960 stated that the licensing of radio stations was the province of the Ministry of Posts, Telegrams, and Telephones (Phipps 1972, pp. 4–5). The elections did not force the establishment of private stations, but the entire atmosphere surrounding Lebanese radio changed after 1972 in that political groups knew that they would not gain access to the state radio.

The elections did create an interesting and short-lived alternative to the Ministry of Information radio outlet. Farid Salman, who owned a cinema newsreel, "Actualité Libanaise," purchased a block of time on the Cyprus Broadcasting Corporation's medium-wave service, which reaches Lebanon with a clear signal. Salman, who appears to have acted out of financial motives as well as a desire for freedom of expression, recorded political messages, including one from the Prime Minister, which were aired on the Cyprus "Radio Magazine." The project lasted only four days. The government jammed the station and caused the practice to be discontinued (Mirshak 1972, p. 7).

By the time the 1975 Civil War started, domestic coverage had improved, although Lebanon had not become an important international broadcaster because short-wave transmitters remained few in number and low in power.

The main domestic service was boosted by the construction of a new 100-kilowatt medium-wave transmitter outside of Beirut in Amsheet.

2.3.2 Television

Television was organized in a totally different manner from radio. In the mid-1950s, a group of Lebanese businessmen approached the government and proposed that they build a television station financed by the sale of advertising. They signed an agreement with the government in 1956 for the construction of a station that would operate two channels, one for Arabic-language and the other for mostly foreign programs. The 1958 Civil War interrupted the station's construction, but the services started in May 1959 (N. Dajani 1971, p. 172). La Compagnie Libanaise de Télévision (CLT) thus became the first nongovernment-operated, advertising-supported television station in the Arab world. Article 21 of the agreement addresses some of the stipulations under which CLT would operate:

1. The government does not give the company monopoly rights.
2. Broadcasts should be under government scrutiny, and should not include programmes which threaten public security, morals, or religious groups, or enhance the image of any political personality or party.
3. Programmes should be restricted to education or entertainment, and advertising should not exceed 25% of broadcast time.
4. There should be at least 20 hours per week of programming, and the company undertakes to broadcast free of charge news programmes and official bulletins provided by the Ministry of Guidance and Information.
5. The first phase of the project will include the construction of a main transmitter with 400-watt power, to be increased later to 4 Kw, and the installation of relay stations to cover the whole of Lebanon.
6. Television is to respect all laws and regulations relating to the rights of the press and of authors, and shall be subject to all laws and internal or international regulations dealing with wireless communications and broadcast institutions. It shall also exchange sound programmes with the Lebanese radio in the sphere of overall co-operation.
7. If the television station stops broadcasting for 30 days on two occasions in one year without a compelling reason which the government considers to be valid, the government has the right to take over the station directly and to operate it on a commercial basis. The government can cancel the license without indemnification by giving advance notice which shall not exceed four years.
8. The agreement, once approved officially, shall be in force for 15 years, at the end of which the government has the full right to buy all facilities connected to the project, at prices specified by two experts, one representing the government and the other the company whose agreement has been ended. In the event of any dispute on the estimates the two parties shall seek an international arbitrator to decide the points at issue. [N. Dajani 1979, pp. 26–27]

The original studios and transmitters and some of the original equipment are still operating in a building in a residential area in Beirut. The transmitters, operating on Channels 7 and 9, and a tower are located atop the building. At first the transmission hours were limited and employees few because the venture was almost totally concerned with making a profit rather than with providing a comprehensive national television service. As the above stipulations indicate, the government placed severe restrictions on the kinds of programs which could be telecast. Obviously, the government had in mind a television service that was not unlike radio where news was guided by the government in power and programming was almost entirely entertainment. The economic situation immediately after 1958 was not conducive to commercial advertising and revenue was small; profits went to investors rather than being returned to the station in the form of training of personnel or buying new equipment and studios for local production.

Shortly after transmissions started, CLT established a separate company to handle station administration and advertising sales. Advision, as the organization was known (Sobh 1971), had the American Time-Life organization as a partner for a short period of time. In 1967, the French government corporation SOFIRAD purchased Advision in partnership with a group of Lebanese investors (N. Dajani 1979, p. 28). CLT modified its transmitters in the late 1960s to transmit SECAM color, but it was not until the mid-1970s that cameras and associated studio equipment were installed for local color production.

CLT faced additional financial problems in mid-1962, when a second commercial station began telecasting. Compagnie de Télévision du Liban et du Proche-Orient (Télé-Orient) reached agreement with the government in 1959 for a second television station in Lebanon. The organization, which agreed to the same conditions as CLT, was partially financed by the American Broadcasting Company (ABC). Later ABC sold its interest in the station to the British Thomson Organization and the Rizk Brothers, a wealthy Lebanese family (N. Dajani 1979, p. 29). Télé-Orient built a studio in Hazmiyeh, about 15 kilometers from Beirut, and telecast one program on two channels, 5 and 11. The Télé-Orient facility was designed to house two medium-sized studios and additional space for administrative offices and equipment such as tele-cine. The 1962 design, which was still operational in 1980, allows one person to operate lighting controls, switching, and audio. When no live studio news or interviews are to take place, only a transmitter, a master control, and a tele-cine operator are needed to run the operation in addition to the "director," who does the job of several other employees.

Until the late 1960s, little local production was done by either station. The Lebanese audience was not large enough to make such undertakings profitable. Some Egyptian films were shown but a substantial percentage of the relatively short telecasting day was devoted to American, British, and

French programs that were broadcast with the original sound, but subtitled in Arabic. Neither the stations nor the Ministry of Education appears to have been interested in any kind of educational programming during those hours when commercial programs were transmitted. The Ministry of Information was not unhappy with the services since they did not telecast political or controversial programs and were essentially free of charge to the government. That advertising sales were allowed on television, it was reasoned, softened the criticism of noncommercial radio.

These two stations were motivated almost entirely by the desire to return a profit to both local and foreign shareholders, and they were not interested in such program development as local news. The Ministry of Information controlled both local and international news; television newsfilm from VIS-NEWS and UPITN were sealed on arrival at the Beirut airport and delivered to each station. The seals were broken in a special viewing room by government censors.[16] The television organizations did not resent this state of affairs because the government-controlled news freed them of responsibility for what was broadcast.

Beginning about 1970, the stations and their employees benefited from increased local musical and dramatic production efforts that were shown in Beirut and then sold to stations in the Gulf states. Some programs were produced under the auspices of the stations. Independent producers often rented the studios and video tape facilities from the stations. Télé-Orient was particularly active in the Gulf television market and served as a distributor of foreign programs in addition to acting as sales agent for Arabic-language material produced in Lebanon.

Despite efforts to increase revenue by producing programs for export, financial problems plagued both stations from the very beginning. Unable to compete successfully for limited viewers and financial resources in Beirut, the two organizations started to cooperate with advertising sales and even broadcasting the same program simultaneously. In 1968 Advision had become the sales agent for Télé-Orient as well as CLT, and in October 1972 Télé-Management was created to undertake complete marketing and advertising sales of all television channels. Advision continued to assume the responsibility for the operation of CLT.

Between 1972 and the outbreak of the civil war in 1975, the television business seemed to stabilize. Both stations were returning a profit. Local production had increased because of the export market for Lebanese taped television programs. Both stations maintained a limited broadcasting schedule of only six hours per day. About one-half of the programming was imported from the west and included such shows as "The Flintstones," "Mod Squad," "Jackson Five," "Peyton Place," "Partridge Family," "Tar-

[16]The writer observed the procedure while at the Télé-Orient studios, Beirut, Lebanon, 3 April 1972. For example of censorship on Lebanese television, see Browne 1975, pp. 695–95.

zan," "Hawaii Five-O," "Bewitched," "Mannix," "I Dream of Jeannie," "Land of the Giants," "Gunsmoke," "Hogan's Heroes," "Abbott and Costello," "The Forsyte Saga," "The Saint," and "Burke's Law," in addition to numerous programs in French from ORTF (Phipps 1972, p. 3; CLT Program Schedule 1972; Télé-Orient Program Schedule 1972).

2.3.3 Broadcasting during the 1975 Civil War

As one might expect, the fighting in Lebanon greatly affected the Ministry of Information radio service and the two commercial television stations. The fighting did not start on one particular day. Rather, a series of shootings and kidnappings led to the acquisition of guns, ammunition, and explosives by the various Moslem and Christian factions. The large expatriate community in Beirut stayed throughout the initial 1975 skirmishes, but when fighting intensified they left and closed the company offices in Beirut. The city seemed to erupt into full-scale war after the destruction of many of the luxury hotels not far from the Ministry of Information building. Beirut became a fractionalized city with predominantly Moslem and Christian neighborhoods fighting each other. The Lebanese police and defense forces were ineffective in controlling the fighting. The various factions continued to support daily newspapers, many of which continued to publish.

The electronic media were clearly not responsive to the needs of the Lebanese population during the Civil War. The radio service attempted to stay neutral: the official Ministry of Information Service broadcast some essential information, and people listened for reports about fighting, news about proposed cease fires, casualty figures, information on where essential services could be obtained, and even personal news about families. But there were times, even during the heaviest fighting in 1975 and 1976 when one would not know from radio programs that the country was in the midst of a devastating war. Television reflected the situation even less. Both stations continued to operate and some companies continued to advertise. The stations reran old programs and telecast censored news as if nothing of great importance were occurring. Both stations lost a great deal of money. The equipment that was not damaged during the fighting deteriorated because of lack of maintenance and spare parts. Normal communications between the two stations was impossible at times, since they were located in different parts of the city. Each station had installed relay transmitters around the mountainous country to fill in areas that did not regularly receive one of the three television programs. Almost all of these facilities were damaged and many were destroyed.

In March 1976, however, the broadcast media became heavily embroiled in the dispute. In the middle of the CLT evening Arabic newscast on 11 March 1976, a Moslem Lebanese Army officer, Brigadier Aziz Al-Ahdab, forced his way into the studios of Channel 7 and demanded airtime for "Communique No. 1." Owing to his status and his armed entourage, he was granted his wish. After televising the statement that proclaimed that he was the new ruler of Lebanon and stating that the President should resign, Al-Ahdab moved to the Ministry of Information radio studios and broadcast what had been said on CLT. Thereupon he returned to CLT to supervise the French-language version of the communique on Channel 9. Employees of Télé-Orient, which had been transmitting the CLT Arabic program, immediately stopped transmission after the statement was read. Al-Ahdab did not become an important force in the civil war, but he sparked a media war that had been avoided until that March evening.

Hearing that these broadcasting facilities had been "occupied" by a Moslem faction, supporters of the Christian president took control of Télé-Orient and the radio transmitters at Amsheet. Thus, each major warring group had a radio and television outlet that could enthusiastically broadcast programming in support of its own side. Although these major facilities became targets for gunners, damage was relatively light. One CLT employee observed that his station was an easy mark for artillery because the tower on the building seemed to provide an easily recognizable homing device. One week after the occupations took place Claude Khoury, a Lebanese journalist and television newscaster, made the following observation in *Monday Morning*, a weekly Beirut English-language magazine:

The Al-Ahdab information forces are entrenched in the Lebanese Television Company (Channels 7 and 9) and the Lebanese Radio Station-Information Ministry (Sanayeh, Ras Beirut).

The Franjieh information forces have dug in at Télé-Orient (Channels 5 and 11, the latter, however, being out of order) and the Amsheet radio relay station near Jbail (Byblos).

For ammunition, they're using contradictory news flashes and endless rounds of threats, insults, "we shall overcome" speeches, patriotic songs and military marches.

Caught in the middle are the listeners and the viewers—and, possibly, the troops themselves, the men and women who are reading the news and the various statements prepared for them by the two camps. [1976, p. 41]

It was not until a new elected government took power and the Syrian-dominated peace-keeping force entered Lebanon in 1976 that the respective transmitters and studios were returned to their owners. The government radio service was reunified on 12 December 1976 (BBC n.d., *Clandestine* Part 4, p.1). The civil war had a more lasting effect on Lebanese radio listeners—particularly those who became regular listeners to the clandestine or rebel radio stations that were operated by political factions. Perhaps a more descriptive name for these stations is "illegal," as their origins and locations were known but they broadcast on frequencies that the Lebanese government had not registered with the International Telecommunications Union, a UN agency.

Several factions tried radio broadcasts in 1975 and 1976. The stations were of course intended to disseminate the views of the faction that operated the station. A partial explanation for the proliferation of stations was the need to provide vital communication to people in light of the inability of the national electronic media to do so. During the 1958 disturbances, three radio stations—"The Voice of Arabism," "The Voice of Lebanon," and "The Voice of the People's Resistance"—had not been very professionally run (N. Dajani 1979, p. 48). When the stations ceased operation in September 1958, "The Voice of Arabism" ended its transmissions by announcing, "The national interest made it necessary to stop this broadcasting station. So we agree to stop it voluntarily as a move for cooperation with the new regime" (Brewer 1958, pp. 1–2).

In 1975 and 1976 some of the former radio rebels reactivated stations that had been dormant for 17 years. Many factions attempted to broadcast, but only the more professional and well-financed operations lasted throughout the civil war and continue. Possibly, they have become permanent additions to Lebanese media. "The Voice of Lebanon," a pro-Phalangist (Christian) station, was first heard on 24 September 1975 (BBC n.d., *Clandestine* WBI/5 and 7, p. 1). One day later, "The Voice of Arab Lebanon," a pro-left-wing station, started broadcasting programs that lasted until 26 January 1976 (BBC n.d., *Clandestine* WBI/5 and 6, p. 1). These were not the only stations that operated during the war; but they are the only ones that were well enough financed and protected to become identifiable broadcast entities. The arrival of the Syrian peace-keeping force apparently renewed interest in rebel radio stations and on 22 May 1977 the pro-Phalangist "Free Radio of the Voice of South Lebanon" started transmissions (BBC n.d., *Clandestine* ME/5520/A/2 and WBI/21, p. 2). "The Voice of One Lebanon," an anti-Syrian station, was first reported on 11 May 1977 (BBC n.d., *Clandestine* ME/5515/A/1 and WBI/20). These stations tended to motivate various other political factions to begin stations, and "The Voice of the Arab Revolution," hostile to right-wing elements in Lebanon, emerged in May 1979. "Free Lebanon Radio," anti-Phalangist, and "Radio of Free and Unified Lebanon," pro-Franjiyah (a former Lebanese president), were first heard in 1978 (BBC, "Monitoring" 129/78, p. 2). On the more unusual side, "The Voice of Hope" started in 1979 in southern Lebanon in an area where some Christian Lebanese, under the leadership of Major Saad Haddad, had been cooperating with the Israelis. The operation is reportedly financed in part by an American religious group that includes Pat Boone and features country and western music and inspirational messages in English.

"The Voice of Lebanon" deserves closer examination. Located in Ashrafieh, in the Christian sector of Beirut that resisted the presence of the Arab League peace-keeping force, what started as an informal operation became a viable business, whose news is respected by listeners and is quoted in the international press. What makes the operation unusual is its size and the fact that it is a successful commercial radio station with over 100 employees in a former apartment complex, which houses one medium- and one short-wave transmitter.[17] There is a published quarterly program schedule and numerous brochures in station media kits that provide programming information and station advertising rates. The modest, well-equipped studios contain some equipment from 1958 and are similar to what one would find in smaller medium-sized markets in the United States. Other stations survived the civil war, but they lack the organization of this station, which is located in an area largely outside government control: Ashrafieh is a city within a city. Another unique feature of the station is the fact that it claims to have a license to operate. Immediately prior to the 1976 elections that resulted in a change in leadership, the President signed a permit supposedly authorizing the station to broadcast. It is this action, claims the station management, that legalizes the operation (Khoury 1979), although the telecommunications authority and Parliament did not act to legitimize the broadcasts.

The radio station is apparently quite popular and its news is respected by some listeners because they know that it is not provided by the government. The news operation is extensive and uses local and international correspondents, who telex and phone stories that are used on the Arabic-, French-, and English-language broadcasts. The station subscribes to the Agence France Presse Arabic wire service. The familiar station signature tune, "Bridge on the River Kwai," can be heard in taxi cabs and radios blaring from shops and apartments in various sections of Beirut. An indication of the station's popularity can be gleaned from a survey done in June 1978 in selected Lebanese cities by Associated Business Consultants of Beirut. Of those surveyed who claimed to have listened to radio the previous day, 20.5% said that they heard "The Voice of Lebanon" between 0800 and 0900. The heaviest time for listening was between 0700 and 1000 (Associated Business Consultants n.d., *Extracts* Part V, p. 1). The future of this and the other stations is uncertain. As long as supporters remain tenacious about their "voices" and have the means to protect them physically, they will probably continue to operate. Until Lebanon is able to muster a strong respected national government, it is unlikely the stations will stop broadcasting. A strong national government, on the other hand, requires the support of the factions that operate the stations and compromise, therefore, is possible—a compromise wherein a selected number of private commercially supported stations are allowed to broadcast legally in return for a pledge to support that government. The more popular operations have become an important part of the national electronic media offerings, and it

---

[17]The writer spent 13 November 1979 at the station. Even though the Ministry of Information does not officially recognize the station, most taxi drivers knew where it was located; and permission to visit it was granted by the Program Director, a former CLT employee, after the Ministry of Information informally arranged the contact.

is possible that listeners would resist closing the stations, because the stations provide an alternative to the Ministry of Information radio service for both entertainment and information.

2.3.4 Post War Television Reorganization

Between late 1977 and 1980, Lebanon concentrated on reestablishing a somewhat normal situation with the return to a pre-war status of the many necessities of life and basic government services. Some rebuilding has taken place in Beirut and other cities, but the peace that has come to this country is an imposed rather than a negotiated one. Because a comprehensive settlement has not been reached and the Arab League peace-keeping force will not stay indefinitely, the various factions still support private armies and stock weapons for the next round of fighting. The economy is recovering. The government, however, does not reap all of the benefits, as Lebanon's virtually open borders invite smuggling of easily marketable items such as liquor, cigarettes, and perfumes. Television sets from the ships hijacked in 1978 and 1979 that were destined for Saudi Arabia are available in Lebanon for a fraction of the cost of sets that were legally imported with customs duties paid. An economy that seems to be recovering as well as changes in the administration of Lebanese television have produced an entirely new television organization. The Lebanese appear to be more enthusiastic about television after 1977 because it provides entertainment in the home and it enables them to avoid the streets during evening hours. Lebanon has joined virtually every other Arab country, where the legitimate electronic media are either heavily influenced or controlled by the government.

In 1974, CLT reached agreement with the goverment for a new license to operate its two television channels. The original contract stipulated that the agreement would last for 15 years. As the civil war deescalated in 1976, the 15-year Télé-Orient agreement was up for renewal. In 1977, both stations asked the government to consider an arrangement whereby the television system could be rebuilt. A devastated economy, damaged transmitters, and sections of the country without electricity for receivers had left both stations at a point where it was amazing that the stations were operating at all. In late 1977, the two television organizations and the subsidiaries, Advision and Télé-Management, agreed to form a partnership with the Lebanese government for the creation of a single new national television system known as Télé-Liban. The new organization is half government-owned, with the remaining half equally divided between the Rizk Brothers and the French government SOFIRAD corporation (Rizk 1979). Télé-Liban's president is appointed by the President of the Republic and reports to a board of directors. While this move is obviously a sound step toward the creation of a national television system, two years of operation have not dramatically changed the two formerly privately owned stations. There is more program coordination than there was and each station specializes in the kind of activity it has the personnel or equipment to do best—local production, taping of satellite feeds, etc. The employees at each station site tend to remain loyal to the former companies rather than to the newly created Télé-Liban. They recall vividly the time when the respective stations were occupied and the staffs were polarized. Because the economy stabilized and the television channels provided national coverage, advertising increased to the point where several rate increases in 1979 alone have not discouraged advertisers. In fact, available slots for either spot commercials or sponsored programs have been difficult to find (Yasmie 1979). New advertising rules have lowered the total amount of advertising time per hour to 12 minutes and have forced the clustering of commercials. These promote products such as cosmetics, candy, disposable diapers, and jeans. Local advertising can be seen for clothing stores, soft drinks such as K-Cola and Miranda, computer schools, and restaurants.

The increased program planning and cooperation under Télé-Liban has resulted in three available television services. They are seen throughout Lebanon on various channels from newly installed relay transmitters, but they originate from Channels 5, 7, and 9 in Beirut, start at 1800, and end at midnight. Channels 5 and 7 occasionally show the same program, which may be in Arabic or a program imported from the west. One of these channels almost always features an Arabic program. Arabic news is telecast nightly at 2030 and a taped replay is shown toward the end of the evening's programs. Channel 9 is mostly a channel for western programs in English or French, which are subtitled in two languages, Arabic and either French or English, depending on the language of the original sound track. This channel features at least one hour daily of programs supplied free of charge from one of the three French television networks. There is no English-language television news, but the news in French is available each night. Imported American programs apparently tend to be among the most popular. Lebanon started showing in 1979 what has become the most popular American program in the Middle East, "Dallas."

Under a grant from the International Communcation Agency, William E. Osterhaus of Varitel Communications of San Francisco, California, spent several weeks in Beirut studying the Télé-Liban operation. His October 1979 final report includes 15 recommendations that, if accepted, could provide a more solid basis for Télé-Liban. The recommendations include the suggestion that services such as Télé-Liban 1, 2, and 3 be emphasized rather than channels that are heavily identified with the previous ownership. He recommends a campaign to promote Télé-Liban more heavily among advertisers, so that sales will be more tied to the concept of Télé-Liban than Télé-Management, which still serves as the main sales organization for television. Another recommendation suggests making one station site a transmission headquarters while the other location produces programs. Still another involves the elimination of the politically expedient but inefficient and disruptive practice of switching weekly the origination of the main

Arabic news program between the former CLT and Télé-Orient studios (Osterhaus 1979).

The mood among a cross-section of television employees is optimistic, as they believe that the new organization will increase cooperation and provide funds for much-needed modernization of equipment. Priority can then be given to the potentially lucrative business of program production for export. The mood in Lebanon can change quickly and each organization has its own contingency plans. In the entry foyer of the former Télé-Orient station in Hazmiyeh are two inoperative vintage Marconi monochrome television cameras. They are there in the event of renewed hostilities. When the Syrians entered Lebanon as part of the peace-keeping force, the old cameras were placed outside the station with the hope that they would provide some reminder to the military that the building housed a television station. The soldiers might think the cameras worked and they therefore would behave themselves. "These," noted an engineer, "are our guns."

The Lebanese television situation became further complicated in July 1980. As the result of armed conflicts in east Beirut between two rival Christian factions—the Christian Phalangist party and the national Liberal party—Charles Rizk, Télé-Liban president, was kidnapped and held for several hours until he agreed to resign. He had refused to stop transmitting on one of the channels used by the Hazmiyeh (previously Télé-Orient) facility. The Phalange Party is interested in using any available channel to broadcast an "illegal" television service. If the government is unable to prevent the telecasts, it is likely that similar television services will start. The most likely sponsors of such undertakings are the same factions that have successfully started illegal radio stations.

It is impossible to predict the future of broadcasting in Lebanon because the country's future is uncertain. Devastating civil war has clearly forced the electronic media to change. Radio listeners have become cognizant of the return of the government's pre-war radio service plus several rebel radio stations that the government is powerless to stop. Television has been reorganized with the government as one-half owner and with a board of directors that is more responsive to the needs of the population. Since television is entirely financed by commercial advertising sales, any renewed fighting could again force the television system into a situation where government may need to take control, at least financially.

2.4 Syria

Approximately 7.5 million people live within 71,498 square miles of what is known officially as the Syrian Arab Republic. Part of the Ottoman Empire prior to World War I, the area includes most of what was known as Greater Syria, which included parts of present-day Turkey, Iraq, Jordan, Lebanon, and pre-1948 Palestine. France administered the country under a League of Nations mandate between 1920 and independence in 1945.

Syrian politics have been heavily influenced by the Baath (resurrection) Party, which was founded in Syria in the early 1940s. The party, which is also strong in Iraq, believes that all Arab lands are essentially part of the Arab nation and should be united into one cultural and political entity. The political situation since independence has occasionally been volatile, with frequent military coups occurring between independence and 1970, when Hafez Al-Assad became president. The country's economic plight has hampered development. With an essentially agricultural economy, Syrian leadership has kept and even encouraged the private sector at times, but has maintained the Baath ideological commitment to socialism. The Soviet Union has been Syria's main military supplier since the ill-fated union with Egypt between 1958 and 1961, when the two countries formed what was called the United Arab Republic (UAR). Syria lost territory to Israel during the 1967 and 1973 Middle East Wars, and the Golan Heights area, which separates the two countries, is patrolled by a third party—a United Nations peace-keeping force.

Syria's neighbors, with whom she has had variously hostile and good relations, are Turkey, Iraq, Jordan, Israel, and Lebanon.

2.4.1 Radio

Radio broadcasting in Syria dates from 1946, when the Syrian Broadcasting Organization was founded. The radio system has expanded since its beginning but it has not achieved the status of systems in other Arab countries. This is due to a lack of funds and a lack of government commitment to radio until the early 1960s. Unlike Jordan and Egypt, Syria has not had the strong, stable leadership that would have enabled planning for orderly expansion of radio personnel, studio facilities, and transmitters.

By 1950, four medium-wave transmitters in the two main cities of Aleppo and Damascus broadcast about nine hours of Arabic programming between the hours of 0600 and 0800, 1300 and 1500, and 1800 and 2300. Foreign-language broadcasts between 2300 and 2400 presented programs in English, French, and Turkish (UNESCO 1951, p. 541). Also, in the 1950s, Hebrew broadcasts to Israel started.

Syria's broadcasting was heavily influenced by the country's union with Egypt between 1958 and 1961. Particularly during the early enthusiastic period of the union, Egyptians came to Damascus, where all broadcasting was headquartered, and Syrians went to Egypt. During this time Egypt alrady had a firm commitment to a large broadcasting system with multiple services and numerous high-power transmitters. Syrians trained in Egypt and in Syria by Egyptian radio employees also learned the Egyptian philosophy of radio propagands, later useful in defending the country against attack from Egypt after the disintegration in 1961 of the UAR. Between 1950 and 1965 important changes took place. The Damascus radio complex, which houses the radio studios, was built. This complex is not on the grand scale of Egypt's or even Lebanon's and basically remains unchanged from its construction in the early 1960s. The most significant expansion was the construction of medium- and short-wave transmitters designed to serve domestic and neighboring audiences with Arabic programming and a wider international audience with Arabic and foreign-language programming. By 1965 the country claimed 16 radio transmitters that broadcast programs for the entire nation, plus other broadcasts in French, English, and Spanish (UNESCO 1965, p. 106).

Short-wave transmitters were built near Damascus in the 1960s and were used to broadcast the domestic Arabic as well as the foreign-language programs. However, the country has not been enthusiastic about beamed short-wave programming and the transmitters were allowed to deteriorate largely because of a lack of maintenance. In 1978, all short-wave transmitters were deactivated and a plan was finalized to install five new 250-kilowatt replacement transmitters with a sophisticated antenna system. No FM facilities exist in the country, but new medium-wave transmitters linked by the national microwave system will help provide better coverage to the less populated regions by the mid-1980s. Syria's one entry into the race to gain superpower transmitter status is a Czechoslovak-made 1500-kilowatt Tesla medium-wave facility with an intricate antenna system that allows switchable omnidirectional and directional transmission. In late 1979, the antenna was oriented to broadcast to Iraq and the Arabian Gulf states, but the transmitter is excessively expensive to operate according to the Ministry of Information. The government must supply 16 tons of oil per day in order to generate sufficient electricity for the transmitter (Karkoush 1979).

2.4.2 Radio Services

Main Program. Not broadcasting between 0230 and 0530, the Main Program operates from the studios in Damascus for 21 hours per day. Coverage within Syria is complete, with medium-wave transmitters in larger cities such as Damascus and Aleppo, as well as low-power stations in other cities. No short-wave broadcasts are possible because of the rebuilding of the short-wave transmitters. Although essentially designed for a Syrian audience, broadcasts are also intended to be heard in neighboring states. Newscasts, drama, interviews, and even music are supportive of the Baath Party and specifically the policies of President Al-Assad. This service has been used by Syria to communicate with neighboring countries in order to defend its role in the Syrian-dominated peace-keeping force in neighboring Lebanon. The main Program is continuously monitored by Jordan and Iraq for clues to possible shifts in government policies that may affect them.

Syria's relations with those countries have occasionally been volatile and Syrian newscasts are therefore closely monitored by many listeners in neighboring countries.

Voice of the People. Relatively new, having started in September 1978, the Voice of the People contains several programs that at one time were featured on the Main Program. This service is designed for a less sophisticated audience than the Main Program. In late 1979 the service operated in Arabic from 0600 to 1000 and from 1700 to 2100 on several medium-wave frequencies. The time between the two Arabic program periods was used to transmit foreign-language programs and some music on medium wave, as shown in Table 11.

National radio coverage is a reality. A Syrian listener has a main national program as his primary source of news, information, and entertainment. The successive government changes during the 1950s and 1960s, however, did not allow or encourage a planned expansion of the radio system. The situation with the short-wave transmitters is a case in point. It is unthinkable that Egypt or Saudi Arabia, for example, would allow the main transmission source for its international service to deteriorate to the point that facilities would have to be completely shut down, and only then have plans drawn for new transmitters. Syria does not import talent for its broadcasting productions or for its engineering staff. The country has a long tradition of drama, writing, and art that has not been tapped to any significant degree to help with the construction of a first-rate comprehensive radio system.

Table 11. Syrian Foreign Language Services

Language	Time
French	1000–1100
English	1100–1200
Western Music Program	1200–1400
Turkish	1500–1600
Hebrew	1600–1700
Russian	2100–2130
German	2130–2200
English	2300–2400
Spanish	0230–0330

SOURCE: Kouhakja 1979.

2.4.3 Television

Syria's construction of a television system in 1960 resulted from its brief unification with Egypt. The UAR contract with the Radio Corporation of America (RCA) for a comprehensive television system included a station in Damascus. It was obvious from the beginning, however, that the Syrian system was not to be developed on the same scale as Egypt's. The studio building in Damascus consists of four studios, two large and two small, and the structure itself has remained virtually unchanged for 20 years. When the station officially started on 23 July 1960 (Helwani 1977), the same date as the beginning of Egypt's television service, a good deal of the programming was live or taped. Egyptian programming comprised a substantial portion of the limited nightly telecasts. Those Syrians who worked in Egypt as part of the exchange-of-personnel agreement and in Syria itself recall that Nasser dominated programming intended for the Syrian station in order to disseminate his point of view. More specifically, they accuse Nasser of having promoted the Syrian television system in order to have an eastern relay for Egyptian television programming. In addition to the main transmitter in Damascus, stations were built during the 1960s in Aleppo and Homs that broadcast "bicycled" tapes and films until these stations were connected in the 1970s to the main station by microwave.

Aside from the construction of these two stations, both distant from the Damascus television headquarters, there was little expansion of physical facilities between 1960 and 1975. The Syrian economy did not permit the luxury of additional television production or transmission equipment or, for that matter, the large-scale importation of television receivers. During this period, Syria was involved in the two Middle East wars of 1967 and 1973, and most of her foreign exchange went toward the war effort or other nonbroadcasting national priorities. As previously noted, frequent changes in government leadership during this 15-year period did not provide the broadcast media with strong direction. Because of the Arab League boycott of RCA in the late 1960s (the Boycott Office is located in Damascus), spare parts were always a problem, and eventually the original RCA cameras acquired in 1960 were replaced with Polish cameras. However, the majority of the equipment in Damascus remained RCA, except for the Ampex video tape recorders, until about 1975, when the decision was made to upgrade the equipment and convert to SECAM color (Haffar 1979). During the mid-1970s, plans were finalized to replace the old monochrome television transmitters and to install new ones to increase coverage in Syria and to provide a signal to neighboring countries.

One motivation for the upgrading and expansion of the Syrian television system was the increasing availability of signals from other countries. Israel, Jordan, and Iraq had increased the number of relay stations, including some near the Syrian border, and Syrians were able to receive more foreign signals. Particularly attractive were the Jordanian channels that featured large amounts of western entertainment programming. New color transmitters and antenna systems have been installed in Hassaka, Aleppo, Slemfe, Damascus, Sheikh Saleh, and Homs. A transmitter has been built in Deirlellour to broadcast the Syrian television service to Iraq, and another in Tabqa to broadcast a directional signal to Turkey. Finally, a new transmitter is planned near Soueda that will broadcast to Jordan (Karkoush 1979).

The Damascus studios have been converted to color, and new monitors, switchers, and cameras have been installed. Syria does not import personnel for its television system, as there appears to be an abundance of technical and artistic talent. What is lacking in Syria is any enthusiasm for creative programming or innovative production techniques. Syria has not attempted to become a television production center for the creation of programming to be sold to other countries. Many of the television employees work in relative isolation from the rest of the Arab broadcasting world. Only a few have been attracted to high-paying jobs in the Arabian Gulf. When studio color transmissions started in 1979, technicians did not understand how to light the news set or to light for a simple chroma-key picture. For a short time in 1979, the United States International Communication Agency supplied an American lighting expert who worked with the lighting problems primarily associated with the news set. Employees of Syrian television learned a great deal about lighting from the American consultant. The news on television, considered to be important by the government, was considerably improved.

2.4.4 Television Programming

Syria operates one national television channel, which supplies programming to about 90% of the population. The broadcast day starts at 1430 and runs until about midnight. On Friday and Sunday, the transmission time is lengthened and programming starts at 1300 (Syrian Television Schedule 1979). Programming done in Syria consists of the same television offer-ings—news, drama, music, and political programs—as found on other Arab world systems. A good deal of time is devoted to interviews and discussions of the Syrian economy and to politics and Islamic religious thought. These programs are relatively easy and inexpensive to video tape, and they provide the government with a means of giving national exposure to those people it believes best reflect the thinking of the Baath political leaders. Some drama is taped and shown. A locally produced children's program is scheduled every day for early evening transmission. Taped music programs ranging in length from five minutes to one-half hour are interspersed with other kinds of programming. These music tapes, some of which date back ten years, are used as "fill" until a program such as news needs to be telecast as scheduled. Films and video tapes from non-Arab countries are shown. Many of these, such as documentaries from the East European countries, are provided without charge as part of cultural agreements. Relatively few programs from the United States and Europe have been shown on Syrian television. An occasional segment of "Kojak" appears, but Syria neither believes that it can afford to purchase large amounts of western programming nor thinks that such offerings are appropriate for Syrian viewers. The Director General of television does believe that the western programs have some social value for Syrians because they show life, albeit in a dramatized form, in other cultures (Bellatt 1979).

Possibly the most important program to both government and viewer on Syrian television is the news. Because so much time during the various newscasts is devoted to the activities of the President and other government officials, television personnel put a good deal of time and effort into television news. Viewer interest in these newscasts derives in part from the fact that government policies and directives are often featured. Actual news items and guidance regarding the basic ordering of stories are supplied to both radio and television by the Syrian News Agency. The first television newscast of the day is at 1900 and is scheduled for 15 minutes, featuring almost exclusively local Syrian news. The main evening newscast is telecast daily at 2030 and runs between 15 and 20 minutes, depending on the amount of news available. When the President travels outside of Syria on official visits, more news is generally available and the newscast is extended beyond its normal length. This main newscast includes local, Arab world, and international items from wire services and the European Broadcasting Union (EBU) daily satelite news feeds. Prior to sign-off the third newscast of the day is aired, consisting mostly of headlines. Local stories are filmed with 16 mm film equipment. Syria is interested in Electronic News Gathering (ENG) and has acquired a Bosch one-inch machine, but no field taping with the unit has been attempted (Hijab 1979).

Television in Syria is financed directly by the government and by advertising time sales. There is almost no contact between those who are responsible for programming television and those who are charged with selling commercial time. A small staff is employed to organize commercials on television—a reflection of the fact that, although commercials have always been allowed, the Ministry of Information is not particularly enthusiastic about them. This is due apparently to the financial arrangement within the government regarding advertising time sales. Thirty per cent of the revenue from advertising is retained by Syrian Television; the remaining 70% goes to the Syrian Ministry of Finance, which supposedly returns that amount and more as part of the government's yearly financial allocation to all ministries (Al-Sharif 1979). A good deal of paid advertising appears to be for state-run industries, which manufacture soap, shoes, clothing, etc. Increasingly, however, commercials that are also seen in other Arab countries are for products such as Japanese watches, imported candy and cosmetics, and processed cheese. The government may reap a kind of psychological benefit from television advertising. The commercials may serve to remind the nation that the Baath Party has not proscribed the concept of free enterprise.

It seems unlikely that Syria will build an elaborate national multichannel television system on a par with that of some other Arab countries. Economic constraints and national priorities appear to be major limiting factors. The country is interested in having its radio services reach neighboring countries, and it will resume short-wave transmissions of Arabic and foreign languages by the mid-1980s. However, Syria has not been and probably will not be an important Arab world radio braodcaster equal to Egypt, Iraq, or Saudi Arabia. The government has not supported research on set ownership or listening preferences. Color television did not start until the late 1970s; and apparently very few color sets are available, although some are featured in stores. Many families are content to acquire a monochrome set to enjoy national as well as neighboring channels.

2.5 Jordan

The Hashemite Kingdome of Jordan consists of 37,738 square miles (including the occupied West Bank) and is inhabited by a population of about 2.8 million people. The term Hashemite indicates that the royal family traces its history to the Prophet Mohammed. Neighboring countries are Syria, Iraq, Saudi Arabia, and Israel.

The original territory was ruled by the Ottoman Empire until after World War I. Great Britain had limited administrative control over what was then called Transjordan and administered a League of Nations mandate in what was then called Palestine. After the 1948 war that followed the departure of the British from Palestine, King Abdullah's territory was increased by an area negotiated by the Arabs and Israel that included part of the city of Jerusalem. Unlike vast portions of the country that are desert, the West Bank is agriculturally rich and has some light industry. That part of Jerusalem that was Jordanian is a popular tourist attraction. In 1951, King Abdullah was assassinated and his son Talal was named king. Talal served as ruler for only a short period of time, allegedly because of a nervous disorder, and was succeeded by his son, Hussein. The country was ruled by a regency council for one year, until the King reached the age of 18 and completed his schooling in Great Britain.

In 1967, during the Six-Day War, Israel gained control of the West Bank. The territory is occupied and administered by Israel and has been the focus of international news since the mid-1970s because of the Jewish settlements that have been built there. The loss of the West Bank was a serious financial loss for Jordan. In addition, the migration of Palestinians from the West Bank to Amman, the capital, increased the already sizable Palestinian population. In 1970, there was a brief but bitter civil war, which pitted the Palestinian forces in Jordan against those loyal to the King. The basic result of the action was that Hussein remained in control of the country. The economy has become healthier during the 1970s largely because of the expatriate salaries that Jordanians who work in the Gulf states send home, and because of foreign aid and loans from countries like the United States and Saudi Arabia.

2.5.1 Radio

Jordanian Radio, officially known as the Hashemite Broadcasting Service (HBS), traces its beginnings to the Palestine Broadcasting Service, which was established on 30 March 1936 by the British government under its mandate authority. The station was an early radio outlet in the Arab world and broadcast limited local programming in three languages—Arabic, English, and Hebrew. Studios were located in Jerusalem and a 20-kilowatt transmitter and tower were placed in nearby Ramallah (*Palestine Department of Posts...1935* 1936, p.5; *Palestine Department...1936* 1937, p. 6). The station was established by the British to facilitate communication with the Arab and Jewish residents of Palestine. The British were also interested in providing an alternative to the hostile Italian propaganda broadcasts from Radio Bari (see 5.2). During and immediately after World War II, the station facilities and transmission time were expanded and the BBC's Empire Service was at times rebroadcast over the station.

When the British left Palestine in May 1948, Jewish forces captured the radio studio complex and the Arab forces took control of the transmitter in Ramallah. After the 1948 peace agreement with Israel, Jordan used the Ramallah transmitter site on the West Bank while Israel refurbished the damaged Jerusalem studio complex, which still serves as the headquarters for its domestic and international radio services. Through Jordanian military authority on the West Bank, Jordan operated an Arabic service from the Ramallah site, to which studios had been added. On 24 April 1950, the West and East banks of Jordan were unified officially, and the military (Hashemite Broadcasting Service n.d., p. 2) gradually handed over broadcasting to the Ministry of Information, which, in a manner similar to other Arab states, administers the radio service. Financial constraints hampered the expansion of the radio service after 1948. At the time, the government did not realize the importance of providing citizens with a viable radio service. This situation changed markedly in the mid-1950s, when Radio Cairo started attacking King Hussein and other government leaders for taking orders from the British—particularly from Glubb Pasha, a British officer who headed the Arab Legion, Jordan's army. When the government realized that Cairo's Voice of the Arabs was in fact having an impact, plans were made to construct a new radio studio facility and transmitter in Amman. On 1 September 1956 King Hussein—himself an avid amateur radio operator—inaugurated the new Amman radio transmitter, which broadcast limited programming of about four hours per day on one short- and one medium-wave transmitter. This station assumed the greater part of the responsibility of counter-programming the Egyptian services while the Ramallah site featured the domestic main service.

In 1958, neighboring Iraq underwent a bloody revolution resulting in the deaths of the Iraqi prime minister and most members of the royal family, which was closely related to the Jordanian royal family. This situation, coupled with the general instability in the Middle East between 1956 and 1960, caused the Jordanian government to take more notice of the need for a reliable, comprehensive radio service that would also serve neighboring states. The basic importance attached to radio in Jordan dates from expansion plans that were drawn in 1955 and 1956 and became reality in 1959. On 1 March 1959, King Hessein dedicated the Amman broadcasting service and on 23 August of that year he opened the studios of the radio service in Jerusalem. During the March ceremonies Hussein said:

As Jordan listens today to its vivid voice, energetically defending Arabism and Islam, with the portraits of glory embodied in its vibrations, and with the guiding light of holiness radiating from within its depth, Jordan finds itself empowered to propagate such lights as would illuminate the way for humanity. The way of Jordan is the path of the Almighty God; the mission of Jordan is unity, amity and fraternity. [Hashemite Broadcasting Service, n.d., p. 1]

After 1960, the Jordanian government's commitment to a radio system was firmly established and plans were drawn for the introduction of a television service. Financial priorities did not allow the government to allocate funds to construct a large radio complex with a large staff like Nasser's in Egypt. A lack of money to operate a system in the 1950s had motivated Jordan to allow commercial broadcasting on radio; an aggressive sales staff, oriented toward research, was organized for this purpose. In the 1950s, the country had asked for American help with its then fledgling radio system and a contract was signed between the Hashemite Broadcasting System and Syracuse University. The contract stipulated that Americans employed by Syracuse University would work in Amman as advisors (Hamilton 1972; Jarrar 1979). This contact with the Syracuse group probably fostered the early research interest of HBS in determining audience size in both Jordan and neighboring countries in order to establish commercial advertising rates. In the 1960s, when little if any media research was being undertaken in the other Arab countries, HBS undertook a radio preference survey in Riyadh, Saudi Arabia, during a period when the Saudi Arabian government was not receptive to this kind of activity. This survey was probably the first of its kind to be done in Saudi Arabia (Associated Business Consultants, "A Seven Day...Survey").

The above-mentioned survey was undertaken by Associated Business Consultants (ABC) of Beirut, Lebanon, which formed an alliance with an American firm by the name of RTV International, with offices in New York City. The company was founded in 1963 by Richard Bertrandias, a former official at Radio Liberty, an American radio organization headquartered in Munich, Germany, which broadcasts to the Soviet Union in various vernacular languages. Originally named Radio Liberation, the station is known to have been started and then operated by the United States Central Intelligence Agency (CIA), until the source of funds became public knowledge in the early 1970s. Radio Liberty and a sister station, Radio Free Europe, which broadcasts to Eastern Europe, but not the Soviet Union, still operate; now they are funded openly by the United States government.

It has become popular to accuse American organizations that operate in the Middle East of having some connection with the CIA. Mr. Bertrandias' background and RTV's interest with ABC in media research and mass communication in Arab countries has led to suspicion that RTV had CIA connections or that it was actually owned by the United States intelligence agency. For a time, RTV held contracts with Arab and African countries; in many cases funding was arranged by the Agency for International Development (Associated Business Consultants/RTV International n.d.). But rumors and speculation about the company apparently hurt its chances for success, and by the late 1970s it had ceased to exist. At one time, RTV attempted to secure a transmitter location on Cyprus for a radio station that would broadcast to the Arab world in a manner similar to Radio Monte Carlo (see 5.3). In 1972, RTV successfully negotiated a contract with Bahrain to start a commercial television station that it operated until the Bahrain government took it over. Other RTV activities in the Arab world included hotel management contracts in Riyadh, Saudi Arabia, and Beirut, Lebanon, as well as the introduction of television in Jordan. When the United States Army Corps of Engineers sought contract bids in the late 1960s for the operation and maintenance of new Saudi Arabian television stations in Qassim and Medina, RTV was financially disqualified because it did not have a firm enough economic base. Speculation about involvement with the United States intelligence community may, however, have influenced the Corps of Engineers' decision (West 1972).

The Hashemite Broadcasting System did not become a strong commercial service in the region. HBS lacked the transmission power to reach large audiences in Syria, Israel, Iraq, or Saudi Arabia. Nevertheless, the commercial income did help pay the bills for a radio service that until 1967 had studios in Amman and Jerusalem. Its international short-wave service provided programs in Hebrew, Spanish, and English. The basic orientation of Jordanian radio has been to defend Jordan's political position in the Arab world rather than to engage in the type of hostile propaganda frequently favored by Syria, Iraq, and Egypt.

The June 1967 Middle East war affected Jordan profoundly. The West Bank was occupied by Israeli forces, resulting in a stream of residents leaving it for Amman, in the economic loss of potential tourists to East Jerusalem, and in the loss of West Bank agriculture and light industry. Jordan also lost the Jerusalem radio studios and the transmitters at the Ramallah site. After the war, operation of HBS was centered in Amman. Plans were drawn to expand the number of transmitters and the studios as soon as the economic situation would permit. The government realized more than ever the importance of a reliable radio system. With this, it could encourage the indigenous population stunned by the loss of its land, and maintain contact with Jordanians living under Israeli occupation, as well as with active Palestinian elements determined to retake the West Bank.

One of the changes following the 1967 Six-Day War was the general cooling of radio propaganda in the Middle East. Egypt had been a leader in suggesting that the Hashemite and Saudi Arabian royal families should be overthrown. The occasional vindictive broadcasts from Iraq and Syria did continue; but many countries, including Jordan, took the position that they should concentrate on the organization of a domestic service as well as broadcasts to reach other countries to help explain Jordan's Arab world position. Although television took some attention from HBS, by the early 1970s plans were made for the transmitters that would have to be added to provide coverage to areas such as Aqaba on the Red Sea. Plans were also made to join the ranks of the Arab countries that had decided to build superpower medium-wave transmitters. HBS operates three basic radio services, which are broadcast on medium-wave, short-wave, and FM transmitters, all of which originate from the broadcasting complex in Amman.

2.5.2 Radio Services

Main Arabic Program.   The main provider of HBS's news, information, and entertainment, the Main Arabic Program broadcasts daily from 0530 to 0130 the following day (Radio Jordan Frequency Schedule 1979). The basic format is similar to Radio Cairo's Main Program and many other services in other Arab countries where programming is presented in blocks that include special features for children, women, and laborers, interspersed with music and regularly scheduled newscasts. This service is also intended to be heard outside of Jordan, as it is broadcast from a 200-kilowatt medium-wave transmitter in Amman and a 1-kilowatt medium-wave facility in Aqaba. At selected times during the day and at night, portions of this service are broadcast by one of several 100-kilowatt short-wave transmitters in Amman.

English Service.   Jordan has always broadcast some English-language programming because of the Palestine Broadcasting Service heritage and the fact that English is widely spoken in an area where Great Britain once had considerable presence. After the 1967 war, HBS discontinued its Hebrew schedule and decided to concentrate on English as an alternative to its Arabic service and as a kind of program that might be popular among both Arabs and Jews in Israel. The service lasts for 12½ hours per day, from 0700 to 1930, and is broadcast from Amman using a 20-kilowatt medium-wave transmitter, an FM transmitter, and, at specified times during the day, a short-wave transmitter. Programming is blocked in a manner similar to the Arabic service, but the overall format is heavily weighted toward music and news. Some drama is broadcast and specific times are set on a published schedule for classical music, American country and western music, jazz, and various request programs ("Radio Jordan English Service" 1979, p. 2). In order to be more competitive with radio services such as Radio Monte Carlo, the very latest popular western music is played from a supply flown weekly from London by Alia, the national airline (Zada 1979a). The service identifies itself as Radio Jordan and does not accept advertising.

FM Stereo Service. The motivation for an FM stereo continuous music service appears to have been King Hussein's interest in such an undertaking. In addition, people with home stereo equipment, imported mostly from Japan, were tuning to such a station that broadcast from Jerusalem. In 1979, a studio in the broadcasting building was renovated for an FM stereo control room and in January 1980 test transmissions were started.

2.5.3 Jordanian Superpower Transmitter

Throughout this study of Arab world broadcasting, the intense interest in high-power medium-wave transmitters has been noted. With neighboring countries either planning or constructing superpower transmitters, Jordan decided that it must also build a powerful facility if its radio voice was to be heard among the clash of broadcast signals that crowd the medium-wave spectrum at night.

The Ministry of Information contracted with Continental Electronics of Dallas, Texas, for the construction and installation of a 2000-kilowatt medium-wave transmitter in Ajlun, near Amman (King 1979; Continental Electronics 1979, p. 1). Such a powerful facility would provide a strong signal to all neighboring countries. As the transmitter was intended to broadcast the HBS Main Program, additional revenue might result from an increased coverage area.

About the same time that the government ordered the new facility from Continental, Saudi Arabia finalized with the same company its Northern Stations Project, which consists of one 1000-kilowatt and three 2000-kilowatt medium-wave transmitters, located at Qurayat and Duba in the northern Saudi Arabian desert. Both countries applied to the International Telecommunications Union International Frequency Registration Board for 594 kHz and were registered as having made the request. The frequency was noted as belonging to both countries. Continental Electronics started building in its Dallas plant two of the world's most powerful medium-wave transmitters that would operate on the same frequency while located only a few hundred miles apart. In the fall of 1979, both transmitters were installed and started test transmissions, at which time both governments realized that serious interference problems existed. Jordanian and Saudi Arabian Ministry of Information officials and broadcast engineers held a meeting that resulted in an agreement that Jordan would not broadcast on 594 kHz (Ashfoura 1979). In return, Jordan received undisclosed compensation, and agreed to a change of frequency at the expense of the Saudi government

(Odeh 1979). The Saudi Arabian Ministry of Information defended its acquisition of the frequency by noting that although Jordan apparently registered the frequency first, it did so with the understanding that considerably lower power would be utilized. Officials took the position that the problem was Jordan's, because Jordan changed the intended power of the transmitter after the frequency had been registered. (S. Nasser 1980).

2.5.4 Patterns of Radio Listening

In a February 1972 study of radio and television audiences in Jordan, Associated Business Consultants of Beirut, Lebanon, made the following major findings (1972, pp. 1–2):

1. In the six cities surveyed there were an estimated 135,000 radio sets.
2. 90% of those surveyed listen to radio daily.
3. 94% of those surveyed own at least one radio set.
4. Adult listeners average two hours and forty-five minutes per day.
5. The most popular hour for radio listening is between 0630 and 0730.
6. The most popular type of radio program is news, followed by music.

The Jordanian radio audience, like that in other Arab countries, listens to foreign radio stations. A survey done in Jordan for the International Communication Agency in May 1977 concluded that 71% of an estimated 426,000 Jordanians listen regularly to non-Jordanian stations. An overwhelming number of listeners say that they listen to foreign radio stations on mediumwave; and among those surveyed who listen "once a week or more often" in Arabic, 34.3% listen to the BBC, 33.6% hear the Israeli Broadcasting Service, and 23.4% listen to Radio Damascus (USICA 1978b, pp. 11–12; Jarrar 1970, p. 16). What these data do not indicate is the effect of these broadcasts on listeners. What seems clear is that Jordanians are similar to other Arabs with respect to a curiosity about hearing what neighbors, whether friends or enemies, are saying. Listeners appear to realize that in most cases the governments are the broadcasters and that tuning to a government radio station provides the listener with the government view. The BBC's news is uniquely popular because it is acknowledged by many to be essentially objective since the British government itself is not the broadcaster.

2.5.5 Television

By 1964 it was obvious to government officials that Jordan must build a television system. Jordan's Arab neighbors had started television broadcasts in the early 1960s—in the case of Iraq, in the 1950s. When Saudi Arabia, the most conservative of the Arab counries, announced its plans in 1963 for a national television system, Jordan had no choice but to begin steps for the expensive undertaking. In 1965 and 1966, the government allocated funds for a feasibility study, which was undertaken by an international team of consultants. About the time that the report was made to the government, a group of local businessmen proposed that they construct a television system along the lines of Lebanon's. The proposed system was to be commercial, but the government was to be allowed a good deal of control, including supervision of programming. The Jordanian Cabinet at last agreed to the basic plan proposed by the businessmen; but when the programming proposal was received and it became obvious that it was to be mostly entertainment, the Cabinet ruled against a private-government partnership and decided to operate a system itself (Jarrar 1970, p. 20). International bids for the creation of a television system were advertised and, by May 1966, bids had been received for the construction of a television system by 16 firms from the United States, Europe, and Japan. A board reviewed the bids and decided to allow several firms to supply and install in Amman various parts of the system. The bulk of the studio and transmission equipment was supplied by Marconi of Great Britain. The government created the Jordan Television Corporation, which would gain income from both commercial advertising and license fees; King Hussein laid the corner stone for the television building outside Amman on 11 July 1966 (Madanat 1976, p. 1).

The June 1967 Middle East war delayed the official introduction of television. During the economic, political, and military readjustments immediately following the loss of the West Bank to Israel, television lost some government attention. The construction of the studio complex and the delivery of equipment were delayed. Also, many western technicians left Jordan during the war, further slowing plans for installation of equipment. In retrospect, the decision to locate the main studio complex in Amman rather than in Jerusalem was a sound one. The initial plan called for a transmitter in Jerusalem to broadcast the Amman signal to the West Bank and to Israel, which at the time had no television. Some television equipment, notably a transmission tower and antenna, had been delivered to Jerusalem and was captured by the Israelis, who later used the equipment for their own service. In the fall of 1967, equipment deliveries resumed and British engineers continued equipment installation. Jordan Television (JTV) contracted with RTV International to supply a team of people to act on behalf of the government in certifying the equipment installation and to provide some production and technical training for those Jordanians who would actually begin the service.

On the evening of 28 April 1968, television officially started from the Amman studio with a three-hour daily transmission on Channel 3. The initial stages of program development included some local programming—news, interviews, and children's programs. After two years of limited transmissions, the daily schedule had been lenghtened to four and a half hours, and increased local programming had been made possible by the addition of a large production studio and lighting equipment, additional cameras, and more video tape recorders. The addition of another transmitter on Channel

6 expanded the service to reach approximately 65% of the combined population of Jordan and the West Bank.

The 1970 Jordanian Civil War, which pitted Palestinian forces in the country against King Hussein's army, temporarily halted the development of television. However, planning continued for more space and equipment. By 1972, the basic administrative structure of the television service and the programming philosophy were established. The first channel to become operational, Channel 3, became the main Arabic service, broadcasting from approximately 1730 to midnight. Channel 6 features mostly foreign-language programs that are imported primarily from the United States and Great Britain. News is presented nightly in French, Hebrew, and English. Both channels simultaneously televise the main nightly Arabic news program at 2000. This is done both to increase coverage and to discourage alternative viewing. Transmissions are extended during religious holidays and on Fridays.

By the mid-1970s, both channels had acquired additional production equipment including outside broadcasting vehicles and video tape recorders. The country became a member of INTELSAT, thus allowing the broadcast of such events as the Munich Olympic games and American space shots. Through the Arab States Broadcasting Union, Jordan became the coordinating center for several Arab countries' participation in the European Broadcasting Union (EBU) satellite news feeds (Boyd 1975b, p. 317). On the sixth anniversary of JTV in April 1974, Jordan began color television transmission using the PAL system. Color brought new television production equipment to Jordan, resulting in an increase in the quality of the signal of both channels. In the mid-1970s, a national telecommunications project was completed that allowed the Amman headquarters to supply repeater stations in Petra, Ma'an, and Aqaba. By 1980 JTV was using 15 transmitters (Jordan Television Engineering Department 1979) that provided reliable color coverage to most of the country. Some of the transmitters have been positioned so that the programming can be seen in neighboring Syria, the West Bank, and Israel.

2.5.6 Links with Other Arab Countries

The size of the administrative, production, and engineering staffs for television increased significantly during the 1970s as new studios and equipment were added and as local production increased. Jordan television, which has never been heavily subsidized by the government, found that there was a market in the Gulf states for some of its productions. The studios in Amman are kept busy with tapings that are used for domestic consumption and then offered for sale to other countries. An interesting by-product of the television system is that Jordan is probably the major exporter of engineering and production talent to the Gulf states. Egyptian actors and directors still tend to dominate the Arabic serial and television play syndication market, but

Jordanians are heavily used in the Gulf in all facets of development. Television is no exception. In 1979, the two large stations in Oman hired some 20 Jordanian engineers and production specialists to replace the Germans and British who were there on contract (Jarrar 1979). The export of television personnel is good for the Jordanian economy because expatriate salaries contribute to the flow of hard currency into the country. However, the continuous departure of trained people means that there is almost always a shortage of competent people to operate the Jordanian television system. In 1978, JTV made the decision to build a television production center adjacent to the existing television complex. The venture, which will include government as well as private money, will undertake the production of commercials and series for other countries (Ashfoura 1979).

2.5.7 Television Programming

The main Arabic program on Channel 3 telecasts productions made in Jordan and Egypt. Imported programs from the west are shown with the original soundtrack but with subtitles that have been added electronically. This process, which is used heavily in Jordan and in a few other Arab countries, allows the soundtracks of films and video tapes to be translated into Arabic and typed on a white scroll by an electric typewriter. When the foreign program is aired, the subtitling is done by a machine that uses a monochrome camera with the polarity reversed, so that the black letters ultimately appear white when superimposed or keyed over the picture. An operator sits in a special booth during the broadcast, listens to the soundtrack, and advances the subtitles on the scroll according to the prepared script. This procedure, because of the human factor, produces erratic results, but it saves the enormous expense of dubbing programs onto video tape or of subtitling films. The procedure is also used on the programs that are telecast on the predominantly foreign Channel 6.

The Arabic newscast at 2000 is a nightly 30-minute program, which features news about the royal family, domestic government news, international news from wire services, and the twice-daily EBU news exchange satellite feed. Imported programs from the last quarter of the 1979 television schedule shown on the Arabic program (see Figure 3) include "Gunsmoke," "Wild Wild West," "The Waltons," "Josie and the Pussycats," "The Incredible Hulk," "Return to Peyton Place," "The New Avengers," "Return of the Saint," "Thrillseekers," "Grizzly Adams," "New Land," "Star Trek," "Eddie Capra," and "Kojak" (Fourth Cycle, JTV 3). The program from Channel 6 is telecast simultaneously on the Arabic channel for special events. The Arabic news is always broadcast simultaneously on both channels. The early evening French-language programming is the result of a cultural agreement between Jordan and France that stipulates that the French government will supply programming on film and videotape and two French citizens who write and deliver a daily newscast.

Figure 3. Jordan Television Daily Schedule, Fourth Quarter 1979

	Saturday	Sunday	Monday	Tuesday
1830	French Series	Varieties	Documentary	French Series
1900	French News	French News	French News	French News
1915	Varieties	Varieties	Varieties	Sports News
1930	Hebrew News	Hebrew News	Hebrew News	Hebrew News
1945	Science World	Sport Magazine	Varieties	Varieties
2000	Arabic News	Arabic News	Arabic News	Arabic News
2030	"Fall and Rise of Reginald Perrin" "Dad's Army"	"Muppet Show"	"Doctor Down Under"	"All in the Family" "The Goodies"
2110	"All Creatures Great and Small"	Documentary	"Power Without Glory"	"The Onedin Line" "Top of the Hill"
2200	English News	English News	English News	English News
2215	Variety Show	"New Avengers"	"The Italian Way" "Rafferty" "Quincy"	"Eddie Capra" "Kojak"
2310	Arabic News	Arabic News	Arabic News	Arabic News
2320	"Bluey"		Continuation of program prior to news	

	Wednesday	Thursday	Friday
1830	French Documentary	French Series	French Series
1900	French News	French News	French News
1915	Varieties	Varieties	Varieties
1930	Hebrew News	Hebrew News	Hebrew News
1945	"Zero One"	"Eva 2000"	"Living Tomorrow"
2000	Arabic News	Arabic News	Arabic News
2030	"It Ain't Half Hot Mum"	"Some Mothers Do 'Ave 'Em" "Taxi"	"How's Your Father?" "Mr. Big"
2110	"The Sullivans"	"Survivors"	"Tycoon"
2200	English News	English News	English News
2215	"Love Boat"	Movie of the Week	"Flying High"
2310	Arabic News	Arabic News Continuation of Movie	Arabic News

SOURCE: "Jordan Television Foreign Program, JTV6."

Although Jordan probably adheres more faithfully to its published television schedule than most other Arab television services, changes do occur almost daily. Occasionally special programs of local interest are substituted for scheduled programming on both channels. Times are only approximate because of the emphasis on foreign programs, which, lacking commercials, do not conform to standard program times. There is often a good deal of fill, slides, and music, to help bring the program times in line with the published schedule. Although the times for the various news services are published, the news does not always fill the scheduled period and is occasionally extended.

On both channels, there are several reasons for the emphasis on foreign programming. First, the television administration believes that the programming is popular among Jordanians. It tries to provide those with television sets with popular entertainment. Jordan Television has, from the start, attempted to attract Arabs from the West Bank and the citizens of Israel to its television service; popular foreign programming was one way of realizing this goal. Whereas Israel, like Jordan, established a television service after the 1967 war, the one Israeli channel has not featured much foreign programming.

The Jordanian services, which are very concerned about expenses and income, apparently use foreign programs to attract advertisers. In 1977, the Minister of Information indicated the effects of foreign programming were minimal, but that some viewers confess a frustration about not being able to afford some of the products that are advertised on television. After watching an episode of "Hawaii Five-0," the Minister said, his son asked why they did not have a house as nice as those of the important people on the program; their present house, the son said, was not good enough for a person as important as a Jordanian minister (Odeh 1977). The Minister apparently had not realized the possible impact of television on his own family.

Because Jordan uses so much western television programming, suppliers are interested in having Jordan show their television series. A showing on Jordan television can help program sales in other Arab countries. Thus, Jordan is in the position to telecast programs first and at a relatively low price. The television administration also gets foreign programming relatively cheaply by allowing its electronic subtitling scrolls to be duplicated and used by other Arab countries. This is attractive to suppliers. An example of a program that has become very popular in the Arab world and that was first shown in Jordan is "Dallas." Viewers and the television administration generally agree that it is the most popular foreign program to be shown on television. Edited to exclude some of the sex, the series is apparently popular because it deals with contemporary Texas and the American West, which holds a fascination for many Arabs. When the Program Director of Jordan Television was asked how the program contributed to Jordan's national development, he replied that in many respects modern Jordan had some of the same cultural problems as those exhibited on "Dallas." Jordan has many wealthy people because of the economic boom in the late 1970s. Arab society, he noted, is changing and traditional family relationships are not as strong as they once were. "Dallas" is consequently believed to be an effective means of indirectly examining some of the problems of modern Jordan (Jarrar 1979).

2.5.8 The Israeli Audience

Jordan discontinued its Hebrew radio service after the 1967 war and has not resumed it. The basic philosophy has been to reach Israeli citizens through English-language radio broadcasts, by popular foreign programming on television, and with a daily Hebrew news program on Channel 6. The newscast started in October 1972 and is intended to provide information about Jordan as well as to disseminate the Arab view of the Middle East problem (Odeh 1979). In addition, the newscast seeks to provide Israelis with an alternative view of events in Israel. Occasionally, items in Israeli newspapers and the foreign press about Israeli society, politics, or the economic situation are included as news items. Many newscasts include a political cartoon drawn on a camera card by an artist at Jordan television.

It is difficult to assess the impact of the Hebrew news from Jordan on Israelis. The newscast is probably watched by those Israelis who are curious or who have sets tuned to JTV for the entertainment programs from the west and do not change channels when the news is aired. Unlike the reaction of some Israelis to the Hebrew radio broadcasts of Egypt, Syria, and Iraq, which they see as propaganda, the JTV Hebrew news is generally given good reviews by many citizens and media professionals. The language is generally accurate; moreover, the basic approach includes an effort not to portray Israeli society in a derogatory light (Bar-Haim 1980). Jordan's basic media policy has always differed from other countries that broadcast to Israel in that the Ministry of Information officials know that inflammatory anti-Israel rhetoric will not attract or keep broadcast media consumers. Not only do Israelis seem to recognize the attractiveness of the two Jordan television channels, but the JTV schedules are published daily in the *Jerusalem Post*, an Israeli English-language newspaper.

2.5.9 The Television Audience

The ability of Jordanians to receive foreign television signals depends on the location of the viewer. Even within the hilly city of Amman, the quality of foreign and domestic signals varies greatly. Signals from Israel and Syria can be received during most parts of the year. During the summer months, the Egyptian, Lebanese, and Cypriot channels can be received in some parts of Amman by people who have installed antennas with rotors, an increasingly popular practice. The last available survey of television viewing patterns in Jordan was done in 1972; since then important changes, such as an increase in the number of owned television receivers, have taken place in Jordanian society. Nevertheless, the main findings of the study are of interest (Associated Business Consultants 1972, p. 1):

1. The estimated number of television sets was 105,000.
2. Average number of viewers per set was 6.5.
3. 73% of surveyed households had a set.

4. 81% of viewers surveyed watched television daily.
5. Most viewers (80%) watched in their own homes, while 17% watched outside the home, and 3% watched both at home and outside.
6. The most popular time slot for viewing was 2000 to 2030—the time of the Arabic newscast.
7. The most popular foreign series included wrestling and "Hawaii Five-0."

The Jordanian television system differs in several respects from the services operated by other Arab countries. The system has always tried to operate with little or no expense to the Jordan government. Financial support comes from license fees and advertising. About 1000 people work with the two channels, a relatively lean staff compared with that of other countries such as Egypt that have built large systems with a vast number of employees. JTV programming philosophy includes the desire to reach a non-Arab country, Israel, with attractive programming and news. Programming that helps with the priorities for Jordanian development has not been totally neglected. However, the percentage of imported entertainment programs from the west is higher on JTV than on any other Arab television system. Finally, Jordanian television serves as the main training ground for television engineers and other technical people who work in the Gulf countries. When the new television production center is completed, Jordan will have the potential to join those who supply Arabic programming to eager purchasers in the Arabian Gulf.

2.6 North Yemen

North Yemen, officially the Yemen Arab Republic, is located in the southwest corner of the Arabian peninsula, with Saudi Arabia to the north and the People's Democratic Republic of Yemen (South Yemen) to the south and east. The population estimates vary between five and six million people, about one-quarter of whom are employed in other countries. Many are in the Gulf states working as laborers and in service industries. The three main cities are San'a (the capital), Taiz, and the Red Sea port city of Hodeida. Agriculture is an important activity in North Yemen, which is a relatively poor country blessed with fertile land. Coffee has been the main source of foreign exchange, but cotton exports are increasing and may soon rival coffee as the most important crop. Qat, a plant whose leaves when chewed produce a mild narcotic effect, is also a source of income for farmers.

Politically North Yemen has witnessed some dramatic changes in this century. After the dissolution of the Ottoman Empire in 1918, Imam Yahya gained control of the country and remained in power until he was assassinated in 1948. Yahya's son Ahmed defeated the forces who had assassinated his father and proclaimed himself Imam. After Ahmed's death in 1962, his son Mohammed succeeded him, but Mohammed's rule lasted only a few days; the military deposed the new leader and proclaimed the Yemen Arab Republic. In 1967 the Yemen civil war ended. Royalist forces (those who supported the Imam), supported by Saudi Arabia, had been pitted against republican forces, supported by Egypt. North Yemen's political stability has been threatened since 1968 by South Yemen (People's Democratic Republic of Yemen), a proclaimed Marxist state. There was open warfare between the two Yemens in 1971, followed by a ceasefire and an agreement between the two countries to merge. This merger, however, did not occur. Occasional changes in the government have continued to take place during the 1970s. Again fighting between the two Yemens erupted in February 1979, and again a ceasefire was signed, along with a pledge to unite the two countries. The United States supplied North Yemen with arms during this fighting, but the country has moved closer to the Soviet Union, with which it concluded an arms deal in November 1979.

2.6.1 Radio

Egyptian radio services, most notably the Voice of the Arabs and Radio Cairo, played an important part in the eventual development of radio in Yemen. During the 1950s, Egyptian services were well received in the southern part of the Arabian peninsula. There was, in fact no real alternative to the Egyptian programming. Local broadcasts from the San'a station were limited in hours and, compared with those of Egypt, unprofessional.

In September 1956, both Radio Cairo and the radio station in San'a broadcast programming that was designed to provoke actions against the British government's presence in the Aden Protectorate (South Yemen). A kind of mini radio war between Aden and North Yemen reached its peak in 1957. The North Yemen government apparently believed that this broadcasting activity would distract attention from its own internal problems (Marco 1968, p. 105).

During the civil war in the 1960s, broadcasting to North Yemen intensified as Egypt and Saudi Arabia openly used their radio services to support efforts of the opposing groups. After the 1962 military coup, the government moved to centralize the mass communication media under a ministry of information. The construction of a viable internal radio system that could be used for national development was not possible until the end of the civil war.

Since 1967, the government has increasingly realized the importance of radio as a means of communicating with the largely illiterate population. Under the administration of the Ministry of Information in San'a, three radio services, all broadcasting only in Arabic, have been built. Each one has taken the name of the city from which it originates: Radio San'a, the main North Yemen station, which transmits for 15 hours per day; and Radio Taiz and Radio Hodeida, each of which daily transmits four hours of programming (Nyrop, et al. 1977, p. 225; The Middle East and North Africa 1980, p. 1170). North Yemen does have short-wave transmitters. They simulcast programs from the domestic service. The government announced that in late 1980 or early 1981 a new 600-kilowatt medium-wave transmitter would be completed and afford better national coverage. Of the three medium-wave transmitters for the three existing radio services, none exceeds 60 kilowatts (*World Radio TV Handbook 1980* 1980, p. 197). There are an estimated one-quarter million radio receivers in the country.

2.6.2 Television

The economic and political situation in North Yemen did not provide strong motivation for the government to start a television system until radio facilities were first completed. In the early 1970s, a group of international businessmen, headed by an American, attempted to gain a government concession to operate a commercial television service in San'a. The businessmen, with the backing of an international television equipment manufacturer, were to provide the station itself and to operate it on a commercial basis, with a percentage of income going to the government. However, government changes during the final stages of negotiations prevented the conclusion of the proposed agreement. Also, the North Yemen government realized that although the station would be built at no cost to the government, there would not be total government control over programming.

The government formally opened its PAL color San'a-based television service in September 1975 (*The Middle East and North Africa* 1980,p. 1170), making North Yemen the last Arab country to start a television service. Programming is usually confined to the evening hours. Most programs are imported from other Arab countries, especially from Egypt. Since 1975, to serve the important population centers, two more transmitters have been built and linked by microwave to the San'a studios (*World Radio TV Handbook 1980* 1980, p. 398).

If North Yemen continues to enjoy amicable relations with its potentially hostile neighbor South Yemen, all facets of development, including the broadcast media, may prosper. If South Yemen again threatens the security of North Yemen, broadcasting activity may increase in order to increase local radio and television programming and provide a more attractive alternative to broadcasts from South Yemen. North Yemen's location, political situation, and economy will not encourage the construction of the powerful transmitters that many other Arab countries seem to believe are necessary.

2.7 South Yemen

South Yemen, officially the People's Democratic Republic of Yemen, is a country with an estimated population of one and one-half million people, who live within 111,000 square miles. Neighboring countries are Saudi Arabia, Oman, and North Yemen.

Historically, the country's fortunes were tied to the British, from whom Aden and the surrounding Protectorate of South Arabia secured independence in 1967. In 1839 the British East Indian Company occupied Aden, a port that was an ideal location for coal storage facilities used by ships traveling to and from India. Because of its port, Aden became a thriving trade center between World War II and independence. South Yemen is not as agriculturally fortunate as neighboring North Yemen, although some coffee, cotton, and fruit are grown.

The loss of British prestige after the 1956 Suez War encouraged attempts to force the British to leave the area. Making a choice between the two main rival political organizations, the British handed power to the National Liberation Front (NFL), which became the only recognized political organization in the country. After independence, the government reorganized the country in order to gain more complete control of most commercial activities. In the early 1970s, banks, insurance companies, and many other businesses were nationalized. The South Yemen government became politically close to the People's Republic of China, the Soviet Union, and the East European countries. The country's Marxist attitudes, combined with its geographical location, have led to increased isolation. The relationship with neighboring North Yemen has varied, depending on the political climate of both countries. In 1972 the two countries agreed to unite, with the new country to be named the Yemen Republic. Following armed conflict along the North and South Yemen border in February 1979, the countries renewed their pledge to unite. Whether these two countries, which have very different political orientations, will be able to create a single political entity remains to be seen.

2.7.1 Radio

Radio broadcasting in Aden started in May 1954 with the local relaying of the BBC Arabic Service and the Cyprus-based, British-operated Sharq al-Adna. Programming from these stations was broadcast locally via a transmitter rented by the colonial government from the British telecommunications company Cable and Wireless. In August 1954, the Aden Broadcasting Service was officially formed as a sub-section of the Public Relations and Information Department. With the creation of the new radio service, local Arabic programming of about two hours per day replaced the relays. By 1960, the daily program lasted for ten hours, three of which were a relay of the BBC Arabic Service from London.

Studio and transmission facilities were expanded during the 1950s. The original rented Cable and Wireless transmitter was replaced by a 250-watt medium-wave transmitter. In 1957, under a British Colonial Development and Welfare grant, two additional transmitters were purchased and installed—a 5-kilowatt medium-wave transmitter to serve the Colony and a 7.5-kilowatt medium-wave transmitter to reach the Protectorate. All broadcasting was done by the British government, and several BBC personnel were seconded for transmitter maintenance and the training of program production personnel (British Colonial Office 1960, p. 8).

The British government's interest in providing a local broadcasting service for Aden was the result of an awakening, fueled by Egyptian radio broadcasts, that took place between 1953 and 1956 among both the urban and rural populations of the Colony and Protectorate. The Voice of the Arabs and Radio Cairo programs encouraged the population to join Nasser's Pan-Arab movement. Programs were designed to provoke anti-British feeling. Great Britain's involvement in the 1956 Suez War further motivated those who were planning to force the British to grant independence and leave the area. The Egyptian broadcasts came at an opportune time for residents of South Yemen. The port of Aden allowed free trade. Transistor radios from Japan were abundant; people purchased them with the hope of finding news and entertainment. With no Arabic local broadcasting available, it was only natural to tune to the popular Egyptian services. The British were at a loss to compete with the Egyptian broadcasts that circumvented the British-influenced local media and went directly to the population. In 1956 the British authorities realized the seriousness of the situation and opened a local Arabic station, but it could not compete in coverage with the Voice of the Arabs (Gavin 1975, p. 333). Another problem was the actual use to which the medium was put by the British.

The administration could not effectively use the radio to propagate broad and general ideas of political integration. Instead, broadcasting became one of the principal means by which popular sentiment was galvanized against British rule. As radios poured into Aden in a mounting flood throughout the 1950s and '60s, legitimacy of the British presence was steadily sapped away. [Gavin 1975, p. 334]

After independence, the government added more radio transmission facilities with the help of the Soviet Union and East European countries. These countries have provided a good deal of the military and civilian aid to South Yemen. South Yemen's radio has not, however, improved technically because the country's economy has not prospered since independence. When the National Liberation Front assumed power upon British departure from Aden, it moved to centralize governmental activities. A 1974 decree established state control of all forms of mass communication. The Minister of Information was given the power to appoint newspaper editors and broadcasting station managers (Nyrop 1977, p. 107). The South Yemen government may have been reacting to increased broadcasting efforts from neighboring North Yemen- and Saudi Arabian-financed clandestine radio. Clandestine broadcasting sought to undermine the government's position much like Egypt's broadcasts in the 1950s and 1960s, but there is no indication that these neighboring broadcasts had any effect on the general population.

The pattern of transmitter acquisition may provide some clue to the country's radio broadcasting priorities. There are two medium-wave transmitters of 50 and 200 kilowatts for local coverage. Four short-wave transmitters—three 100-kilowatt and one 7.5-kilowatt (*World Radio TV Handbook 1980* 1980, p. 397)—are apparently used to reach the rural population, but they also beam programs to North Yemen, Saudi Arabia, and Oman. These facilities broadcast a daily program, Aden Voice of Oman Revolution (see 6.5).

2.7.2 Television

The idea for the introduction of television in Aden dates from the period in the 1950s when the British authorities realized that Egyptian radio programs were popular and that no effective means of countering them existed. By 1963, the British government had made the preliminary decision that a local television service would be beneficial. The medium, it was apparently reasoned, could provide an attractive alternative to external radio broadcasts. This reasoning was not, of course, unique to Aden. As noted elsewhere in this study, governments have attempted to use television as an alternative to foreign-radio listening, particularly at night. Saudi Arabia is a case in point.

In 1963, the British obtained television channel assignments at the African VHF/UHF Broadcasting Conference held in Geneva (*VHF Television Assignments obtained for Aden* n.d.). In 1965, programming started, but coverage was limited to the populated areas surrounding Aden that were served by four low-power transmitters (see Table 12). Programming during the period between initiation and independence consisted of films obtained from United States and British television services. Because of limited local production facilities—there were no video tape recorders—Aden-based programming consisted of news in Arabic and English and live interviews. The original equipment, obtained from Great Britain, consisted of Pye and Marconi components (Patel 1980).

Table 12. South Yemen TV Channels and Locations

Channel Number	Location
4	Little Aden
7	Crater Pass
10	Barrack Hill
5	Hiswah

SOURCE: *VHF Television Assignments obtained for Aden . . .* n.d.

After independence, the television service deteriorated because of lack of spare parts and maintenance. The government emphasized radio broadcasting. However, the television service, which interestingly enough accepts commercial advertising, continued to operate a monochrome service. At least one additional low-power transmitter has been added since 1967 (*World Radio TV Handbook 1980* 1980, p. 398), and the service, still confined to the Aden area, operates a limited early afternon and evening service.

The differences in the use of mass communication in South Yemen and neighboring Oman, Saudi Arabia, and North Yemen are due mainly to philosophy and economic constraints. The government decided to emphasize radio and maintain the status quo on television, since the country has limited resources to devote to its broadcasting services. South Yemen's information activities, including local and regional broadcasting, are likely to increase during the 1980s. The country's strategic location provides a military advantage for the Soviet Union and other countries that have negotiated treaties allowing access to South Yemen ports and airfields. In the event of a threat to the Gulf states' oil supplies to the west, the Soviet Union and the United States and its allies may find themselves sparring from military bases negotiated with respective friendly nations. South Yemen may yet be thrust into the information forefront of the Arab World.

3   The Arabian Gulf States

3.1 The Gulf States: Introduction

The importance of the Arabian Gulf states was generally unknown until the early 1970s. The name itself—Arabian Gulf—is relatively new, having been coined by those Arabs who felt that "Persian Gulf" was a geographer's term that added credibility to Iran's claim of influence. Countries that border on the Gulf and whose people speak Arabic qualify for membership in the Gulf states' seven-member fraternity: Bahrain, Iraq, Kuwait, Oman, Qatar, Saudi Arabia, and the United Arab Emirates (UAE). During the 1970s, these countries emerged as an international economic force because of their petroleum exports. Only two states, Bahrain and Oman, are not major oil exporters, but they play an important part politically and economically in the area as a result of either their strategic location or their involvement with petroleum shipping and services. Common factors identified by the states themselves include religion, land, environment, culture, the Arabic language, history, mutual interests, and common will (*T.V. in the Gulf States* 1979, p. 3). Of these similarities, Arabic and Islam are the most important. The states vary greatly in their political environment, national economic priorities, and income.

The one country that does not fit politically into the group is Iraq. Nevertheless, Iraq is included in this chapter because it is active in efforts by ministers of information of all seven countries to cooperate in various information activities, particularly in the dissemination of information regarding Arab culture. Iraq is a member of what is probably the most visible result of information-cooperation efforts, Gulfvision. Iraq is the only country that is not governed by a powerful head of state whose family historically ruled or otherwise was recognized as having influence, in the bedouin tradition, over its geographical area.

Prior to the discussion of individual media systems, several factors that are important to broadcasting developments need to be mentioned. As is the case in the other Arab world countries in this study, the Gulf states' electronic media are either directly or indirectly government-controlled. Residents of one country have reliable access to the radio and television programming of other countries. The powerful medium-wave radio signals from these countries are usually available in other countries. Because of a phenomenon known as over-the-horizon propagation or "tunneling," normally line-of-sight FM radio and television signals travel long distances over warm salt water during hot, humid summer months. Viewing of television channels and listening to radio stations of Gulf states other than the one in which one resides is apparently a standard practice.

With the possible exception of Iraq, the Gulf states have almost no artistic tradition. Painting, sculpture, and drama were discouraged because many states, most notably Saudi Arabia, were influenced by a traditional interpretation of Islam that forbids reproductions of human forms. Nor did the bedouin culture, which dominated these countries until modern times, encourage artistic development because of constant tribal wanderings.

Except for Iraq, Gulf states radio and television systems are operated and maintained mostly by Arabs from Jordan, Lebanon, the Sudan, and Egypt. Most states do not have qualified personnel to undertake sophisticated broadcast equipment maintenance, and local talent is very limited for radio and television program production. Each country has an expatriate community that works with oil, shipping, and other industries. Kuwait and the United Arab Emirates have a population that is only about one-half native-born. The governments directly employ large numbers of nonindigenous Arabs, Pakistanis, and Indians as civil servants. In the case of the ministries of information and subordinate broadcasting organizations, Jordanians, Egyptians, and Palestinians hold some senior government positions and have policy influence as well as day-to-day operational responsibility.

Radio and television receivers are available at fairly low prices. Most countries in the Gulf do not feel that they need income from import taxes on consumer goods, including home entertainment systems. Home video recorders have become so common in residences in Kuwait, Saudi Arabia, Qatar, and the UAE that these countries probably constitute the largest home video cassette market in the world. A substantial portion of the available cassettes are pirated films and television programs from the United States and Europe. Many tapes of American programs are crudely edited, leaving intact entire commercials and even station identification. Also, residents of the Arabian Gulf appear to be frequent listeners to international short- and medium-wave radio broadcasts from non-Arab countries.

The ordering of countries in this chapter is geographical. Starting in the north with Iraq and working down the Arabian Gulf, the remaining six countries are: Kuwait, Saudi Arabia, Bahrain, Qatar, the United Arab Emirates, and Oman.

3.2 Iraq

For several hundred years prior to World War I, Iraq was part of the Ottoman Empire. After the war, sections of the country were occupied by Great Britain, until it was given a League of Nations mandate to administer Iraq. This lasted until 1932. Faisal, brother of Abdullah, the first king of Jordan, was proclaimed king in 1921. Descendants of this Hashemite family maintained a royal house until 1958. During the preceding twenty-six years, the country underwent various changes that included or were influenced by the death, under suspicious circumstances, of Faisal's son, King Ghazi; political rivalries between pro- and anti-British factions and between communists and supporters of the Baath Party; rebellions by the Kurdish minority; military coups; and religious friction between Shiite and Sunni Moslems.

In July 1958, Abdul Karim Kassem, an Army officer, staged a military coup that resulted in the death of King Faisal, a second cousin of King Hussein of Jordan, and many other members of the royal family. Killed too was the pro-British Prime Minister, Nuri as-Said. Kassem was but one of a series of leaders who came to power during various military coups after 1958. The political situation was unstable during the 1960s and 1970s, with the power largely vested in the military, which has been influenced by communists and Baath Party philosophy that believes Arabism should pervade all political and economic thinking.

The country has close relations with the Soviet Union and the East European countries, important Iraqi arms suppliers. Iraq, a major oil exporting country, started using income from increased oil prices in the 1970s to foster national economic development. After Egypt signed a peace treaty with Israel in 1979, Iraq emerged from relative isolation in the Arab world to take part in the call for the boycott of Egypt. One result has been better relations with Saudi Arabia and Kuwait, neighbors with whom Iraq has not traditionally had close relations.

Eleven million people are estimated to inhabit the country's 167,925 square miles, which share a border with Syria, Jordan, Saudi Arabia, Kuwait, Iran, and Turkey.

3.2.1 Radio

The first radio station in Iraq started as a government enterprise in either 1935 (UNESCO 1951, p. 533) or 1936 (*Present-Day Iraq; Culture* 1970, p. 12), depending on the source consulted. Radio programming began from a lower-power medium-wave transmitter connected with the Telegraph and Mail General Administration, but administered by a government committee including a representative of the Ministry of Education. However, the government allocated insufficient funds to operate a reliable service and eventually a tax of one-half Iraqi dinar was imposed on the sale of radio receivers to help pay the seven full-time employees (Adwan n.d., pp. 2–3).

Shortly after the government station began, King Ghazi, who was interested in things technical and was known to be anti-British, started a privately owned station in the royal palace. He apparently operated the station irregularly, depending on his mood. The King was the only announcer and was known for his pro-Nazi broadcasts, including news bulletins supplied by the Germans (McKenzie 1940, pp. 200–1). The station ceased to exist when Ghazi died in April 1939.

The original government radio service operated until about 1939 for approximately five hours per day in Arabic. In 1939, a daily 15-minute program in Kurdish was started for the Kurdish minority located mainly in the northern part of the country. During World War II, radio transmissions were lengthened with the help of British program advisors and technicians. In 1945 the Arabic program contained a limited offering of music, news, poems, and some drama, from 1625 to 2205 hours. The Kurdish program had been expanded from its original 15 minutes to one hour between 1525 and 1625 (Adwan n.d., pp. 6–7).

Between the end of World War II and the 1958 revolution, no major developments occurred in Iraqi radio. The government made little effort to comunicate with minorities within the country, except for the Kurds. The pro-western civilian government and the royal family apparently believed that they had support from the Iraqi citizenry and from other Arab countries as well. The government did not become concerned about hostile broadcasts from other Arab countries until Egypt's Voice of the Arabs started a campaign against Nuri as-Said, then Prime Minister, who was encouraging Arab support for the pro-western Baghdad Pact. Baghdad was apparently taken by surprise by the viciousness of the Egyptian radio attacks and did not have the skilled radio personnel to mount an effective counter attack. More importantly, Iraq did not have sufficient transmitter power to cover its own country completely with an Arabic service, much less to reach neighboring Arab countries with a reliable signal. In the mid-1950s as-Said approached the American Ambassador to Iraq with an urgent request that the United States supply high-power short- and medium-wave transmitters. The Prime Minister wanted transmitters "in a matter of days, or a few weeks at the latest," because the country's transmitters were inadequate to match the Egyptian signals. In return for American help—which incidentally was not supplied because of United States State Department bureaucratic inefficiency—Iraq offered to grant the Voice of America use of any American-supplied facilities (Gallman 1964, pp. 49–50). In addition to the Voice of the Arabs, Egypt also had at least one clandestine station beamed to Iraq that identified itself as Radio Free Iraq. Some observers believe that Egypt's radio propaganda helped inspire the 1958 revolution. This may be true, although the broadcasts alone did not bring about the military coup on 14 July 1958 that dramatically brought an end to the Iraqi royal family.

The Iraqi character, which tends to be unpredictable and occasionally violent, showed itself in connection with the coup. The King, many other members of the royal family, and the Prime Minister were killed. Abdul Karim Kassem, the coup leader, became the head of government until he, in turn, was killed in 1963 in another coup. Kassem appears to have realized the importance of the electronic media to gain popular support internally and to communicate with other Arab countries. He also knew that the Egyptian broadcasts had been well received in Iraq and that his government had to take steps to increase radio transmission power. He turned to the Soviet Union for several powerful medium- and short-wave transmitters. The new $3.5 million facility was dedicated by Kassem as part of a celebration marking the third anniversary of the 1958 revolution (Schmidt 1961, p. 7; Adwan n.d., pp. 11–12). The new transmitters gave Iraq transmission power equal to Egypt's. The Kassem period marks the beginning of present-day Iraq's interest in broadcast dissemination of its political philosophy to the Arab world.

An example of how quickly loyalties can change in the Middle East is the turn of events under Kassem regarding Egypt. Radio broadcasts had been pro-Nasser after the revolution, but when Iraq declined Egypt's invitation to join Syria in the UAR, broadcasts turned violently anti-Nasser. Egypt and Iraq entered into a radio propaganda war more violent than Egypt's had been against the King and Nuri as-Said years before. While many Iraqis undoubtedly admired Kassem for having brought an end to the monarchy, the majority believed that his tenure as national leader brought disgrace and fostered internal corruption. One observer comments on Kassem's use of the media:

After the 1958 revolution, more publications appeared and cultural activities increased. Radio broadcasts were expanded to fifteen hours per day and the programs became revolutionary and anti-imperialist in nature. Yet, this freedom led to confusion and conflict developed between papers and political parties. Kassem closed most of the opposition papers and only left the papers which supported him. He turned radio and television into tools for his government and personality. He selected the announcers who supported him and imprisoned those who disagreed with his policy. Radio and television became devoted to Mr. Kassem. His speeches and other information occupied most of the transmission hours. Only songs which glorified him were telecast and broadcast on radio. During the five years Kassem was in power he used the media extensively for his own purposes. [Adwan n.d., p. 10]

The political leaders who followed Kassem maintained an interest in radio. The broadcasting complex in Baghad, which houses both radio and televison studios, has been expanded and modernized over the years. The radio studios date from the late 1950s and appear well maintained. New American Ampex audio tape recorders have been added, but the audio consoles and other equipment are over 20 years old. There are some production facilities elsewhere in addition to the main radio studios in Baghdad. The majority of production, however, takes place in Baghdad under the supervision of the Ministry of Information, which is responsible for the electronic media.

The main expansion of radio in postrevolutionary Iraq has been in transmitters rather than studio equipment. The political leaders who followed Kassem in the 1960s and 1970s have continued to install transmitters to provide better signals both inside the country and to the rest of the Arab world. The external short-wave service uses 12 transmitters, which are placed in various parts of the country. There are six medium-wave transmitters, five of which are over 100 kilowatts. A 2000-kilowatt facility located in Babylon is primarily used for the Voice of the Masses Program and can be heard clearly at night from Oman to Egypt.

By 1970, Iraq had become more internationally minded and was broadcasting 189 hours per week in Arabic, 70 in Kurdish, 28 each in Turkmanian and Persian, and 7 hours each in Urdu, Turkish, English, German, French, Hebrew, and Russian (Ali 1980).

The basic program schedule in 1980 consisted of the following programs and languages.

Main Program. Iraq's major effort is devoted to the Main Program, which operates for 22 hours per day, from 0200 to 2400. The general tone and approach of this radio service is similar to the main radio service transmitted by most other Arab countries. News times are fixed and there are music programs, drama, interviews, and discussions. A good deal of time is devoted to political discussion, a dominant program type on Iraqi electronic media. News, music, drama, and interviews tend to promote the stand that the government is taking in the Arab world. Changes that have taken place in the tenor of radio programming since 1978 are reflected in this important service. Radio broadcasting employees told this writer that in 1978 the President of Iraq had issued a directive to media officials to dwell less on the "sad" and "negative" aspects of Iraq and to make radio and television programs more entertaining and happy. When asked, the Ministry of Information denied that this had been ordered by the President but did admit that some lightening of program style had occurred. One reason for this change may have been that Iraqi officials believed people were turning to more attractive foreign radio stations.

Voice of the Masses. The Voice of the Masses is broadcast on both short- and medium-wave and is intended for both domestic and Arab world consumption. The service, entirely in Arabic, parallels the 22 hours per day of the Main Program. The schedule is occasionally interrupted to broadcast special programs intended to be heard in other countries such as Egypt. Between 1800 and 2000 hours each evening the Voice of the Masses carries the Palestine Program, which is produced under Iraqi supervision by Palestinians. It is over the Voice of the Masses frequencies that one of the more interesting radio programs in the Arab world, the Voice of Egypt of Arabism, is broadcast. Observers have compared this program with Ahmed Said's style from the Egyptian Voice of the Arabs.

Possibly because of the relative isolation of Iraq prior to the Egyptian-Israeli Peace Treaty in 1979, there had been some clandestine broadcasting from Iraq directed mostly against neighboring counties—Kuwait, Saudi Arabia, Jordan, Syria—with whom at times it did not have good relations. Iraqi radio services have tended to broadcast rather strong political rhetoric. Occasionally, they have been known to transmit inaccurate information to see what the effect would be. It was as though Iraq were returning to the mid-1960s when violent radio propaganda was used. However, increased sophistication and the availability of radio programs from other countries have enabled Arab radio-listeners to check the accuracy of news reports; and this has reduced the effect such broadcasts used to have.

On 27 May 1979, the Voice of Egypt of Arabism was first heard over three short- and two medium-wave frequencies (Foreign Broadcast Information Service 1979). The use of two frequencies—1035 kHz 2000 kilowatts (Babylon) and 692 kHz 1200 kilowatts (Basrah)—ensured that the nightly two-hour program could be heard by the majority of Arabs with a standard radio receiver. The Ministry of Information denies that the program originates from Iraq. The transmission is divided into blocks that feature mini-programs about such subjects as peasant life, Islam, and music. The entire theme of the service is anti-Sadat and listeners report that the programs are appealing in part because the announcers are Egyptian. Egyptian officials state that the Iraqi program poses no threat to the stability of Anwar Sadat's government. Taking no chances, however, Egypt jams this program.

Kurdish and Other Minority Language Programs. The Ministry of Information expanded the amount of time devoted to Kurdish broadcasts during the 1970s. The Kurdish minority has been a serious problem for Iraqi governments, which have alternately fought and signed peace agreements with them. The number of broadcast hours in this language appears to be dependent on the interest that the government has in communicating with Kurdish speakers. In 1980, the daily number of hours was approximately 20 (Ali 1980). Assyrian and Turkmanian languages in Iraq also receive some attention from the radio authority. Programming in each language is transmitted for about two hours per day.

Foreign and Beamed Programs. Most of the expansion in the number and duration of foreign languages occurred during the 1970s, although broadcasts in Russian, English, and French date from the 1960s. About two hours per day are devoted to programs in French, English, German, Russian, Turkish, Persian, Hebrew, and Swahili. After the Shah left Iran in 1979, more attention was given to the Persian broadcasts because of the increased tension between the two countries and the resultant skirmishes at the border.

The two main factors that will determine Iraq's future as an Arab radio broadcaster are money and the country's future role in Arab politics. If Iraq continues to move from relative isolation and increases its leadership role in the Arab world, it will probably extend its ability to be heard in other countries. As a major oil-exporting nation, the country has the financial capacity to do so. Philosophically, increased expansion is consistent with Baath Party policy, which states that all Arabs are "part of one nation both in the cultural and spiritual sense. . . . The different [Arab] countries . . . make up a politically and economically united fatherland" (Shibli-L-A'Ysami 1977, p. 9).

3.2.2 Television

Iraq was the first Arab country to establish a government-operated television service in the Middle East. As part of a trade fair, the British Pye electronics firm brought television equipment to Baghdad in 1956. The government was impressed with the equipment and purchased the studio facilities and low-power transmitter. The service officially started on 2 May 1956. Programming at first was experimental and irregular. Only a few television sets existed in Baghdad at the time and a regular service did not seem feasible. Television assumed importance in Iraq immediately after the 14 July 1958 revolution. Kassem, sensing that television like radio could facilitate social change, ordered an increase in the power of the Baghdad station. In 1959, a new 2-kilowatt transmitter was put into service (Fakery 1980). Between 1958 and 1963, while Kassem was president, some updating of studio equipment took place; but political and economic conditions prevented construction of a country-wide network. Iraq did not, at that time, have national telecommunications relay facilities to distribute the Baghdad signal. Kassem made his mark by developing Iraqi programming rather than by expanding facilities.

Following the revolution, the Kassem regime established a Special Supreme Military Court, or People's Court, presided over by Fadhil Abbas Al-Mahdawi, Kassem's cousin, who possessed no legal qualifications (Penrose and Penrose 1978, p. 220). Because of the broadcasting of the trials on both radio and television, Mahdawi became well known for his showmanship rather than his juridical leadership. Generally referred to as the Mahdawi Trials, the trials were an outlet for people's feelings against the old regime and served as a substitute for mob action. Khadduri makes the following observation about the televised events:

The proceedings of the court were fully reported in the press and broadcast on radio and television, so that Mahdawi's name was familiar in almost every home and coffee shop. The people watched the trials as if they were watching a theatrical performance. They noted how he arrogantly entered the court at the head of a band of officer-lawyers, taking his seat amid the loud applause of the spectators. He opened each session with a resounding 'In the name of God and the People.' Before the trial began he always made a speech giving his opinion on the question of the day. He would then make a speech and shower insults on the men at the dock, treating them all as guilty and making no distinction between plaintiffs and defendants. He was often interrupted by one of the spectators, who asked him to recite a poem specially prepared for the occasion, and the recitation was likely to excite some of the spectators who would rise and perform a *dabka*, a form of folk-dancing, in support of the cause to which the poet had addressed himself. [1969, p. 80]

The Iraqis have not generally been very successful users of the broadcast media. They lack the talent and humor of the Egyptians and the attention to detail often possessed by the Jordanians. Richard Cawston made the following observation after a trip to Iraq in the early 1960s:

At seven o'clock every evening, there was what is called the Government Program. This consisted of two unshaven army officers arriving at the station at five minutes to seven—script in hand. They walked straight into the studio and addressed the camera about anything from politics to personal hygiene for twenty-five minutes nonstop. The television authorities never had any idea what the officers were going to talk about. [1963, p. 5]

An era in Iraqi political and broadcasting history ended when Kassem was overthrown in 1963. He was killed near the television studios and his body was displayed on live television.

After 1965, additional television stations capable of some local production were constructed. Stations were opened in two major cities north of Baghdad: one in Kirkuk in 1967 and one in Mosul in 1968. In 1968 a powerful station was opened in Basrah, a city located near the border with Kuwait. This station was built during a period when there were hostile Iraqi-Kuwaiti relations because Iraq had claimed Kuwaiti territory during the Kassem regime. The station is received clearly in Kuwait and during the warm summer months as far south as Bahrain. Additional transmitters have been constructed, including one in 1974 to transmit programming mainly in Kurdish. Two additional stations, at Qaim and Haditha near the Syrian border, were planned in 1980 to provide coverage to those cities as well as to reach a Syrian population with Iraqi television (Yousef, 1980). Most of the programming supplied to these stations originated in the main Baghdad studios.

In the early 1970s a second television channel was started and in 1976 limited color broadcasts using the SECAM system were begun (Fakery 1980). Additional studios capable of color origination were built in the early 1970s in connection with the inauguration of the second channel.

Unlike most other Arab television systems, Iraq's uses relatively little western television programming. The general philosophy of the government

since the 1958 revolution has been to down-play things western and imperialist. The country broke diplomatic relations with the United States
during the June 1967 war and has not reestablished them. However, some
western programming is shown with subtitles, the need for such programming having increased when the second channel was added. Old American
and British feature films, purchased in the 1950s and 1960s, are shown on
Friday afternoons and late at night. American series are scheduled intermittently rather than regularly. Examples of programs telecast during 1980
include "Little House [on the Prairie]," "Mannix," "Lucy," "Love Boat,"
"Eight Is Enough," and "Dallas." Television officials told this writer that
"Dallas" was popular because people like to see contemporary American
clothing, hair styles, and cars.

Each of the two channels operates from approximately 1800 to midnight,
seven days per week. Transmissions are extended on one of the two channels on Friday afternoons and during afternoons when local soccer matches
are being played. The Ministry of Education tapes morning educational
programs tied to the national school curriculum. These are telecast by the
national facilities.

The most important nightly news program comes at 2000 hours on Channel 9, the main national channel. The Iraq News Agency provides guidance
on specific news items and story ordering. International stories are provided
nightly by the European Broadcasting Union satellite feed, taped in Baghdad at 1900 and quickly edited for the main Arabic news program. The news
in English comes at 2200 hours and is a direct translation of the Arabic news
two hours earlier. On the three newscasts that this writer observed in
January 1980, a considerable amount of time was devoted to anti-Egyptian
stories about President Sadat. On the English newscast each time Sadat's
name was mentioned, the announcer preceded it by the word "traitor."

President Saddam Hussein has provided some thoughts on the role of the
Iraqi media:

Information is one of our revolutionary democratic means for enlightening, informing the people and acting as a surveillant. To function properly, information media needs great care, not only on the part of those
directly responsible for it, but also on the part of all of us. We are required to attend to it but not to spoil it, to guide it and to cooperate
with it, to criticize it in case it errs and to provide it with all possible
means of power and development so that it can properly play its role in
enlightening and acting as a surveillant. [Hussein 1977, p. 8]

Iraqi television is heavily political, and devotes a great deal of time to
documentaries about the progressive stance taken by the government.
Discussions and interviews with party officials and government leaders are
presented almost every evening. An example of political programming on
television is "Behind the News," a weekly broadcast that provides, accord-

ing to television officials, an Iraqi perspective of international situations and news events. Building on the government's anti-Anwar Sadat theme, the program on 20 January 1980 featured old film footage of Egypt—crowded Cairo, primitive conditions in the countryside, pollution. These conditions, the commentator said, were brought about by the Sadat government.

With the continuation of a stable government in Iraq, television may become an even more important medium. A national multi-channel service is now in place and more stations are planned or are under construction. A new television complex was to be completed in 1981, adjacent to the existing television studios in Baghdad. The main motivation for the modern facility was to provide coverage of the 1982 Iraqi-hosted meeting of the nonaligned countries. After the gathering, Iraq will be able to undertake more local production than was previously possible. In terms of facilities, at least, Iraq has been in a position to assume equal status with members of the Arabian Gulf television community.

3.3 Kuwait

The State of Kuwait is small, comprising 6,880 square miles in the northeastern corner of the Arabian peninsula. It is located between Saudi Arabia and Iraq. Only about one-half of the approximately one million inhabitants are native-born Kuwaiti nationals. The resident alien community consists of Pakistanis, Indians, and citizens of other Arab countries, who work with the oil industry and in service jobs.

In 1899, the ruling Sabah family established a relationship with Great Britain for the purpose of protection and international representation. Kuwait became a British Protectorate in 1914, further strengthening the relationship with Great Britian. The country became independent in June 1961, and in 1963 the government adopted a constitution. By law, the head of state is a member of the Sabah family, which has been a political force since the 1700s.

Kuwait is a major petroleum-exporting country, ranking second in the Arab world to Saudi Arabia. The capital, Kuwait City, features modern buildings and wide, well-planned streets. The country is small and its relatively well-educated, organized Kuwaiti civil servants and businessmen appear able to manage projects that in many other Arab countries would become delayed due to bureaucratic inefficiency. An interesting feature of Kuwait's foreign policy is its financial involvement abroad. The government makes loans and gives financial aid for development projects to other Arab countries and to African nations. Kuwait's per capita GNP is the highest in the world.

3.3.1 Radio

During World War II, the British operated a low-power radio transmitter in Kuwait. One purpose of the station was to counter Nazi broadcasts in Arabic as well as occasional pro-Nazi transmissions from neighboring Iraq. An official, identifiable Kuwaiti radio station dates from 1961, when Kuwait became independent (Monsour 1980). Because Kuwait is so small and flat, the country has not had the radio coverage problems of larger Arab world nations. A service could be provided to all within the Kuwaiti borders with a single medium-wave radio transmitter. However, during the 1960s and 1970s, as the country became increasingly wealthy and assumed an important leadership role in the Arabian Gulf, the number and power of transmitters rapidly increased. The government wanted to reach a large, regional audience with a Kuwaiti message. The Ministry of Information, under which both broadcast media function, appears to have decided that a state can partially overcome the psychological disadvantage of smallness by having a powerful radio and television service.

Using a variety of FM, medium- and short-wave transmitters, Kuwait provides several radio services.

Main Program. The Main Program is intended for local as well as Arab world consumption. Operating from 0200 to 2200 hours, the service features a mixture of news, drama, music, discussions, and educational programming. On mediumwave, the program is transmitted continuously on two frequencies, using one 750-kilowatt and one 1500-kilowatt facility. The latter transmitter on the low end of the medium-wave band renders the program accessible in most parts of the Arab world at night. An even wider reach is made possible by the use of nine short-wave frequencies during the day. This ensures reliable reception in all parts of the Middle East for those with short-wave radios and the motivation to tune to Kuwait.

Second Program. Intended to be an Arabic alternative to the Main Program, the Second Program broadcasts from 1000 to 1600 daily. The six-hour schedule is broadcast by a 200-kilowatt medium-wave and one short-wave transmitter. Programming on the service is similar in format to the Main Program, but it is intended for a local and regional audience rather than a larger Arab world audience.

English Program. The English Program operates from 0800 to 1000 and from 1800 to 2100 on the same medium- and short-wave frequencies as the Second Program. Most of the program time is devoted to music, with occasional news and interview programs. Kuwait is one of many Arab countries that operate an English-language radio service for its own citizens. English is widely spoken in the Arab world, particularly in the Arabian Gulf, and many countries apparently believe that such a service lends them prestige.

FM Music. Kuwait's newest service is continuous FM stereo "beautiful" or "background" music, only occasionally interrupted by news. It is apparently quite popular among Kuwaitis. One reason for this is the availability of a variety of multi-wave receivers.

Koran Program. Special radio programs that feature religious discussions and readings from the Koran have become a means of providing religious programs to Moslems as well as a way of reminding citizens and neighbors that Islam is still important. Kuwait's population is mostly Sunni Moslem but a sizable Shiite Moslem population also exists. The Iranian revolution has helped bring an increase in conservative religious activity in the Middle East and this daily program, 0500 to 0800 on the same facilities as the English and Second Programs, provides a reminder that the modern State of Kuwait is a dedicated Islamic nation.

Persian and Urdu Service. For approximately two hours per day, Kuwait broadcasts Persian and Urdu language services on medium- and short-wave transmitters. Programming is intended for speakers of these languages who reside in Kuwait and for listeners in Iran and Pakistan.

The radio and television studios in Kuwait are housed in a modern Ministry of Information building, located in the downtown area of Kuwait City. The formidable structure has become a landmark. The radio studios were occupied in June 1978, after being completed by a French company. Fifteen studios, all of which are equipped for stereo recording, contain Schlumberger audio equipment. Because the Ministry of Information was attempting to build for the future, more studios were built than are used, ranging in size from compact booths for news reading to large drama studios with "dead" rooms. The French technicians who installed the equipment have trained engineers in operation and maintenance. Although some Kuwaiti radio operators work with the equipment, the majority of those who work in radio engineering are non-Kuwaitis.[1]

3.3.2 Radio Audience

The percentage of foreign-radio listening in Kuwait is high mainly because of the large resident alien population interested in hearing transmissions from home. Data from an April-May 1974 survey commissioned by the United States Information Agency indicated that the BBC's Arabic Service and Radio Baghdad (Main Program) were almost equally listened to. Of those surveyed, 22.4% reported listening to Radio Baghdad during the previous seven days while 22.3% said that they had listened to the BBC. The third and fourth most listened to stations were Egyptian—Radio Cairo (Main Program) and Voice of the Arabs (USIA 1975a, p. 10). Data provided by Radio Monte Carlo from a February-March 1979 McCann Erick-

---

[1]Technical and other information about radio studios and equipment was provided by staff engineers at the complex on 16 January 1980.

son Middle East Media Study indicate that Radio Monte Carlo Middle East (RMC) is the most listened to foreign commercial radio station. Nineteen per cent of those surveyed said that they had listened to RMC during the past seven days. The second and third ranked commercial stations in terms of popularity in the study were Cairo's Middle East Program and Bahrain Radio ("Audience, Penetration, and Listenership" 1979, p. 1).

3.3.3 Television

Television had an informal beginning when the local RCA television receiver dealer started a low-power American-standard transmitter in Kuwait City in order to promote set sales. At independence in 1961, the Ministry of Information became the television broadcaster and changed the system to the CCIR European standard. In about 1967, residents in the Eastern Province of Saudi Arabia and Bahrain started purchasing dual-standard receivers so that the Kuwaiti channel could be viewed. Until 1970, the only television station serving the Dhahran and Dammam, Saudi Arabia, area had been an Arabian American Oil Company (ARAMCO) station that operated on the American (525-line) standard. It was observed by many Saudi viewers who were anxious to receive more than the one channel that the Kuwait station could be received in that part of Saudi Arabia during the warm summer months. The availability of Kuwaiti and other channels in the Gulf states has played an important part in television development in the area.

The transmission capability of the Kuwaiti Main Channel has been increased since the 1960s. A separate transmitter, Channel 6, rebroadcasts the Main Channel specifically toward Basrah, Iraq, in order to provide a television presence in a country that threatened in the early 1960s to invade Kuwait.

The expansion of television in Kuwait took place in 1973 as part of the completion of the radio broadcasting complex mentioned earlier. Kuwait started color television transmission in 1974 using the PAL system. When it moved to a new television studio building in 1979, Kuwait started a second television channel, which, like the first, uses color. The television studios are impressive. The Kuwaiti facilities were the most modern and extensive in the Arab world until they were surpassed by the new television complex in Riyadh, Saudi Arabia. The equipment, with the exception of a few British Marconi cameras from the old studios, is French-supplied by Thomson-CFS. Some of the equipment, such as bi-lingual character generators that can produce subtitling in Arabic and English, is specifically designed for Kuwait Television. There are six studios, three for on-air programming such as news and interviews and three larger studios for video tape production. One studio, 800 square meters in size, is spacious enough to accommodate several sets at the same time; it was used for the production of "Iftah Ya Simsim," the Arabic "Sesame Street," discussed in the last part of this chapter.

There are no radio or television receiver license fees in Kuwait. The government is wealthy enough to provide radio and television programs for citizens. Commerical advertising is allowed only on the Main Channel for a maximum of 15 minutes per day between programs. The commercials are permitted because the government wishes to endorse the free enterprise sytem as well as to help viewers make choices about the kind of products they want to buy (Al-Fieli 1980). Television officials do not know the amount of income that the commercials generate. Television advertising in Kuwait is similar to that seen in other Gulf countries where television advertising is allowed. Advertisements promote candy, Japanese watches, automobiles, processed cheese, disposable diapers, and products such as food processors and other small home appliances.

Kuwait Television operates two television channels. The first channel (KTV One), an updated version of the original service started in the 1960s, is considered to be the main program. The second channel started in 1978, preceded by research to determine listener needs and preferences (Ragheb and Haddad 1979).

Kuwaiti television viewers apparently watch their own channels. The propagation phenomenon that sends television signals long distances does not bring the signal northwards as easily as it does south. While the main Kuwaiti television program is generally available in Bahrain, the Eastern Province of Saudi Arabia, and at times in the United Arab Emirates, the signals from these countries do not tend to reach Kuwait. One channel from the Basrah, Iraq, station and another from Iran are easily received in Kuwait; but the political nature of Iraqi television and the rather bland educational and religious programming from Iran since the 1979 revolution do not seem to attract many viewers.

Main Channel (KTV One). The Main Channel is predominantly in Arabic. Locally produced entertainment programs as well as those imported from other countries are shown. There are two newscasts nightly at 1700 and 2100. Regular daily hours of operation are from 1700 to 2330, but the broadcasting day is occasionally lengthened for special events, during religious holidays, and on Fridays.

Foreign programming is very popular. Two programs on the 1980 schedule are "The Waltons" and "Dallas," a program that fascinated Arab viewers as much as it did Americans.

Second Channel (KTV Two). Generally referred to as the cultural service, the second channel might more appropriately be called the foreign cultural service. Although it does feature some Arabic programming, the majority of the offerings are imported from Australia, Great Britian, and the United States. The service starts daily at 1900 with western cartoon series, some of which have been dubbed into Arabic. To complete the second half hour, programming suitable for children is shown. Examples include "Big Blue Marble," "Wild, Wild World of Animals," and "Bewitched." From 2000 to

2030 the news in English is featured. From 2030 until about 2300, selected Arabic films and serials for television are scheduled. However, the majority of programs are western programs and made-for-television films. Programs aired during the 1980 season include "Starsky and Hutch," "Ascent of Man," "The Pallisers," "Family," "Wolfman Jack Show," "Eight Is Enough," "Donny and Marie," "Police Woman," "Nana Muskouri," and "Survivors" (Kuwait Television Schedule 1980). Officials are not concerned about the cultural effect of imported programs because they believe that it is up to the viewer to make a choice between what is offered on the two services. They indicate that even if western entertainment programs were not offered on Kuwait television, they are available in local cinemas or on video tape for home video systems.

The prevalence of home video tape systems is noted at several points in this chapter. The Kuwait concrn about the pervasiveness of tapes is slightly different from that of other Arabian Gulf countries. Since independence, public cinemas have been widespread. The country's 11 major movie houses show both Arabic (mostly Egyptian) films and western films with Arabic subtitles. Many of Kuwait's cinemas are in financial trouble, though, be- cause, according to their owners, television and home video tapes have reduced attendance (*Gulf Mirror* 1980a, p. 3).

Of the countries in the Arabian Gulf, Kuwait has the most developed radio and television system. The country is small enough readily to achieve complete signal coverage; the broadcasting complex built in the late 1970s provides adequate facilities into the 1990s. The television organization plans to increase local production, although there is no intention to undertake production projects for profit. Kuwait is sufficiently affluent to underwrite the cost of any indigenous production that it believes is in the national interest.

3.4 Saudi Arabia

Saudi Arabia shares with North Yemen the rare distinction of never having been colonized or otherwise dominated by a foreign power. Even the Ottomans could not occupy the whole of Arabia on a continuous basis. The area's modern history began when Abdul Aziz ibn Saud captured the old walled city of Riyadh from the Rashid family in 1902: over the next thirty years, his sons and followers conquered various sections of the country, which occupies most of the Arabian Peninsula and borders on Jordan, Iraq, Kuwait, Qatar, the United Arab Emirates, Oman, and North and South Yemen. In 1932, that land was proclaimed Saudi Arabia.

The two factors that have most influenced Saudi Arabian society are religion and oil. The kingdom is the most conservative of all Arab countries, adhering to the basic beliefs of a Sunni Islamic sect that follows the teachings of Mohammed Abd-al-Wahhab. The consumption of alcoholic drinks is illegal and public cinemas are not allowed: the country's legal system follows the teachings of the Koran closely. In the 1930s, oil was discovered in the Eastern Province, but almost no revenue was realized by the government until after World War II. Income then increased steadily, during the 1950s and 1960s, but not until the rapid increases in OPEC oil prices after the 1973 Middle East War did the country accumulate enormous wealth and put into effect its remarkably energetic development plan. An important supplier of oil to the United States, Europe, and Japan, Saudi Arabia is the largest oil exporter of the Arab countries. Estimates of its population, between six and eight million, have remained the same since 1960.

3.4.1 Prebroadcasting Developments

Before the contemporary development of the electronic media in Saudi Arabia is discussed, some background information is necessary. By the mid-1920s, the followers of Ibn Saud had captured the Hijaz, the Western Province, which contains the holy cities of Mecca and Medina: its former ruler, Sharif Hussein of Mecca, was expelled. (His sons Abdullah and Faisal were to become the kings of Jordan and Iraq respectively.) That part of the peninsula had been heavily influenced by westerners, and the Turks, who had had nominal control over the area until World War I, had left behind Telefunken wireless stations and a telephone line between Jidda and Mecca (Philby 1952, p. 173). The king realized that he would need the help of wire and wireless communication facilities in order to rule effectively over such a vast, sparsely populated country: he purchased and installed a network of transmitters in various cities in the kingdom and also acquired—from his friend the British Marconi agent H. St. John Philby, arabist and historian—portable transmitters that would accompany him when he traveled (Williams 1933, p. 248; Philby 1955, p. 316). But he realized at the same time that he and those who followed him would need to strike a delicate balance between modernization and Islam, for the Wahhabi religious supporters of his family—especially the *ulema*, the religious leaders—were grimly opposed to the Western gadgetry that would almost surely change the traditional bedouin ways of the area. Their objections to wireless communication were more absolute even than their objections to automobiles and telephones: being unable to see the manner of its working, they had to suspect that it was literally the work of the devil (Philby 1955, p. 316). Ibn Saud's way of proving that it was not was characteristic of him: he devised an "experiment" to satisfy them. He asked a group of *ulema* to travel to Mecca, where they were to await a wireless transmission from his headquarters in Riyadh. At the appointed time he had passages from the Koran read to them over the system and then had the men in Mecca read sections of the Holy Book to others of their sect with him back in Riyadh. He then reportedly observed in the presence of the religious leaders that, as the devil could not pronounce the word of the Koran, the "miracle" they had just witnessed had to be the work of man and nature rather than the devil (Eddy 1963, p. 258; see also Benoist-Mechin 1958, p. 205; Nadir 1971; Walpole *et al.* 1971, p. 182). Although music and photography continued to be forbidden for the time being, opposition to wireless communication ceased. In 1927, its future was sanctioned by an official *fatwa*, or legal opinion, in which the religious leaders decided not to rule on the legality of radio technology: "we abstain from answering the question and without knowing about science we will not discuss it from the viewpoint of the teachings of God and His Prophet" (Nallino 1939, p. 119). Television, however, was to be another matter.

3.4.2 Radio Broadcasting before 1960

It is said that very early ibn Saud listened, occasionally, to Arabic-language radio broadcasts from Europe, and that he had transcripts made of them in the late 1930s and during World War II. But there had been no such early need for a radio broadcasting service, in Saudi Arabia, as in Egypt, Lebanon, and Iraq. No foreign power was at the time influencing government decisions. The king ruled the country with an ongoing system of interpersonal communication, visiting the various tribes on a regular basis and often inviting tribal leaders to meet with him when he traveled to the kingdom's major cities. But by the end of World War II, when he was showing signs of age and had begun to give some administrative responsibilities to trusted advisors and to those of his sons who might potentially come to the throne, he may have reasoned that when he became older and found it difficult to travel extensively, radio could be a substitute for his visits. Also, Saudi citizens started acquiring radios after World War II, and they listened to Arabic programs on foreign stations in order to get news and other programming. The Minister of Finance arranged in May 1949 for International Telegraph and Telephone, Inc., to build a medium-wave transmitter and studio in Jidda, and ibn Saud put his son Faisal, later crown prince and king, in charge of the station ("Saudi Arabian Broadcasting: A Synopsis" 1980, p. 2). Service was at first restricted to five hours—two hours in the morning, and two 90-minute periods in the afternoon and evening; neither women's voices nor music (military marches excepted) was allowed on the air. Most of the broadcasting time was devoted to religious programming, including some broadcasts that originated from Mecca ("Saudi Arabian Broadcasting: A Synopsis" 1980, p. 2).

The original 3-kilowatt transmitter in Jidda was soon replaced by a 50-kilowatt RCA facility and the hours of programming were expanded; Faisal was influential in 1953 in establishing the first identifiable office within the government to handle broadcasting and information activities—the Directorate General of Broadcasting, Press, and Publications—an organization later given the status of a ministry of information. But no other major broadcasting developments took place in Saudi Arabia in the 1950s, though the number of Saudi radio receivers increased because of growing affluence and the new availability of electricity. Smaller, more reliable battery-operated transistor sets also appeared on the market and, as was the case in many other Arab countries, coffee house owners acquired radios to attract customers. As the decade ended, the radio service was still restricted to the Western Province and operated for only a limited number of hours per day. Listeners interested in news events tuned to the BBC; those more interested in entertainment, especially popular Arab music, tuned to one of the Eyptian radio services. And when, in the late 1950s, the Egyptian services (most notably the "Voice of the Arabs") started attacking the Saudi royal family and suggesting revolution, the government was initially power-less to counter them. The popular Egyptian radio services, which were only to grow more hostile during the 1960s, were therefore probably the single factor most responsible for the expansion that took place in Saudi Arabian radio in that decade.

3.4.3 Radio Broadcasting, 1960s

Primarily because of increased listening to foreign broadcasts, the government announced in 1957 that it would build a station in Riyadh (*Business Week* 1957, p. 48). The first Saudi radio station outside the Western Province, the Riyadh Domestic Service was on the air about 16 hours per day (Walpole *et al.* 1971, p. 183). Then in the early 1960s construction started on a new broadcasting studio complex back in Jidda: its service was to be known as Radio Mecca even though it did not originate from there, and it operated for about 17 hours per day. In 1965, these two domestic radio services were operating quite separately, 500 miles apart, with no means existing—other than the low-quality radio-telephone link that was used for special announcements or speeches by the king—to connect them. They reached only their respective cities and the surrounding towns: national coverage was not yet a reality. Indeed, the only radio broadcasting in the large and oil-rich Eastern Province was done by ARAMCO, the American oil company later acquired by the Saudi government. Not until the late 1960s did the Ministry of Information inaugurate a medium-wave transmitter, in Dammam, to serve the eastern portion of the country. But it had been announced in 1964 that a series of 1-kilowatt transmitters would be built in major Saudi Arabian cities to rebroadcast the Mecca service, and plans for a series of short-wave transmitters had been commissioned: construction had begun in Riyadh, in the middle 1960s, on a 1200-kilowatt medium-wave superpower station orginally meant to broadcast a "Voice of Islam" pro-gram to compete with the anti-Saudi Egyptian radio services. The last plan was frustrated by failure of the French-built transmitter to operate as designed until it was refitted in the early 1970s—by which time, after Nasser and King Faisal had met in the wake of the 1967 war and reached agreement over the chief source of friction during the 1960s, the civil war in Yemen, the need to counter Egyptian broadcasts had diminished.

As the 1960s ended, the fact that the kingdom was no longer under constant radio attack by other countries gave planners an opportunity to review the future of radio broadcasting in Saudi Arabia. During this period, a plan was conceived to provide a strong signal to the sparsely populated northern portion of the country and to reach countries such as Egypt, Lebanon, Iraq, and Jordan (Kingdom of Saudi Arabia Central Planning Organization 1970, p. 140). All major government offices except for the Ministry of Foreign Affairs, which has traditionally been located in Jidda, were moved to Riyadh: the Ministry of Information was relocated in 1967, and plans were consolidated to centralize radio administration and most production and transmission there as well. The United States Army Corps of Engineers, which had built the initial television facilities in the kingdom, was asked to supervise the design and construction of the new central radio studio and administration building: that project was completed in 1972 and became operational in 1974. The chief problem of the period was that the Ministry of Information had grown dramatically and it was hard to find enough qualified Saudis to fill the major management positions in expanding radio and television services. In Saudi Arabia those positions were reserved for natives of the country—as was not true in gulf states such as the United Arab Emirates—though it had always been the practice to use non-Saudis to do equipment installation, maintenance, announcing, and program production. All too often, those who assumed administrative responsibilities had no previous media experience, although many had been university educated.

3.4.4 Radio Broadcasting, 1970s

The October 1973 Middle East War had a great effect on Saudi Arabia and consequently on its radio system. Though not directly involved in the armed conflict between Egypt, Syria, and Israel, the kingdom for a time joined other Arab countries in stopping shipments of oil to the west, quadrupling the price upon resumption of shipping. Saudi Arabia found itself with more oil income than it could absorb—and a new international role. The increased income was earmarked for an energetic development plan that included additional high-powered radio transmitters, able to reach other countries: Ministry of Information planners reasoned that Saudi Arabia's pro-west orientation and moderate stands on increases in OPEC oil prices would necessitate a particularly strong external radio service, one able to defend the kingdom's political, religious, and economic policies to its neighbors.

In the mid-1970s, the completion of a Saudi national telecommunications system made networking possible. Originally planned in the late 1960s, the project was delayed because of its expense and the Ministry of Communication's indecision as to what kind of technology should be used. After an International Telecommunications Union study, the decision was made to utilize a combination of underground cable and microwave links. The desire to distribute radio and television signals was only a small part of the motivation behind the construction of the system, which was designed also to be used for military and commercial telephone communication within the country; but with the networking capability it supplied, the Jidda and Riyadh radio studios would be able to feed to any combination of medium- and short-wave transmitters and thus at last provide a national service. Moreover, the country had lacked sufficient high-power medium-wave transmitters capable of reaching neighboring countries during the day as well as at night: with the increased oil income following the 1973 Middle East War, Saudi Arabia could afford to purchase, at a price of between four and five million dollars each, superpower medium-wave transmitters to do that job. As part of what had first been conceived as the Northern Stations Project, the Ministry of Information purchased from Continental Electronics one 1000-kilowatt and three 2000-kilowatt medium-wave transmitters, to be located at two sites (Continental Electronics 1979), and linked to the Riyadh and Jidda studios to transmit the General Program. In addition, Continental installed one 2000-kilowatt and one 1000-kilowatt transmitter in Jidda and another 2000-kilowatt transmitter in Damman. In 1980, a superpower facility was planned for Jizan in the southern part of the country. With all this transmitter construction completed, Saudi Arabia may have the most powerful medium-wave transmitter system in the Arab world. Between 1979 and 1981, 12,000 kilowatts of medium-wave transmission power were added to a country that at one point not very long before had not had the ability to reach its own population with a radio signal: it can now be heard reliably throughout the Arab world, except in the North African countries. Radio services have expanded ahead of studio space and a new addition is planned to the Riyadh radio studios built by the Corps of Engineers.

3.4.5 Radio Services

Dependent on announcers and producers from other Arab countries, Saudi Arabia can claim little that is uniquely Saudi about its programming: Egyptian, Jordanian, and Lebanese personnel particularly have had a major influence on programming style and format, and some of the recorded music and drama broadcast in Saudi Arabia was taped in other Arab countries prior to the time when the kingdom built adequate studios for its own productions. By the early 1960s, the initial restrictions on music were gradually changed, one reason for that being that popular songs could easily be heard on the Egyptian radio services. Religious leaders did object to the introduction of female announcers on the Jidda-based radio service in

1963—but King Faisal reportedly told the protesting *ulema*, "You'd better get used to women's voices on the radio, because you'll be seeing their faces on television soon" (Holden 1966, p. 117). The first part of this prediction was fulfilled and women's voices are an every day part of Saudi radio programming.

The following discussion covers the Saudi Arabian radio services as they operated in 1980.

General Program. The General Program is transmitted for 20 hours per day on the powerful medium-wave transmitters, and at various times during the scheduled broadcasting period over 12 short-wave transmitters. It originates from the studios in Riyadh and Jidda with a certain number of hours going out from each location each day. Intended to be the country's main domestic and international Arabic radio voice, the General Program is structured so that special programs appropriate for military personnel, children, women, students, and housewives are aired at appropriate times. These special programs occupy approximately one-third of the service's total times. Another one-third of the program time is devoted to music, with the remaining one-third used for news and religious programs ("Saudi Arabian Broadcasting: A Synopsis" 1980, p. 3).

Much of the religious programming offered on the General Program is supplied by another radio service that, originating from the holy city of Mecca, is heard on the frequencies of the interrupted General Program, at the times of the daily prayers. Besides the actual calls for prayer from the Mecca Mosque, this service—called "The Voice of Islam" like that projected anti-Egyptian Riyadh service of the previous decade—broadcasts news and features about Islam. In 1980, plans called for it to become independent from the General Program and to assume with its Islamic religious character, a separate existence.

Holy Koran Broadcast. The Holy Koran service traces its origins to 1972 and is actually two separate services, one from Riyadh, the other from Mecca, transmitting on both mediumwave and shortwave. Designed for listeners in Arab, Asian, and African Islamic countries, the Riyadh service lasts for 18 hours per day, 0600 to 2400. The Mecca service broadcasts from 0600 to 1200, and then from 1600 to 2400; it does most of the short-wave broadcasting, on six frequencies ("Saudi Arabian Broadcasting: A Synopsis" 1980, pp. 5–6). The Holy Koran Broadcast appears to differ from the Voice of Islam in that the latter is more oriented toward news and information about the Islamic world than the former, which is designed rather to broadcast serious religious discussion and lectures, as well as readings from the Koran.

International Foreign Language Programs. Saudi Arabia's external language services are beamed primarily to Islamic countries. Two of the services, the Indonesian and Urdu, were started as early as 1949 and were transmitted for a short time each day on the facilities constructed for international telegraph traffic. The original enthusiasm for this kind of broadcasting did not continue because of limited facilities, and the higher priority given to the establishment of a domestic service in the 1950s and 1960s. Essentially a product of the 1970s, then, the language services shown in Table 13 feature religious subjects and some information about Saudi Arabia as an international economic entity.

European Service. In January 1965 the Ministry of Information began an English service in Jidda in the hope both of reaching the large foreign community there and of communicating Saudi news, views, and other information to diplomatic missions that might not (it thought) have personnel to translate the daily Saudi newspapers from the Arabic. For the first two years of the service, the staff consisted of two full-time British ex-BBC announcers and one full-time American announcer; special programs were taped on a weekly basis by native English speakers who were employed part-time.[2] The hours of the service have fluctuated, depending on availability of transmission time and programming personnel. During the first five years, there were two one-hour transmissions, one in early morning and one in early afternoon; the evening program lasted for three and one-half hours. On Friday, the afternoon transmission was lengthened to include a program of popular western music for people at the Red Sea beach, introduced with patter by a popular Saudi Arabian disc jockey. Between 1966 and 1968 the Jidda service was broadcast simultaneously from Riyadh, using the radio link supplied by the telephone authority: the link was of poor quality, a fact that discouraged listening in Riyadh, and the rebroadcast was discontinued when a separate Riyadh-based English service was started. In 1980, that Riyadh service broadcast from 1400 to 1600 and 2100 to 0100 daily: the Jidda English service included an afternoon and evening transmission for a total of four hours per day.

The Jidda French service, which began in 1965, has not recieved much attention because French is not an important language in Saudi Arabia. The kingdom has close relations with France, however, and appears interested in continuing the service locally for public relations purposes.

Although intended mainly for listeners within the kingdom, at specific times the English and French services are broadcast on shortwave for listeners in the rest of the Middle East and in Europe.

3.4.6 Television before 1970

Although relatively late in establishing a government-operated television service, Saudi Arabia is the location of the second television station in the Arab world.[3] On 17 June 1955 station AJL-TV went on the air in Dhahran on the Arabian Gulf (*USAFE Television Story* 1955, p. 3). It was operated

---

[2]This writer was the American announcer.
[3]The U.S. Air Force established a television station in Libya at Wheelus Air Force Base that broadcast its first program on 22 December 1954. See *USAFE Television Story* 1955, p. 1.

Table 13. Saudi Arabian Foreign-Language Broadcasts

Language	Duration (local time)
Persian	0600–0800
Turkish	0700–0900
Indonesian	1400–1600
Bengali	1600–1700
Urdu	1700–1900
Swahili	1900–2000
Somali	2000–2100

SOURCE: "Saudi Arabia Broadcasting: A Synopsis" 1980, pp. 4–5."

by the United States Air Force and was intended to provide entertainment for the American personnel stationed at Dhahran Air Force Base, then a Strategic Air Command facility: some local production was done by base personnel, but programming came mostly from American networks. Program fare included "Jackie Gleason," "Ed Sullivan," "Studio One," "Groucho Marx," and "I Love Lucy." Another station, operating on the same American 525-line system as the Air Force station, opened in September 1957 on the Dhahran ARAMCO compound (*Aramco World Magazine* 1963, p. 6). Station HZ-22-TV, which still broadcasts (see 3.4.13), telecast American programs and some locally produced Arabic-language productions. Until the station became an entirely English-language operation after the government opened its own television station in the Eastern Province, all English programs were dubbed into Arabic: the Arabic sound was transmitted with the picture, and the English sound was provided by FM radio. ARAMCO's American employees, for whom the service was originally started, used a standard American television set with an FM radio tuned to the ARAMCO frequency—but few Saudis, in those early days, had sets of any make.

The Saudi government had several reasons for announcing, in late 1963, that it would build a national television system. First, it needed to provide the population with an innovation that was at least symbolically modern. Despite the fact that the Wahhabis had interpreted sections of the Koran to mean that any kind of cinematic art was a form of idolatry, wealthier Saudis had by that time traveled to Lebanon and Egypt and had become enamored of television. National television, it was reasoned, would at least give the government some control over the kind of news, developmental, and entertainment programming that was provided to Saudis at home. The second reason for the introduction of television was the preoccupation of the Ministry of Information with hostile broadcasts from Egypt's radio stations: a television service operating during evening hours would provide an attractive alternative to Radio Cairo and the Voice of the Arabs, which were thought to be widely heard in Saudi Arabia at night. Third, the government counted on using television for educational purposes—to help with basic health and literacy training as well as to support classroom teaching. Finally, television would help provide a sense of unity not before possible, a unity also being promoted at the time by increasing numbers of inter-province domestic airline flights and new telephone and telex systems. No longer would the Eastern Province be isolated from the capital and the cities near the Red Sea.

Television was and is still organized in a manner almost identical to radio. It is operated by the Ministry of Information, and all funding is provided by the government: there is no license fee, and advertising is not permitted.

For the first eight years, the United States was deeply involved in television planning and operation in the kingdom. The American connection started when then Crown Prince Faisal, who later became king, made a visit to American Ambassador Parker T. Hart: he asked for American help in "solving the problem of contracting for a reliable television system" (Hart 1970), believing that the United States could build stations for him quickly, bypassing the Saudi Arabian commercial firms, which could be expected to slow the introduction of television and increase the cost of the project. Ambassador Hart passed the request for help to the State Department, which in turn contacted the Federal Communications Commission (FCC). Edward W. Allen, then the FCC's chief engineer, came to Saudi Arabia, and after visiting various locations wrote a report that served as a blueprint for television facilitites construction throughout the 1960s (Allen 1963, p. 1). The implementation of the Allen Report became the responsibility of the United States Army Corps of Engineers (COE), whose efficiency in constructing the Dhahran airport facility and several small projects involving the Saudi Arabian military had impressed the Saudi government. Their responsibility was formally defined in an agreement signed in January 1964 by Ambassador Hart and Omar Sakkaf, Saudi Deputy Minister of Foreign Affairs (United States Department of State 1964, pp. 1864–75).

The Corps of Engineers hired an American firm to construct two buildings, one in Riyadh and one in Jidda, to house the studios and equipment. Contracts were awarded to RCA to supply the equipment; another contract went to the National Broadcasting Company International (NBCI) for the operation and maintenance of the stations. American television engineers and production specialists were stationed in each. Test transmissions started at both stations early in the summer of 1965: on 17 July 1965, the date generally accepted as the formal beginning of Saudi Arabian television, both stations went officially on the air (Watson 1965, p. 1).

3.4.7 Opposition to Television

It is unlikely that the full story of the opposition to television from conservative religious elements in Riyadh will ever be known. What is certain is the profound and far-reaching effect that one incident had on the country many years later.

Interestingly, the Saudi religious establishment had not objected to the early American Air Force and ARAMCO broadcasts in the Eastern Province, just as it had given only minor opposition to early programming on the first radio station in Jidda in the Western Province. Those two areas had been more exposed to the outside world, specifically to the west—the western oil companies having been present there since the 1930s—than had the central area of the country, the Nejd, which is more religiously conservative. But essentially the same religious leaders who had opposed radio broadcasting opposed television, and television was a more serious problem because of its visual element. Even still photography had been unacceptable to the *ulema* until the early 1960s, when ibn Saud had exercised his own masterful brand of ratiocination on the point:

Islam takes seriously and literally the Second Commandment to make no graven image nor any likeness of any living thing. Sculpture and painting, impudent attempts to imitate the Creator, are proscribed, sweeping away the idols of the polytheists who flourished in Arabia before Muhammed, but also casting a blight on all the fine arts so far as live subjects are concerned. And yet, Ibn Sa'ud was convinced by the engineers that photography was essential, especially aerial photography to locate roads and geological foundations. When American photographers began to operate with his permission, he was denounced by bigots for perfidy to Islam.

He summoned his detractors and convened the 'ulema . . . and put forth questions: Painting and sculpture are idolatry, but is light good or bad? The judges pondered and replied that light is good; Allah put the sun in the heavens to light man's path. Then asked the King, is a shadow good or bad? There was nothing in the Qur'an about this, but the judges deduced and ruled that shadows are good, because they are inherent in light, and even a holy man casts a shadow. Very well then, said the King, then photography is good because it is nothing but a combination of light and shade, depicting Allah's creatures but leaving them unchanged. The battle was won in the King's characteristic way, by persuasion and not by force. [Eddy 1963, p. 258]

Saudi Arabia was changing only slowly, however, and television continued to be seen both by theologians and by radical religious zealots as blasphemous: moreover, it was potentially corrupting in their eyes as yet another western influence. In the summer of 1965, during the test transmission period in Riyadh, a conservative royal family member named Khalid ibn Musad gathered supporters for a march on the television station, intending to destroy its transmitting equipment. What happened next is still a matter of speculation. Several sources reported that the transmitter had been destroyed: this was not true. When police dispersed the crowd, Khalid returned to his house—where he was shot and killed during a struggle with an official of theMinistry of the Interior.[4] Though Khalid's immediate family appealed to King Faisal to punish the person who shot him, Faisal ruled that the man had acted appropriately, and his identity was never officially disclosed.

But the incident was not really over. Almost ten years later, Faisal ibn Musad, Khalid's younger brother, shot and killed King Faisal while he was receiving guests in Riyadh: *Newsweek* reported that after the shooting Faisal ibn Musad had shouted, "Now my brother is avenged" (1975, pp. 21–23). King Faisal's death came when his leadership was badly needed in the kingdom. He was a moderate who had attempted to balance social progress with the constraints imposed by conservative Islamic beliefs, and it is one of history's ironies that he was thus killed over an incident involving television—a medium he had supported and helped to develop.

3.4.8 Television Expansion

In 1967, two years after the opening of the Jidda and Riyadh stations, a second television project was completed by the COE: a series of microwave relays was built to send the Jidda station signal to transmitters in Mecca and the adjacent city of Taif, the government's official residence during the summer. (No additional programming facilities were needed in Mecca and Taif, as all transmissions were still to originate at the Jidda station.) In that same year an operation called the "Training Transmitter Project" was also completed—one which the COE and RCA undertook only reluctantly. The innocuous name of the project notwithstanding, its four transmitters in a building near the Jidda television station were in fact intended by the Ministry of Information to jam Egyptian television signals, broadcasting on the same channels as the Egyptian channels most likely to "tunnel" across the Red Sea. The importance of this project to the government can only be understood within the context of the anti-Saudi Egyptian radio propaganda that was so virulent prior to the 1967 Middle East War; and indeed by the time the transmitters were operational, improved relations between Saudi Arabia and Egypt had made them—like the Riyadh "Voice of Islam" radio transmitter—unessential. As no television signals from Egypt ever reached Jidda, there was no opportunity even to test the system.

In early 1968, two more television stations came on the air. Designed for limited local production only, these stations in Medina, north of Jidda, the second most holy city in the kingdom, and Qassim, a conservative Islamic area northwest of Riyadh, were smaller than the Jidda and Riyadh facili-

[4]Shobaili 1972. Dr. Shobaili attempted to obtain clarification of the incident from the Minister of Information, who, at that time, was Deputy Minister of Interior. The Minister declined to clarify the story, stating that he thought it best not to resurrect the incident. Various inaccurate accounts are available. See, for example, *The Economist* 1965, p. 742; and Walpole *et al.* 1971, pp. 185–86.

ties—though they contained living quarters for the foreign engineers who were needed to operate them. The Jidda and Riyadh stations supplied most of the programming on video tape and film, until they were connected to the national television network for direct rebroadcast in the 1970s: the usual contractors, RCA and National Broadcasting Company International (NBCI), built and operated them.

The final Saudi television project involving the United States Corps of Engineers was the construction of a powerful television station in Dammam in the Eastern Province: the good working relationship that the COE had had with the Ministry of Information soured when the station became operational. The Saudi government had placed a high priority on the completion of the Dammam station: neighboring countries were building stations that might reach the Eastern Province. A Kuwait station was already available there during the warm months; and Saudi Arabia, which had traditionally had a friendly rivalry with Kuwait, wanted especially to make a similar showing in that neighboring oil-rich state. ARAMCO, moreover, was tired of providing the sole television service in the area, and of trying to find programming that both its own employees and its Arab hosts would find enjoyable and appropriate. With uncharacteristic speed, then, a letter of credit for the $3.25 million needed for the construction of the station moved through the kingdom's financial bureaucracy to the Chase Manhattan Bank in New York and to the United States Treasury Department. The Minister of Information also approved the use of RCA as the prime supplier of equipment, despite the fact that the company was on the Arab League boycott list: the Ministry assumed that no violation of the boycott agreement had occurred inasmuch as the RCA Damman contract was not a new one but rather was written as an amendment to an older, pre-boycott, contract. RCA supplied two 12.5-kilowatt transmitters, designed to operate in parallel and to feed an antenna mounted atop a 1200-foot guyed tower. The effective radiated power of the station at that time was possibly the highest in the world (Radio Corporation of America 1969, p. 1). But apparently the Corps of Engineers had misunderstood some of the technical advice provided by RCA—and its transmissions did not reach Kuwait. The government was furious, and with the cooling of relations between the COE and the Ministry of Information, the Corps stopped contract work on broadcasting in the kingdom. Furthermore, by 1971, the COE had numerous contracts with the Ministry of Defense and Aviation, its original Saudi employer, and had lost interest in the other (and always secondary) type of work that it had found in Saudi Arabia.

3.4.9 Television in the 1970s

Considerable changes had taken place in Saudi Arabian television by 1974. After nine years of experience with television, the Ministry of Information felt more comfortable with the medium. With the assistance of the Corps of

Engineers, in its approved days, a small number of Saudi television employees had been sent to the United States for training in all facets of television: students had taken production courses, English-language training, graduate work in broadcasting, and electrical engineering degrees.

In 1969, NBCI had lost a competitive bid to AVCO, an American corporation then owning broadcasting stations, for the operation and maintenance of the kingdom's television stations: AVCO, which had underbid NBCI in order to get a start in Saudi Arabia, was to contract directly with the government after the Corps of Engineers withdrew from television there. But most notably, by 1974, the entire television system was Saudi-managed: a local Saudi company, BETA, had taken over the AVCO contract. In 1980, BETA still had the operations and maintenance contract with the Ministry of Information—though the technicians and engineers who worked for the company were virtually all non-Saudi Arabs. European personnel generally supervised the work done by Jordanian, Egyptian, and Lebanese engineers.

Before any additional stations could be built or existing stations upgraded, the government had to make a decision about the type of color system it would adopt. The feeling in Saudi Arabia and many other Gulf states was that the German PAL system ought to be the common Gulf states color standard. In 1971, the Ministry of Information hired Hammett and Edison, a San Francisco, California, consulting firm, to study the SECAM and PAL systems to determine which one would be better for the kingdom: they too concluded, in their 1972 report, that PAL should be the choice. Despite this, the country decided on the SECAM system, invented and promoted by the French, who have been successful in some countries in tying SECAM-standard acceptance to various economic, military, or cultural agreements.[5] The SECAM decision was thus political rather than technical (Edison 1979), and was made by the Saudi Arabian cabinet, possibly at the request of King Faisal. In any case, whatever length the French went to in order to secure the acceptance of the SECAM color system in the kingdom, it was worth it to them: most of the color equipment bought by the Saudis since, whether for new stations or for upgrading older ones, has been purchased from French manufacturers. In 1982, for example, a new broadcasting complex, the largest and most technically advanced in the Arab world, was due to be completed in Riyadh—using French equipment exclusively. The main consulting group for the project was a French state-owned organization. Inconveniently for the Saudis, of course, the remaining Gulf states (with the exception of Iraq) use PAL—and PAL is incompatible with SECAM for color transmission. In order to compete in international television in the Gulf states region, Saudi Arabia had to convert its powerful twin RCA transmitters in Dammam to PAL so that those outside the kingdom

[5]For a discussion of the French effort to have other countries adopt the SECAM system, see Crane 1979.

could see the Saudi signal in color. Another transmitter (UHF) was constructed in 1976 to broadcast the Dammam signal locally in SECAM (Al-Warthan 1979).

In August 1977 a new television facility was opened, in Abha, in the southern part of Saudi Arabia ("Saudi Arabian Television: A Synopsis" 1980, p. 3). The station is used to broadcast the national television service and has the capability of producing local programming. But it is the only station with production facilities that has been built since the Dammam station was completed: the growth in Saudi Arabian television has been in the increase in coverage provided by transmitters that broadcast the Riyadh signal, by a leased INTELSAT system satellite transponder to 20 ground stations scattered throughout the kingdom. The same system is planned to link the new industrial towns that are under construction. Thus, although behind other Gulf states such as Kuwait on the construction of production facilities, Saudi Arabia has expanded its television coverage to include the entire country; and, moreover, two ground stations linked to the INTELSAT system—Taif and Riyadh—are used to receive and transmit television signals internationally. (Radio also uses the INTELSAT satellite for stand-by purposes for linking the Jidda and Riyadh stations and the powerful medium-wave stations that form the Northern Stations Project. In December 1979, when the national telecommunications network malfunctioned, the satellite circuit was activated so that the distribution of radio signals would not be interrupted [S. Nasser 1980].) Saudi Arabia is an active participant in the ARABSAT project—headquartered in Riyadh—in which members of the Arab League will particpate in the launching of a satellite in order to improve all forms of communication, including the distribution of broadcast signals among Arab countries. Finally, Saudi Arabia has plans under way to design, build, and launch a satellite for its own exlusive use. The government apparently believes that having such a satellite will lessen its dependence on INTELSAT for circuits, and the $500 million voted for the project by the Council of Ministers in December 1979 (S. Nasser 1980) is apparently believed to be a notably good investment of excess funds gained from oil exports.

The 1982 completion of a new one-half billion dollar Riyadh television complex will further centralize the distribution and production of Saudi Arabian television: the facility will provide adequate space for a planned second channel and studios to accommodate additional Saudi program production.

3.4.10 Television Programming

It is easier, given sufficient funds, to acquire hardware than to produce software, and generally speaking the Saudi Arabian television administration has been more successful in managing the equipment-related aspects of television than the programming side. The Corps of Engineers and NBCI were ready to provide production advice when asked by the government, but programming decisions have been the responsibility of the Ministry of Information—and, when television was first introduced, very little thought had been given to the kind of daily schedule that the Ministry would provide. It was after the incident in Riyadh, which showed how militant the opposition to the medium could be, that officials became concerned about the possible consequences of the start of actual programming.

In July and August 1965, the test pattern was telecast in the morning; in the early evening about an hour's worth of programming was provided, including Koran readings, background music, and scenic slides of various sections of the kingdom. Mighty Mouse cartoons were shown, and off-camera announcers read the news while still news pictures appeared on the screen. By almost any measure, these first television signals were received with tremendous excitement by the citizens of Riyadh and Jidda, the majority of whom had not seen a motion picture before films were shown on television. This writer remembers the scene in downtown Jidda during the brief evening transmissions in August 1965: people stood five and six deep on the sidewalks to catch a glance of the television sets in shop windows. Every morning when the test pattern transmission stopped, the station's switchboard was flooded with calls wanting to know where the "programs" were (Watson 1965, p. 2). The Minister of Information would drop by the station at night to see how the programming was progressing. On one occasion he came to the station with a press delegation and decided on the spot that the visit should be televised: on that evening, the programming was extended to 70 minutes (Watson 1965, p. 1).

Early planning by the Ministry of Information and NBCI projected that nightly programming was to be limited to about two hours; and the programming, maintenance schedules, and number of personnel to be hired were arranged accordingly. But receiver sales soared. Those who could not afford to buy, such as males from lower-income families and expatriate workers, watched television in the coffee houses and restaurants at night. By the end of the first year of operation, the stations were each operating between five and six hours daily.

The Jidda and Riyadh stations had only one studio each; and although the studios were large, only limited amounts of local programming could be produced in a single studio, which could be used only when the station was off the air. Programs were moreover limited by the lack of production, engineering, and artistic personnel. Some dramas were taped, then, but most locally produced programs consisted of interviews with officials and religious leaders. Children's programs and dramas were (and still are) written and produced by Arabs from other countries, most of them from Syria: because of the Yemen Civil War, Saudi Arabia did not have close relations with Egypt, and Jordan had no television system at all at the time. The only live programming consisted of the news and press reviews, announcements of the evening's schedule (which was not yet published in Saudi newspapers), and transition announcements.

Religious programming, important in all Arab countries, has special importance in the country in which the two most holy cities of Islam are located. Each telecasting day starts with a Koran reading. Evening prayer calls are heard over a slide or short film of the famous mosque in Mecca. King Faisal reportedly promised religious leaders, when he was trying to secure approval for the construction of the system, that television would be used as an important means of disseminating religious doctrine (Eilts 1971, p. 27); and one of the first programs to be video taped at the Jidda station, a popular religious series that continued into the 1970s, therefore deserves special mention. The former United States ambassador Hermann Eilts described it and its creator thus:

At least one distinguished *alim*, Shaykh Ali Tantawi, is demonstrating the value of television in the cause of religion. Possessed of an engaging television personality, this savant conducts a regular question and answer program on religious subjects. He invites written questions, reads them before the television camera, and with homely anecdotes about and relevant allusion to contemporary everyday life instructs his viewers. Lacking his imagination, some of his colleagues shortsightedly criticize him. He deserves more credit. [1971, p. 28]

When the Jidda station acquired a mobile broadcasting unit, it began originating both live and taped broadcasts from Mecca during the important religious days of Ramadan and Hajj: before the completion of the national telecommunications system, the programs were taped and distributed to other stations. As of 1980, about 25% of unified programming was devoted to religious subjects ("Saudi Arabian Television: A Synopsis" 1980, p. 5), while the Qassim and Medina stations, in traditionally conservative areas, had formerly programmed as much as 50%. There is some evidence to suggest that the kingdom's commitment to religious television will increase. The revolution in Iran and the attempted mosque take-over in Mecca in 1979 were reminders that the country should move cautiously toward modernization, which might be perceived by conservatives as rejecting (or even as encroaching on) traditional Islam.

The increase in programming hours during the first year of operation required buying material from other countries. Egypt, as previously noted, was not considered to be an acceptable supplier: not only were relations between the two countries at an all-time low between 1965 and 1970, but the material that Egyptian television made available to other countries often contained objectionable references to Nasser's various Pan-Arab themes. Some programming, generally of low quality, was purchased from the two Lebanese stations. At that time, Arabic programming was not being taped in Europe, and the Arab production centers in Jordan, Bahrain, and Dubai had not been constructed. The only answer to the immediate need of even more additional programming, then, was to purchase packages of old movies from the United States and Great Britain. Some of these films were shown, but many proved to be unacceptable because of unsuitable themes. During the first five years of television in the kingdom, imported western made-for-television programs were limited to those that had been sold to other Arab countries and therefore were already dubbed or subtitled in Arabic, among them "Private Secretary," "Bonanza," and "Combat." These programs proved to be so popular that the Ministry of Information was willing to purchase additional such programs to help fill the expanded television schedule: by 1968, purchases had included "Car 54," "Wackiest Ship in the Army," "The Flintstones," "Dennis the Menace," "Wrestling," "The Fugitive," "Loretta Young," and "Rin Tin Tin." Until about 1972, the percentage of imported western programming on the Saudi Arabian television system ranged from 25% to 33%. After 1972, the kingdom started purchasing large amounts of Egyptian programming while continuing to buy from Lebanon; and by the late 1970s, it was also buying programs from Jordan, Bahrain, and Dubai, in addition to special productions done by Egyptian producers working in Europe. While the percentage of imported, mostly entertainment programming has not decreased, the percentage of imported western programming has decreased. This is due not only to increased program production in the Middle East but to the new permissiveness in television programming in the west: the earlier programs had been more acceptable and had required little editing.

3.4.11 Censorship

One of the advantages of television over public cinemas was that television could more easily be controlled by the government. News and other information about the royal family and the country itself could be—and was, and is—placed first on the news: the royal family and ranking government dignitaries have thus always been assured a great deal of exposure on the medium. The government believes moreover that it must regulate cultural trends toward modernization, and controlled television is one means of expressing and affecting, often indirectly, the prevailing mood. The use of the medium itself, of course, reflects a government orientation on the question of how quickly society should move away from traditional Islamic practices. The alternations of cultural liberalism and conservativism in Saudi Arabian society since the introduction of television have been clearly seen on it: for example, women were only gradually allowed to be seen on television, and there remains a kind of double standard on the national channel. Western women are considered to be properly attired when their arms are covered and their skirts are not above the knees. On the other hand, Arab women are usually more conservatively dressed, with at least a scarf covering the hair. Following the 1979 Mecca Mosque incident, Saudi women were banned from television altogether for a short time.

Every program purchased for Saudi television, whether bought from an Arab or a western country, is reviewed by a special department within the Ministry of Information that must screen both its visual and its audio portions. For example, some words on the English sound track of an American-made program may be deleted even in a subtitled program because the original sound track can be heard. The basic guidelines established in the late 1960s for censoring imported programs still apply, prohibiting:

1. Scenes which arouse sexual excitement
2. Women who appear indecently dressed, in dance scenes, or in scenes which show overt acts of love
3. Women who appear in athletic games or sports
4. Alcoholic drinks or anything connected with drinking
5. Derogatory references to any of the "Heavenly Religions"
6. Treatment of other countries with praise, satire, or contempt
7. References to Zionism
8. Material means [meant?] to expose monarchy
9. All immoral scenes
10. References to betting or gambling
11. Excessive violence [Shobaili 1971, pp. 272–43].

Of course, Saudi Arabia is not the only Arab country to screen programs before showing them on television, and these criteria are generally used by all the Gulf states; but they are more strictly applied in Saudi Arabia. An example of what can happen to a program when they are applied to an ordinary American western film was related to this writer by an employee of the film department in 1966:

The town sheriff walks into a bar—censored because alcohol is forbidden. Sheriff talks to woman who is unveiled—censored because woman's face is shown. Sheriff pets dog as he walks down the street—censored because the dog is considered an unclean animal. Finally all scenes involving the sheriff are omitted because it is discovered that the sheriff's badge closely resembles the Star of David and is unacceptable because of the association with Israel. [Boyd 1970–71, pp. 76–77]

Except for residents of the Eastern Province, viewers have little opportunity to compare the Saudi television service with that of other Arab countries and are therefore unaware of the extent of program censorship. But now, fewer programs are imported from the west—and those that are, such as "The Rockford Files" and "Columbo," are considered to be easily edited for Saudi television. Because the kingdom is such an important market for Arab television programs, particularly dramatic programs dealing with Islamic history and bedouin culture, many are conceived and made with the requirements of the Saudi system in mind.

3.4.12 Television Programming; the 1980s

Riyadh is now the center of program transmission, providing the bulk of programs for all stations and relay transmitters in the kingdom. The cities with studios large enough to tape programs—Jidda, Riyadh, Dammam, and (to a limited extent) Abha—are each assigned the task of specializing in the production of certain kinds of programs that are then placed on the national network. Both Riyadh and Jidda tape some programming for children: quiz programs are taped in Dammam, as is a program about Saudi Arabia that is made as part of a Gulf states cooperative programming arrangement. Riyadh is the originating center for almost all news.

The telecast day is similar to that established in the late 1960s. The service starts at about 1700 and continues until about midnight. On Fridays the transmission is extended, starting about midday with sports programs and an Arabic dramatic series. News headlines usually come at the beginning and end of the daily transmission period: the nightly newscasts, 30 minutes of which are in English and fifteen in Arabic, reflect the thinking of the government on both domestic and foreign policy. The government has commissioned several studies on how the television medium can be used for educational purposes, but relatively little educational programming is shown, except for a few programs on health, safety, and literacy: the Ministries of Information and of Education have never been able to agree on which has primary responsibility over such programming. At one time the television service considered employing a company to produce a series on basic adult literacy, but that plan did not come to fruition. The Ministry of Education, which closely controls the national school curriculum, has expressed an interest in a comprehensive television instruction program to be shown in schools with the goals of improving the quality of teaching and of furthering unity in the curriculum: this plan too has been shelved, apparently because the Ministry of Education wants its own production studios and transmitters. But after the Riyadh television complex is completed and a second national channel is started, the ministries may be able to reach an accord on the subject of instructional programming. Some form of televised supplement to classroom instruction is likely to be given national priority in a country that is very concerned about education and that must import the majority of its teachers from other Arab countries.

Some of the government's programming choices have unquestionably helped unify the country. The visual medium has been able to do what radio was unable to do, for lack of transmitters, even into the late 1960s: to provide a sense of national direction and to explore various ramifications of the kingdom's culture and history. National leaders, most of whom are members of the royal family, have been given the kind of national visibility not possible before the introduction of television. The medium has been used with some degree of effectiveness during periods of crisis, the first instance being in 1967, when a series of bombings occurred in Riyadh.

Yemenis, allegedly supporting Egypt's role in the Yemen Civil War, were arrested and executed; but first they were shown on television in an interview during which they admitted their role in the bombings. These telecasts were apparently well received by citizens. Seeing the people responsible for the acts somehow added credibility to the government's statements about the nationality of the bombers and their motive, and stopped rumors and speculation about the causes of the explosions. More recently, during the November 1979 Mecca Mosque incident, television helped again in a national crisis—though it began the exercise less than smoothly. The take-over of the large mosque on the day corresponding to the end of the Islamic fourteenth century caught Saudi Arabian authorities by surprise: for several days, Ministry of Information officials withheld information about the "incident," and Saudi citizens listening to foreign radio reports began to suspect that the government was minimizing the seriousness of the situation in the mosque. When the government decided to release specific information about the extent of the fighting, television was unable to react promptly: pictures of what was actually happening were difficult to obtain because no trained Saudi national was available to take the necessary news footage, and Arab expatriate employees of the film department hesitated to undertake the assignment until their security in Mecca could be guaranteed. But as soon as film of the fighting became available, it was included in newscasts and some was released to the television services of other countries. Following his capture, the leader of the take-over was interviewed on television. The Ministry used this and other footage to produce a one and one-half hour documentary that was shown on the national channel and was offered to the services of interested Arab countries:[6] it showed Mecca and provided some history about the mosque itself; then the fighting was shown, followed by footage of the final group of holdouts, including the leader, being given medical attention in prison. As the interviews with the Yemeni bombers had, thirteen years earlier, this program defused rumors—and it apparently helped satisfy Saudi concern about the extent of damage to a holy Islamic structure.

3.4.13 ARAMCO Broadcasting

A discussion of the broadcast media in Saudi Arabia would not be complete without further examination of the broadcasting activities of the Arabian American Oil Company (ARAMCO). This organization was originally owned by major American oil companies that first participated in Middle East petroleum exploration in the 1930s: company headquarters are in Dhahran, in the Eastern Province, where almost all oil activity is centered. During the 1970s the kingdom purchased the company, but it continues to

[6]Programs concerning the mosque incident were seen by Americans and Saudis interviewed by this writer. The writer viewed the tapes produced after the incident on 29 December 1979 at the Dammam, Saudi Arabia, television station.

contract with a consortium of American oil firms to manage and market the country's entire output—and, of course, the country is the Arab world's largest oil producer. Americans have always played an important part in Saudi Arabia's oil industry, and acquisition of control by the kingdom has not decreased the number of its American personnel. Indeed, the country's booming oil business during the 1970s increased the American presence in the Dhahran area: by January 1980, 3,000 Americans were directly employed there by ARAMCO and 3,600 more were employed by various company subcontractors. Also resident were many employee dependents (Nawwab 1979). The ARAMCO Compound in Dhahran, then, could function as a model American community, complete with cinemas, a bowling alley, supermarkets, beauty shops, and a school system with an American curriculum; women, not allowed to drive in the rest of Saudi Arabia, were there permitted to do so. Naturally, in such a setting, an American-type broadcasting system would operate.

It was noted earlier that ARAMCO started television transmissions from HZ-22-TV in September 1957 and soon was providing entertainment not only for its American employees but for Saudis in the surrounding area who could receive the signal—broadcasting its soundtracks in two languages, both English and Arabic. In 1963 the station's coverage was extended by a transmitter built in the Hofuf area, about 60 miles from the main ARAMCO compound; and in 1964 the company moved its studios from their previous location above a snack bar to a larger building, specifically to accommodate an increased local production schedule including religious programs, drama, a children's series, and a bedouin show (Al-Warthan 1979)—mostly in Arabic. Several American production specialists have been employed by ARAMCO television to advise on local production and to work on the various public relations films that the oil company has produced. (Programming is under the direction of the ARAMCO Public Relations Department.)

When the government Damman station went on the air in 1970, HZ-22-TV ceased all Arabic-language transmissions. ARAMCO actually welcomed relief from the responsibility of being a major television broadcaster in Arabic, never really having sought that role, but its station still continued to send out American programming in English from its 525-line monochrome transmitter. Local Saudi nationals continued to receive this predominantly entertainment-oriented programming by purchasing dual-standard sets that were able to receive not only both the ARAMCO and the government station but, in the summer months, the services of other Gulf states as well. In November 1976, ARAMCO modified its transmitter to broadcast NTSC color. In March 1979, a new Harris 625-line PAL color transmitter became operational, thus making ARAMCO TV's signal compatible with the neighboring Gulf states and the Damman high-power PAL transmitter. The station operates daily from 1630 to approximately 2200, featuring those American and British programs that the company believes conform to local Saudi cultural standards. Indeed, all programs are censored by the ARAMCO Public Relations Department in spite of the fact that most offerings purchased for the station are intended for a western audience. Minimal editing is usually required. The station features mostly entertainment programs that come on ¾ inch U-Matic cassettes. Public service announcements and some safety and training films are televised daily between programs such as "Sesame Street," "The Muppet Show," "Lou Grant," "Strange Report," "Different Strokes," "Anna Karenina," "Electric Company," "Grizzly Adams," and "Secret War." Station HZ-22-TV is bigger than ever, then—but all programming is in English and Arabic subtitles are no longer provided.

Like its television services, ARAMCO's radio broadcasting dates from the 1950s: not until the mid- to late 1960s did records and tapes become generally available for sale in the kingdom, and ARAMCO reasoned that FM radio music would fill a real void. So too would a 15-minute newscast of international news from United Press International (UPI)—read by an employee of the ARAMCO PR department at 1145, with taped repeats at 1245 and 1745—incorporating items about American sports activity and the weather forecast for the Eastern Province. But the original small radio operation of the 1950s has, like the company itself, greatly expanded. By 1963, popular and easy listening music services were available on both FM and mediumwave. After 1970, the company decided that more variety was important and designed a new system to broadcast four separate 24-hour FM stereo music services: the operation, assembled wholly from components, resembles an American automated radio station down to its automatic system of voiced time signals. The four music services, some of which are purchased prefabricated from American suppliers of tapes, feature popular music, country and western music, classical music, and easy listening music respectively. The first two services were broadcast by 1-kilowatt and the second two services by 10-kilowatt FM transmitters; the popular and easy listening programs are also broadcast from 0.25-kilowatt medium-wave transmitters (Skowrowski 1979). These programs are popular among the large western expatriate population in the Eastern Province and are particularly welcomed by the large hotels there and in neighboring Bahrain, where the services are provided as a free amenity to most hotel rooms.

The ARAMCO broadcasting services are available to only one area of the country, the Eastern Province, and their effect is not known; but they do provide more diverse program offerings on both radio and television than are available in any other section of Saudi Arabia.

3.4.14 Video Cassettes

The business of providing equipment for home video recorders and cassette programming in the Gulf states, particularly in Saudi Arabia, is flourishing. This area may constitute the largest home video cassette market in the world; it is surely one of the world's largest outlets for pirated tapes of first-run American and British films and television programming. Part of the explanation for this situation can be found in the cultural and economic conditions that exist in the kingdom. Only a few private cinema enterprises have been allowed to operate—small businesses that rent 16-mm projectors and older Egyptian and western films for home showing—and no public cinemas exist, though companies such as ARAMCO and some large defense contractors such as Raytheon and Lockheed have been permitted by the government to import films for showing before their own employees. In most areas of the country, excluding the Eastern Province, the only television programming available is the one national Saudi Arabian television channel. Yet, from their travels in Europe, the United States, and other Arab countries, upper- and middle-income Saudis have become accustomed to a diverse film and television diet. That Saudi Arabia's is a culture that is fascinated by modern gadgetry also boosts business, as does the fact that import duties on home entertainment equipment are low to non-existent. Saudi Arabians in such large cities as Jidda, Riyadh, and Damman had also been accustomed, since the 1960s, to buying audio cassettes of western music illegally recorded from the BBC or the Voice of America, and Arab music illegally recorded from Radio Cairo or the Voice of the Arabs.

The video cassette business, more technically advanced and profitable than the audio, started in Saudi Arabia in about 1972, with the sale of Sony U-Matic machines. At that time Sony was making these recorders available mostly to the United States market, and consequently the first machines sold were 525-line NTSC American color standard: they were used with the Sony dual, and later triple, standard (NTSC, PAL, SECAM) 525/625-line sets that were becoming so popular. The American standard U-Matic sets were purchased both by individuals for home entertainment and by foreign businesses that wanted to provide employees with entertainment in construction camps located in isolated areas. When the VHS and Sony (Beta) home video recorders became available in the kingdom, however, interest in these larger and more expensive U-Matic units declined.

Once cassette machines became popular, the immediate problem was to provide enough programs on cassettes to meet the demand. At first, cassettes were openly imported into the kingdom: before the arrival of copying equipment, a company would acquire the rights to programs and then have the duplicates shipped to Saudi Arabia. The customs inspectors and the Ministry of Information, which is responsible for approving such material, were initially accommodating: they did not understand what the cassettes were and had had no means of previewing the programming. When they awoke to the realities and required that all material be censored, the importers simply circumvented the system by smuggling. At least two businesses operate in Saudi Arabia selling selected television programming taped in various American and British cities: so little attention is paid to the editing of their tapes that in many instances identifications from stations in New Orleans, Louisiana, and San Francisco, California, may be heard. Even commercials are often left in the programs. And after the advent of copying machines, pirated American and British first-run films were regularly shipped to Saudi Arabia for duplication and local sale or short-term rental. Eventually, the pirating importers almost wholly prevailed over those who were purchasing the rights to programming. Foreign business firms in the kingdom became their willing customers because their wares cost so much less than legal equivalents. That the tapes for VHS and Beta units are considerably smaller than those for U-Matic recorders had much to do with the supplantation of the latter machines by the former: their programming was not only less expensive but was more easily smuggled past the censors in customs.

The video cassette business has, then, circumvented the government's policy of controlling the kind of visual material shown in the kingdom. One need no longer rely wholly on Saudi Arabian television for entertainment. Indeed, in some instances the censored western programming shown on the national television channel is locally available in full on video cassettes. The efficiency of the cassette pirates is evident from the speed with which the controversial British program of April 1980, "Death of a Princess," reached the kingdom. Purporting to detail the death of a Saudi Arabian princess and her lover for adultery, the film was flown to the Eastern Province the morning after its showing on British TV: copies were duplicated and made available in Dammam for sale the same day. Though luggage is thoroughly searched by Saudi customs authorities, a compact VHS or Beta tape may—as before noted—be carried through customs in a coat pocket: and so, doubtless, came the "Princess" to Arabia. The video cassette business is still growing rapidly throughout the Middle East. Though Saudi Arabia is the liveliest market, because of its prevailing cultural conditions and the economic position of its citizens who want video programming, the kind of activity described above occurs in many other Gulf states. Since 1978, the sale and duplication of cassettes has increased even in the less affluent countries such as Jordan and Egypt.

3.4.15 The Broadcasting Audience

Little audience research has been done in Saudi Arabia. First, the government has been hesitant to allow foreign companies to come to the kingdom and ask questions that might, by local standards, be sensitive. Second, when permission has been granted for survey work, it has been given with the stipulation that women not be interviewed—even by trained female interviewers. Whatever reliable data are available, then, regarding radio and television audiences in Saudi Arabia, apply only to the male half of the population. The Hashemite Broadcasting Service of Jordan may have done the first radio research in the kingdom—apparently without official permission—in 1965. In December 1972, Associated Business Consultants (ABC) of Beirut, Lebanon, did a survey of the radio, television, and print media habits of priority audience groups in the kingdom: this study was sponsored by the United States Information Agency and the BBC. Extensive surveys were also done in Saudi Arabia by Cyprus-based Middle East Marketing Research Bureau as part of the 1977 and 1979 McCann Middle East Media Study: McCann refused to grant permission to quote from its studies but Radio Monte Carlo, one of the McCann participants, released some material to this writer.

It is impossible to know exactly the number of radio and television sets in Saudi Arabia. Customs figures on the importation of sets are not helpful because many of the imported receivers are purchased by Arab expatriate workers, mostly Egyptians and Jordanians, and taken home to their families and friends. Even a low-paid laborer from another Arab country can afford to buy an imported radio in Saudi Arabia; and the same statement may apply to television sets, as many workers come to the kingdom without their families and several men, often renting a small apartment or room, pool their financial resources to purchase a stove, refrigerator, and television set.

Since Saudi Arabian television is not commercial, one common reason for undertaking research to determine audience size and makeup does not exist. The 1972 USIA survey did ask respondents some questions about television viewing habits: 87% said they owned a television set and 52% said that they watched television daily (USIA 1973, pp. 8–11). But the only known comprehensive study of television use in Saudi Arabia was done in 1972 by Boyd and Shobaili. This project involved 120 interviews conducted in Riyadh among middle-class and upper-class Saudis. Below are some of its major findings.

1. 90.8% of respondents owned a television set. 29% owned two television sets.
2. 60% of respondents said that they watched television daily.
3. The average number of viewing hours per week among those samples was 14.8.
4. The average number of people who watched television with the respondent was 5.9.
5. The most popular programs among respondents included the Egyptian films and programs shown on Thursday and Friday, over the Arab weekend.
6. 98% of respondents believed that television had an impact on Saudi Arabian society, most people noting that it provided information of an overall educational nature to viewers. Secondly, respondents said that television served to keep the family together: they reported fewer instances where the adult male family members had to leave home to seek entertainment with male friends. Television appeared to be a family-centered form of entertainment which could be enjoyed by all. [1972, pp. 269–302]

The 1972 USIA survey of radio listeners indicated that 88% of those sampled tuned to the Saudi service at least once per week. It is apparently, then, as common a practice in Saudi Arabia as in other Arab countries for people to tune to the government stations to hear what the government is saying—but the survey also indicates how very usual it is to tune to foreign radio stations. Seventy per cent of respondents said that they tuned at least once a week to Radio Cairo and 53% to the Voice of the Arabs; at least once a week 73% listened to the BBC, 62% to Radio Kuwait, and 37% to the Voice of America. Radio Monte Carlo (RMC) is apparently the most popular among the commercial radio stations that can be received in Saudi Arabia, but Jordan (HBS), Egypt (Middle East Program), and the Bahrain Commercial service are also well liked (Pan Arab Computer Center 1978, pp. 1–6; "Audience, Penetration and Listenership" 1979, pp. 1–10). The government seems to be aware of the popularity of Radio Monte Carlo: during the fighting that followed the November 1979 Mecca Mosque incident, the government jammed RMC, which was reporting the incident more thoroughly than were the Saudi Arabian radio services. It took several weeks and a considerable amount of work by RMC officials in Saudi Arabia to get the government to cease jamming (Regnier 1980).

The kingdom faces, in the 1980s, the difficult problem of coping with an accelerating demand for appropriate programming. But the future of radio and television broadcasting in Saudi Arabia depends on many factors, including the stability of the present government, the future level of oil incomes, and the kingdom's position internationally and within the Arab world. By 1985, the country will have completed the installation of the most extensive system of radio and television transmitters in the Arab world; added studio space will allow the production of as much locally produced radio and television programming as the government deems appropriate. The proposed second television channel will allow a choice of programming for those viewers who do not have access to alternatives from other countries: that additional service could also be the opportunity for the Ministries of Information and Education to cooperate on educational broadcasting, particularly instructional programming designed to help alleviate the kingdom's lack of qualified native teachers.

But, the country's development has been so rapid since 1965 that the government has not been able to install within the Ministry of Information a cadre of skilled administrators able to establish, and then effect, a consistent broadcasting policy. Most particularly, the government has not agreed on the manner in which it will present itself to its own citizens, to the Arab world, or to the rest of the world. The government's practice has always been to react to events, usually after a period of silence during which rumors abound: the information apparatus of the kingdom must then act to attenuate the rumors and minimize the incident or situation that started them. This procedure may be culturally Arab in nature, but the government appears to be interested in making changes in it, in light of its present position in the international political and economic community.

The event that caused leaders to re-think their way of reacting to events was the November 1979 Mecca Mosque incident: though Saudi reporting on it was ultimately extensive, the limited amount of information available from the government media during its course—not to mention the jamming of Radio Monte Carlo—gave rise to speculation among western and Arab countries that it was actually part of a larger plot to change the form of government in the kingdom. Saudi leaders admit that some of the speculation could have been avoided or negated if the government had itself provided more information about the situation from the beginning, not waiting to react to external comment on the state of affairs. In an interview published in a London-based Arabic-language magazine, *Al-Hawadith*, Crown Prince and Deputy Prime Minister Fahd was to admit that Saudi Arabia had not then had an information philosophy, adding that clearly the country should "facilitate the task of the [foreign] press instead of neglecting to put the facts to it" (Al-Lawzi 1980). The government realizes, then, that it must be more aggressive and prompt in providing information about internal matters. An example of such a possible change in the previous policy is the manner in which the media handled the Saudi Arabian Airlines jumbo jet disaster at Riyadh airport in August 1980. Immediately after the catastrophe, the state radio and news service released information about its extent and speculated about the cause of the fire, which killed over 300 people. Film of the burning plane taken by Saudi Arabian television was fed by satellite to all interested television organizations—and quickly appeared on American network television news.

The acquisition of the broadcasting infrastructure has been the easy, albeit expensive, part of the establishment of a comprehensive Saudi Arabian radio and television system. More difficult to achieve will be lasting, practical agreement on the way in which that nation's broadcasting facilities will be used.

3.5 Bahrain

Bahrain, eight islands situated about 15 miles off the coast of Saudi Arabia in the Arabian Gulf, is the smallest Arab country. Approximately one-quarter million people live within its 231 square miles. Bahrain Island is the largest island, and it is here that the capital, Manama, is located. In the 1500s, the Portugese established a presence on the islands, but the British and the Khalifa family have influenced the country in more recent times. Great Britain became responsible for Bahrain's protection in 1861, having established a relationship that lasted over 100 years. Following the 1968 British decision to leave the Gulf area, Bahrain declared its independence in

1971. For a period of time Bahrain discussed with Qatar and the United Arab Emirates the possibility of forming a federation, but this did not come about. In 1973 a constitution was promulgated that established the country as a constitutional monarchy, with Emir Al-Khalifa as the head of state. The nation is ruled by an administrative body comprised of the heads of various departments and ministries.

Oil was discovered in Bahrain in 1932, but production has steadily declined and the economy increasingly depends on the service industries that support the petroleum exports of neighboring countries. During the 1970s, the country became an important tourist center in the Gulf—an area where western and Arab residents of the more conservative countries, most notably Saudi Arabia, could come to relax, to enjoy live entertainment imported from Europe and Asia, and to enjoy an alcoholic beverage. By the mid-1980s, Bahrain will be connected to the Arabian peninsula by a causeway financed largely by Saudi Arabia. This project will make the country more accessible and will increase the tourist business from Saudi Arabia.

Lacking the funds to do otherwise, Bahrain started broadcasting on a small scale in 1955. The island group has not felt the need to use the broadcast media to make its presence felt outside its boundaries. With a small, concentrated population, the country had no internal communication problems that might have motivated a large investment in broadcasting.

3.5.1 Radio

In 1955, the Bahrain government started an Arabic-language radio station on Bahrain Island, which provided limited news, music, and dramatic entertainment. The station gradually increased the hours of transmission, up to 14 hours per day by 1980. The studios are still at the original site near the capital, Manama, although they were refurbished and new equipment was added in 1972 (Suliman 1980). The 20-kilowatt medium-wave station can be heard in neighboring Gulf states, but its power does not compare with that of stations in the area that have joined the race to acquire superpower transmitters. This situation apparently reflects the government's lack of interest in competing with regional Arabic-language stations and its contentment with providing an essentially local service. The one national Arabic service provides various kinds of programming similar to those that most other Arab countries provide on a Main Program.

In 1977 the Ministry of Information, which operated all broadcast media, started an English-language radio service. There appears to be more interest in fostering this radio service than the Arabic one. Because English is widely spoken in Bahrain, it was believed that a commercial English-language service would be popular on the islands and in other Gulf states that could receive the signal. Furthermore, income derived from such a station would help finance activities of the Ministry of Information. The service, known as Radio Bahrain, operates daily from 0600 to midnight on both FM and mediumwave. The basic format is similar to that of a popular United States music station. Disc jockeys (DJs) host blocks of time, featuring popular music almost exclusively. News is regularly scheduled and throughout the day there are short features about sports, books, cinemas, etc. Most of the personnel consists of housewives who have been trained at the station—native English speakers who are married to expatriate Britons or Bahrain nationals. The other employees are the DJs, most of them male, who came to the country from Great Britain to work as disco DJs and who were trained locally to work at the more lucrative job of announcing for Radio Bahrain (Suliman 1980). The most expensive air time is during the popular "Radio Bahrain Top 20" program (Radio Bahrain Commercial Rate Card No. 5). The service broadcasts commercials for local businesses, including hotels, restaurants, and clubs, and in this respect serves as a type of promotional voice for the tourist activities that many people from other countries find attractive. International companies are attracted to this service primarily because of the potentially large audience in Saudi Arabia's Eastern Province, only a few miles away. Because of the neighboring Saudi market and the fact that Saudi Arabian broadcasting does not permit commercials, products such as small home appliances, cold drinks, food products, and automobiles are advertised on Radio Bahrain. Of course, the main audience of the station consists of those who speak English, and in this respect the audience is quite different from and smaller than that of commercial Arabic services in the area: in the McCann and PACC surveys, Radio Bahrain ranked consistently behind Radio Monte Carlo and Egypt's Middle East Radio (Pan Arab Computer Center 1978, pp. 1–6; "Audience, Penetration and Listenership" 1979, pp. 1–10). Probably the main competitor of Radio Bahrain is ARAMCO's popular music service that provides similar music without commercials.

3.5.2 Television

In several respects the introduction of television in Bahrain is more interesting than radio, although the service now operates in a manner similar to the English-language service. The activities of the American company RTV International have been mentioned previously in this study with regard to the introduction of television in Jordan. (See 2.5.1.) RTV International also attempted to start a commercial radio station to broadcast to the Arab world from Cyprus, and tried to bid on an operations and maintenance contract in Saudi Arabia. In 1972, RTV International signed a contract with the Bahrain government giving the company a concession to operate a color commercial television service (Hamilton 1972). A small studio was completed in 1973 and telecasts, using the 625-line system, started the same year. Viewers in Bahrain and Saudi Arabia were apparently enthusiastic about the station at first because it provided an interesting alternative to the then monochrome ARAMCO 525-line service and the Saudi Arabian national channel. The color signal was clearly an advantage. Initially, advertisers were attracted to the service because of the audience in the Saudi Arabian Eastern Province. During the initial two years of operation, most programming was imported from the United States, Great Britain, and Egypt. Little local production outside of news and interviews was done because of the limited studio space and equipment. RTV had started the station with as little money as possible and much of the equipment first used was not of broadcast quality—U-Matic machines used without timebase correctors, and 8mm film chains. Apparently acceptable by local standards, the signal was not of broadcast quality at first. Moreover, construction of a new building and purchase of associated equipment to increase local programming and improve the quality of the broadcast signal led RTV into financial difficulties. This situation, coupled with Bahrain's desire to have its own television service rather than one operated by an American company with rumored CIA connections, motivated the Ministry of Information to assume operation of the station in 1976. The original studios now house Radio Bahrain. The Ministry of Information is expanding the building that houses the new television studios. This will provide larger studios for Radio Bahrain and new studios for the Arabic service, which will move from its old location when the project is completed.

Bahrain television has continued the commercial orientation started by RTV International. Relatively little local advertising is done and most commercials feature the kinds of products promoted on other television stations in the area. Bahrain is in an advantageous position because of its proximity to the Saudi Arabian market: the advertisements are often for the kinds of luxury items and consumer goods purchased in Saudi Arabia more frequently than in Bahrain itself. The importance of Saudi Arabia to the commercial success of the station is evident from advertisements that Bahrain television places in newspapers that serve the Gulf states. Usually appearing on the same page as the radio and television program listings, they remind readers to view the station—"Bahrain Television: Best in News and Entertainment"—and seek to attract advertisers:

Click! TV. It's an appeal to the senses. Showing, telling, selling. Presenting your product story to over 400,000 households in Bahrain, Eastern Province of Saudi Arabia, Qatar and U.A.E. Click! Advantage Two: TV has your audience captive. Talking to them in their homes, in a relaxed mood. Switch to Bahrain TV. It's quite clearly the most powerful medium of today. And tomorrow. [*Gulf Daily News* 1979, p. 6]

Bahrain television operates for about 52 hours per week: daily from 1700 to about midnight and, on Thursday and Friday, from 1600 and 1500 hours respectively. Programming consists of limited local production; imported Arabic serials from Egypt, Dubai, and Jordan; and American and British series subtitled in Arabic. There are two daily newscasts, in Arabic at 2000

Figure 4. Schedule of Bahraini Television Programs

Saturday

1700 Koran
1710 Religious Talks
1715 Program Preview
1720 Cartoons and Children's Program
1830 "Fire House"
1900 Daily Arabic Series
2000 Arabic News
2030 "Duchess of Duke Street"
2130 English News
2145 Tomorrow's Programs
2150 Arabic Weekly Series
2250 Local Program

Sunday

1700 Koran
1710 Religious Talks
1715 Program Preview
1720 Cartoons and Children's Program
1900 Daily Arabic Series
2000 Arabic News
2030 Wrestling
2130 English News
2145 Tomorrow's Programs
2150 Arabic Musical Program

Monday

1700 Koran
1710 Religious Talks
1715 Program Preview
1720 Cartoons and Children's Program
1900 Daily Arabic Series
2000 Arabic News
2030 Musical Show
2130 English News
2145 Tomorrow's Programs
2150 Local Program
2240 "Rush"

Tuesday

1700 Koran
1710 Religious Talks
1715 Program Preview
1720 Cartoons and Children's Program
1900 Daily Arabic Series
2000 Arabic News
2030 Local Program
2130 English News
2145 Tomorrow's Programs
2150 English Film: "Drumbeat"

Wednesday

1700 Koran
1710 Religious Talks
1715 Program Preview
1720 Cartoons and Children's Program
1830 "Pretenders"
1900 Daily Arabic Series
2000 Arabic News
2030 "Executive Suite"
2130 English News
2145 Tomorrow's Programs
2150 Local Musical Program
2240 "Baretta"

Thursday

1600 Koran
1610 Program Preview
1615 Cartoons
1645 German Soccer
1730 Children's Program
1800 "It's About Time"
1900 Daily Arabic Series
2000 Arabic News
2030 "Little House on the Prairie"
2130 English News
2145 Tomorrow's Programs
2150 "Dallas"
2240 Arabic Film

Friday

1500 Koran
1510 Program Preview
1515 Cartoons
1530 Children's Film
1630 Arabic Film
1800 "Circus"

Friday (continued)

1900 "Tarzan"
2000 Arabic News
2030 Local Program
2130 English News
2145 Tomorrow's Programs
2150 English Film: "Dr. Cook's Garden"

SOURCE: *Gulf Mirror* 1980b, p. 16.

and in English at 2130. Bahrain news is furnished for the most part by the state news agency; international news comes from the major wire services and EBU satellite news feed. Figure 4 gives the television schedule for one week in January 1980.

To a large extent, the broadcast media in Bahrain have been organized by the government to reflect the basic economic orientation of the country: to attract people to the tourist-associated industries on the islands and to gain income from the petroleum-rich neighbors. The commercial radio and television services are economically sound largely because of the Saudi Arabian market that attracts advertisers to Bahrain media.

The country probably will not become a major broadcasting force in the Arabian Gulf because it lacks the funds for the extensive facilities it would take to gain this status. The greatest potential for expansion lies in the production of television series that can be sold to other Arab countries. The Bahrain television organization already is active in program taping, but it has not been as active as Dubai or Jordan. In order to be competitive, a considerable investment in studios and equipment will be necessary, in addition to more aggressive and creative management and promotion.

3.6 Qatar

The state of Qatar contains some 100,000 inhabitants within its 4,250 square miles. Qatar is actually a peninsula that protrudes about 100 miles into the Arabian Gulf; it is bounded to the southwest by Saudi Arabia and by Abu Dhabi, which is part of the United Arab Emirates.

The Ottomans occupied the area for four decades until World War I. In 1915, Great Britain recognized as rulers the Al-Thani family, with whom it signed a treaty that stipulated that Great Britain would handle external political affairs for the country. Petroleum was discovered in small amounts in the 1940s. Since then, oil production has increased steadily with the discovery of new oil fields—many offshore. The economy of the country is heavily dependent on oil income, and the traditional pearling and fishing industries have all but disappeared. There is some agricultural development; however, the basically desert country is not self-sufficient in the production of food. The oil industry has created the need for skilled labor and large numbers of people from Jordan, Lebanon, Iran, and Pakistan have settled in Doha, the capital.

After the British decision in the late 1960s to leave the Gulf area by 1971, Qatar and Bahrain discussed the possibility of forming a federation with the Trucial States—now the United Arab Emirates. However, this was not to be, and Qatar, like Bahrain, declared its independence in September 1971 and joined the United Nations. The country, now an important oil exporter, is an independent Sheikhdom with a constitution that provides for a con-

sultative assembly. The ruler is a member of the Al-Thani family. Culturally, Qatar is as conservative as Saudi Arabia because it has been influenced
by Wahhabi religious doctrine.

3.6.1 Radio

Two major developments motivated Qatar to begin a radio broadcasting
service: the announcement that the British were leaving the area, and
increased income from oil. The service was inaugurated on 25 June 1968,
with five hours of Arabic programming per day from a 10-kilowatt medium-
wave transmitter. Since then there has been a steady increase in the number
of transmitters, radio services, and studio facilities. Six months after the
initial Arabic service began, the medium-wave transmission power had
increased to 50 kilowatts and in 1969 to 100 kilowatts (Said n.d., p. 1).
Qatari nationals hold responsible positions in the Ministry of Information,
under which the broadcast media function; however, much of the program
planning and production and virtually all of the technical operation and
maintenance is done by nationals of other countries.

After the introduction of radio in the late 1960s, and more earnestly after
independence in 1972, the government decided to use the electronic media
in order to make its presence felt in the Gulf area. Unlike its less affluent
island neighbor, Bahrain, Qatar had the funds to support a major broadcast
facility.

The following describes the radio service in 1980:

Arabic Programs. The main Arabic service is broadcast for 18¼ hours
per day, from 0545 to 2400. Similar to the various main radio programs of
other Arab world countries, the daily schedule includes blocks of news,
music, drama, government announcements, and educational features. This
program is broadcast by two 750-kilowatt medium-wave transmitters on 954
kHz. The superpower station can be heard clearly throughout the Gulf area,
particularly at night. This service is also broadcast by means of a 100-
kilowatt short-wave transmitter operating in the 31 meter band. There is a
second Arabic program that is broadcast by two low-power medium-wave
transmitters, primarily for residents within the country. Known as the
Colloquial Service, the two-hour, 1600 to 1800, daily program features
programming in a local dialect, including some of the local folklore music
that has been recorded.

Urdu Program. A one-hour daily program in Urdu is broadcast locally
on mediumwave for Pakistani residents.

English Services. Aside from the main Arabic program, the Qatari
English Services are the most extensive. There are two separate transmissions, FM and mediumwave. The FM program is continuous automated
easy listening music. From 0600 to 2400 hours the medium-wave service
operates. Two transmitters are used to broadcast the program, one for the
morning and one for the afternoon/evening transmission. This program

features a great deal of western popular music within a DJ format. There are regularly scheduled segments for classical, country and western, and music requested by listeners (*Gulf Mirror* 1980b, p. 17). Newscasts and some drama and short features about beauty, health, and education are broadcast. Some of the informational programs are produced locally by Ministry of Information employees and some are imported, mostly from Great Britain. Between 2000 and 2400 hours, music from the automated FM music service is simulcast. In 1980, the evening automated segment of the English Service on FM was expanded into a separate program that provides continuous and essentially uninterrupted easy listening music.

Qatar is in the unusual position of having excess transmitter capacity, in that many of the low-power but still functional facilities have been replaced with new, high-power transmitters. A new Doha radio studio complex is scheduled to be completed in 1982. The additional studio space will be utilized, according to the plan, to add separate religious and educational radio services (Said n.d., pp. 3–4). These will be broadcast on existing, but currently unused, facilities.

3.6.2 Television

Qatar started television on 15 August 1970 with a daily monochrome three- to four-hour transmission (*T.V. in the Gulf States* 1979, p. 84; Ibrahim 1980). This first television effort was intended to be temporary, as it provided a period of time to train local staff and to hire nationals of other Arab countries, upon whom the system heavily relies. During this initial introductory stage of television, new color facilities were being readied. A new three-studio complex housing American and European equipment was completed in late 1973, and on 1 July 1974 Emir Sheikh Al-Thani opened the PAL color service ("State of Qatar: Qatar T.V." n.d., p. 8). Between this official opening date for color television in Qatar and the beginning of the 1980 program schedule, many important changes have taken place. Those in charge of scheduling appear to have finalized a sequence of programs that balances imported western and Arab productions with some local production of entertainment and information programs.

The one national program is telecast on two channels, 9 and 11, and provides complete national coverage. The program can also be seen year-round in Abu Dhabi, Bahrain, and the Dammam-Dhahran area of Saudi Arabia. During the summer months, the signal occasionally reaches Kuwait and areas of the United Arab Emirates. The television service averages 63 hours per week. Transmission time is increased during the summer months to include a four-hour 0900 to 1300 series of programs, presumably for the entertainment of school children who are at home during this time. On Friday, as is the practice in virtually all Arab world television systems, the transmission is extended. Qatar concentrates on programming for children on Friday mornings, featuring cartoons and "The Wonderful World of Disney."

The normal telecast day starts at 1600 with the Koran reading, a religious discussion, and the daily television program review. From approxmately 1630 to 1730, cartoons and other programs for children are featured. The 1980 schedule features "Iftah ya Simsim," the Arabic "Sesame Street," from 1630 to 1700. From 1730 to 2030, there is a mixture of educational and informational programming and often a short religious dramatic series. At 2030 until 2045 the nightly Arabic newscast is presented. The news closely duplicates the established format for other Gulf state countries; news about the activities of the Emir and about Qatar itself are then followed by other Arab world news and international stories that rely heavily on EBU satellite feeds. Musical features and imported western and Arabic productions follow the news until 2200, when the nightly English news is telecast. This news is almost identical to the Arabic news in both format and content. Usually, Arabic and western entertainment programs are shown between 2015, when the English news ends, and the final newscast (usually headlines) at midnight. During this period, western programs such as "Paper Chase," "Roots," "Incredible Hulk," and "Centennial" have been shown (*Gulf Mirror* 1980b, p. 17).

Qatar television accepts commercials, most of which are for locally available products from Europe and Japan. They do so despite the fact that the majority of funds needed to operate the television system is provided by the government. There is no receiver license fee. Perhaps an obvious question is why a relatively wealthy country like Qatar permits advertising when that small amount of income is not needed. One answer is that the Ministry of Information, which controls television advertising, wants the television system to help communicate to its citizens that the country still embraces an essentially free-market economy—reasoning similar to that used in Kuwait. In addition, advertising helps the local merchant families, who are most likely to benefit from television commercials. Advertisements meet established standards before being accepted. No alcoholic beverages may be advertised, and there is a prohibition against comparative advertising, gambling, and products of a personal nature that may be offensive to a family audience. Commercials are clustered between programs and may not be shown adjacent to religious programs or political commentaries ("Advertising Rates and General Conditions Effective April 1, 1980" n.d., pp. 3–4). Fifteen-, thirty-, forty-five-, and sixty-second commercials are accepted, with a premium price charged for commercials adjacent to popular international sporting events.

As a relative latecomer to both radio and televison broadcasting in the Gulf area, Qatar has progressed fairly rapidly—particularly with the construction of radio and television transmitters and studios. Both broadcast media schedules are extensive for a small Arab country with a correspondingly small population. This situation necessitates the use of large numbers of nationals from other Arab countries in order to maintain and operate equipment and to provide some local programming.

3.7 United Arab Emirates

The 1968 decision by the British government to leave the Gulf area affected the collection of sheikhdoms known as the United Arab Emirates (U.A.E.) much the same as it did Bahrain and Qatar. On 1 December 1972 these entities—previously known as the Trucial States—ended their relationship with Great Britain; the U.A.E. was officially formed on 2 December, when six of the emirates, Abu Dhabi, Dubai, Sharjah, Ajman, Umm Al Quwain, and Fujeirah, declared themselves a federation. In 1972, another emirate, Ras Al Khaimah, joined the U.A.E. as the seventh member. Bahrain and Qatar, as has been noted, considered joining the federation but decided against it.

The British came to the area in the 1800s to stop the pirates who operated from the coastal areas; hence the original term Pirate Coast. British presence is still strong in the area and English is widely spoken.

About one-quarter million people live within the federation's 32,280 square miles. Saudi Arabia, Qatar, and Oman border on the U.A.E. The oil industry, centered in Abu Dhabi and Dubai, has necessitated the importation of skilled labor for petroleum operations. There are Arabs from other countries as well as Iranians, Pakistanis, and Indians, who work with the oil, oil service, and local businesses. The expatriate population exceeds the indigenous inhabitants.

The fact that the U.A.E. is a federation greatly complicates government administration, including control of the electronic media. Abu Dhabi is the official capital and is the largest emirate with the most oil. Dubai, the traditional capital of commerce, is the second largest emirate, which has some oil. The remaining five emirates are not oil-rich, but they vie for a share of the national wealth. The country embraces a monarchical form of government. The rulers of the seven emirates comprise the Supreme Council of the U.A.E., of which the ruler of Abu Dhabi is the president and the ruler of Dubai vice president. Oil was not commercially available until the early 1960s; since then money from this industry has permitted rapid development and some drastic cultural changes. In Abu Dhabi it is not unusual to see camels tethered near new Mercedes automobiles; in Dubai there is an ice rink where bedouin in traditional dress may be seen skating.

The result of the federation system is that broadcasting in the U.A.E. is unique in the Gulf states. A radio and television system is operated by the federal government. In addition, broadcasting is done by individual emirates.

3.7.1 Radio

British forces first brought radio broadcasting to the area by establishing a station for their own use in Sharjah. Abu Dhabi was the first emirate to introduce Arabic radio broadcasting when limited programming started in 1969. After the creation of the U.A.E., this facility became the headquarters for the official federal Arabic radio service. Upon independence, the service changed its identification from "Abu Dhabi Radio" to "United Arab Emirates Radio from Abu Dhabi" (Mubarak 1980). After 1971, new modern studios were added to the complex. The transmission power of this station was increased with the addition of a superpower (1500-kilowatt) transmitter. Other lower-power facilities rebroadcast the main (and only) national service throughout the federation. One short-wave transmitter is used to reach the Arab world. The linking of these additional transmitters was made possible when the national telecommunications network was completed. The service, which is the usual mixture of blocks of news, drama, music, and informational programs, operates for 19½ hours per day.

The second radio service operated by the federal government is a foreign language program, originating from Abu Dhabi and heard widely, but not as extensively throughout the federation as the Arabic program. English, one of the three foreign languages broadcast, is featured from 1300 to 1600 hours over a single medium-wave transmitter. Music is an important part of the daily offering on mediumwave, but a good deal of informational programming is also provided. Besides news and commentary, daily programs inform residents and visitors about activities, receptions, and other social events. Originally, several full-time British contract employees were brought to Abu Dhabi specifically to work with the English service. However, as of January 1980, only part-time employees were working with the English section. Between 1600 and 1700 there is an hour of French programming, followed from 1700 to 2000 by Urdu, a language spoken by Pakistani workers in the area. Additional English programming is broadcast from an FM transmitter between 1600 and 1900 (Hellyer 1980). The three-hour nightly program consists of music played by a disc jockey who solicits requests by mail and by phone. This service is staffed by many of the same part-time people as the medium-wave service. The setting of the FM studio and transmitter is unique in the Arab world. The Ministry of Information radio and television compound, like the others in the Arab world, is heavily guarded by the national armed forces and one needs to have permission to enter this complex. By contrast, the FM facilities are housed in the same building as the television transmitter and are completely unguarded.

3.7.2. Television

The first transmissions were started under the auspices of the Abu Dhabi sheikhdom as a monochrome service on 6 August 1969, prior to the formation of the federation. When Abu Dhabi became the U.A.E. capital, the system became the national television channel, owned and operated by the federal government in a manner almost identical to that of radio. The Abu Dhabi broadcasting complex was expanded after 1971 and new PAL color equipment was installed, enabling color television to start on 4 January 1974 (*T.V. in the Gulf States* 1979, p. 18).

Because of a serious shortage of skilled people in the U.A.E., television had to rely heavily on outsiders to start and continue to operate the system. Nationals are in charge of various departments of the Ministry of Information that supervise television, but over half of the planning and production staff and virtually all technical staff are from Jordan, the Sudan, Egypt, and Lebanon. The first two successive directors of television were from Jordan and the Sudan. The result—not at all unique to the U.A.E.—is that the television service is not entirely programmed with the local culture in mind. There is also little local production aside from news and other informational programming, the majority coming from other countries in the Arab world and the west.

The daily television schedule starts at 1700 and continues until midnight. After the traditional opening and Koran reading there is a period of programming for children—cartoons and "Iftah ya Simsim," the Arabic "Sesame Street." Then comes an Arabic feature, often a program in a 13-part series, and a locally produced informational program. At 2100, the main Arabic daily news is telecast. It usually includes stories about the activities of the U.A.E. president and vice president and items about the emirates. Arab world news and international items from the EBU satellite feed follow. After the news, a locally produced film or video tape feature about some aspect of the U.A.E. is shown. At 2230, the news is presented in English. This is almost always identical to what was shown one and one-half hours earlier on the Arabic news and is read by two native English speakers, one of whom is usually a part-time employee of the radio service. The closing program is an entertainment feature, either in Arabic or in English.

Using a series of repeater television transmitters, the federal television service reaches about 80% of the population. The national microwave telecommunications system provides network interconnection.

There is competition for viewers in the U.A.E. from other television services within the federation, in addition to signals that can be received from Oman, Saudi Arabia, and Qatar. The federal Ministry of Information is aware that its service has a responsibility to uphold and promote the national interests of the entire federation. Thus, entertainment programming is not emphasized; informational and cultural programming, within personnel and budgetary limitations, must take priority. The broadcast media have problems similar to those faced by other branches of the Ministry of Information. The federal government, in an attempt to include personnel from all seven emirates, has been forced to appoint people who are not educationally or administratively qualified. In addition, these employees from other emirates, though working in Abu Dhabi, continue to maintain their residences in the other emirates. Therefore travel time between home and job often means loss of two days per week. The four-day work week for commuters adds to the responsibilities of the nationals of other countries who, in reality, do most of the planning and actual work. All federation members realize that a national radio and television service plays a necessary role in the unification of the country. However, individual emirates have the right to broadcast; and in one emirate, Dubai, commercial radio and television programming is a major business.

3.7.3 Dubai and the Federation

The creation of the federation of emirates in 1971 did not remove the right of members to undertake certain activities that they believe important to their own development. Indeed, there is competition among the seven for the more visible aspects of development such as airports, hotels, schools, etc. Dubai, though not oil-rich, has been a thriving commercial and banking capital since the 1950s. The city itself is a blend of old and new buildings and modern western-owned hotels that cater to the international business traveler. Dubai probably has more international bank branches per capita than any other city in the world. The economic health of this city is due in large measure to the U.A.E. vice president and local ruler, Sheikh Rashid, who is an aggressive businessman. One of his advisors, Riad Shuabi, a Palestinian, was the main force behind the initial introduction of radio and television as well as its later expansion into what is now the most aggressive production and marketing organization for Arabic television programming outside of Egypt. Shuabi has increased his financial holdings in both print and electronic media, as detailed below (see 3.7.4), to include an interest in advertising and in *Eight Days*, a London-based English-language magazine that specializes in the Arab world.

3.7.4 Dubai Television and Radio

Dubai television started broadcasting a commercial monochrome service from Dubai in 1972 (Robertson 1980). Essentially operated during the evening hours, the station showed imported Arabic and western entertainment programs that would attract a large audience for those who were interested in advertising on the station. Relatively little local production was done at first, except for limited news broadcasts. This Channel 2 service was popular among the large expatriate population in Dubai and Abu Dhabi as well as with the local population. Advertisers were attracted to the service, which seemed to be a natural part of the thriving commercial activity in Dubai. With the success of Channel 2, plans were made for a more extensive service, which by the late 1970s had produced two separate commercial channels—one Arabic and one English—a commercial FM radio service, and a major television production and marketing company. The contrast between the radio and television services in Dubai and Abu Dhabi is striking, primarily because of the completely different orientations of the two services. While the Abu Dhabi-based national service programs respond to the needs of all seven emirates, Dubai concentrates on commercially oriented broadcasting. The Dubai radio and television services rely exclusively on expatriates. Even some management positions are held by British citizens. The television facilities are superbly maintained and among the most elaborate and modern in the Arab world.

Program One. Program One is a PAL color station intended mostly for Arabic speakers. The signal does not reach all of the country because it is essentially a regional service that is operated by a company controlled by Sheikh Rashid—in effect representing the Dubai government. The signal is received reliably in Abu Dhabi, Sharjah, and Umm Al Quwain on one of three channels, 10, 2, and 33. The service operates daily from 1700 to midnight and from 1500 to midnight on Friday. There is some limited local programming in the form of news, interviews, and religious programs. Yet, the majority of the schedule is a mixture of imported subtitled older western programs and relatively new Arabic features. Examples of the imported programs seen in 1980 are "Daktari," "Little Lulu," "Ironside," "Batman," and various sports programs such as wrestling and soccer. Occasionally, the facilities of the two services are linked to transmit the same program, such as a popular western film ("Dubai Radio and Colour Television Program Schedule" 1980, p. 2). Program One, however, caters almost exclusively to speakers of Arabic, and most of the Arabic programming that is telecast is produced in the adjoining Dubai production center.

Program Two. In June 1978, a second television service started. The audience for this English-language color channel is primarily the expatriate population and western-oriented local residents. The station operates daily from 1800 to midnight, except on Friday, when the transmission starts one hour earlier. The only programming that originates live from the television center is the news—a 10-minute bulletin of local news at 2000 hours and a 20-minute newscast that features world news at 2200. Like the other channel, Program Two is heavily commercial.

Advertising may be purchased to run within the imported programs rather than between programs; however, there is a 50% surcharge for the former option ("Radio and Colour Television Advertising Rates Effective January, 1980" n.d.). Programs telecast during the first quarter of 1980 provide some idea about what a viewer may see on Channel 33: "Sons and Daughters," "Upstairs, Downstairs," "Bob Newhart," "Blind Ambition," "Flaxton Boys," "Charlie's Angels," "Happy Days," "Petrocelli," "Anna and the King," "The Bold Ones," "Night Gallery," "Green Hornet," "Sierra," "The Onedin Line," "Hart to Hart," "Grizzly Adams," "Police Woman," "Long John Silver," "Flying High," "Starsky and Hutch," "Barney Miller," "Fantasy Island," and "Star Trek" (Dubai Radio and Television Program Schedule" 1980, p. 2).

These two television services operate from separate control rooms and use one of two studios available for news and for other limited local informational programming. The Dubai radio and television complex also contains a new studio, "C," which is used exclusively for the taping of Arabic productions. Completed in December 1978, this facility constitutes the main production facility of the Arabian Gulf Production Company. The organization was created by Riad Shuabi to produce programming for Arab world television stations and to market productions from Dubai as well as those done in other Arab world studios. Only the main 1100 square meter studio in the Egyptian television complex is larger than studio "C." This Dubai studio was designed to allow 1050 square meters of studio floor space—intentionally 50 square meters more than the main BBC television studio in London. It is equipped with the latest television production, lighting, and video tape editing equipment. The studio is usually in continuous operation, with as many as four separate sets in the studio at one time. Often as one scene from a series is being taped, a different part of the studio is being readied for another scene from the series or for another series.

The economic conditions that motivated the creation of this business have been noted in the chapter on Egypt (see 2.1.12). There is a basic need for more Arab world productions among Middle Eastern television stations— particularly those in the Gulf states that can afford to pay the prices such productions demand. Also, the marketing efforts of the official Egyptian television sales organization have been hampered by that country's peace agreement with Israel and the resultant attempts by Arab countries to boycott Egyptian products and services. The Dubai production center is frequently rented by Egyptian directors and producers who bring Egyptian actors to the facility to make programs. Egyptian material is still the most popular in the Arab world; moreover, Egyptians who produce and appear in productions that are not taped in Egypt are not subject to the boycott. The Arabian Gulf Production Company has helped the Egyptian television organization sell programs taped in Egypt by editing that makes them appear to have been shot elsewhere. This highly professional facility includes an adjoining hotel and restaurant that caters exclusively to artists who come to Dubai to undertake television productions.

Dubai Radio—Arabic Service. The Dubai Radio—Arabic Service started in 1971 and operates between 0630 and 0030 hours the following morning. Using a staff that is comprised of over 50% Arab expatriates, the service is essentially music-oriented with some news and brief features (Ahmed 1980). The medium-wave signal can be heard throughout the United Arab Emirates and the commercial rates are slightly higher than those on the sister English radio service.

Dubai Radio—English Service. This service is broadcast exclusively on FM between 0630 and 0030 hours the next morning. Western popular music is played throughout the day by DJs who are native English speakers, and record requests are taken. Between 2100 and sign-off, continuous stereo music is played from prerecorded tapes.

The commercial success of the two television and the Arabic and English radio services in Dubai has made the U.A.E. an important broadcasting center. Even more significant is the impressive Dubai-based Arabian Gulf Production Company, which supplies facilities for the majority of taped syndicated Arabic productions sold in the Middle East. The success of the Dubai operations has given rise to imitators in at least one other emirate. There is a station in Ras Al Khaimah that operates like the first Dubai television station, with nightly transmission of imported western programs and no local production. It is, however, unlikely that Dubai's fellow federation members will become competitive threats. The smaller emirates to the south of Dubai do not have the economic base or the capability to organize production activities on the scale of what has been built in Dubai.

The unique political and economic nature of the U.A.E. has produced two distinct systems of radio and television broadcasting. One, operated by the national government headquartered in Abu Dhabi, features a noncommercial radio system and a commercial television system. The programming philosophy of both media is oriented toward the tastes and interests of the population of all seven emirates. The Dubai system, the second major one in the country, is run as a profit-making venture. Its programming is designed to attract a large audience for potential advertisers. The Arabian Gulf Production Company is a major production facility for the Arab countries and provides an example of how quickly the media have developed in the Arabian Gulf area.

3.8 Oman

Approximately one million people live in Oman, an independent sultanate of 82,000 square miles in the southeastern part of the Arabian Peninsula. Oman's neighbors are South Yemen, Saudi Arabia, and the United Arab Emirates. The small Musadam Peninsula, separated from the main portion of Oman by the U.A.E., is strategically located on the Strait of Hormuz, through which 40% of the world's oil passes.

Known until 1970 as Muscat and Oman, the country was one of the less developed in the Middle East until a 1970 coup, organized by Qaboos bin Said, resulted in the exile of his father to London. The country's development since 1970 has been impressive, particularly when one considers that progress has been accomplished largely without the oil income that most other Gulf states have. Oman does have some petroleum, but the amount only meets domestic needs, with little left over for export.

In the nineteenth century, Oman and Great Britain established a special relationship that, to some extent, still exists. British civil servants and military officers hold important positions as advisors at the request of the ruler, himself educated at Sandhurst. Qaboos believes that these and other western advisors are necesary to help organize the country in light of its location. South Yemen has been a particularly hostile neighbor: the Marxist government there supported a separatist movement that was militarily active for about ten years in the Dhofar area until successful Omani military efforts brought the fighting to a halt in 1975. Oman faces no significant internal threats: the military concentrates on security along the 1000-mile coastline and along the border with South Yemen.

The two major cities that constitute the capital area, Muscat and Matrah, are probably the most picturesque on the Arabian coastline. Old Portuguese ruins, a reminder of a former European influence, and modern buildings combine to create an unspoiled effect not found in neighboring countries.

3.8.1 Radio

The attitude of the government toward the broadcast media changed immediately after Qaboos bin Said took power. Prior to 1970, the country lacked many elements of modern development. The first medium-wave transmitter, built near Muscat, had a power of one kilowatt. Programming was limited to a few hours per day. In 1973 the power was increased to 100 kilowatts, and on 17 November 1974 a new Muscat medium-wave transmitter was inaugurated. In Salala, a 100-kilowatt medium-wave facility was built to serve the section of Oman near South Yemen. The national Arabic program is also transmitted from a short-wave transmitter, providing coverage to all parts of the country not already served by the medium-wave signals. English, the only other language used on Radio Oman, replaces Arabic daily from 1300 to 1500 hours (Siyabi 1980). Programming emphasizes news and information concerning government development policies and accomplishments. Most of the program and production personnel of the station are Omani, but Arabs from other countries help with equipment, transmitter operation, and maintenance. British advisors help with some of the program and technical planning. One British advisor is hired by the Omani government to work with the Minister of Information.

The ruler is concerned about the lack of radio coverage. As a result, plans are being made to increase the number of medium-wave transmitters (Ashworth 1980). Not only does the government want to reach all citizens with its development message, but it wants to provide a viable alternative to frequent hostile broadcasts from South Yemen on behalf of the Popular Front for the Liberation of Oman. South Yemeni transmitters have broadcast anti-Oman propaganda for years; activity increased in 1979, when

Oman was reported to be considering providing military facilities to the United States, which was seeking a stronger military presence in the Middle East.

Masirah, an island off the Omani coast in the Arabian Sea, is the location of the BBC's Eastern Relay medium- and short-wave transmitters that rebroadcast the Arabic, Hindi, Persian, Urdu, and English services originating in London. The Omani government does not use any of these transmitters.

3.8.2 Television

Television is considered by the government to be an important part of development. The medium's development has gone according to a plan whereby, first a station would become operational in the capital area, then a second station would be built in the Dhofar region, and finally the signal would be provided to major population areas by microwave and satellite. On 17 November 1974, the Muscat station went on the air with limited programming. For five years this station was operated and maintained by a German company that had a contract with the Ministry of Information. In 1975, a second and almost identical station became operational in Salala. This facility was operated under contract by a British company. In 1979, when both contracts expired, the government determined that it was capable of operating the stations itself with the help of Arabs from other countries. In late 1979 Oman hired about 20 Jordanian television engineers and technicians, who became responsible for both stations under the supervision of a few Europeans employed under the original contract. The distribution of the Omani televison channel is at least as widespread as Omani radio. This is accomplished by a leased satellite circuit, which distributes the signal to 11 ground stations and transmitters in addition to the main transmitter sites located at the two major stations ("Oman Colour Television: TV Transmitters in Operation" n.d.). The same distribution network makes it possible for the two stations, Muscat and Salala, to feed local news items and productions to each other.

The organization of televison is relatively streamlined. A director general of radio and televison reports to the Minister of Information. The Director General, in turn, appoints and is responsible for various engineering, administration, and programming heads. There is no license fee for broadcast receivers in Oman. The entire budget for these operations is supplied by the government. Advertising is not permitted.

3.8.3 Television Programming

The one Omani national PAL color program operates from 1700 to midnight daily, except on Friday, when programming starts at 1500 hours. Imported programs from the Arab world and the west constitute the bulk of the daily schedule. Oman has been supportive of the Egyptian peace treaty with Israel and the government therefore has not supported the Egyptian boycott. Hence, programming is purchased directly from the Egyptian Radio-Television Federation. Imported western programming is deemphasized and limited to serious documentaries and entertainment programs such as "Star Trek," "Project U.F.O.," "Kung Fu," "Chopper Squad," and "The Odd Couple" ("Oman Television Schedule: January 1 to March 31, 1980"). There are two daily 30-minute newscasts—Arabic at 2100 and English at 2200 hours. International news is taken almost exclusively from the daily EBU satellite news feeds.

Thirteen programs are scheduled for production each week, mostly from the Muscat studios. These include a family program, a quiz show, a musical variety program, a children's program, and various programs of an educational nature on, for example, health, traffic, and the country's history. Religious programs are also taped and telecast each week. When television was first started, there was concern among government officials that there would be opposition to the medium from some conservative elements, in a manner similar to fears of Saudi Arabian officials in the mid-1960s. However, the concerns of religious leaders were allayed by the government when they were told that television would be used to extend the religious message (Siyabi 1980).

There is almost no interest in making Oman a production center to compete with Dubai or some of the other countries that rent studio space for Arabic program production. The Ministry does not believe that it is a sound financial investment. In addition, for security reasons the government has been very hesitant to grant visas to Arabs from other countries. In the late 1970s, there was one exception. People were brought from other Arab countries to direct and act in a series of locally taped programs that dealt with Oman's history as a maritime country. Some of the programs were shown in other Arab countries, but this is the only effort of this kind that Omani television has undertaken.

3.8.4 The Audience

The official estimate of the number of television sets in Oman is 40,000 to 50,000. Set ownership is pervasive among upper-middle and above income brackets. In an effort to make television available to those who cannot afford a set, the government has placed large-screen color receivers in public places that are in range of one of the transmitters. Oman is the only Gulf state to undertake a program of placing sets in populated areas. The other countries apparently feel that citizens have the financial means to acquire a receiver. One of the public sets in Muscat is located at a major intersection on the harbor road. The large crowds attracted cause some traffic congestion at night.

Oman does not intend, in the short run, to become an important international radio broadcaster to the Arab world. The country's radio goal is to provide most citizens with the national service on mediumwave. This goal, when accomplished, will spread the Omani message of development and will offer a viable alternative to the hostile broadcasts from South Yemen, directed primarily toward the Dhofar area. Probably no television service in the Gulf states is more aware of the necessity of linking programming to the government's goals. Imported programs from the west are shown but not as extensively as in some other countries in the area. Local production of a nondramatic nature is accomplished with a small staff that achieves relatively high-quality results.

3.9 The Gulf States: Some Conclusions

Each Gulf state has developed a broadcasting system that it believes best suits its needs and that is different from the system of other states. However, there are many similarities among these countries in the way they program their electronic media. These similarities may also apply to the systems in other countries in the Arab world, but, for reasons noted at the beginning of this chapter, the Gulf countries have banded together to cooperate in areas where they feel common interests exist.

The following observations are offered after extensive on-site examination of the Gulf states systems.

Gulf television is entertainment oriented. Programs that are imported from the west or from other Arab countries or those that are taped locally are essentially for entertainment. Some programming of an educational/developmental nature is done for each country's television system; but music, drama, and other forms of entertainment dominate television. Probably the major reason for this situation is a lack of understanding on the part of programmers about how television might be used for purposes other than entertainment. Officials are often too busy keeping the stations running and coping with technical expansion to plan programming that will meet educational/developmental goals. This also applies to radio.

Another observation is that Arab expatriates are used extensively in the Gulf states. Jordanian engineers and technicians are employed extensively in all area countries except Iraq. Egyptian, Lebanese, and Sudanese radio and television personnel have been used in the technical operations of broadcasting. Arab expatriates are found in programming, commercial sales, news, and local production and administration. They are attracted by the high salaries in the Gulf states.

Also, the Gulf area has become a major production center. Due primarily to the Dubai television production studios, the Gulf states have attracted top Egyptian writers, directors, and actors, who have produced programs that rival those made in Egypt. Factors that have allowed this development include the move among Arab countries to boycott Egyptian-made television productions, the increased desire among Gulf countries for Arabic productions that they do not believe they can produce themselves, and the willingness of Egyptian and other artists to come to the Gulf, where high salaries and professional facilities permit a short production schedule. Abu Dhabi and Bahrain rent studios to those who wish to undertake productions, but these locations do not have the facilities or the atmosphere to rival the Dubai operation.

International radio and television broadcasting is pervasive. The climate and proximity of the Gulf states means that citizens of one country can and apparently do receive broadcasts from neighboring countries. Depending on the time of year, as many as seven different television channels can be seen in Saudi Arabia's Eastern Province, Bahrain, Qatar, and the U.A.E. Radio signals from these countries are receivable on mediumwave as well as on FM. Some countries such as Saudi Arabia have intentionally built stations that will reach other countries in order to extend influence, while other stations, such as the one in Bahrain, attempt to reach neighboring markets in order to make their service attractive to advertisers.

English-language programming and news are used extensively. Each Gulf state system broadcasts a daily television newscast in English. All countries in this region have radio services that broadcast domestically in English. Some states—Bahrain, Dubai, Qatar—operate full-time English services. Most of the program time on these services is devoted to music, specifically British and American popular music, including country and western. There are also imported television programs from the United States and Great Britain. Programmers believe that these programs are popular among viewers and are relatively inexpensive to show. Television programming in English tends to be used more heavily on systems that have two channels, such as in Kuwait and Dubai, and on systems that permit advertising, as is found in Qatar and Bahrain.

Still another similarity is that news items from outside the Arab world are alike. All systems in the Gulf area feature nightly television newscasts. There is usually one major newscast in addition to scheduled times when headlines are read. For international news, each country receives, tapes, and uses items supplied by the EBU daily satellite feeds. The second of the two daily feeds occurs about 2000 hours—depending on the local time in summer and winter. With little time before the Arabic news, news personnel view the feed as it is taped and note the stories that seem appropriate for use. The stories are used in order of taping as the tape is put on fast forward during the on-air transition provided by the newsreader. The effect is to create international newscasts that are similar and, in some cases, identical.

The video cassette markets in Kuwait, Bahrain, Saudi Arabia, Qatar, and the U.A.E. are thriving. There are sufficient numbers of people with both the financial means and the motivation to purchase equipment and to purchase or rent mostly pirated tapes of first-run films and television programs. Saudi Arabia sees the most activity of this kind in the Gulf area, and possibly in the world, because of the few entertainment choices available to people who do not live in the Eastern Province.

Beginning in the 1960s, some of the Gulf States began coordinating telecommunication, defense, banking, petroleum, and civil air transportation policies. One part of their overall attempt to promote communication and cooperation is their cooperative efforts in the broadcasting field. In the early 1970s, cooperation was encouraged within the framework of the Arab States Broadcasting Union for news and program exchanges (Boyd 1975a, pp. 311–20). Because of similar interests in the information field, the Gulf Ministers of Information started meeting to discuss ways in which cooperation in radio and television broadcasting could be increased. By the second ministers' conference in 1977, Gulfvision had been formed to promote news and programming among member states. Gulfvision is an organization to which all seven Gulf states belong. The wealthier states believe that cooperation is in their best interests, and countries such as Saudi Arabia, where Gulfvision is headquartered, subsidize membership of the less wealthy countries. These excerpts from the Gulf States Television Charter reflect some of the basic concerns of the member countries with respect to television programming standards:

One of the targets which the Gulf States Television endeavour to achieve is to maintain the local cultural characteristics as these are considered among the major tributaries of the Arab culture.

In all its programs the television service should maintain the moral and social values of conduct originating from the Islamic Faith, which are the corner stone of the spiritual, educational, and cultural basis of this region.

Obscene or vulgar expressions injurious to any public taste should under no circumstances be used. Any scene or term inviting degradation, nudity or provocating sexual instincts or vice should be deleted.

When selecting foreign programs it should be taken into consideration that these do not include any offense to the religious, social or cultural values of the viewers or any insult to their national or human feelings, or any embarrassment to the political authorities of the states.

Foreign programs based on provocation of sexual desires or violence, or causing fear or displaying violence in contradiction with common human values shall be excluded.

Care should be taken that the program shall not include anything which may lead in words or picture to teach the public new criminal methods which can be imitated even if the criminal and the crime are condemned at the end of the program.

Care should be taken when presenting foreign programs to the children or youth so that no specimens conflicting with their upbringing according to the society's objectives are presented. [*T.V. in the Gulf States* 1979, pp. 119–25]

Once per month, on a rotating basis, each Gulfvision member country tapes a program about its country. Copies are distributed to member states, which, in turn, attempt to telecast the program at a specified time and day. Other plans for cooperation have been discussed; however, the most tangible effort made by the Gulf states has been in the area of children's programming.

In 1976, the Kuwait-based Arabian Gulf States Joint Program Production Institution was formed. This organization is an outgrowth of the cooperative efforts among the Gulf states, with the exception of Oman ("Facts about Iftah Ya Simsim" n.d., p. 1; Al Yusuf 1980). The organization produces documentaries about the region, and dubs western cartoons into Arabic for the use of members and for sale to other Arab countries. This most ambitious effort has established a new standard for children's programming in the Arab world.

The idea for an Arabic "Sesame Street" appears to have originated with Abdulrahman Shobaili, a former director general of television in Saudi Arabi. Shobaili was impressed with the program while he was completing his graduate work in the United States. Consequently, he purchased the program to be shown without subtitles or dubbing in Saudi Arabia in 1972. The possibility of producing an Arabic version of the program was discussed in Riyadh, Saudi Arabia, with representatives of the Ford Foundation and Children's Television Workshop, which owns the rights to the program. Initial financial support was supplied by the Ford Foundation and the Kuwaiti Arab Fund for various linguistic studies. The result is a visually impressive and extremely popular 130-program series, which was taped in the modern Kuwait television production center. "Iftah Ya Simsim" was first telecast in all seven Gulf states in the fall of 1979 and is available for sale to other countries.

Before the series was taped, extensive research was done in several Arab countries after pilot programs had been made. Even before the pilots were planned a team of linguists attempted to devise a form of modern standard Arabic that would be acceptable in all Arab countries. The various educational goals of each program were finalized with a group of Arab educators and psychologists representing several regions of the Middle East. The final product has some obvious similarities to the American counterpart: the setting is Street No. 26, where various adults live and interact with children; there are some muppet characters; and Noaman, a cross between a camel and a bear, serves as the Arab Big Bird. All Gulf countries telecast the program between 1530 and 1830 hours, with somewhat predictable results. The production is so superior to the various children's programs done by individual stations that it has set a new standard for children's programming. As with the initial reaction to "Sesame Street" in the United States, some of the most ardent fans of the program are parents who watch it with their children. The reaction to the program in Saudi Arabia was so enthusiastic that the government suspended the production of locally produced programs for young children.

The program is not without its critics, however. Dr. Nawaf Adwan, who heads the Arab State Broadcasting Union Research Center in Baghdad,

Iraq, agrees that the program is visually exciting, but also observes that it tends to reinforce one of the main features of the traditional Arab systems of education—rote learning (Adwan 1980). The Arab countries outside the Gulf region have been hesitant to purchase the program for a variety of reasons. Egypt, a country that could possibly benefit most from televising the program, resisted purchasing it even though the Gulf Production Center arranged a special low price for the package. The Egyptians say, among other things, that they do not like the language. However, they are also concerned that "Iftah Ya Simsim" would reflect unfavorably on their children's programs. In addition they are not purchasing programs from countries that support the Egyptian boycott. Whatever the criticisms, the productions are the largest cooperative television effort in the Arab world. The fact that the shows were taped and are being shown in the Gulf states is an important achievement for states concerned about maintaining their unique cultures.

4   North Africa

4.1 Algeria, *by Michael Pilsworth*

Algeria lies on the coast of North Africa, between Morocco to the west and Tunisia and Libya to the east. Its vast land area (900,000 square miles) consists mainly of mountains and desert (87%). The population at the 1978 census was 18.25 million, increasing annually at a rate of 3.2% overall, though the rate is 6.5% in urban areas. Although only 10% of the land is cultivated, just under half the population is based in the agricultural sector, located mostly in the fertile northern coastal strip that extends 750 miles along the Mediterranean. The southern part of the country is hostile in terms of both climate and terrain. The Atlas range of mountains in the north acts as a barrier to radio and television signals, necessitating the use of medium-wave radio for national coverage and satellite distribution for television. The Saharan region is very sparsely populated, containing approximately one million people in an area twice the size of France. The official language is Arabic, but French still tends to dominate the business

Michael Pilsworth is a co-author (with Elihu Katz, Dov Shinar, and George Wedell) of *Broadcasting in the Third World* (Cambridge, Massachusetts: Harvard University Press, 1977). He has written widely on broadcasting policies in the Third World, and has worked as a consultant to the BBC on social research policy. He now writes on broadcasting policy issues in Great Britain and is currently working on a regular television program about the British televison industry, broadcast by London Weekend Television (LWT). The greater part of the research on which this section is based, and all of the field research, was conducted as part of the joint University of Manchester/Hebrew University of Jerusalem research project, The role of Broadcasting in National Development, which was supported by a grant from the Ford Foundation under the auspices of the International Institute of Communications. This section is a revised and up-dated version of the Case Study Report on Algeria originally written for the research project by Michael Pilsworth and George Wedell ("Algeria Case Study," [Manchester, England: Department of Adult Education, University of Manchester, 1974], unpub. internal report, 54 pp., litho.).

and administrative sectors. About 18% of the population speak a variety of Berber dialects, the most significant being Kabyle.

Since independence in 1962, Algeria has attempted to steer a middle course between the west and the countries with centrally managed economies. The constitution describes Algeria as a one-party Islamic socialist state. The party, the Front de la Libération Nationale (FLN), has been a battle ground for struggles between the left, oriented to Moscow, and the "moderates," oriented more toward the west. However, the situation is much more complex than a simple left/right dichotomy.

Although Algeria's oil reserves are not large, it has a huge amount of natural gas (12% of world reserves) and is also rich in iron ore and phosphates. Spending on oil and gas exploitation is planned at the level of $33 million in the next 20 years. Almost all commerce and industry is state-run by nationalized enterprises.

The emphasis of economic planning has now shifted from capital-intensive, export-oriented heavy industry toward light industry, rural development, infrastructure, and the preservation of the oil reserves. One million Algerians work abroad, and over one million are unemployed; Gross National Product per capita in 1976 was $990.

Broadcasting has been accorded a central role in Algeria's development plans, and the dominance of technocrats in the management of the country and in the civil service has assured the rapid technological expansion of both radio and television transmission and production facilities. However, broadcasting in Algeria has consistently fallen short of the aims set for it. The software component was neglected for many years; spending and training were concentrated in the technical sector, while the production sector was neglected. This problem and several others in broadcasting in Algeria today derive mainly from the colonial legacy, the struggle for independence, and the political power struggles within the ruling party.

4.1.1 Broadcasting during the Colonial Period

The French annexed Algiers in 1830 and the remainder of the country in 1842. Consistent with the established French colonial policy of *la mission civilisatrice* (civilizing mission), the main centers in the north were colonized and incorporated into France. From 1881, the three northern regions were regarded as an integral part of France, with the southern Saharan territories forming a separate area, known as French Sahara, under direct rule. With the massive influx of over one million French colonists into the fertile coastal strip, the French language and bureaucracy came to assert a hegemonic influence on the elite strata of the indigenous population. This was one of the most regretted aspects of French colonial rule. Long before independence was granted, much of the effort of the nationalist movements was expended on the encouragement of the use of Arabic. There was a long struggle against *maraboutism*[1] in the latter part of the nineteenth century, and one of the independence movements, Oulemas, based much of its work in the early part of the twentieth century on the spread of the Arabic language. For these reasons, language policies have marked both the colonial period in Algeria (when the French imposed their own language and culture in order to counter nationalist groups) and the postcolonial period (through the policy of *arabisation*).[2]

When radio broadcasting first began in Algeria in 1937, the French government initially designated it as a service for the one million French colonists. Production facilities were very limited and the majority of the programs were relayed directly from Paris. The network was called France Cinq, or the Fifth Channel. After World War II, local production facilities were expanded. Three studios were built, in Algiers, Oran, and Constantine. A local service, Emissions des Langues Arabe et Kabyle (ELAK), was introduced, though it is claimed that these broadcasts were designed to expedite a divide-and-rule policy, setting the interests of the various linguistic groups against one another. The coverage was limited. During the early 1950s, three radio channels were operational in French, Arabic, and Kabyle. Transmission facilities at this time included 100-kilowatt transmitters for the French and Arabic channels and a 20-kilowatt transmitter for the Kabyle service. These transmitters were located in Algiers. There were smaller transmitters (20 kilowatts) in Oran and Constantine. The incentive to increase the area covered by radio came with the commencement in 1954 of the armed rebellion against French colonial rule. By the end of the decade most of the populated areas in the north of the country were covered mainly using many small one-kilowatt transmitters.

The rebellion also provided the impetus for the establishment of television. The first transmissions began in 1956, two years after fighting began. The French broadcasting organization Radiodiffusion Télévision Française (RTF), installed transmitters in Algiers (50 watts), Blida (100 watts), Constantine (50 watts), and Oran (100 watts). At first, programs were imported from France and consisted solely of films or telerecordings that were shown by means of telecine machines. However, in 1958 RTF engineers introduced a tropospheric transmission system that enabled programs to be relayed directly from France. As television receivers were owned almost exclusively by the colonists, local production was very limited and was predominantly in French, with some news programs in Arabic and Kabyle.[3]

---

[1]The acceptance of a francophone version of Algerian culture.

[2]*Arabisation* is the French term used to denote the process of the reassertion of Algerian culture and language. In practical terms the policy had the effect of reducing the use of French in official business, and increasing the amount of Arabic translation. The education system was restructured and the tradional French-modelled institutions replaced.

[3]Until independence in 1962, the French government allowed only 15 minutes of local origination per day.

The armed rebellion led by the FLN lasted for over seven years and cost over one million Algerian lives. It was President de Gaulle, finally, who granted Algeria its independence on 3 July 1962 in the teeth of strong and militant opposition from many of the French settlers. By October 1963 all agricultural land held by foreigners had been expropriated, and by 1965 more than 80% of the French colonists had left Algeria. But those figures do not begin to reveal the full extent of the struggles that surrounded the granting of independence. The French withdrawal was almost total. The government ordered all its officials to leave the country and to remove all records, plans, and maps. The communications infrastructure was actually left intact by the departing government, but the colonists' secret terrorist organization, Organisation de l'Armée Secrète (OAS), blew up or burned down telephone exchanges, radio and television transmitters, power plants, libraries, bridges, factories, and stores in their attempts to prevent a peaceful transfer of power (Ottaway and Ottaway 1970, pp. 9–10). This physical damage to the communications infrastructure was compounded by the massive and abrupt departure of most of Algeria's professional and technical staff, who were predominantly French. Until 28 October 1962, broadcasting was still carried on by the French,[4] but the internal situation worsened considerably between July and October; and at the end of October RTF in Paris ordered all of its French staff in Algeria to withdraw immediately. Broadcasting virtually came to a halt (only one French engineer remained in the country) until January 1963, when an Algerian service was established.

4.1.2 Independence and the Establishment of Radiodiffusion Télévision Algérienne

The statutory position of Radiodiffusion Télévision Algérienne (RTA) was not defined until 1 August 1963, when a govenment decree defined RTA as being "under the authority of the Ministry of Information. It is a financially autonomous Public Authority, of a commercial and industrial character (*Journal Officiel 1963*). It is enormously significant, though perhaps not surprising, that the formal organizational status of RTA was virtually a carbon copy of the organizational status of the French broadcasting authority at that time, RTF. In 1959, RTF was defined officially as a "financially autonomus public authority, of commercial and industrial character, placed under the authority of the Ministry of Information."[5] Thus the French model of governmental control "at one remove" was translated to the newly independent nation's broadcasting system without any inquiry into possible alternative forms.[6] This perhaps gives some indication of the degree to which

---

[4]On 5 July 1962 a provisional executive (a Franco-Algerian caretaker administration) took over the running of the country.

[5]This formulation was not actually made statutory until 1964. See *ORTF '73* 1973, p. 25.

[6]One has only to compare Algeria's broadcasting system with that of, say, Nigeria (based on the British model) or Brazil (based on the U.S. model) to appreciate the enormous importance of

the French colonial system had implanted its values and assumptions within elite Algerian society. Moreover, the tight control that the Minister of Information was, according to the French model, allowed to retain over the system was thought to be suited to the uncertain conditions of Algeria following independence.

Thus from its inception RTA was subject to close ministerial control. The Director General and all other directors were to be appointed by ministerial decree, and the coordination of informational programs and artistic production fell under the jurisdiction of the Conseil Supérieure de la Radio Télévision, a body whose composition and functions were fixed by decree of the Minister of Information. Finance was controlled, as in France, by the Ministry of Finance. The Director General could not appoint or dismiss the directors of RTA, whose suitability for appointment seems to have been based primarily on political considerations. General matters of policy were determined by the Conseil, also under the authority of the Minister of Information.

During the period that followed, the development of the French broadcasting system was again mirrored in Algeria. The constitution of RTF had been redrafted in 1964 in an attempt to assuage critics, many of them on the staff, who complained about excessive government interference. An "Administrative Council" was interposed between the state and RTF (*Journal Officiel* 1964, p. 6552), which was renamed l'Office de la Radiodiffusion-Télévision Française (ORTF) in order to emphasize its supposed independence. In practice the Council acted as an intermediary body between government and television staff. The government controlled the body, and could give orders to or remove from office even the most senior staff of ORTF (Smith 1973, p. 162).

This structure was only slightly modified when it was translated to the Algerian broadcasting system. The Administrative Council of RTA was constituted under a 1967 government decree that set out the reorganization of RTA. The Council was composed of representatives from five ministries, a representative from the Presidential Council, three members of the Ministry of Information, a representative of the Algerian Press Service, a representative of RTA, and one other person selected on the basis of his interest in broadcasting. Although the formal changes in the structures of control of ORTF and RTA were almost identical, the Algerian system remained more overtly linked to the government than did the French system. The 16-member French council had eight members not formally connected with the government, whereas RTA's 13-member council had only three non-governmental members. In both cases, though, governmental control was exercised over the appointment of members.

---

colonial links or spheres of economic influence in the determination of approaches to broadcasting policies in developing countries.

The broadcasting legislation in Algeria in 1967 also slightly changed the nature of the relationship of RTA to the Minister of Information. Formerly under his *authority*, the new decree laid down that henceforth RTA would be placed under his *tutelage*.[7] This change in RTA's constitutional status actually preceded an identical change in France by one year, instead of following in its train. These changes in their constitutions gave both ORTF and RTA more freedom over the day-to-day management of their operations as well as more financial independence. Thus, in 1967 RTA became more independent at the managerial level, but government control over editorial policy was just as powerful as before.

The real reason for this constitutional alteration was the very poor performance of RTA in the production of local television programs. Apart from news and studio discussions, little local material had been produced, partly because of bureaucratic inertia (which the changes were designed to remedy), but also because of lack of financial and artistic resources. After the reorganization RTA attempted to reduce its heavy dependence on French television programs that had been provided until then by ORTF at nominal rates, and began to initiate its own buying and selling operations in the open market. Even so, the growth of local programming was terribly slow. In 1969 only 25% of RTA's television output was locally produced, most of it being information and news programs.

4.1.3 Boumédienne's Third World Policy and the Development of "Arabisation"

In the late 1960s, Algeria's President Boumédienne gradually placed himself at the forefront of the nonaligned movement. In speeches at regional and international meetings and at the United Nations, he outlined his new Third World Policy (Ottaway and Ottaway 1970, pp. 272–81), which was to have profound repercussions on RTA. This policy shift gave the initiative to the essentialists[8] in the polity who were suspicious of the French-speaking intellectual elite, and who were the spiritual heirs to the Oulemas movement.[9] They promulgated a policy of *arabisation*, the emphasis of Arabic and traditional Algerian culture and the concomitant diminution of French language and culture. In 1970, RTA was again reorganized in order

---

[7]The French word "tutelle" was used. This is not a precise term in translation. Tutelage means "guardianship" in legal terminology. However, colloquial uses of "tutelle" include "taking under one's wing," or even "under the thumb of" someone. The nearest English words are perhaps "control," "supervision," and "guidance."

[8]Clifford Geertz distinguishes between *essentialists,* who are oriented to traditional values, the family, and conservative traditions, and *epochalists,* who are oriented to secular values and modernity, occupational roles, and mobility. For example, in Geertz's terms, Khomeini in Iran is an essentialist, whereas the Shah of Iran was an epochalist. See Geertz 1975.

[9]The early independence movement that made the use of Arabic language a major feature of its campaign.

to expedite this policy, to facilitate a more rapid increase in domestic program production, and to ensure a more integrated approach to the programming for the different services. A circular from the Director General's office (Cheriet 1970) outlined the changes. There was a huge influx of Arabic-speaking managerial staff from the Ministry of Education who were charged with the task of reducing the dependence on imported programs, increasing the amount of local production that was in Arabic rather than French, and increasing the production of programs that would assist Algeria's ambitious development plan.[10]

The reorganization in 1970 certainly had the effect of dramatically increasing the proportion of locally produced programs, as well as the proportion of programs in Arabic. In the four years 1970–73, RTA domestic television production rose to 49% of the output, and the appointment to key positions of several Algerians who spoke little French and whose outlook was distinctly Arab resulted in increased arabization. The television audience, however, did not appreciate these efforts, partly because of the rather low production standards of the programs produced by the Ministry of Education staff, but partly also because they simply did not fully understand the Arabic used in the broadcasts: the French had so successfully acculturated Algeria's elite that many still spoke only French with fluency. At the end of 1975, some of the changes effected in the cause of arabization were reversed and less emphasis was placed on Arabic-language programs on television. There was a slight reduction in the number of locally produced programs, and films and plays in French were discouraged less. Current affairs programs were allowed to cover topics that could not have been mentioned previously. The news programs produced by Ministry of Information staff, however, remained tightly controlled.

The constitutional and policy changes reflected internal power struggles between the various factions within the leadership of the country throughout the 1960s and 1970s. In Algeria, as already noted, there is not only a gap between the intellectual elite and the mass of the population, but also a gap within the elite. On the one hand, there are those who are committed to non-alignment, Third World membership, Arabic culture and language, and Pan-Arabism; and, on the other, there are those who continue to regard the francophone cultural universe as their natural milieu. The latter look to Europe and the west as Algeria's natural partners, seek to establish the country internationally, and favor a technocratic and state-socialist approach to the management of the country. The role of the party, the FLN, is significant in this tension. The changes in 1970, when the policy of *arabisation* was first introduced, reflected an initiative by the left wing of the party, which tended to regard itself as the guardian of the principles of the

[10]Algeria has had three national plans, each to cover four years. The fourth is due to begin in 1982. The first plan, beginning in 1970, was quite successful, and GNP rose by about 10% per annum. Subsequent plans have not been so successful.

popular revolution. RTA, on the other hand, was staffed by French-speaking intellectuals who were oriented to Europe rather than to the Arab world.[11] There was a feeling among some of the FLN leadership that the service was pitched intellectually and culturally at too high a level. Even the use of Arabic can cause problems in this direction, as there are marked differences between "high" Arabic and "low" Arabic, and between modern and archaic forms. These tensions became more acute as television coverage expanded beyond the urban centers in the 1970s and particularly when the southern part of the country began to be covered. Since the early days of independence the party has been synonymous with the government. The takeover by the army and the technocrats in 1965, the establishment of administrative institutions, and the concomitant commitment to high technology and centralized planning has caused the party to come to play a more indirect role in the political life of the country. It increasingly acts at the local and regional level rather than intervening at the center. While the party retains its concern for the strategy and orientation of the country's development, the technocrats in the ministries have come to assert much more control. The consequences for broadcasting have been both to strengthen RTA's position and to assign more resources to the communications infrastructure.

4.1.4 Broadcasting and Development Priorities

Another feature of the legacy of French rule has been the bureaucratic legitimation of the ascendancy of the technocrats within the state's planning process. Broadcasting in Algeria has benefited greatly from the support of the Sécrétariat Au Plan,[12] which draws up the national development plans. The first ordered approach to national development, introduced in 1967, was a three-year plan, set within a broader range of development objectives for the seven calendar years 1967–73. The plan put major emphasis on both the electrification program and the development of transmission coverage for broadcasting, particularly television. A contract for a microwave link between all the main towns in the north was awarded to Télécommunications Radioélectriques et Téléphoniques (TRT) of Paris. The development of this system assured coverage by television of the whole of the northern coastal strip, and also linked Algeria by microwave to Tunisia and Morocco. This arrangement, known as Maghrebvision, is technical, given the linkage of the three North African (Maghreb) television systems, and cultural, given the exchanges and co-production of television programs. The TRT contract allocated under the plan also included the provision of a return TV link to France through a tropospheric relay system, thus ensuring two-way television transmission, rather than the one-way (France-Algeria) system that

---

[11]RTA is a full member of both the European Broadcasting union (EBU) and the Arab States Broadcasting Union (ASBU), a fact that reflects the dual loyalties of RTA staff.
[12]See Republic of Algeria 1970, 1974, 1978.

was operational until 1969. Production equipment was expanded and the planners were careful to purchase color-capable television equipment during the first plan period so that conversion to color during the second national plan could be achieved without undue difficulty.

The first four-year national plan (1970–73) allocated a major cultural role to broadcasting, and set out three objectives: the extension of the transmission network, the increase of Algerian program production, and the multiplication of links to facilitate interregional and international program exchanges.[13] On the transmission side, the plan provided for the investment of $50 million for the installation of a high-power medium-wave radio transmitter near Annaba and the uprating of existing transmitters to improve their overseas coverage; the extension of television coverage through the installation of new transmitters at Medea and Tindouf and the expansion of microwave transmitters; the installation of new television production equipment so as to increase the amount of locally originated material; and, finally, the expansion of the headquarters of RTA in Algiers by the addition of purpose-built television facilities.

The second four-year national plan (1974–77) saw the total expenditure of $15 billion, part of which was allocated to two major television developments: the installation of a satellite distribution system to ensure full national coverage, and the full colorization of the television system. The satellite used was INTELSAT IV (in fact, Algeria was the first user, leasing one transponder). Fourteen earth stations with 11-meter antennae were installed, one in each of the main centers of the districts of the two southern regions. Color television transmissions began on an experimental basis in 1973, and both the French-designed SECAM system and the German-designed PAL system were eveluted. This evaluation coincided with the improvement in east-west relations which allowed diplomatic relations for the first time with West Germany. In April 1974, Chancellor Willy Brandt visited Algeria, at a time when relations with France were strained due to continuing trade imbalances. A year later, Franco-Algerian relations had reached their nadir. In November of the same year, RTA announced that under the 1974–77 national plan they would introduce the German PAL color television system. This was a logical technical decision made possible by political developments. However, this decision in the television production sector did not affect decisions over the transmitter network that continued to favor French contractors, though the satellite and its ground stations were American supplied. Further American contracts are being

---

[13]By 1973, 49% of all programs were locally produced, but much of the imported material came from Egypt and the Lebanon, or via the Maghrebvision link from Morocco and Tunisia. The severing of diplomatic relations with Morocco (1976) and Egypt (1977)—over the Saharan war and the Sadat peace initiative respectively—has caused this supply of imported programs to be restricted.

planned, since the United States has replaced France as the main trading partner.

Under the plan the progress toward full colorization is proceeding rapidly. RTA announced in June 1980 that it had ordered four outside television broadcast vehicles valued at approximately $3.5 million and custom built to RTA's specification by the American company, RCA. Two of the vans, equipped for VTR operations, have already been placed in service for the colorization of existing TV channels in Algiers and in the surrounding provinces. Two additional vans, scheduled for delivery in late 1980, are to be employed for on-location assignments throughout the country.[14]

The national plan scheduled to begin in 1982 includes the provision of a second television channel on UHF that will be used for "educational and cultural" purposes, thereby releasing Channel 1 for more entertainment-oriented programming.

There has been considerable investment in television in Algeria, and it is certainly regarded as a cultural priority, receiving as it does 70% of the budget of the Ministry of Information and Culture. But in 1978 fully two-thirds of this budget was still being committed to transmission equipment, production equipment, capital expenditure, and technical training; only one-third was allotted for the production of programs. Although the Algerian planners have wisely given priority to the expansion of the transmission coverage and of production equipment, the programs themselves have been less well funded, with deleterious effects on quality. However, a new director general, appointed in 1978, has for the past two years sought to reverse this proportion, so as to increase both the quality and amount of local production. In the sector that was most poorly supplied by home-produced programs—telefilms, plays, and drama series—this policy has already produced results: while only 20 hours were locally produced in 1977, 48 hours were produced locally in 1978 and over 60 hours in 1979. The early emphasis on technology at the expense of programming, has now given way to an emphasis on production of local programs. Only when local production is adequate will permission be given for the second television channel.

4.1.5 Reaching the Audience

As already noted, both radio and television cover the whole of the territory, in theory at least. Almost all of the radio coverage is by medium-wave transmitters. The International Service, aimed primarily at Algerian migrant workers in Europe, uses a 1500-kilowatt long-wave transmitter broadcasting in both French and Arabic. Domestic services are mainly in Arabic (Home Service), but there is also a Kabyle network and a French network.

---

[14]The use of outside broadcast vehicles makes the production of authentically local cultural programs more attainable; the purchase is a sign of the new commitment to improving local production facilities and standards.

Television signals are distributed by microwave links and by satellite. Seven main transmitters in the north are linked by the terrestrial microwave systems, with 33 low-power repeaters. As already mentioned, there are also 14 satellite ground stations in the south of the territory.

Reception of radio and television is more difficult to determine. Precise information is difficult to obtain in the absence of systematic audience research and given the reluctance of the broadcasting organizations to provide accurate information. Although both radio and television receivers are subject to a license fee, the collection of this fee is not very efficient. Radio licenses cost between 30 and 50 dinars ($8–13), while television licenses cost 85 dinars ($22) per year. The fees are collected directly by RTA. It is estimated privately by RTA officials that over three million radio sets are in use. Although only 525,000 licenses have been issued for television, penetration is currently estimated at over 50%, that is, one million sets for two million homes. Sets are assembled locally by the state electricity company, Sonélec, and color sets retail for about 3,000 dinars each ($785). An American-built factory has recently been opened for the manufacture of color sets. As per capita income was only $876 in 1976, the purchase of a set is a major item of expenditure for most Algerians and is likely to remain beyond the means of many for some time.

As mentioned above, RTA now comes under the jurisdiction of the Ministry of Culture, though news programs are still supervised by a separate Information Division staffed by Ministry of Information personnel. Its structure today resembles that of the *sociétés nationaux* (e.g., Sonélec), the state-owned and state-controlled organizations in the nationalized industrial sector. RTA is administered by a director general appointed by governmental decree, formally on the nomination of the Minister of Information and Culture. In practice, the President takes a close interest in the appointment, which is regarded as politically central.

RTA is mainly financed by government subvention through the Ministry of Information and Culture. The recurrent budget in 1979 was 169 million dinars ($44.24 million). About 30% of the budget comes from license revenue, the majority from the government, and a very small percentage (less than 5%) from advertising.[15]

RTA's radio and television production studios are located in Algiers, Oran, and Constantine. The headquarters of RTA are located in Algiers, in large purpose-built premises on a steep hill on the edge of the city, a matter of a few hundred yards from the hotel used as a headquarters by General Eisenhower during the African campaign in World War II. In 1966, new radio studios were added to the main complex—itself completed by the French in 1957—and new regional studios in Oran and Constantine were

---

[15]Although advertising is forbidden, the state industries do pay for time that they use to introduce new products such as detergent.

added in 1968. There are now nine radio studios and three television studios. Radio production equipment is mostly French (Belin and Schlumberger), though some equipment installed recently is of Czech manufacture (Desselin). The original television equipment installed in 1957 and uprated in 1963, 1967, and 1970 was predominantly French (Thomson-CSF) and German (Siemens). The first PAL color equipment was British (Pye), though more recently German (Siemens, Fernsehen) and American (RCA) equipment has been installed.

RTA is a full member of both the Arab States Broadcasting Union (ASBU) and the European Broadcasting Union (EBU), and is linked into both the Maghrebvision and Eurovision TV exchange systems (Eurovision by INTELSAT).

Radio programs on the Home Service (Arabic) are broadcast for 24 hours a day, with news on the hour. The Kabyle network broadcasts for 9 hours a day, and the French network for 16 hours a day. All three main services are also relayed on short wave. Algeria broadcasts externally in both English and Spanish and also provides broadcast facilities to various groups in exile: Voice of the Palestinian Revolution (PLO), Voice of the Free Sahara (Polisario), Maghreb of the People (Morroccan group), and Voice of the Chilean Resistance are the main services, all of them in Arabic except the last, which is in Spanish.

Television programs are on the air for eight hours a day, from 1500 to 2300, though on Thursday, Saturday, and Sunday programs are transmitted from 1300 to midnight (Friday is the day of rest, since 1975). Forty-two per cent of the programs in 1979 were informational (education, news, discussion, current affairs, documentary, etc.), the remainder entertainment and religious (see Figure 5). In the same year, 53% of television programs were imported, mainly from America (14%), France (6%), Great Britain (5%) and West Germany (5%). The remainder were imported from Arab countries and from the United Nations (informational and educational films) and various Eastern European countries (documentaries). The proportion of imported programs is to be reduced to 25% as soon as possible, though it should be said that this target was set over ten years ago.

The quality of Algerian television varies markedly, as it does in all countries. Algeria has always enjoyed an international reputation for its small film industry. In the early 1970s, RTA cultivated good contacts with the nationalized cinema organization ONCIC, and in 1978 three feature films were co-produced. However, that relationship was terminated as a matter of policy in 1979, when RTA began to look farther afield for co-production partners for feature films. Two of the films made since then have won international recognition.[16]

---

[16]"Nahla," directed by Farouk Beloufa, and "La Nouba des Femmes du Mont Chenoua," directed by Assia Djebbar (both RTA co-productions).

Figure 5. RTA Television Program Structure

News	14%	
Talks and current affairs	7%	
Documentaries	5%	Information
Schools broadcasts	10%	(42%)
Adult education/Information	6%	
Music	6%	
Plays	5%	
Series and serials	11%	
Feature films	11%	Other
Religion	4%	(58%)
Variety and comedy	4%	
Children's programs	8%	
Sport	9%	

SOURCE: Notes compiled by Pilsworth.

Although the daily news ("Le Journal Télévisé") is still under tight control, the recent liberalization has meant that some subjects can be discussed for the first time. In 1979 current affairs programs dealt with housing problems, juvenile delinquency, property speculation, the status of women, alcoholism, *bidonvilles* (shanty towns), *arrivism*, the remnants of feudalism, corruption, official prevarication, religious controversies, opium addiction, private enterprise schemes, and abuses of ministerial power. Two series in particular—"el Ard" (The Land) and "el Fellah" (The Farmer)— were remarkably objective and imaginative in their description of rural development problems.

However, it is still the case that most of the peak hours are taken up with imported American action-adventure series including "L'Homme de Fer" ("Ironside" dubbed into French), "Kojak," and "Starsky and Hutch." Often old series such as "Perry Mason," "Star Trek," "The Fugitive," "The Virginian," and "Green Acres" can be seen, assuaging the medium's insatiable appetite for material at the expense of indigenous cultural values, their stars speaking perfect Arabic or French, though slightly out of syncronization.

On average, 16% of RTA's television output is devoted to educational broadcasts, mostly aimed at older students and adults. Subjects taught at high school level include mathematics, physics, natural sciences, history, and geography. However, the main emphasis is on nonformal and informal education that is coordinated by the Centre Nationale d'Enseignement Généralisée (CNEG), an agency set up in 1969 specifically to harness the broadcast media to educational goals. The broadcast media are used a great deal in the process of legitimating the rule of the technocrats. The new

National Charter that was introduced in 1975 at first caused an outcry, but, largely through a fairly open process of discussion of the charter through radio and television (50% of broadcasting time was allocated to discussion of the charter for some time) several changes were introduced, notably a softening of the socialist line and a hardening of the Islamic line. Over 14,000 letters were received by RTA during this great debate.

As in many countries, it is often difficult to discern the dividing line between informal political education and indoctrination; but the staff of RTA are sensitive to such problems, and educational objectives are usually well distinguished from the (on occasion) legitimate objectives of national propaganda. There is close cooperation in the field of information education between RTA and the Ministries of Health, Agriculture, Youth and Sports, and Religious Affairs. All these have claims on RTA for the production and transmission of informal educational programs directed to better farming, health education, and other aspects of out-of-school education.

The dominance of Westen European and American formats in television throughout the world has been well documented.[17] At present, western conventions and professional standards are as sought after at Algeria's RTA as in other television stations in the developing countries. The plans for a second television channel and the conversion to full color transmission are indications of this acceptance. RTA is faced with the task of advancing the nation's development in cultural, educational and political terms, while at the same time encouraging and nurturing an historico-political perspective that has been weakened and is largely ignored by the most vocal element of the television audience—the Europeanized, urban middle classes. Together with the basic conflicts between socialist industrialization and Islamic fundamentalism, these considerations, which impinge on linguistic, cultural, political, and even moral modes of expression, have profound implications for RTA's production policy. The successful resolution of these problems and the related problems of television reception and local production will depend on the extent to which Algerian broadcasters are willing and able to assert their independence from the bureaucracy, to develop confidence and maturity in their approach to program production, and to innovate and adapt. The selection and training of production staff is crucial. Now that national coverage on both radio and television is assured, and now that color conversion is almost complete, RTA may be able to invest sufficiently in resources for local production, so that imported material and its *ersatz* Algerian copies can be much further restricted. If this is achieved before the second channel is opened in 1982, Algerian television could establish itself as one of the most independent, creative, and innovative broadcasting organizations in the Arab world.

---

[17]See Katz and Wedell 1977, ch. 2.

4.2 Libya *by Drew O. McDaniel*

It was called the breadbasket of the Roman Empire. For more than four centuries, the two provinces of Tripolitania and Cyrenaica, which now comprise most of Libya, were prosperous African outposts of Caesar's domain. And yet, at the dawn of its independence, Libya was commonly viewed as the the poorest nation-state in the world. Today, the Sahara desert has pushed forward, squeezing the agricultural lands into a thin strip along the Mediterranean. Petroleum and a cash economy have supplanted the food crop and barter system dominant during the first half of this century. Libya has become an influential nation by virtue of its new economic power and its role in regional and global political activism.

Like much of the Arab world, Libya fell under the control of a list of successive invaders and settlers that includes the Phoenicians and Greeks, as well as the Romans. Until 1912, Libya was a part of the Ottoman Empire; for three subsequent decades it was an Italian colony; following World War II, it passed to Allied administration, before it finally won independence in 1951.[18]

Libyan Arab and Berber cultures are extremely adaptive. Each contact with a new power affected Libyan society in sometimes profound ways. A diner at a typical Libyan restaurant would, for example, be able to choose a variety of pasta dishes borrowed from the Italian tradition, as well as Greek and Berber specialties, and of course some foods from the Maghreb, including the national favorite, cous-cous. This ability to absorb and regenerate its culture has created a fascinatingly complex but sometimes contradictory national social pattern.

Libya is now, since the 1969 revolution, officially known as the Socialist People's Libyan Arab Jamhiriya. Its main cities are its captial, Tripoli, situated in the west at the eastern extremity of the Magreb; Benghazi, in the eastern region formerly called Cyrenaica; and Sebha, the desert south called the Fezzan. The country's population is believed to be over three million, including about 400,000 aliens temporarily residing within its boundaries (Nelson 1979, p. 67). Libya's area is roughly one-sixth the size of the United States, consisting mostly of desert lands (*Rand McNally Illustrated World Atlas* 1975, pp. 62–71). Libya has been the largest petroleum producer on the African continent, and thanks to this, the per capita GNP is extremely high, around $6,000 annually (*World Bank Atlas, 1978* 1978, p. 6).

Broadcasting in Libya is a function of the state. The broadcasting agency is the People's Revolutionary Broadcasting Company (PRBC), attached to the Secretariat of Information and Culture. Support for broadcasting comes

Drew McDaniel is Professor of Radio-Television and the Director of the School of Radio-Television at Ohio University. His principal research interest is in mass communication and national development, especially on the African continent.

exclusively through governmental appropriations. No receiver license fees are assessed, nor is advertising permitted on radio or television.

4.2.1 The Media and National Development

On Christmas Eve, 1951, Libya was given its independence through complex negotiations conducted within the United Nations. This decision was a compromise among numerous alternative plans considered by the Allied powers, including a division of the country into its constituent regions with a trusteeship role for the United States and other Allies or a return of the country to Italian control (First 1974, pp. 59–74). The form of government chosen was a constitutional monarchy. Mohamed Idris al Sanusi was selected to lead the nation largely on the basis of his role as patriarch of the Sanusi Islamic order—a sect similar to the Wahhabi of Saudi Arabia.

At the time of independence, the country found itself ill-equipped for its new status in the world community. Internally, the nation had the debilitation of decade upon decade of conflict with the Turks and the Italians; its regional divisions were sharply drawn; and, economically, its situation seemed hopeless, with no apparent natural resources of consequence and with a serious need for land reform. The most dramatic shortage, however, was not in physical but human resources. Despite efforts at education during the six years between World War II and 1951, Libya began its independence with only 33,000 students enrolled in primary or secondary schools (Farley 1971, p. 83). Worse still, there were only 14 Libyans holding college degrees (Keith 1965, p. 11) and only 32 persons studying at an institution of higher education (Farley 1971, p. 83). The difficulties of mounting a development effort with such a lack of manpower to plan and guide programs can hardly be exaggerated.

Perhaps these circumstances, more than any other, account for the delay in the implementation and growth of Libyan media. The wish to satisfy the more basic needs of the nation such as education, as well as housing, food, and transportation, seems to have taken precedence. The government seems to have given little encouragement to the media; the monarchy was an inward-looking regime with its natural vision created from a cloistered, nineteenth-century perspective. At any rate, estimates shortly after independence placed the number of radio receivers at a mere 5,000 for a population of about one million inhabitants (*WRTH*).

Events that would transform Libyan society and economy began unfolding with commercial oil discoveries in 1959. To the reader familiar with the country's petroleum riches, it may be hard to imagine that there was a balance of payment deficit in excess of $100 million in 1960 (Farley 1971, p. 129). Since those oil discoveries, it has been petroleum, nearly alone, that

[18]For an excellent treatment of the early history of Libya and North Africa, the reader is referred to Abu-Nasr 1971.

has fueled the national economy. In 1978, Libyan oil export revenues totalled nearly $10 billion, and in the following year revenues probably approached $16 billion (*United Nations, Statistical Yearbook* 1978 p. 88). Essentially all Libyan development activities, including those of broadcasting, are funded from income provided by petroleum exports. Total planning is in the hands of government agencies, because oil companies operating within the country have been nationalized.

King Idris diverted some of the resources available through oil exports into efforts at social development, most notably in education. In 1954, illiteracy among Libyans was about 81% (Farley 1971, p. 129). But gains came slowly; a decade later, the official estimate was 78% illiteracy, despite a four-fold increase in the number of students in primary and secondary instruction (*UNESCO Statistical Yearbook 1977* 1978, p. 43). Even with this impressive growth, it was believed that only 59% of children eligible for instruction were enrolled in school (Farley 1971, p. 90).

While wealth provided the nation many unquestioned benefits, the rapidity of its influx gave rise to numerous economic and social dislocations. With the increasing flow of cash into the country, there was the familiar rush from the many villages to the main urban centers. Coupled with this movement, thousands of foreign nationals emigrated to Libya to fill jobs vacant because of a lack of appropriately trained native workers; most settled in Tripoli or Benghazi. Naturally, these trends immensely complicated efforts to provide new public services, especially among city dwellers.

The primary development objectives, both before the revolution and especially afterwards, were improvements in agriculture, electrification, transportation, industrialization, and, above all, housing. Approximately one in four Libyan families had no housing in 1963 (Farley 1971, p. 58), and many others were living in substandard dwellings. So impoverished was the life of the common person at the outset of national economic planning that the scope of development activities was necessarily narrowed to the most basic undertakings.

As a result, the media have never appeared to figure very prominently in national development. The model of Arab development through communication, so evident in Egypt, does not seem to have inspired Libyan planners. In the 1963–68 development plan, only about $10 million was allocated to "news and guidance," a sum that amounted to only 1.5% of the total budget (Farley 1971, p. 199). Development programs since the revolution do not seem to have placed a much higher priority on the media. In the development budget for 1969–74, the Minister of Information and Culture was responsible for an allocation of $46.8 million, or about 1.3% of the entire development budget (First 1974, p. 154; see also pp. 152–186). In the five-year development plan for 1976–80, only 1.3% was set aside for Information and Communication (*Middle East Economic Digest* 1976, p. 22).

Another factor that may account for a relatively limited investment in broadcasting and other information activities was the absence of motivations common in Third World communication undertakings. In such nations, media tend to be perceived as channels of mobilization—usually to bring about improved capital formation and national unification. In Libya this "bootstrap" approach has never been necessary due to the ready access of capital and to the general lack of a need to combat ethnic or linguistic divisions.

4.2.2 Prerevolutionary Broadcasting

Like so many other aspects of social and technical development, broadcasting came late to Libya. The first indigenous radio service commenced just after independence. In 1955, a single medium-wave 1-kilowatt transmitter was in service in Tripoli, providing just two hours of daily programming in Arabic (*WRTH* 1955, p. 75). A UNESCO project in the late 1950s was mounted to develop the fledgling service, but the scale of the operation was very small (Codding 1959, p. 81).

Likewise, Libya was slow to develop television. While in francophone Maghreb there existed detailed plans to exploit the visual medium by the early 1960s (Pigé 1966, pp. 148–51), no Libyan TV service was available until 1968, when regular broadcasting was begun on the national independence day, 24 December (*New York Times* 1968, p. 38). Installation of the Tripoli television facilities was by French technicians. Most of the operational staff were from abroad, and the majority of programming was imported (Souriau 1975, p. 156).

A few TV sets were in use before that time. Irregular reception from Europe—mainly from Italy—and from Tunisia was possible. Also, there were daily telecasts from Wheelus Air Base, one of the first television stations in the Arab world. The military broadcasts from the United States base near Tripoli played a role of some significance during the first two decades of independence. In the beginning, the Armed Forces Radio Service employed for its radio broadcasts a low-power transmitter that could be heard over much of the vicinity around Tripoli (*WRTH* 1955, p. 75). The United States military TV service of the 1960s offered the usual fare of local news and a mixture of shows from the American networks. The fact that all broadcasts were in English was not a great deterrent to the creation of a small Libyan audience: those who could afford a set were likely to speak English. At the time of the revolution, there were two radio transmitters in operation at Wheelus (*Guide to Broadcasting Stations* 1970, pp. 58–59). In addition, the eastern area of Libya could receive transmissions from facilities operated by the British Forces Broadcasting Service in Tobruk (*WRTH* 1970, p. 131).

4.2.3 The Revolution and the Media

The revolution of 1 September 1969 halted all foreign military broadcasting and the United States forces were required to evacuate Wheelus Air Base by June 1970. There were several reasons for the revolution. In many respects, the takeover of the government by a group of junior officers, known loosely as the Free Officer Movement, was modeled along the lines of Nasser's assumption of power in Egypt 17 years earlier. But the motivations in the Libyan coup were rather different. First, the infusion of oil money into the economy under the King's management did not bring advantages to all sectors of society; rather, the tendency was to create greater disparity between the poor and the influential wealthy. Moreover, the Idris regime was seen as being aligned with the Europeans and other foreigners who had colonized the nation and about whom much bitterness persisted. Finally, it appeared that in addition to a more egalitarian society, the ruling group known as the Revolutionary Command Council, or RCC, wished to promote fundamental principles of Islam in all areas of the country's life (see First 1974, pp. 75–118).

Formally at first, and later *de facto*, the country has been led by Mu'ammar Al Qadhafi, the key person in organizing the overthrow of Idris, and the personality whose presence is felt everywhere in Libya. It is his political thinking that has guided the nation on its novel path in international affairs. The ideology that fostered the revolution was made public in the form of the "Third University Theory" by Qadhafi a few years after assuming power. This political philosophy rejects both capitalism of the west and communism of the Soviet bloc. Instead, it attempts to create a positive neutralist stance for Third World nations based upon principles of Islam. Eventually, these concepts were drawn together in a publication called the *Green Book* (Qadhafi n.d.).

The political dogma of the *Green Book* outlined a structure for Libya in which governance at the national level is given to a body known as the General People's Congress (GPC). Its membership would be drawn from participants of local "popular congresses" as well as "people's committee, syndicates and unions." (Qadhafi n.d., p. 63). The Revolutionary Command Council was replaced by the GPC in 1977.

The status of congresses and committees as administrative and policy-making bodies throughout political and social life is central to the philosophy espoused by Qadhafi. He says, "The masses of those basic popular congresses choose administrative people's committees to replace governmental administration. Thus all public utilities are run by people's committees" (Qadhafi n.d., p. 61).

For broadcasting, the shift to the authority of public committees occurred on 2 June 1973, when people's committees took control of the radio operations in Tripoli and Benghazi (*New York Times* 1973b, p. 3). By this time, hundreds of such committees had assumed responsibilities for the operation of schools, universities, hospitals, and the like. The imposition of control by the people's committee was intended to make the broadcasting system more directly responsive to the broad public interest. To the extent that a citizenry that had never had a national election nor wide political activity could express itself through representative committees, the system has been functional. Much of the influence of the committee emanates from its chairman, who also is the highest-ranking staff member. In his role as a committee head he is essentially a politician and as such is subject to the usual pressures of power centers within government. On the other hand, most of the remainder of the staff are not especially active politically. Yet staff members are aware of the need to be sensitive to political issues, even though only a small proportion of decisions is directly affected by politics.

If the broadcasting system did not appear to be a primary instrument for economic development, it does seem to have been used as a vehicle for political development. The content of the media shows a commitment to political issues and to the objectives of the polity. Sometimes this is shown in a highly dramatic form as in the televised trials *in absentia* of King Idris and his court (he was condemned to death, though he had taken asylum in Egypt) (First 1974, p. 122). It was reported that the TV stations were besieged with requests for rebroadcasts of these prime-time court proceedings. More commonly, the conventional approach of speeches and discussions was employed in broadcasts. One example was the "Revolutionary Intellectuals' Seminar," the broadcast of a series of public discussions just months after the RCC assumed power. These televised meetings focused on "a definition of the working forces of the people who have an interest in the revolution" (First 1974, pp. 124–28).

Beyond this, the objectives of the PRBC, as stated by the Ministry of Information, have been the projection of Arab socialism and Arab unity to a national audience (El Sheki 1975; see also Elgabri 1974a, pp. 28–29). The concern for politicization of the Libyan public was possibly a legitimate one, for the nation had had no previous tradition of popular participation in governance whatsoever. In a recent study of political activity among rural Libyans, 74.8% of those persons sampled were rated low or very low in predisposition toward participation in political affairs (El Fathaly et al. 1977, pp. 68–69). At any rate, the nature of the people's committee responsible for administrative oversight and the apparent commitment at the highest levels of national leadership have implicitly made radio and television significant forces in Libyan political life.

4.2.4 Organization of the Broadcasting System

The structure of the People's Revolutionary Broadcasting Company (PRBC) is similar to ones used in radio and television agencies throughout the world. Contact with highest governmental levels, along with fiscal and policy oversight, is provided by the Secretary of Information and Culture. This secretariat position is essentially a cabinet-level post within the General People's Committee that reports to the General People's Congress (Nelson 1979, p. 178).

Beneath the information secretariat is the Director General and Chairman of the Broadcasting Committee. This structure integrates both radio and television so that, for example, programming for TV and programming for radio are administered by the same department. Each department head is stationed at the national headquarters in Tripoli, while his deputy department head is located in Benghazi. If a department head is to be out of the country or otherwise unable to fulfill his regular duties, the deputy is temporarily seconded to the Tripoli broadcasting offices.

During the late 1970s, staffing of the three main broadcasting centers was approximately as follows: Tripoli—800, Benghazi—550, and Sebha—50. Only these locations have production capacity for radio and television. While there are transmitter locations elsewhere, just a few technicians are stationed at these operating sites (Oun 1975, 1976).

In theory at least, all persons from the Director General downward are professional broadcasters with some experience at operational levels of the organization. But the swift expansion of the system in the years since the revolution has resulted in shortages of qualified personnel at various levels. Overcoming this problem has been one of the main objectives of the planning and training department.

Training for the PRBC has been accomplished by a variety of means and, as has been the case in other areas of the civil service, has required staff development at all levels. Both communication studies and technical training are now available at the University of Benghazi for those aspiring to a career in radio or television, but an effort has been made within the Libyan broadcasting system to extend training opportunities. Technicians have often been permitted to train at European centers such as those operated by Thomson in Great Britain. A number of staff members have taken college studies in the United States. In 1975, agreements were reached with representatives of the University of South Carolina and Ohio University to institute college-degree programs for broadcasting staff members. So far, several dozen employees have come to the United States under these programs.

4.2.5 Radio Programming

The necessity of extending at a moderate cost a complete service to a nation of Libya's proportions and of initiating the service within a very short time frame has caused difficulties. The population density is among the world's lowest at about 4.5 persons per square mile, with the preponderance of the residents in the three urban centers of Tripoli, Benghazi, and Sebha. However, there are many tiny settlements throughout the country, either along the coastal rim or in oases scattered in the south. Provision of local service to the many remote population clusters has proven impractical. Instead, the effort has been made to transmit to all parts of the country a national service by two high-power facilities on opposite sides of Libya. At

Sabrata and Tripoli in the west and El Beida in the east are transmitters that broadcast each day's national Arabic service and virtually blanket the entire country. Non-Libyan audiences can receive these transmissions also; much of Egypt, Tunisia, and Algeria are covered by the broadcasts because of the antenna locations close to national boundaries (*WRTH* 1980, p. 169).

The national service is broadcast each day from 0400 until 2300. There are eight major daily newscasts supplemented by a variety of what might be called public affairs programs. Radio programming is done in blocks, with shows of 5-, 10-, 15-, or 30-minute lengths. A formatted program approach is not utilized. Contemporary and traditional Arabic music is broadcast in specific blocks of time. Dramatic programs are quite common, frequently based upon historical themes or personalities (Megri 1975).

Each evening there is a "European Service" in Tripoli and Benghazi. About two hours of this service are in French and about two and one-half hours are in English. Generally, the programs consist of news and recorded (mainly European pop) music shows. Other kinds of informational programs include, for example, a series explaining religious beliefs and practices of Islam.

Some regional programming is broadcast from Benghazi, Tripoli, and Sebha. In addition, regional services are further distributed by low-power transmitters in Tobruk and Misurata. There are two other specialized services broadcast from Tripoli. The "Radio Voice of the Koran" transmits Koranic readings and religious services from early morning until evening, and the "Voice of the Arab Homeland" is transmitted each evening.

4.2.6 International Radio Programming

In Libya, as in the Arab world generally, there tends to be no sharp distinction between domestic and foreign broadcast services. Very frequently, broadcasts to other Arab countries are treated just as though they were beamed to listeners within national boundaries. This approach to programming is employed on the grounds that Arabs are a single people, regardless of political divisions. The previously mentioned "Voice of the Arab Homeland" is an example of a service that is targeted for both internal and external listeners.

Libya offers a separate program service for external broadcasting known as the "Voice of Friendship and Solidarity." This service is produced by the overseas broadcasting department of the PRBC at its Malta headquarters. The facilities and offices of Libyan international broadcasting are housed in a rural villa on the island. A bilateral agreement provides for this arrangement, as well as other special trade and diplomatic ties between the two Mediterranean countries.

Until mid-1980, short-wave transmissions by the "Voice of Friendship and Solidarity" were handled by the relay station of Deutsche Welle, also located on Malta. Programs were originated locally or were received from

Tripoli by tropospheric scatter on microwave. The material was packaged into taped broadcasts that were then delivered to the transmitting station for airing at the appointed hour.

In 1975, the overseas broadcasting department began operation of local AM and FM stations in Malta. Programming for these stations was in Maltese; at times a full 12-hour schedule was broadcast daily, consisting mainly of news and recorded European music. Several well-known local personalities, once staff members of the Maltese national service (Xandir Malta), were employed by the Libyan government for its Maltese radio service.

The relationship between the Maltese and the Libyans is a complicated and sensitive one, and intergovernmental frictions have periodically disrupted the operation of the "Voice of Friendship and Solidarity." The Maltese share many cultural values with Arab peoples, but at the same time are repelled by certain aspects of Arab life, for example Islam—an anathema in predominantly Catholic Malta. Also, Malta depends heavily on Libyan oil, tourism, and grants-in-aid. Foreign aid from Libya probably totaled in excess of $40 million in 1980, and tourism is still one of the island's leading sources of foreign currency (Richardson 1979, pp. 40–41).

In 1979, broadcasts from the Libyan local radio stations on Malta were halted when pressure was applied by the Maltese opposition Nationalist Party. The problem began when the opposition filed an application for a license to operate a station of its own, claiming that the two existing radio services on the island were either pro-government or pro-Libyan. The Nationalists professed a desire to "balance" radio programming in the country. Further, it was argued that the Libyans were utilizing a frequency assigned to the Maltese people by international agreements. Although AM and FM services of the overseas broadcasting department were resumed in 1979, relationships between the countries remained uneasy (Sweiden 1979).

In June 1980, both the shortwave broadcasts from Deutsche Welle transmitters and the local broadcasts on AM and ꞁM were suspended altogether by the Maltese authorities. This decision followed a worsening of Libyan-Maltese relations resulting from a number of issues including disputes between the two nations about off-shore oil drilling rights in the Mediterranean. Since cessation of transmissions, the studios have been used to produce programming in Maltese that is recorded, then shipped to Tripoli for broadcasts from Libya back to Malta. The staff has also begun the recording and production of transcriptions in Arabic and English for distribution and rebroadcasting (Sweiden 1980).

From the outset, long-range plans always envisioned the relocation to Libya of the short-wave services. The abrupt turn in relations with Malta has hastened that move. The staff of the "Voice of Friendship and Solidarity" is largely intact; by the time broadcasts were suspended it had already started English, Italian, Arabic, and French services. It is expected that the move to

Tripoli will be made when the national broadcasting center has been fully implemented and sufficient production and transmitting capability can be allocated to this unit.

4.2.7 Television Programming

The television program service in Libya has undergone a remarkable evolution since its inception in 1968. The number of channels has grown from one to two, the hours of transmission have been greatly expanded, and local programming has become a significant part of the schedule. Since 1975, the three production centers have been linked by microwave interconnection, thus providing a national network for television. Programming ordinarily is originated in Tripoli, but the other centers are also equipped to feed the network when a locally produced show is to be seen nationally. The microwave system also connects with Tunisian television in Tunis, and thereby with other nations of the Maghreb. By means of this hookup, Eurovision programs can be routed to Tripoli and Benghazi through ties in Morocco (Oun 1975), although the PRBC does not hold membership in the European Broadcasting Union.

The main service of television begins each day at 1600, when schools are in session, with instructional programs supporting varied subjects in the national primary or secondary curriculum. General programming commences at 1700. On Fridays, the station signs on about noon for religious programming, prior to a broadcast of the main prayer service, and continues with regular programming afterward.

The television schedule on the first channel revolves around the main evening newscast, which is broadcast nightly at 2200. This program, customarily employing both male and female announcers, is, by western standards, quite formal and rather staid. Because of cost and logistic factors, there is little field reporting included in these broadcasts; most stories are simply read by the presenters, but efforts to use stock slides, maps, wirephotos, and other visual materials make the newscasts a little livelier. Wire services employed include Reuters and JANA, the Libyan national news agency.

In concert with the political and cultural objectives of Libyan broadcasting, the content of the first channel tends to be serious. Discussion, commentary, documentary, and programs focusing on history and folklife are staples of the main television service.

Prior to the Lebanese civil war, the PRBC depended heavily on Beirut television syndicators for Arabic programming and subtitling. Since 1976, the PRBC has actively sought new sources of programs and has increased its own production capacity. Bilateral program exchanges with other Arab nations occasionally provide programs, but political considerations often complicate matters. For instance, Egyptian television—once a major program supplier—can no longer exchange its shows with Libya. Cooperative productions in which the PRBC has been involved include the Arab States

Broadcasting Union's programs "The Arab Encounter" and "The Great Homeland" (*ASBU Review* 1975, pp. 16–28; *ASBU Review* 1979, pp. 34–35). The majority of local programs fall into three general categories: music, documentary, and news. Imported programs subtitled in Arabic are still seen on the main channel, about five to ten hours weekly, including feature films and children's cartoons. For most of the first decade of TV service in Libya, imported shows from the United States were a significant part of the daily schedule. Among those aired were "Hawaii Five-0," "The Brady Bunch," and "The Untouchables."

The regular transmission of the first channel concludes with a feature film around 2300. Usually this is an Arabic movie, but once or twice a week a French film may be shown. Following the film, a special service called "The French Program" is broadcast. This transmission is between one and two hours in length and is intended for the French-speaking community in the country. These programs can also be seen in French-speaking Tunisia.

The second channel began broadcasting in early 1980. The function of this service is to offer an alternative to the programs available on the first channel, mostly in the form of entertainment shows. All programs are in English, usually imported from the United States or Great Britain, and are not subtitled. This service begins each evening about 1700 and concludes just before the evening newscast on the first channel (El Shweikh 1980).

The telecasting of second- and third-language services may seem odd, but one must remember that the population of non-Libyans resident in the country approaches 15%. Among a very large number of these people, French or English is spoken. Furthermore, Libyans typically have had six years of compulsory English-language training by graduation from secondary school. While the quality of instruction is sometimes uneven, sufficient skill is often acquired to be able to follow television dialogue.

4.2.8 The Libyan Audience

By all accounts, radio is the dominant medium in the country. As in most nations, it is a mobile means of mass communication: listeners frequently carry radios with them while they work or travel. In a society in the process of development, this is a real advantage, since the use of radio does not interrupt the long day's activities demanded of laborers and employees.

The distribution of radio receivers is officially calculated to be approximately 7.5 per 100 population (*United Nations Statistical Yearbook 1978* 1979, p. 950), but unofficial estimates are rather higher, around 15 sets per 100 listeners. Radio receivers are freely available both in shops and in traditional *souks*. Pocket sets sell for as little as $6, while popular multiband sets are in the range of $30.

Radio has served as the primary source of information and news. It was radio, for example, that projected the news of the 1969 revolution to the public and remained the principal source of information during the first confused weeks (First 1974, p. 120). In addition, the many external services of the region are easily heard everywhere in Libya, including the ubiquitous BBC Arabic Service and Radio Cairo's "Voice of the Arabs." Because the majority of radio receivers in use are capable of short-wave reception, it is probable that a considerable audience exists for international broadcasters.

Television sets are much less widely available as the cost of even inexpensive receivers continues to discourage use by those with low incomes. Recent official estimates are unavailable, but the figure at the end of the 1970s was very likely less then 2 sets per 100 population.

Television is, by its nature, an activity that requires greater attention than radio, and it is normally nonportable. Television is thus a leisure activity and usually, as a consequence of Libyan life styles, involves the whole family. However, the viewing of certain programs in groups that are of mixed age and sex can often cause embarrassment when the content offends values or customs of family elders. These shows are watched by the younger members of the family alone. The influx of programs from abroad along with the quick pace of social change has seemingly created this double standard in taste.

Audience research has rarely been undertaken by the broadcasting system. Those reports that may exist are not publicly available and there is doubt that any findings have led to a great impact on the operation of the services. It appears that the administration of the PRBC relies on the opinions and attitudes of the People's Broadcasting Committee as the main feedback mechanism for the programs of radio and television.

4.2.9 Technical Facilities

As noted earlier, the PRBC relies on only three combined radio and television production centers, apart from the studios operated by the "Voice of Friendship and Solidarity" in Malta. The Tripoli and Benghazi centers are of moderate size and a much smaller facility is operated in Sebha. Production studios at each site are not fully integrated, but are in close proximity, in the interest of convenience and security.

Through the first decade after the revolution, investment in equipment and physical amenities seems to have been modest. In Tripoli and Benghazi, the television studios were converted radio studios. Likewise, other areas in the centers appeared to have been modified from their intended usage as the growth of the system and changing technology demanded. Some items of broadcast equipment have been more than a few years old; however, the maintenance was meticulous. A steady upgrading of broadcasting equipment has been evident; and while changes have been gradual, they were in keeping with the number of qualified technicians available during the period. For instance, color broadcasting, employing the SECAM method, did not begin until the late 1970s.

In the decade of the 1980s, the outlook is for a faster rate of technical development in the broadcasting system. For years, plans had been on the drawing boards for a completely new broadcasting center for national production, administration, and programming. Construction of the project was delayed by various problems, including charges of bidding irregularities among certain European contractors. However, the building was completed and the first phase of the new facilities implementation was begun in 1980 (Sweiden 1979).

Nearly all equipment used by the PRBC is of American or European manufacture. British, West German, and Swiss items were commonly used, but no equipment from the Soviet bloc is in evidence.

One area in which the broadcasting system has invested heavily in current technology is in the area of high-quality video tape recording equipment. This is a requisite for Libyan broadcasting, as it is in most Third World countries, because virtually all programming must be supplied from video tape. There is some use of film, but films from non-Arab nations frequently require subtitling; and this is generally done by making dubs, with titles, onto video tape. This factor has also meant that the PRBC must maintain an extensive and relatively costly tape library.

The opening of the national microwave system was an important achievement for it not only linked all the production centers in Libya but also broke the broadcast isolation of the country. A further step in this direction was taken with the opening of a satellite earth station in 1980 to connect with the INTELSAT global system. This facility is located near Tripoli and ties into the terrestrial microwave network.

4.2.10 The Decade Ahead

For those who find the social and political objectives of the national leadership perplexing, it must be recalled that at the time of the military takeover, Mu'ammar Al Qadhafi was merely 28 years old. He and his colleagues represented something completely new in Libya—an educated elite. Libyans who attained 40 years of age before 1980 were not only of another generation than the present leadership but were the product of an anachronistic society in which education and a global perspective were largely missing. The revolutionary government found that few Libyans of middle age and older had the needed literacy skills or the ability to perform other tasks required within the new technocracy. The civil service and government administration demanded capabilities that were possessed by only the very young, educated, but often inexperienced, Libyans. It is this phenomenon that has made organizational development so difficult in the broadcasting system.

Still, in the coming decade, the fruits of the past years of investment and development will begin to be enjoyed in Libya; and, as this occurs, a maturity in broadcasting as well will prove inevitable. The maturity will be reflected in new facilities that will be, or will approach, state-of-the-art technology. Many of those who spent years in educational institutions outside the country will return to assume positions of leadership within the PRBC organization. There should be a reduced dependency on programming imported from abroad. Most importantly, the reach of the mass media is almost certain to extend to all sectors and levels of society.

In the final analysis, political priorities will dominate the future of broadcasting. A massive involvement of the citizenry in the innumerable people's committees and congresses is essential for the effective operation of the government envisioned by Qadhafi. Radio and television will continue to be important instruments of political development. Indeed, the success of the new government structure may well depend, to a significant extent, on the ability of the media to mobilize the Libyan public for active participation in its political life.

4.3. Morocco, *by Claude-Jean Bertrand*

No Arab country lies farther west than Morocco and none closer to Western Europe. Morocco experienced Roman rule and Vandal invasion in ancient times; it occupied Spain between 711 and 1492; from the eighteenth century it had many contacts with European nations; from 1911 to 1956 it was a colony of France and Spain. Morocco thus looks upon itself as having a special calling to act as a bridge between two cultures. On the other hand, Morocco suffers from an internal split between the partly Europeanized middle class in the coastal cities and the more tradition-bound rural population of the interior. Moreover, about 40% of the population, mainly in the northern and eastern mountains, consist of Berbers who lived in Morocco long before the Arabs arrived in the eighth century and who normally speak one of their own dialects.

Unlike most other African states, Morocco has been a nation for many centuries. All Moroccans share the same religion, Islam, and nearly all share a language, Arabic. With the exception of Libyans, all Maghrebians share the legacy of long years of colonization by France, French as a second language, and the memory of the struggle for independence. Yet Morocco is different. It has retained freedom of enterprise within a planned economy. Its old-fashioned authoritarian monarchy has tolerated some degree of political pluralism; and, though Morocco does support Arab and Moslem causes, it has kept close to Western Europe and to the United States.

Claude-Jean Bertrand was born in Algeria, where he spent over 20 years of his life. He studied at the University of Algiers and then at the Sorbonne. He now teaches at the University of Paris-X (Nanterre) and at the Institut français de presse. His fields of interest are American civilization and media. He has maintained an interest in the Maghreb, which he has visited several times since independence, most recently in November 1979, as part of a USICA-sponsored lecture tour of West Africa. He is the author of numerous published articles in French and English.

Morocco is more developed than most Third World nations and growing at a more rapid rate; nevertheless it still faces problems. Its demographic growth rate is one of the highest in the world (3.2%): its population has grown from four million in 1900 and six million before World War II to an estimated 20 million in 1980. Since agricultural productivity and industrialization do not keep up with this, the result is continuing poverty: its per capita GNP is under $600. Another problem is rapid urbanization and proletarianization. Though over 60% of the population are still rural, there are now 14 cities with over 100,000 inhabitants, plagued with shantytowns and unemployment.

Another problem is social inequality. The lower 20% of the population gets 7% of the national wealth, while the upper 20% gets over 65%. To some extent that corresponds to the economic split between a traditional and a modern sector: on the one hand quasi-feudal large land-owners who grow commercial crops on irrigated land, as opposed to small farmers, 87% of whom own fewer than nine acres; on the other hand, a quantity of craftsmen and an overabundance of tradespeople, as opposed to a relatively small number of industrial concerns often controlled by foreign corporations.

After France granted independence in 1956, a series of conflicts began between the monarchy and the Istiqlal Party, which had been fighting against colonialism since the 1930s. The political crisis that erupted in 1971 coincided with two attempts on the King's life. King Hassan II sought and received diverse support. In the mid-1970s, the Saharan conflict erupted when Spain left that area. The Green March to the South in 1975 generated a "sacred union" of all Moroccans around the King.

4.3.1 Radio

A state Office chérifien des PTT had been set up by Franco-Moroccan agreement in 1913 and had been granted a monopoly over the post, the telephone, and the telegraph. A 25 November 1924 executive order enlarged its monopoly to include all electronic communications. It was in February 1928 that the first radio broadcast was made from Rabat with a 2-kilowatt medium-wave transmitter, the power being later increased to 5 kilowatts (1932), then 20 kilowatts (1935). A 2.5-kilowatt short-wave transmitter started relaying the medium-wave signal in 1942. After World War II, Morocco began building its communications infrastructure in earnest. In 1947, separate production and transmission facilities were given to the French and the Arabic programs—though at that point still only the major cities of Rabat, Casablanca, Fez, and Meknes were covered. Also, in 1947, Radio Maroc was granted by executive order a degree of legal and financial responsibility within the Post Office.

A 1948 conference in Copenhagen authorized Morocco to use eight transmitters. The next year, two new 20-kilowatt transmitters were inaugurated, one for the French, one for the Arabic program. Then, in April 1953, the large Sebba Aioun transmitting station began operating with two 120-kilowatt medium-wave transmitters that, at night, covered almost the whole territory. FM was started in Casablanca in 1954. In 1955, an administrative and production center, La Maison de la Radio (Radio House), was opened in Rabat. In 1956, Sebaa Aioun was equipped with four short-wave transmitters. By the next year, Moroccan radio could use an aggregate 559 kilowatts of transmitting power for its three programs, the "A" Program in French (75 hours per week), the "B" Program in Arabic (60 hours) and Berber (20 hours), and the "C" Program in Spanish (10½ hours) and English (5½ hours).

Under the French Protectorate, the mission of radio was to serve French interests, those of the settlers and those of the Empire. News and other programs were tightly supervised by the Résident Général. He appointed the Director of Radio Maroc, who, in the absence of a board of governors or a board of management, had direct authority over all seven departments. If radio played a part in the fight for independence, it was through Cairo's Voice of the Arabs.

After 1956, the Moroccan government wished to unite a country long divided between a large French zone and a small Spanish zone in the north, and it wished to be heard on the international airwaves. Above all, it wanted to ensure its central control. French capital and experts were flowing out of the country, so little change could be brought in immediately. In 1959, the "A" Program was in Arabic (100 hours per week), the "B" Program in French (75 hours) and the "C" Program was given to Berber, Spanish, and English. As part of successive three- or five-year national development plans, technical facilities were expanded. By 1965, there were 24 transmitters including three in Oujda in the east, two in Safi, and one in Agadir in the south. Expansion slowed down from the mid-1960s, except for two 400-kilowatt long-wave transmitters set up at Azilal (altitude—5,500 feet), and accelerated again as part of the 1973–77 Plan.

Radio Maroc was not the only broadcasting institution in the country. In Spanish Morocco, the Sultan's deputy had granted the right to broadcast to a firm controlled by Torres Queveda, who already enjoyed a monopoly on the colony's telephone and telegraph. Its station, Radio Dersa Tetuan, used two medium-wave transmitters (25 and 5 kilowatts).

In Tangier, as early as 1937, in spite of French opposition, private entrepreneurs and hostile nations (e.g., Italy) had moved in. A first local station was soon taken over by French interests, then by the state. In 1939, Spaniards built a station that was protected so long as Spain ruled over the city (1940 to 1945), but in 1947 it was taken over by Radio Africa, whose principal owner was a Frenchman linked to Radio Andorre.[19] A year earlier,

---

[19]Until it stopped broadcasting in April 1981, the station was one of the so-called French "peripheral stations," an American-style commerical outlet like Europe No. 1, Radio Luxembourg (RTL), or Radio Monte Carlo (RMC)—stations whose transmitters stand just outside

an American had launched Radio Tanger, of which 49% was owned by Spaniards and 33% by Americans.

When independence came in 1956, there were three private concerns in Tangier. Radio Africa owned five transmitters, two medium-wave for Radio Africa Maghreb (125 kilowatts) and Radio Africa Tanger (12 kilowatts), and three short-wave for Radio Inter Africa. The Spanish-speaking Radio Pan American operated a 2-kilowatt transmitter, and Radio Tanger International used two (50 and 10 kilowatts) medium-wave and two (10 kilowatts) short-wave transmitters.

In 1948–49, the French government had yielded to United States pressure and given the Voice of America (VOA) a ten-year lease on broadcasting. VOA set up 12 short-wave transmitters with a combined power of 820 kilowatts to relay its broadcasts to Eastern Europe 24 hours a day. A condition was that it also relay programs of Radio Maroc and of the French radio.

An international conference gave Tangier back to Morocco in 1956. A ministerial decree then abolished all stations outside the state monopoly. Only three years later, however, the government decided that all those stations should go off the air by 31 December 1959 and, until then, would be strictly supervised. Radio Dersa and Pan American readily sold out. The Radio Africa people secretly shipped out all their equipment. Radio Tanger was bought by the Moroccan government in 1960 and integrated into the state system. The Moroccans extended the VOA lease until 1963, provided it stopped relaying third-party (i.e., French) radio and that it loaned them two transmitters. In 1964, the United States transferred all the equipment to Morocco, which, in return, let VOA use it for a two-year renewable period.

4.3.2 Early Television

Television started earlier in Morocco than anywhere else in Africa. In 1950, two French firms obtained from the Office chérifien des PTT a 50-year monopoly on Moroccan television, as well as the right to take advertising *ad libitum* and to retain 85% of the annual fee on receivers. A year later another firm took over, TELMA. In March 1954, two years late, it started broadcasting 30 hours a week in Arabic and French, using a 4-kilowatt transmitter in Casablanca and another in Rabat. In May 1955 it stopped, and went bankrupt in 1957, being ten million (new) francs in debt. Circumstances could hardly have been worse for the TELMA project. With the Sultan exiled, agitation for independence was peaking. The French were getting ready to leave; few Moroccans could afford the sets; the Istiqlal had ordered a boycott of all French products. Of course, the newspaper press fought the threat to its advertising revenues.

---

the French borders in Saar, Luxembourg, and Monaco, and are now all controlled by SOFIRAD, a (French state) holding company.

In late 1960, the government bought the equipment, much of it outdated, for one million francs. For two years, the Moroccans studied a relaunching with French experts—then suddenly initiated it in 1962 to cover the International Fair in Casablanca. For some years television was to be an improvised operation of Moroccan radio. As late as 1970, only four hours a day were broadcast (one and one-quarter hours in French) over a restricted area, the large cities in the north.

4.3.3 Broadcasting Reorganization

For a few years after independence, the status and structures of broadcasting changed only marginally. Several drafts of a constitution were proposed but to no effect. In the absence of a clear statute or rules and regulations, a tacit understanding enabled broadcasting both to function as a branch of the Postal Ministry and, politically, to be directly controlled by the Prime Minister.

A 19 January 1962 executive order resolved the ambiguity by creating the Radiodiffusion-Télévision Marocaine (RTM) and shifting it to the Ministry of Information, Fine Arts, and Tourism. In the 1960s, various modifications were introduced, yet by 1980 RTM's legal standing and missions were still unclear. It was described as a separate government agency, legally responsible and financially autonomous, placed under the authority of the Minister of Information. There had been ministerial declarations (e.g., one in 1978 stating that the object of RTM-TV was both to preserve Moroccan and Islamic culture and to present a balanced picture of the world), but no specific Broadcasting Act had yet filled the "juridical vacuum" in which Moroccan radio and television are often said to be operating.

Originally, the budget of RTM was a *budget autonome* voted upon by the Board of Directors, not by Parliament, the expectation being that it balances its accounts. Now it is a *budget annexe*, discussed in Parliament like the national *budget général*, because RTM both needs extensive financing by the state and has extensive revenues of its own. In 1977, for instance, its income came from an annual fee on TV receivers (21%), advertising on TV (17%), and a state grant (62%).

The annual fee on radio receivers was eliminated in 1971. The television fee in 1980 was 60 DH (approximately $13.20) for a black-and-white set and 100 DH ($22.00) for color, double what it had been for about 15 years before 1979. Advertising on radio had been allowed by a 1928 governmental order. It was decided in 1961 that not only Radio Tanger could take commercials but also television when it came. Morocco was thus the first country in Africa to authorize radio advertising as a source of financing, and commercials appeared on TV in March 1970. Six minutes a day were allowed; but for some years four was the norm. In 1980 there were about six breaks an evening, between 10 and 15 minutes of advertising. A special bureau attached to the Ministry of Information screens the material, most of which comes from foreign firms (like Goodyear or Coca-Cola) or their local subsidiaries. As France is the country's major economic partner, Havas, the leading French advertising agency, is a major client.

In the 1979 RTM budget, 76.2 million DH were appropriated for operating expenses—27.5 million for staff (RTM has about 1600 employees), 31.8 million for equipment, 16.5 million for finance charges, 0.4 million for unexpected expenses—and 39.9 million DH went to investments. In 1980, 90.4 million DH and 22.7 million DH were respectively budgeted, the aim being to improve programming.

Except for Oujda on the Algerian border, the more important cities sit within an amphitheater of mountains, with Rabat and Casablanca in the center, on the Atlantic coast. They can easily be covered. The problem is with towns and villages in the mountainous Rif area (maximum altitude 8000 feet) to the north and beyond it on the Mediterranean coast, and in the long Atlas chain (maximum altitude—13,660 feet) to the southeast and beyond it on the margins of the desert.

Since 1975, moreover, Morocco (446,000 square kilometers) has been fast extending to the southwest over the vast, sparsely inhabited former Spanish Sahara (226,000 square kilometers). Since cooperation on a Maghrebian satellite has not materialized, RTM has had gradually to add transmitters so as to reach the whole population. By 1976, however, only the long-wave transmitter at Azilal (about 150 kilometers northeast of Marrakech) covered the whole country (not including Western Sahara). Only 18% was reached on mediumwave in the daytime by the "A" radio network, 12.3% by the "B" network, 5.5% by the "C."

At the turn of the 1980s, RTM had the following transmitting capacity (see Table 14): two 400-kilowatt long-wave transmitters that could be coupled; 1986 kilowatts mediumwave; 700 kilowatts shortwave (to which can be added the eight Tangier transmitters operated by VOA but technically the property of the Moroccan state); and 12 kilowatts FM.

The radio system, consisting of three networks based in Rabat, seven regional stations, and "La Voix du Maroc" in Tangier, could use 7 studios and 6 mobile units in Rabat, 3 studios and 2 mobile units in Tangier, 2 studios and 2 mobile units in Casablanca, 3 studios and 1 mobile unit in Laayoune, 2 studios and 1 mobile unit in Marrakech, 2 studios and 1 mobile unit in Agadir, and 2 studios and 1 mobile unit in Fez.

The "A" or "National" Network broadcasts 22 hours a day in Arabic on long, medium, and shortwave, and FM. The "B" or "International" Network broadcasts 19 hours a day on mediumwave and FM. The "C" or "Berber" Network operates on mediumwave 18 hours a day; 3 hours in Spanish, 3 hours in English and 12 hours in Berber. The regional stations in Oujda, Rabat, Casablanca, Fez, Marrakech, and Agadir air their own productions three hours a day (from 1500 to 1800), and the "A" program the rest of the time. The Laayoune originates more—a two-hour Spanish program and a six-hour Arabic program.

The three-network pattern reflects the inherited linguistic pluralism.[20] Out of about 40,000 hours of programming a year, 62.6% is in Arabic; 18.5% is in French; 12.5% is in Berber; 3.7% is in Spanish; and 2.8% is in English (Chakroun 1979, pp. 12–20). Each of the major networks corresponds to one of the cultural polarities, the traditional-rural on the one hand and the modern-urban on the other. As one Tiznit high school boy put it, "Arabic radio reminds me that I am Moroccan while French radio entertains me with programs all young people want." As far as subject matter is concerned, overall airtime is allocated as follows: entertainment, 67.44%; news and public affairs, 15.88%; education, 5.89%; culture, 6.39%; religion, 4.14%; and advertising, 0.26% (Tangier) (Chakroun 1979, p. 12–20).[21]

The National Network is the most important medium for that mass of the people who cannot read, cannot afford a television set, or know little or no French. It is more slow-paced and rambling but more diversified and popular than the others. Its format has not changed much over the years. Music fills over two-thirds of the airtime. RTM has several orchestras, for "classical" (i.e., Andalusian) music, modern (Arab) music, and popular "malhoune" music; regional stations have some orchestras too. RTM also has several companies of actors to produce serials and plays. Among the more appreciated programs are the morning programs for women (sometimes lively discussions on problems of family life) and the phone-in programs introduced in the late 1970s on themes inspired by songs. Most programs are taped, yet none is precisely scheduled except the news and press review, whose length may vary unpredictably. Nearly two-thirds of the nonnews, nonmusic programming (14% of the total) is imported or obtained from United Nations agencies. Generally speaking, though, the National Network cultivates traditional values. On political and social subjects, it tends to sound rigidly Islamic and rather parochial.

The International Network caters to the younger, more educated, western-oriented audience. Almost three-quarters of its airtime is devoted to music, much of it American pop, interspersed with world news. The format is more strict: the day is sliced into periods entrusted to one of several disc jockeys, who model themselves on their colleagues of the French peripheral stations. Quite a few of the programs are borrowed in their entirety from

[20]It may also reflect the fact that 150,000 foreigners lived in Morocco in the late 1970s, including 60,000 French people, and that tourism is a major industry: in 1978 the official figure for tourists was 884,000, including 31,000 French people.

[21]"It is not easy to be precise about Moroccan programs for the RTM is so discreet that newspapers, whether in French or Arabic, do not publish listings" (Pigé 1966, p. 93). That is still true for radio. The RTM publication *Idaa wa-telvaza*, supposedly a monthly, comes out irregularly.

Table 14. Moroccan Radio Transmitters

Type	Place	Frequency	Power
	"A" Network		
	(broadcasts in Arabic from 0500 to 0300)		
Longwave	Azilal	209 kHz	800 kW
Mediumwave	Agadir I	936 kHz	1 kW
	Casablanca I	1080 kHz	1 kW
	Ksar es Souk	864 kHz	15 kW
	Laayoune	657 kHz	50 kW
	Marrakech I	972 kHz	1 kW
	Ouarzazate	1116 kHz	15 kW
	Oujda	594 kHz	100 kW
	Rabat I	819 kHz	25 kW
	Safi I	1026 kHz	1 kW
	Sebaa Aioun	612 kHz	300 kW
	(Meknes)		
	Sidi Bennour	540 kHz	600 kW
	Tan Tan	657 kHz	20 kW
	Tanger II	1116 kHz	1 kW
	Tarfaya	711 kHz	10 kW
	Tetouan I	1053 kHz	10 kW
Shortwave	Tangier	609 kHz	50/100 kW(VOA)
	Tangier	6170 kHz	100 kW
	Tangier	9540 kHz	50/100 kW
	Tangier	15155 kHz	100 kW
	Tangier	15160 kHz	100 kW(VOA)
	Tangier	15335 kHz	100 kW
	Tangier	15360 kHz	50 kW
	Tangier	21735 kHz	50 kW
FM	Casablanca	96.1 mHz	3 kW
	Rabat	92.1 mHz	3 kW
	"B" Network		
	(broadcasts in French from 0600 to 0100)		
Mediumwave	Agadir II	774 kHz	50 kW
	Agadir III	1197 kHz	20 kW
	Casablanca II	1188 kHz	1 kW
	Marrakech II	1152 kHz	1 kW
	Oujda II	828 kHz	100 kW
	Rabat II	1026 kHz	5 kW
	Safi II	1323 kHz	1 kW
	Sebaa Aioun II	1044 kHz	300 kW
	Tangier III	1017 kHz	1 kW
FM	Casablanca	90 mHz	3 kW
	Rabat	87.9 mHz	3 kW
	"C" Network (broadcasts in Spanish from 0600 to 0900, in English		
	from 0900 to 1200, in Berber dialects from 1200 to 2400)		
Mediumwave	Agadir III	1197 kHz	20 kW
	(1600–0100)		
	Casablanca III	1485 kHz	1 kW

Table 14. (continued)

Type	Place	Frequency		Power
	Marrakech III	1593 kHz		1 kW
	Rabat III	1296 kHz		1 kW
	Sebaa Aioun III	702 kHz		140 kW
	Tetouan II	918 kHz		5 kW
	Radio Tanger ("La Voix du Maroc")			
Mediumwave	Tangier I	1233 kHz		200 kW
	External Services (to the Middle East, West Africa, Europe)			
Shortwave	Tangier	1000–1800	15360 kHz	50 kW
		1000–1600	15335 kHz	100 kW
		1100–2200	21735 kHz	50 kW
		1600–2200	15160 kHz	100 kW(VOA)
		1800–2200	9540 kHz	100 kW
		2200–0100	6170 kHz	100 kW
		2200–0100	15155 kHz	100 kW
		2200–2400	6095 kHz	100 kW(VOA)

SOURCE: This information was gathered from a variety of sources including *World Radio TV Handbook*, the BBC Monitoring Service, Télé-diffusion de France, and the Moroccan broadcasting services.

Radio France. Only about 1.5% of the nonnews material is locally produced.

With Spanish on the decline and English never having been the tongue of either natives or invaders, the "C" network was first and foremost meant for some 40% of the population who speak Berber and do not know classical Arabic. Four hours a day (up from three hours in the mid-1970s) were devoted to each of the three dialects, *tachelhit* (in the southwest), *tamazight* (in the central mountains), and *tarifit* (in the north). What is most appreciated, especially by those Berbers who have migrated to the big cities, is the rich traditional music.

Up to 1980 at least, Tangier's "La Voix du Maroc" was apparently popular, even in the south. Though Arabic was used far more than French or Spanish, its tone was more international (if only because of the commercials) and more cultural than that of the "A" Network. News, relayed from the networks, was not emphasized. Much time was given to religion, education, music, and sports.

The VOA facilities in Tangier are used by RTM for a combined total of 300 hours a week to send some of its regular programs on short wave to distant countries.

4.3.4 Television

RTM television was launched in March 1963 on 625 lines, using studios in Rabat, the modernized TELMA installations in Casablanca, and seven relay stations in Tangier and major cities in the interior. Only in the mid-1960s did expansion really start. Until then, the government seemed voluntarily to underfinance the new medium.

In 1980, RTM's 18 transmitters and 16 low-power repeaters, linked by microwave, covered all major urban areas. As early as 1972, it was claimed that 80% of the population were within reach of the RTM-TV signals—a claim that, even if accurate, ignored the fact that many town dwellings and many villages did not have electricity.[22] As late as 1980, a large part of the population remained untouched by television, especially in the mountains. Unlike Algeria, Morocco did not distribute by satellite. As early as January 1970, Morocco became the first African nation to own an earth station. It was set up at Souk El Arba by the PTT in cooperation with INTELSAT; but the station was normally used for telecommunications and occasionally to receive Eurovision programs.

Whereas radio was somewhat decentralized, all TV programming in 1980 came from the Ain Chok center near Casablanca and, predominantly, from Rabat. Rabat had 2 small studios, 3 video, and 15 film mobile units. Casablanca had two production studios and four film mobile units. Color was introduced in 1972 using the French SECAM system, yet in 1979 still less than 3% of licensed receivers were color sets.

In 1980, the single television network was on the air an average of 35 to 40 hours a week, rising to 55 hours in a festive period like Ramadan. Moroccan production capabilities were not equal to the transmission facilities, so over 40% of the programs (over 50% of the nonnews programs) were imported, including most of the entertainment. Originally, much came from France, whether it had been made there or was American material dubbed in France. Since oil capital had greatly increased Middle Eastern (mainly Egyptian) production of films and serials, Arabization had progressed.[23] But not so Moroccanization: RTM produced little apart from newscasts, taped songs, and a few plays—much of it looking, said local critics, like "televised radio."

A glance at the listings for a normal week (Figure 6) will give an idea of the programming. The absence of sports that week was abnormal. A few days later, the June 21–27 week (during Ramadan) featured several hours a day from the Moscow Olympics. Among other items commonly presented in the spring of 1980 were visits of the King to the provinces, patriotic songs, Andalusian music, and locally produced plays.

In 1978, Chakroun found the following distribution of program types: advertising, 4.35%; religion, 5.56%; education, 8.41%; culture, 11.22%; news and public affairs, 22.34%; entertainment, 48.12% (1979, p. 19).

---

[22]In 1971, that meant 32% of urban households and 97% of villages.
[23]The Institut national de l'audiovisuel (INA) sends French-made programs selected by RTM, which French State Department subsidies make inexpensive. It sent 706 hours in 1973, 440 hours in 1976, and only 289 hours in 1979.

Entertainment consists to a large extent of serials and movies from Egypt, Lebanon, Jordan, France, and the United States. American series are particularly relished: "Social calendars are re-arranged to accommodate 'Rich Man, Poor Man,' " reported an American who lives in Rabat. Yet what the Moroccan in the street enjoys most (apart from sports perhaps) is locally produced entertainment, like a famous weekend variety show that, for several years in the late 1960s, was produced at the Mohammed V Theatre in Rabat. An interesting 1980 compromise was an Iraqi serial that systematically incorporated music hall items done by Moroccan artists.

Spanish and English were granted only a few minutes on Sundays. Berber appeared only occasionally as folklore performed by a singing *rais* with his orchestra. French, on the contrary, was heard some 40% of the time, exactly 38.8% when Kallati monitored RTM-TV in January 1978 (1973, p. 183).

4.3.5 Educational Broadcasting

Instructional radio was experimented with in 1960 and launched in October 1961 with the help of French broadcasting and UNESCO. Over 1000 sets and 1000 loudspeakers were distributed to schools. The main purpose was to retrain primary school teachers. There were six hours a week in French and ten hours in classical Arabic. The next year, for lack of a clear constitution and adequate budget, the project was gradually paralyzed. For similar reasons, educational television, which started in 1965 with a daily half-hour aimed at adults (housewives especially), stopped in 1967. When revived in 1968–69, it was intended only for high schol students about to graduate.

In 1972 came the creation of the Radio Télévision Scolaire (RTS), placed under the authority of the Minister of Education. The same year educational TV was relaunched mainly to provide primary school teachers with re-fresher courses. This could not be claimed to be a success (Cassirer 1975). Programs and schedules were unpredictable, and at the scheduled time (1830) teachers were busy with their second wave of afternoon students. The quality and relevance of the programs was unattractive. Local needs were not taken into account, and little feedback was obtained. In addition, accompanying literature was ill-distributed.

In 1977 the new Minister of Education, who belonged to the Istiqlal, announced that he wanted to promote RTS. It did move to new larger premises in 1978, but austerity struck: in 1979 RTS was granted only 200,000 DH for staff and 300,000 DH for equipment. Meanwhile, Arabization-cum-Moroccanization (which the Istiqlal champions) did not ease the problem of lack of expertise.[24] The training of specialists and the development of suit-able software had only just started being tackled by the Hassan II Center for Educational Television (1977), built in Ain Chok with the assistance of the French Institut national de l'audiovisuel (INA).

[24]Before 1974, the RTS was practically run by the French Cultural Services.

Figure 6. A Week's TV Programs

Monday, June 2, 1980

1830 Sign on; Reading of Koran;
Presentation of evening's programs
1845 10th episode of (French) serial "The
Separation"
1915 News in French
1940 "Artistic Encounter" with
Mohammed Al Mouji
2030 News in Arabic
2130 12th episode of (Egyptian) serial "My
Dear Children, Thank You!"
2210 "Pictures of Life" (Moroccan)
2300 Last news bulletin; reading of Koran;
Close down

Tuesday, June 3

1830 Sign on; Reading of Koran;
Presentation
1845 Children's program: "Uncle Driss"
1915 News in French
1930 Educational TV: natural sciences,
"Wild Animals" (imported)
1950 Religious program
2000 "Between Yesterday and Today"
(about leather-tanning)
2030 News in Arabic
2110 (U.S.) movie (dubbed) in French
"Histoire d'un amour"
2245 Variety (songs)
2300 Last news; Koran; Close down

Wednesday, June 4

1830 Sign on; Reading of Koran;
Presentation
1845 Children's Program
1915 News in French
1930 Educational TV: "Drawing"
2000 "From One Object to the Next," a
program by Hassan Talbi (Moroccan)
2030 News in Arabic
2115 13th episode of serial "My Dear
Children, Thank You!"
2215 Literary Review
2300 Last news; Koran; Close down

Thursday, June 5

1830 Sign on; Reading of Koran;
Presentation
1845 "The World of Dance" by
Mohammed Lotfi (Morocco)
1915 News in French
1930 Literacy Assizes (Egyptian)
2030 News in Arabic
2115 4th episode of (Italian) serial
"Leonardo da Vinci" (in French)
2215 "The Seven Dice" by Mohammed El
Bouanani (games)
2300 Last News; Koran; Close down

Note: On Wednesday June 4 will be played the King's
Cup final between Real (Madrid) and Castilla, at 1830.
Let us hope that the RTM will show the game (of
soccer).

As far as adult education is concerned—important in itself but also,
through women, for the education of children—vast projects were
announced in 1963 and 1965. By 1980, little effort had been made, especially
little concerted effort, with RTM, RTS, and the Hassan II Center all
theoretically involved. Very little was done on TV, not much on radio. In a
country that is predominantly rural, for instance, only 1% of radio time was
devoted to agriculture. The Ministries of Education, of Agriculture, of
Health and Family Planning, and of Islamic Affairs did employ broadcasting
but not in cooperation with the users, and never in dialectal Arabic.
"Morocco does not care to emulate Italy in its use of television to fight

Friday, June 6

1830 Sign on; Koran; Presentation
1845 Children's program: "Sindibad"
1915 News in French
1945 5th episode of the (Moroccan) serial "Roses Fade"
2005 Religious program
2030 News in Arabic
2115 "Thoughts and Theories" by Dr. Ben Aboud (Moroccan religious program)
2200 A feature film in Arabic
2215 Last news; Koran; Close down

Saturday, June 7

1830 Sign on; Koran; Presentation
1845 Children's program: "Drawings" by A. Filali (Moroccan)
1915 News in French
1920 "The Little [music] Conservatory of Abdenbi Jirari" (Moroccan)
2030 News in Arabic
2115 A new episode of the (British, dubbed in French) serial "Upstairs, Downstairs"
2015 4th episode of the serial "Men on the Way" (*Nass ala Tarik*) (imported)
2300 Last news; Koran; Close down

Sunday, June 8

1500 Sign on; Koran; Presentation
1515 10th episode of the (Egyptian) serial "Samra"
1615 "The Third Time" (a knowledge competition between two high schools)
1715 The Week in Review in English
1730 The World of Circuses (The Bulgarian Circus)
1850 The Week in Review in Spanish
1900 Variety (songs)
1915 News in French
1930 A new episode of the serial "Little House on the Prairie" (U.S. dubbed in French)
2030 News in Arabic
2115 Cine-Club (quality movie and discussion); Last news; Koran; Close down

SOURCE: *Le Matin (du Sahara)* 1980a, translated by the writer.

illiteracy," wrote Jibril—although the task was such that it would by itself justify the opening of a second TV channel (*Lamalif* 1977, p. 31).

4.3.6 Broadcast Journalism

Information has always been looked upon as the primary mission of Moroccan broadcasting. Thirteen hours of "news" were produced daily in the late 1970s, 9% of all programming. It seems all the more important for RTM as so little is produced in other fields. One explanation given is that "interest in broadcast news, a characteristic of Maghrebian audiences generally, seems even intensified here." (Elgabri 1974, p. 34). Actually it is official policy that national attention must be focused on the King and his ministers.[25]

The centrally important National Network gives six 10- to 30-minute newscasts a day (the most important at 0700, 1300, 1800, and 2300) and 3- to 5-minute summaries every hour on the hour. The other radio services take their cues, and usually their texts, from the "A" Network, as does TV. The early evening 45-minute TV news, read in classical Arabic with few pictures, can expand to two hours. Most of the news is domestic, the hierarchy of subjects being the King's activities, national news, news of the Arab world, news of Africa, news of the rest of the world, then sports and weather. The sources are the Royal Cabinet, the Ministry of Information, correspondents in the major cities, and the national news agency, Maghreb Arab Press (MAP).

RTM has links with the outside world other than MAP. It is connected to Spain by microwave and to France by cable. It has been receiving Eurovision programs since the mid-1960s. It is a member of the European Broadcasting Union (EBU), the African URTNA, and the Arab States Broadcasting Union (ASBU). It has at various times cooperated with nations in Western and Eastern Europe and in North America. Pooling resources with Algeria and Tunisia seemed an obvious move. A Maghrebvision network was discussed from 1966, started operating by microwave in 1970, but was promptly stalled by political conflicts.

Actually the closest cooperation has always been with France, in spite of friction between the governments. Following such agreements as the conventions signed in 1963 and 1972 (supplemented in 1976) France has supplied equipment, technicians and consultants, training, and programs. The 1975 fragmentation of the monolithic French ORTF into seven distinct and specialized units made for much confusion. For instance, TDF, the technical unit, for some years stopped working with Morocco while INA (part of SFP, the independent production unit) was helping at the Ain Chok center. In 1980, TDF resumed its assistance. Quite separately, the Antenne 2 unit (the second French TV network) began collaborating with RTM in 1976.

4.3.7 The Moroccan Public

The 1971 census indicated that 87% of women were illiterate, as were 87% of rural men and women. In 1978 the national average was estimated to be 75%. This alone could account for the extraordinary popularity of radio. But also to be considered are the geographical isolation of many villages, the social segregation of women, and the general paucity of entertainment, especially outside the cities. Other factors are the ancient Moslem and local tradition of oral communication, commonality of language, and, of course,

---

[25]This was evident in 1963, when, to prepare for the December referendum on the Constitution, the government had 4,000 TV sets distributed to cafes, hotels, and other public places.

transistorized receivers that appeared on the market just when radio stopped serving exclusively the French, the wealthy, and the intellectuals.

A 1973 survey[26] showed that 92.1% of city dwellers listened to radio regularly, and 75.4% of the rural population, with many sets blaring away in cafes and shops. There being no license fees for radio now, not even a minimum number of sets in use can be specified. In 1980, three million was considered a reasonable figure, as opposed to 133,000 licensed sets in 1950 and 512,000 in 1960, the actual numbers being about double. In the late 1960s it was believed that about half the sets were equipped for shortwave.

Statistics for television are more precise. In 1980 RTM reported to the European Broadcasting Union 726,420 black and white and 20,770 color licensed sets. The number of receivers actually used was, of course, higher, probably by 10–25%. Even before RTM-TV went on the air, Moroccans are said to have owned about 95,000 sets to watch foreign broadcasts. In the 1960s, the government variously encouraged the sale of low-priced sets, but the sale of TV sets did not dramatically increase until the early 1970s.[27] At that time, several factors coincided: an economic euphoria (due to general salary raises, the 1973 Investment Code, etc.); a better-educated post-independence generation coming of age; and a government effort in favor of broadcasting triggered by the Saharan conflict.

In the upper classes, a set will be acquired for the children and the domestics. For the middle classes, purchasing a set (on credit) is a priority: it provides prestige and tightens the traditional family bonds. Poorer men, the younger ones particularly, will view television in cafes, as the price of a black and white set still represents four to five times the minimum monthly salary. Television has so much become part of the cafe scene that prices go up when people come in for the shows after the news,[28] and rise even more when sports are on. Though less than 60% of the territory (not including Western Sahara) was covered by television in the late 1970s, it was estimated that about 60% of the population had access to a set at least occasionally, i.e., over ten million Moroccans. The 1973 SOPEM survey found that over 20% watched every day, 17% at least once a week, and 37% seldom or never (Abderahim 1978, p. 56). Home-bound women tend to watch more than men. Though moving pictures and stereotyped story-lines make television relatively easy for all to follow, the young in particular find it more attractive, partly because they can, being better educated, understand classical Arabic and French.

[26]This was a survey done in 1973 by SOPEM (Paris) on the audience of Radio Tanger, which was financed by advertisers (Service autonome de publicité; informations et publicités Maroc; Agence Havas Marocaine; and Univers Maroc). See Abderahim 1978, p. 56.
[27]In 1970, there were only 190,000 licensed sets (probably 250,000 in use), 58% of them in the Casablanca-Rabat area and 34% in the next four largest cities.
[28]A July 1974 survey showed peak viewing time was 2100 to 2330, with a maximum between 2130 and 2300. See *Lamalif* 1977.

4.3.8 Problems of Broadcasting

Moroccan television is an institution that breeds obscurantism. . . . It serves as a garbage-can for the worst foreign programs. . . . It presents an abominable image of our country. . . . Not even our fiercest enemies could have invented such a mill of anti-national propaganda . . . *Al Asas* (June, 1980) [Lamrhili 1980, pp. 6–7]

Though not all criticism of RTM is as shrill as that of this radical monthly, much of it does carry a similar message. Negative judgments come not only from French, American, or German consultants. Research work by Moroccan academics, assessments in the press, and speeches in Parliament[29] have been remarkably outspoken in recent years. Strictures are clearly inspired by a patriotic desire for improvement. In a nutshell, RTM is accused of being politically shackled, professionally mediocre, and culturally alienating.

At RTM, apart from the fact that the journalists' scripts are read by speakers, "self-censorship becomes an obsession . . . to avoid any risk of even vaguely alluding to any taboo topic" (*Lamalif* 1977, p. 30). Whatever discontent there is with governmental policies (or lack of them), with bureaucratic abuse, with speculation and corruption, it never is heard on the air, not even under the guise of police blotter news items. RTM will not even accept free high-quality documentaries on remarkable achievements in other Arab countries (e.g., educational TV in Kuwait) for fear of generating disaffection toward the Moroccan regime. In 1978–79, RTM-TV did produce a very successful weekly program called "Samar" in which VIPs from every section of the political spectrum (including the socialists and communists) were in turn invited, with guests of their choice, to talk about their experience of preindependence history. Even that atopical show seems to have come as a refreshing shock (*Lamalif* 1979b, p. 15).

As late as 1980, it was taken for granted that all news was scrutinized beforehand, if not dictated, by the Palace and that the main task of broadcast journalism was to support king and government. The effect, everyone agreed, was that the "news" was uninformative—and unexciting. In cafes, customers will only interrupt their games and conversation when at last the evening entertainment starts. During the Green March in 1975, the news did become lively and popular because it then reflected the words and concerns of the ordinary people. Critics maintain, however, that the lesson was not learned. "To a large extent, the electronic media are bad," says Zakya, "because they have to give the full text of the least official speech, and even sometimes repeat it," while a crucial issue, like the war in the Sahara, "does not produce any information. There's complete silence" (*Lamalif* 1979a, p. 6).

[29]"Protest is developing against the media. . . . [N]ot only does it come from opposition members [of Parliament]. The most virulent criticism issues from the Independents [a new party of moderates that has held the majority in Parliament since 1977]" (Zakya 1979, p. 4).

Ostensibly, state control is motivated by the need to keep the whole nation gathered around the throne and active in the effort to develop the economy; but mobilization for development necessitates feedback. "The total absence of relationship between the RTM and its listeners and viewers," Abderahim notes, "represents a major obstacle to its action" (Abderahim 1978, p. 49). More specifically, RTM "seems to pay no attention whatsoever to the general and permanent dissatisfaction" with its services (Jibril 1977, pp. 26–34).

Given the close governmental attention, it is the more surprising that clear policies for RTM were never articulated or vigorously enforced. The resulting lack of quality is such that in July 1980 RTM was denounced in the semiofficial *Le Matin (du Sahara)*. "We too often forget," wrote the Grumbler in his column, "that our enemies too are listening and making great fun of our lack of discipline and our slovenliness as broadcasters." He added, "We would like every evening to watch an international movie. . . . Certainly we appreciate that so much air time is devoted to movies in Arabic—provided they be not lemons, which they usually are" (1980b, p. 2).

"The organization of the RTM is archaic, unadapted and it should be reformed to face the new needs of television," a (confidential) official report affirmed not long ago. Apart from the absence of a precise legal framework, broadcasting has long suffered from a lack of leadership and expertise. Top executives have too often been political appointees, ignorant of radio and television, who did not stay on long enough to learn, but who, critics say, brought in untrained or hastily trained protégés who *have* stayed on. Hence, they claim, a "mafia" developed within the RTM monolith that has institutionalized muddling through and that resists any change. RTM management, according to French consultants, is definitely inferior to that of the huge RTA (Algeria) and even of the RTT (Tunisia). For instance, constant complaints are heard about insufficient funding; yet, in the 1974–77 period, RTM spent only 60% of the 244 million DH the Plan had budgeted for it. In December 1979, for the first time, an engineer risen from RTM ranks was appointed its director general. This, however, was not considered totally satisfactory, for one problem with RTM is that investments have too often gone to transmitters (with little long-range planning) rather than to production facilities or to the training of administrative, technical, and artistic staff. Little was seriously done until the late 1970s to fight the general shortage of mature, well-trained producers, scriptwriters, and journalists.[30] The result is that RTM cannot produce more than 15–20% of its programs, aside from the news, even though it overworks its equipment and personnel.

---

[30]With support since 1971 from the German F. Naumann Foundation, the Training Center for Journalists in Rabat has developed into the Institut supérieur de journalisme (1977), which graduates twenty to thirty students a year.

Too much of the hardware is old and old-fashioned. Eurovision pictures of international events can be shown the same day; but, for lack of video equipment, films of domestic events may be up to three days late. When some apparatus breaks down, it is too often discarded because no one can repair it or cares to. Technicians are so relaxed, notes a British visitor (Garrett 1978, pp. 46–48), that they commonly ignore schedules (except for the sacrosanct newscasts, which will come on even if the previous show is far from finished). They miss cues, cut to a blank screen, or forget the sound. Low salaries and ill-defined functions do not breed professional fervor. Programs and schedules do not seem to be anybody's prime concern. "No one can tell you who exactly is responsible and on what criteria programming is determined," writes Jibril (1977, p. 29). Nor does anyone know precisely, or really care about, what the public needs and wants. The situation is such that, RTM having in early 1980 systematically shown the great matches of the European soccer season and viewers having loved it, several newspapers wondered aloud if the government had finally articulated a policy for television. Too frequently some cheap foreign material is acquired and scheduled, and then the time is preempted by officialdom. A Rabat cab driver told the writer glumly in November 1979: "To choose, the only thing you can do is to turn off the set. No movies. Always the Green March and the celebrations of Independence. Mohamed V is dead. Like De Gaulle, it's finished. There are songs, yes, but not many. And also a little soccer."

Political control of broadcasting is far more common in the world than broadcasting freedom, and Morocco is in no way exceptional. Failure to respect professional standards set by the more developed countries is unavoidable in developing nations. What then of the cultural complaints Moroccans make against television?

To many illiterates, much of TV entertainment, though fascinating, is irrelevant, especially as they cannot understand the dialogues. Even the sentimental Egyptian serials, which they are accustomed to by now, seem a little silly and alien to them. What they would most enjoy is local productions set in an environment familiar to them and dealing with their joys and concerns. The most traditional people object to TV programs for puritanical, even religious, reasons. Fathers, if uneducated, find them a threat to their authority, if only because children are prompted to ask questions that they are unable to answer. While only a few parents may object to the Syrian or Egyptian words, accents, and attitudes that some young people adopt, many adults hold TV responsible for youth's rejection of their values and ideals. Television is commonly accused of leading the younger generation to abandon the fields and forsake manual labor to seek conspicuous consumption as pictured on the screen.

Certainly broadcasting deepens the cultural gap between Arabic-traditional and French-modern. The Istiqlal Party has vigorously pressed for arabization, particularly since 1973. But here Morocco faces two problems.

One is that neo-classical Arabic, though it has developed into an international idiom for media, still sounds foreign to many and, in its purer forms, can even be incomprehensible, especially to the children. The more colloquialized classical Arabic, used in variety shows, for example, would be welcome, but popular experiments with news in dialectal Arabic have not been followed through. The second problem is set by the Berberophones. Since 1977, they have become more vocal in their opposition to the absence of their language on the major radio network and on television. Difficult as it is for a foreign observer to appreciate, many Moroccans simply do not clearly understand much of what is said on Moroccan radio and television.

In more sophisticated circles, it is vehemently regretted that broadcasting, TV above all, has done so little to conserve and enrich the national culture (Jibril 1977, p. 32). It could, for instance, have stimulated the growth of a Moroccan cinema. Local investors find films too risky as compared to real estate, while the government-controlled Centre Cinématographique Marocain (CCM) is too propaganda-oriented to promote creativity.

4.3.9 Foreign Media in Morocco

Just as many of the 450,000 Moroccans in France will listen to RTM's National Network on mediumwave at night, Moroccans in their homeland consume foreign media, including TV.[31] Inhabitants of Oujda and the eastern border view Algerian television. Spanish TV is normally received in the north. A special antenna makes it possible to watch it, together with Portugese TV, as far south as Rabat.

As for radio, older people who formerly listened for Arab music to Cairo on shortwave or to Algiers had probably, by 1980, switched to the Arabic program of the British Broadcasting Corporation (BBC). Radio France Internationale (RFI) broadcasts in French but, unlike the BBC, RFI is more interested in Africa than in the Middle East. Hence its "24 heures en Afrique" has had the favor of many, especially students, since the Moroccan concern has shifted to the Sahara. VOA seems to have a small following and Radio Moscow, which is clearly audible, appears not to be credible. Far less than 10% of the population regularly listen to anything apart from RTM; but those are people interested in news, opinion leaders, whether they are intellectuals or small tradesmen and craftsmen. Quite different are the young educated people who at night tune in on longwave to the pop music of the French peripheral stations like Europe Number One or RTL (Luxembourg).

4.3.10 Conclusion

For years Moroccan broadcasting was considered inferior to that of Algeria or Tunisia. State control was tight and negative. A turning point in RTM history may have come with the 1975 Green March, for which it mobilized a

---

[31]For a historical survey, see Boyd 1976, pp. 183–96.

mass movement and unified the nation as the media had never done before. Apparently this came as a shock both to the authorities and to the public. Things slowed down afterwards, if only for economic reasons,[32] but seemed to be still moving in 1980.

Planned for the immediate future were the extension of TV coverage, the renovation of transmitters, the expansion of production facilities (at the Casablanca station and in a new Maison de la Radio in Rabat), and the better training of personnel.

In July 1980, SOFIRAD, the French state-controlled holding company announced that a powerful long- and short-wave, French-speaking commercial radio station was about to be built in Nador in the northeast of Morocco. Radio Méditerranée Internationale (RMI) would start broadcasting in late 1982. Meanwhile it would take over the management of Radio Tanger. Thus what in 1969–70 had been a Dutch-Swiss project, had become a Franco-Moroccan (49–51%) joint venture aimed at exploiting a market neglected by RMC (Radio Monte Carlo): Morocco, North Africa, and Black Africa. Morocco also looked upon it as a tool to build up its international image.

In July 1980, too, the decision seemed to have been finalized to open, within a year, a second television channel. This commercial network would also be a joint venture of the Moroccan state and private interests. Its purpose, among other things, would be to shake RTM's first channel into life.

Such big business undertakings seemed unlikely to cure many of the ills that plagued Moroccan broadcasting. The 1973–77 Plan had called for better, more diversified programming, adapted to the needs of society by use of audience research. It had called for more educational broadcasting and for lively news shows based not on speeches but on field reports. That was wise but it was not done.

Many of the attacks on Moroccan broadcasting, whether voiced by foreigners or by natives, derive from a comparison of RTM with its institutions in Europe or North Ameica. That comparison is unfair and could be crippling. A developing nation does not have the means to create a BBC or CBS, and it should not try. On the other hand, at the turn of the 1980s, the ever-increasing volume of criticism aimed at RTM and the real efforts made at improving its performances did show both an increased awareness of its problems and a budding desire to solve them.

---

[32]The 1978–82 plan had to be scrapped in favor of a triennial 1978–80 "Austerity Plan," mainly because of the oil crisis and the Saharan war.

4.4 Tunisia, *by Donald R. Browne*

Tunisia has generally suffered by comparison with its North African neighbors. Smaller by far, and possessing none of the oil wealth of Libya or Algeria, it has gone largely unnoticed in the turmoil of world or even regional politics. Yet this modest-sized nation has won a considerable reputation for its resourceful approach to national development—an approach in which broadcasting plays an important, if not necessarily constant, role.

The history of modern Tunisia is quickly told. It became independent of French rule in 1956, after a struggle that saw a number of Tunisian intelligentsia jailed but very few killed. In the following year it became a republic. Thereafter, it has been governed by one political party, the Destourian Socialist Party, and led by one chief of state, Habib Bourguiba. There have been various antigovernment protests and riots, some over religious issues and some over political, but little has changed, including the men who surround Bourguiba and rotate from one ministry to another. To its immediate neighbors it is remarkably placid; one North African proverb has it that "Morocco is the lion, Algeria the warrior, and Tunisia the woman." For the most part, change has come quietly and is not, at first glance, always obvious. The Tunisia of today, however, is a remarkable contrast with the newly independent Tunisia of 25 years ago, especially when one takes into account the limited resources with which it has had to fashion this transformation.

Not only is Tunisia not abundantly blessed with oil (although explorations continue), but other natural resources are also in short supply. Phosphate is the country's only major exportable natural resource. Other mineral deposits are hardly worth mentioning. Agricultural produce, chiefly olive oil, citrus fruits, and dates, finds its way to foreign markets, but the uncertain climate, with its long droughts and sudden torrential downpours, hampers maximum exploitation of this resource. Tourism has become a major source of foreign currency. As a result, hotel and resort construction has boomed; however the country's frequently rocky coast and general scarcity of water, combined with limited capital and hotel expertise, restrict development of this sort.

The two resources that have led to progress for the country are its people and its governmental policies. President Bourguiba has often called Tunisians "the nation's greatest resource"; and even if one makes allowances for a certain degree of political hyperbole, the description seems apt. Tunisians

Donald R. Browne is Professor of Speech-Communication at the University of Minnesota. He has written numerous monographs, book chapters, and articles about foreign and international broadcasting, including articles on Lebanese and Palestinian broadcasting. He lived in Tunisia from 1960 to 1963 and visited the country again in 1977.

are, on the whole, hard-working, even-tempered, and resourceful. Tunisia's governmental policies have aided the development process, too, in that the country has been able to seek the assistance of other nations, France and the United States in particular, without accepting priorities or philosophies that might accompany this assistance.

This does not mean that the country is without serious problems. The fickleness of the weather, combined with the aridity of much of the land in even the most favorable years, means that Tunisia lacks a stable agricultural base for the feeding of its own people, much less production for export. Two elements of progress—increased health care and educational opportunities—have led to further problems: rapid growth of population and of a specific segment of that population that is over-educated and/or underemployed. As President Bourguiba's health appears to grow worse by the year, predictions concerning the country's uncertain future circulate more and more freely—although not in the Tunisian mass media, which are either under direct government control or strongly subject to its influence. Indeed, the mass media themselves, with broadcating in the vanguard, appear to have conditioned the people to expect and desire stability and to see progress in evolutionary, rather than revolutionary, terms. And this itself has come about through a gradual process of evolution.

4.4.1 Radio before Television

The French were, on the whole, slower to develop broadcasting in their colonies and protectorates than were the British. Development of the media came earlier and progressed more rapidly in those colonies where comparatively large numbers of French citizens settled; and Tunisia was certainly one of these. Its proximity to France, the relative arability of land on or near the Mediterranean coast, the comparative docility of the Tunisians themselves led tens of thousands of French nationals to settle there. The colonial government licensed a broadcast service in 1930; it was intended primarily for the French colonists, and consisted largely of material imported from France. The service was based in Tunis, and few efforts were made to extend it beyond the areas where French colonists lived (primarily the northern third of the country). At the time of independence, there were an estimated 100,000 radio sets in the country, most of them in French households, the majority in and around Tunis.

The Tunisan government lost little time in developing broadcasting facilities. A number of French advisors stayed on to help operate Radio Tunis, and these included adminstrative, technical, and artistic personnel. This would have been necessary in any event, since there were few Tunisians trained to step in and take over, but it also stemmed from the fact that the Franco-Tunisian independence agreement contained numerous provisions guaranteeing the rights of French citizens living in Tunisia, including certain cultural rights:

The French shall continue to enjoy in Tunisia the cultural advantages from which they have benefitted up to now in the fields of thought and art, especially as concerns the entry, circulation and dissemination of all their means of expression. The Tunisian Government may nevertheless forbid publications which might jeopardize law and order or morals, with due respect for freedom of opinion and information. [*Le Monde Economique* 1956, p. 196.]

Thus, for the next several years, the French language service of Radio Tunis maintained its preindependence nature and scope: 8½ hours per weekday, 12½ hours on Saturday, 16 on Sunday as of 1960 (Voss 1962, p. 223), and with a program schedule featuring such educational fare as Mallarmé's poetry, "Athens Before Democracy," and the Stoic philosophers (Celarie 1962, p. 127). However, broadcasting in Arabic, which had taken second place to broadcasting in French in the preindependence period—6 hours per weekday as compared with 7½ hours in 1952—surged ahead during the late 1950s, and by 1960 the average weekday included 12 hours of Arabic broadcasting. Transmitters were also strengthened and services expanded. The southern city of Sfax received a 5-kilowatt transmitter in 1961, and a short-wave transmitter, intended to relay the Arabic service to southern Tunisia and to other parts of the Arab world, was installed in 1959. In 1960, the government initiated a plan to modernize and improve broadcasting facilities, at a cost of nearly four million dollars (*Republic of Tunisia: A Communications Factbook* 1964, p. 23).

Programming in the initial years of independence was something of a problem with respect to the Arabic service. Whereas the French service was able to draw upon the resources of ORTF in Paris (an October 1962 schedule lists such imported fare as a serialization of Dostoevski's *The Idiot*, jazz from the Champs Elysées, and "The Adventures of Tintin," a popular French comic book hero), the Arabic service had to fashion a schedule out of locally available resources. Some program material might have been available from Egyptian radio, but Nasser and Bourguiba were on poor to indifferent terms during much of this period. Certainly Egyptian popular music, widely available on disc, was played, as was a good deal of music by popular artists from Europe and the United States. Interviews with Tunisians from the world of the arts were also prominent, and not surprisingly, since Tunisians pride themselves on their achievements in poetry, illustration, ceramics, and numerous other manifestations of cultural life. Visiting artists from the Arab world, Europe, and elsewhere were also interviewed, and their visits were frequent enough so that few weeks went by without a guest appearance.

News broadcasting, too, posed relatively few problems. Tunisia's governmentally controlled news agency, Tunis Afrique Presse (TAP), drew upon the major American, European, and Arab news agencies, plus its own domestic reporters, to furnish a reasonably comprehensive service: and, with the aid of that service and its own reporting staff, the Arabic service of Radio Tunis was broadcasting news reports some 12 times a day by 1961. President Bourguiba's voice was frequently heard in these early days as well. His declarations and explanations of policy, his exhortations to the people to apply their collective efforts to the cause of national development, his reviews of progress made since independence, were weekly features in the broadcast schedule (Elgabri 1974a, p. 31).

But broadcasting as an arm of national development was another matter. Radio Tunis staff members were aware of the role that radio could play in this respect—UNESCO and other official and unofficial reports provided plenty of examples—but they had no tradition of their own on which to draw, since the French administration had rarely employed radio to this end. Gradually, and with the collaboration of various ministries (e.g., Agriculture, Public Health) and organizations (e.g., the General Unions of Tunisian Students and of Tunisian Workers), the staff developed a number of weekly broadcasts designed to answer listeners' questions concerning national development and to induce listeners to think more deeply about these issues. There were also special daily broadcasts for women, dealing with subjects ranging from education to fashion (Celarie 1962, pp. 126–27).

4.4.2 The Introduction of Television

Although broadcasting in the early years of independence was synonymous with radio, television was under active consideration by the late 1950s, and its imminent introduction was rumored yearly in the early 1960s. It was seen as "contributing to the creation of a national soul, to the political and civic education of the public" (*La Presse* 16 October 1962, p. 2). Although recognizing that the venture would be expensive, the government was overtaken by events. The Italian government had erected a television relay transmitter on Pantelleria, an island just east of Tunis, in order to reach Italians on the island as well as the Italian community then in Tunisia. Wealthy Tunisians were beginning to purchase sets, both to receive the Italian signal and in the hope of soon being able to do the same with the Tunisian service. As many of these individuals were well placed in Tunisian society (several were high government officials), their hopes had the effect of further stimulating the government to take action.[33] However, several years passed before the government committed the funds necessary for the introduction of television. The service was finally inaugurated on 31 May 1966, Tunisia's National Day.[34]

---

[33]I can recall several conversations with Tunisian businessmen and government officials in the course of which these feelings and desires were disclosed, during the latter part of my service in Tunisia with the United States Information Agency (1960–63).

[34]Not all of the time in the intervening years was spent in merely contemplating television. Training of television personnel had begun in the early 1960s, and a small practice studio was set up in 1963. Experimental broadcasts, both in Arabic and French, began in early 1966.

From the beginning, Tunisian television offered both information and entertainment: programs were both local and imported, some in French and some in Arabic. Broadcasts were generally limited to the early to mid-evening hours. The area of national development received considerable attention, and some of the new programs bore resemblance to certain of the radio programs already mentioned: "Women and Society" and "New Home" stressed the rights and duties of women in national development, while "Young People's Club" attempted to prepare younger viewers for "future participation in the national effort."[35] Those in charge of the new medium also began immediately to lay plans for television programs on agricultural and industrial development, despite the fact that there were as yet few sets available in the villages, and coverage was limited to a relatively small segment of the country. According to official Tunisian estimates, there were only some 5,500 television sets in Tunisia as of the end of 1966.[36]

4.4.3 From the Tenth Anniversary to the Present

Ten years after Tunisian independence, then, radio broadcasting was firmly in place as an instrument of national development, while television was in its infancy but displayed every sign of enjoying a healthy future. Plans were in place for the development of a relay system that would carry the new medium to all but the southernmost parts of the country, where, in any case, few people lived. The growth of both media since that time, in physical terms at least, has been impressive, and television's has been almost phenomenal. Table 15 shows the figures for set ownership from 1966 to 1979, and that growth has certainly been stimulated by the concomitant growth of both number and power of transmitters. Where in 1966 there were six radio transmitters—mediumwave, shortwave, and FM—most of them located just outside Tunis, and with a total power of a little over 200 kilowatts, by 1979 there were nine radio transmitters, near Tunis, Sfax, Gafso, and Monastir, and with a collective power of nearly 3000 kilowatts. Television, for its part, went from one 100-kilowatt transmitter just outside Tunis to a 1979 total of 11 transmitters all across the country, with a combined total of just over 1200 kilowatts.

Along with these increases in transmitter power, there has been dedication to the production of Tunisian programs, as opposed to imported fare.

[35]Akrout 1966, p. 64. There was a considerable French role in the development of Tunisian television, including assistance with preliminary audience surveys and the dispatching of a team of 27 experts, in August 1965, to help prepare Tunisian staff to operate the new service. See Hirsch 1968, pp. 10–12.

[36]This and other official figures on sets in use, from 1966 to the present, are drawn from the yearly statistical charts on radio and television licenses, as they appear annually in the *EBU Review,* generally in the March issue. One must bear in mind that, in any country where there are license fees and taxes on sets, as is true for Tunisia, there will also be a certain degree of evasion of payment and black market trade in illicit receivers. It is impossible to judge the extent of this trade in Tunisia.

Table 15. Set Ownership in Tunisia (by number of licensed sets)

Year	Radio	Television	Combined
1966	370,000	5,500	—
1967	370,000	35,000	—
1968	370,000	37,000	—
1969	374,000	50,267	—
1970	380,000	72,000	—
1971	248,408	92,416	18,446
1972	251,085	109,569	20,946
1973	277,145	147,104	22,627
1974	283,727	165,841	23,775
1975	287,841	191,043	Not reported
1976	290,446	207,742	25,060
1977	290,446	207,742	25,060
1978	294,826	Not reported	282,248
1979	295,333	Not reported	291,330

SOURCE: Statistics furnished by government of Tunisia to *EBU Review*. No explanation furnished for abrupt decrease in figures for radio licenses between 1970 and 1971. Unofficial figures for radio set ownership at present run as high as 1,500,000. The change in numbers for the last three years is a reflection of a new reporting procedure.

Agreements with France ensure the provision of radio ("Tribune of History," "Crossroads of Knowledge") and television ("History in Judgement," "Dossier on the Screen") series, but these are few in number, as are British ("Anna Karenina") and American ("Grizzly Adams") shows. Egyptian films and series (e.g., "Ahlam el Fata Etair") are more numerous, and Lebanon has in the past furnished many programs; but well over 50% of the television schedule and over 90% of the radio schedule is Tunisian, making allowance for the fact that much of the popular music on various programs comes from abroad, as do news clips.

The range of Tunisian-produced programs is considerable. The June 1980 schedules include individual shows and series dealing with Tunisian history, economics, letters and music, original Tunisian drama for radio and television, in French and in Arabic, youth talent shows, serial dramas for preschool children, broadcasts from the Carthage Festival, medical and legal advice, quiz shows, Arabic poetry, tips on road safety, etc. News plays a prominent role in both media; radio carries it 13 times a day in Arabic and 12 times a day in French, while television carries it once a day in each language.

Radio provides two separate services: the National Service, in Arabic, which is on the air for 20 hours per day, and an International Service, in French for 16 hours a day and in Italian for 1 hour a day. There are also brief regional services from Sfax and Monastir, and the National Service is relayed to North Africa and Europe on shortwave. Television has one combined service (about 75% Arabic, 25% French) that is on the air from mid or late afternoon to 2300 or 2400, for an average of between seven and eight hours per day.

Although Tunisian Radio and Television is a government-operated service and is partially financed by the government, radio set owners (an estimated 295,000 as of July 1979, although this figure is probably far too low) pay an annual license fee of two dinars ($4.20) and radio-television set owners (an estimated 291,000 as of July 1979) pay a fee of five dinars.[37] There is no advertising on either medium, although it has been considered. A new law was enacted when the National Assembly discussed the 1980 budget that mandates that four millimes (about one U.S. cent) be added to consumer electricity bills. The amount is not to exceed 1200 millimes (about $2.50) every two months and is expected to provide an additional two million dinars for radio and television.

In contrast with most Western European systems of broadcasting, there are no citizens' advisory councils or boards, although the service does conduct surveys of the extent, nature, and degree of satisfaction of listening and viewing. The successive directors general of Tunisian Radio and Television have generally come from within the government, and few have had previous media experience. The Director General in 1980, Moncef ben Mahmoud, was previously the Director of Political Affairs in the Office of the Prime Minister. Previous directors general have included a governor of a province, deputy ministers, and, in one case (Slaheddine ben Hamida), a former chairman of Tunis Afrique Presse.

4.4.4 Broadcasting and Tunisian Development

Tunisian radio and television serves many needs—for entertainment, information, and education. Well over half of the broadcast time for both media is taken up by entertainment, with music playing a major role. Information, primarily in the form of newscasts, analyses, and press round-ups, takes perhaps another quarter of the total hours. Something less than a quarter of the time, then, is devoted to education, most of it informal. Each of these three general categories of programming can contain developmental messages, so it is useful to examine how they were designed to enhance political, economic, and educational development.

Political development was a part of the mission of Tunisian radio from the first days of independence. The nation was not deeply divided along political lines—indeed, there were no serious challenges to Habib Bourguiba and the Neo-Destour Party (as it was then called)—but it was the opinion of Bour-

---

[37]Statistics from *EBU Review* March 1980, p. 45. Because of conditions noted in note 36, above, and because transistor radios are especially easy to smuggle, it is presumed and even acknowledged by Tunisian officials that the number of undeclared radio sets may be considerable. One undated (probably early 1980) United States International Communications Agency factsheet on Tunisian Radio and Television cites a figure of 1,500,000 radio sets, or roughly one for every four Tunisians.

guiba that the majority of Tunisian citizens lacked "political awareness," especially in terms of what they should expect of their new government and what parts they themselves should play in that government. Accordingly, not only did Tunisian radio provide accounts of what the government and its leaders were doing; it also prepared programs in which citizens could raise questions and make comments about the government, within reasonable limits. (Certain elements within the Tunisian press have at times been critical of government policies and personalities, although some newspapers and magazines that carried their criticisms too far, in the opinion of the government, have been closed down. The broadcast services have never gone this far.)

But the real star of political broadcasting was President Bourguiba himself. Although he had not used radio often prior to independence (for one thing, he had spent considerable periods of time in jail), he made frequent and effective use of it thereafter. He covered a wide range of topics, from how to treat foreigners who visited the country to why it was no longer necessary or even respectable for women to wear the veil.[38] His manner of speaking was warm, yet direct, and very colorful: in one talk concerning the veil he referred to it as "filthy rag." He seemed often to search for the correct word to catch the precise meaning of what he wanted to convey when in reality he knew it all along. He punctuated his remarks with questions directed at his listeners, discussing their problems in specific enough terms so that he seemed really to know them. He enlisted their help in the task of national development by placing that help in concrete terms and within the realm of possibility.

As President Bourguiba's health declined in the mid to late 1960s, he appeared less and less frequently on radio and seldom on television, although his activities, as well as excerpts from his pronouncements, continued to receive full attention on the newscasts of both media.[39] None of his

[38]See Duvignaud 1970, *passim*, especially p. 291, for some interesting observations on Bourguiba's "national development" speeches and the role of radio in bringing them to the nation. Duvignaud is somewhat critical of the government, and, by implication, of Bourguiba, for having aroused a number of false hopes by the broadcast of these speeches. Bourguiba's use of radio and television has not been the subject of scholarly analysis, but something of his background and his approach to working with the Tunisian people is shown in Knapp 1970, ch. 8. This book, though dated, is an excellent introduction to the country. Considerably drier in style but more up-to-date is *Tunisia: A Country Study* 1979. Also, Bourguiba's speeches have from time to time touched directly upon the role of the media in national development. For example, in an April 1974 speech, he talked about the dissolution of moral values through "the texts of songs, which, on the whole, support base instincts." Cited in "L'Enjeu socio-culturel du Cinéma en Tunésie," *Interstages*, October 1979, p. 6.

[39]One example of a different mode of conveying the President's words and thoughts to the nation was a radio series entitled "With the Great Struggler" (1969), which featured excerpts from past speeches by Bourguiba, and which was designed to give Tunisians, especially younger ones, a better sense of the history of the national movement (Radio Tunis in Arabic, 3 July 1969, cited in *BBC Summary of World Broadcasts*, ME/W527/B/1, 11 July 1969).

cabinet ministers or other close political associates appears to have possessed the same charisma where radio broadcasts are concerned, and it may even be that the period of maximum effectiveness for such broadcasts is long since past. Radio where the average Tunisian citizen was concerned, was a new medium of communication in the late 1950s and early 1960s, and Bourguiba's employment of it was fresh and vital. Now it is an open question as to how long such freshness and vitality can be sustained or whether a "new" political personality could recapture or rekindle the spirit of earlier times. In any event, the point seems moot.

Economic development has been absent from Tunisian broadcasting in certain forms commonly found in developing nations—e.g., the rural radio forum. However, it has appeared in connection with two sectors of activity that are of considerable importance in the Tunisian economy: family planning and literacy training. Radio has been employed to both ends in numerous developing countries, and Tunisia's use of it in each case can hardly be described as pioneering. Still, formal family planning programs, especially those involving mass media campaigns, are not common in the Arab world, and the initiation of such an effort in Tunisia took a certain amount of courage and resourcefulness. Unfortunately, the effort was not successful and is more interesting in terms of what it tells us about failures than successes.[40]

Discussions about family planning had begun in 1962, and an official, albeit experimental, family planning program was launched in 1964. Several family planning centers were set up around the country, mobile units served more distant centers, and President Bourguiba gave his support to the effort through various speeches and brief remarks, some of them broadcast. In 1969, it was decided that family planning information should be introduced to the primary schools, and that television would be the medium to do so. The plan called for 10,000 television receivers to be placed in schools throughout the country; a small studio was constructed and a group of Tunisians was sent to France for training in program production and equipment maintenance. (The French government gave the program considerable financial support.) The studio was finally ready in February 1971, but was not inaugurated until May, when ten television receivers had been installed in classrooms in Tunis only. In the meantime, Tunisian financial commitments to the project had lessened; ministerial commitments were no longer as strong as they had been (partly, it seems, because there were five different ministers of education during the period 1969–71); and the result was that a projected series of 13 programs emerged as one film and one slide story. The film was incorporated into a television program and was quite enthusiastically recieved, but the effort stopped at that point.

[40]See Mahjoub 1976, pp. 217–30. For a more detailed account of some of the problems and successes in Tunisia's overall family planning effort during the 1960s, see Lapham 1970, pp. 241–53.

Where Tunisian broadcasting is concerned, educational development has been largely confined to adult education. The Ministry of Education appears to have taken relatively little interest in the direct use of radio and television in the classroom, although there was an interesting short-term experiment in 1972 that involved the use of "TV programs of educational interest" from France, Canada, the United States, Sweden, and Niger. In this experiment, the programs, plus introduction and other elements, were copied onto 16 mm film and were shown directly in classrooms if they could not be received directly through transmission of the television signal. Teachers were a bit put off at first by the "unmanageable" nature of student response to the programs (meaning that responses were nowhere near as predictable as they had been for more traditional classroom fare), but the programs appeared to promote a good deal of classroom participation, and some teachers found that the programs sparked fresh student interest in certain subjects (e.g., French, mathematics). The experiment was financed by UNESCO and the French-based Agence de Coopération Culturelle et Technique (Egly 1974). The emphasis on a transnational approach to education should have been especially welcome in Tunisia, given the country's openness to other cultures, but there is no indication that it has been continued in any form, on television at any rate.

There have been a few examples of more or less formal adult education through radio and television, although these have not been tied in with formal credit-granting institutions. Certain series, especially of Tunisian and Arabic culture (music, poetry, etc.) have been offered as self-study courses, and accompanying printed material has been made available for those wishing to purchase it. Tunisia has also participated in the International Radio University, a European-based organization that produces tapes on international topics, predominantly in French, for broadcast.

Tunisia's "literacy through radio and television" efforts were somewhat more successful, although they were plagued by some of the same problems as was the family planning series. The Tunisian government had launched a literacy campaign in 1966 with the announcement of a series of five-year plans running until 1997. Initial efforts did not involve the broadcast media, but in January 1968 radio and television were employed on an experimental basis for a period of six months, during which time various problems concerning their utilization were discovered, analyzed, and, in some cases, solved. A second and larger experimental effort involving radio and television ran from October 1968 to June 1969. In it, radio and television literacy lessons (the two media essentially duplicated and reinforced one another) were to be followed by people in various circumstances. Some were in highly organized study centers, others were in less formal study centers, and still others followed the lessons at home. The Tunisian Office of Social Education conducted a survey in June 1969 in which it discovered that over 25,000 people had followed the course of a regular basis, almost half of them children of school age. The hour of broadcast—1730—turned out to be unfavorable for the attendance of adults working outside the home, but nearly 9,000 women claimed to have followed the program regularly.

A report made for UNESCO in January 1971 (Allebeck *et al*, 1971, pp. 41–51) on the literacy series pointed out that the commitment of educational and financial resources to the project by the Tunisian authorities was hardly overwhelming. Budgets were cut back sharply. The presenters themselves often showed up to do the programs at the last minute ("et même plus tard," according to the report) because they were not given release time from their regular teaching jobs. Many of the study centers were not properly staffed since too many facilitators were trained, if at all, in theoretical aspects of working with the illiterate and a special series of seminars had to be organized to introduce them to the more practical aspects of this work. Also, the necessary support material did not always reach the centers.

Despite all of these problems and drawbacks, the experiment appears to have been successful and has continued, although not on the massive scale originally envisaged back in 1966. Radio has been made more independent of television, and the special requirements of educating the illiterate have become more clearly understood through a series of research studies conducted by the Economic and Social Research Study Center of the University of Tunis. The virtual collapse of the Tunisian agricultural cooperative scheme at the end of the 1960s was harmful to the literacy training effort, since the latter was closely tied in with the former; but the provision of literacy lessons through radio and television also enabled a large number of Tunisians to follow the lessons on their own, without depending on the study centers that had often been developed in conjunction with the cooperatives.

The past decade has seen no further broadcast programs of the scope or ambition of the two already described. There are regular daily and weekly programs for farmers, women, businessmen, etc., but these are generally brief (5 to 15 minutes) and not coordinated with other media of communication, such as pamphlets, discussion meetings, etc. Furthermore, their effects, derived from assessment of reception to assessment of impact, are rarely measured. It is quite possible that these programs are very successful: the average Tunisian appears to be more prepared to consider innovation than are his Maghrebian neighbors; radio and television set ownership is widespread; and the government generally enjoys the confidence of the people. However, more specific indications are generally lacking.

One might well assume that classroom use of radio and television would be widespread in Tunisia. That it is not could be explained by the aforementioned lack of interest in these media on the part of the Ministry of Education, but this begs the question. Lack of interest may itself be explained by a tendency on the part of the Ministry to follow certain of the more traditional French approaches to education, in which the audio-visual media play a very minor role. It may also be due to lack of financial commitment for such activies on the part of the goverment, perhaps again because the Ministry itself sees more pressing needs. There is also little doubt that many teachers, especially in rural areas, feel threatened by educational radio and television, which may approach some subjects with greater knowledge or sophistication than the teachers possess. Whatever the reason, efforts in this particular sphere have been modest.[41]

As Tunisia begins its second quarter-century of independence, it seems apparent that its broadcasting system has been an important element in national development in certain respects, notably political and cultural development, but that it is currently underutilized in other respects, notably economic and educational development. The relative excellence of Tunisian political and cultural broadcasting should be examined in light of one important factor: the country had strong political and cultural unity at the time of independence that spared Tunisian radio, and subsequently television, the fierce battles that raged over these issues in many developing countries and in their broadcast systems. Nevertheless, President Bourguiba's use of broadcasting was quite remarkable, and the commitment to broadcasting virtually every facet of Tunisian culture gives Tunisian broadcasting officials justifiable pride.

The relative poverty of effort and of success of Tunisian economic and educational broadcasting should also be examined in light of certain factors. Two of the major attempts at economic development—family planning and literacy training—were exceptionally ambitious: the first was at that time virtual *terra incognita* for Arab countries, while the second has been one of the most difficult types of developmental broadcasting for any nation to execute successfully. The general lack of in-school educational broadcasting may be due as much to a lack of interest on the part of the Ministry of Education as it is to a lack of interest on the part of broadcasting officials,[42] and interministerial cooperation has not been common in Tunisia. Finally, the strong opposition in rural Tunisia to most collectivization efforts, notably the one launched by Minister of Planning Ahmed ben Saleh in the late

[41]An elaborate plan for the expansion of educational broadcasting in Tunisia was prepared in 1971 by a joint team from UNESCO and the Swedish International Development Authority (SIDA). It called for the expenditure of several million dollars for the creation and equipping of new studios and for increased production and distribution of television receivers (Tunisia assembles receivers from parts supplied by European firms, thus making it possible to offer the public relatively low-priced sets) etc. The plan was not put into operation, for reasons unknown to me. See Allebeck *et al.* 1971, pp. 85–151, for an outline of this plan.

[42]There also appears to be a tendency on the part of Tunisian broadcast officials to view radio and television first and foremost in terms of political and cultural broadcasting. This may be something of a legacy from the French, whose broadcast system emphasizes the same things: most Tunisian broadcast staff who receive overseas training do so in France, which helps to perpetuate the tradition. Also, cultural broadcasting is a relatively "safe" area, compared with economic or educational broadcasting.

1960s, has had its impact on the few Tunisian attempts to organize broadcast forums of the sort that have been quite successful in many developing countries.

Tunisia's relative poverty must also be taken into account when assessing the uses made of broadcasting for national development. The modest license fees charged to listeners and viewers are inadequate to support an already well-established technical infrastructure, much less an ambitious program of developmental broadcasting. During the 1960s, the country was able to interest certain donor groups in sponsoring a few efforts at developmental broadcastng, but such aid has been harder to come by in the 1970s, perhaps because Tunisia is now considered to be one of the better-off developing countries.

Regional cooperation might be of some help to Tunisia, and in fact there is an organization that promotes such cooperation: Maghrebvision. Founded in 1970 by Morocco, Algeria, and Tunisia, it features a microwave hookup between the capitals of the three countries. However, most of the material exchanged through the system or co-produced by its members has been cultural in nature: economic and educational development have received little attention.[43] Tunis is also the new headquarters of the Arab League, following the removal of the League's offices from Cairo as a result of the Egyptian-Israeli Peace Treaty (1979); as such, Tunis has also become the headquarters of the Arab States Broadcasting Union (ASBU). It is too early to determine whether this will have any notable impact on Tunisian broadcasting.

In sum, the Tunisian approach to broadcasting has been characterized by the usual mixture of successes and failures enjoyed by most developing nations. While broadcasting does not appear to have a high position in the list of national priorities, it has been used with resourcefulness in certain spheres of activity. Its failures could in some cases be considered noble. But if it is to progress over the next 25 years, it will require a higher level of financial support, a greater degree of interministerial cooperation, and the flexibility to deal with a post-Bourguiba Tunisia.

---

[43]The early years of Maghrebvision are described in El Shafei 1974, pp. 26–30.

Part 3 International Radio Broadcasting in Arabic

5   Broadcasting to the Arab World

This chapter and the following one discuss international radio broadcasting—that is, the attempts of one nation or group to reach populations in other nations through transnational radio signals. A great deal of international television broadcasting also takes place in the Arab world: however, for the most part television programming is intended primarily for the population of the originating country and is received outside its borders inadvertently.

Chapter 5 examines radio broadcasts from outside the Arab world. The importance that a country attaches to the Middle East can be inferred from the emphasis it places on its international radio broadcasting to the area. The chapter explores the degree to which and the reasons why non-Arab countries broadcast in Arabic to the Arab world. It also analyzes the relative popularity of some of the international services and updates a 1975 survey of Arabic programming (Boyd 1976, pp. 183–96). In the fall of 1979 this writer sent letters to 44 broadcasters who were known or thought to be Arabic-language broadcasters; the response rate was 83%. All data were cross-checked with information provided by monitoring services, short-wave listening reports, and other sources such as the *World Radio-TV Handbook*.

International radio broadcasting among Arab countries is discussed in Chapter 6. The subject has been mentioned throughout the preceding chapters, and what follows will not duplicate what has already been presented. A closer examination of one Egyptian radio service, however, will serve as an example of how radio was used to promote a particular political philosophy. The Voice of the Arabs still serves as a model for other countries that hope to emulate its reported successes. Also to be discussed is the Arabic language itself and how it has been effective in reaching an often enthusiastic audience. Finally, the subject of unofficial or clandestine broadcasting among Arab countries will be examined. This kind of activity is not unique to the Middle East, but it is possibly more pervasive there than in any other part of the world.

5.1 Introduction

One observer clearly lists some of the reasons for the general receptivity to international Arabic programs in the Middle East:

1. There is high appreciation for oral culture in the Arab World.
2. Radio surmounts both the physical and political barriers which hamper the distribution of printed matter, and the obstacle of illiteracy.
3. The historical primacy of external broadcasting has turned listening to foreign stations into a tradition and a habit.
4. There is a saturation of shortwave receivers in most Arab countries.
5. In sharp contrast to countries where the cultural elites have inherited the ex-colonial languages, there is a comparative lack of such linguistically alienated elites in most Arab countries.
6. For technical, political, and geographical reasons, little or no high-frequency jamming is carried out in the Arab countries. [Wood 1979, pp. 117–18]

Two factors must be considered when discussing the generally favorable conditions for international broadcasting. First, broadcasting in the Arab world is done directly by the government or by organizations in which the government has a majority financial interest or outright control. There apparently is a good deal of listening to available foreign radio as a means of validating government-originated news. Second, many international radio broadcasts in Arabic are available to the Arab world listeners on medium-wave frequencies both during the day and at night. Therefore, a listener does not need a sophisticated short-wave radio in order to receive foreign radio broadcasts.

From the broadcaster's perspective the Arab countries have common interests that facilitate programming to a large geographical area in spite of the countries' unique histories, political orientations, and economic climates. The Arabic language is common to all countries; and although each country or region has its Arabic dialect, modern standard Arabic—that generally printed in newspapers and magazines and used on radio—is universally understood. Arab countries have many cultural similarities in that music, drama, poetry, and literature are widely shared. Despite the perception among non-Arab countries of disunity in the Arab world, most Arab states share a sense of common origin that probably dates from the spread of Islam (Shalaby 1979, pp. 3–11), a unifying religio-cultural force. With the possible exception of Egypt, which formally ended its state of war with Israel in 1979, Arab countries oppose the Israeli presence in the Middle East and feel that a solution to the Palestinian problem must be found.

5.2 Early Broadcasting Efforts

Arabic broadcasting to the Middle East started during the 1930s and was done exclusively by Italy, Britain, and Germany. Italy, the first to transmit in Arabic, started in 1934 from the Prato Smeraldo Radio Center in Rome (Radiotelevisione Italiana 1979). Early experimental broadcasts were apparently not blatantly political, until Mussolini focused his aspirations on North Africa and Ethiopia in the mid-1930s. Radio Bari, as the service was known, faced several obstacles as the first non-Arab-language broadcaster, such as lack of radio receivers in the target area and timing difficulties with listeners in a region where few clocks existed and where time still has a different dimension than in the west. As Rolo notes, the Italian government distributed radios and announced program times in terms of sunrise and sunset, and he well describes a scene that probably happened often:

> When the day's work was done both the fellaheen (peasants) and the city dwellers would betake themselves to their favorite cafes, huddle together under a fuming oil lamp, and stolidly smoking their water pipes play game after game of backgammon until the communal loudspeaker gave forth the voice of the Bari announcer. [1941, pp. 45–46]

Between 1935 and 1937, Bari was the only external service available in the Arab world. During this period, the tone of the transmissions turned decidedly anti-British. The broadcasts, while apparently well received among some listeners, did not cause undue concern among British diplomats, who tried to analyze the effect of the Italian programs.[1] But by 1937, in view of the pervasive British presence in Egypt, Palestine, Trans-Jordan, Iraq, and the states in the Arabian Gulf, the British government had become increasingly worried about the entire range of Italian anti-British propaganda in the Middle East and established several committees to determine how best to counter these efforts (Briggs 1965, pp. 398–99). Late in 1937, the government authorized the BBC to broadcast in foreign languages, including Spanish and Portuguese; Arabic was to be the first. There is some evidence that indicates that the Spanish and Portuguese services were authorized in order to avoid giving Mussolini the impression that Great Britain was starting the Arabic service specifically to counter the Bari broadcasts (Clark 1959, p. 173). The BBC Arabic Service started on 3 January 1938. The first program featured messages of good will by Sir John Reith, BBC Director General, the Egyptian Chargé d'Affaires in London, the Ministers of Iraq and Saudi Arabia, and the Governor of Aden (Mansell 1979; see also "Arabic Broadcasts from London" 1938, pp. 46–47). During the initial stages of the service, problems of personnel, dialect, and a suitable format were resolved;[2] from its beginnings until now, the service has

---

[1]See, for example, diplomatic correspondence in FO 395/663 and FO 395/557–60, File 2, Commonwealth and Foreign Office Archives, Kew Gardens, London, England.
[2]For a discussion of dialects and an overview of an early program schedule see Hilleson 1941, pp. 340–48.

been a reliable source of news and information. Its success has encouraged imitation: it was the proving ground for a format of Arabic foreign programming that would feature a mixture of Koran readings, news, drama, and music in Arabic. The British and Italian radio war officially ended 16 April 1938 with the signing of the Anglo-Italian Pact, which called for an end to hostile propaganda (Grandin 1939, p. 54). The agreement had important implications for the British government because it marked a new policy that recognized the significance of radio propaganda as a diplomatic instrument (Mackenzie 1938, p. 191).

Italian anti-British propaganda from Bari started again in late 1938, but thereafter Italy turned its attention to Europe, and the Germans took over the role of transmitting anti-British propaganda to the Arabs. Nazi broadcasts started in 1938 and greatly intensified during the last month of the year. The German broadcasts, more hostile than those from Italy, were strongly anti-Jewish, anti-Russian, and anti-British (McKenzie 1940, p. 210). The British were successful in recruiting announcers, poets, and musicians from the Arab world. The Nazis employed an Iraqi named Yunus al-Bahri, who, according to many who both worked with and listened to him, was a skilled announcer and propagandist whose microphone arts were unmatched even by those of Ahmed Said, the famous Voice of the Arabs announcer during the 1950s and 1960s. By 1939, the French had entered the field of Arabic broadcasting, but not to the extent that the Italians, British, and Germans had. The French were essentially concerned with their North African colonies, where transmissions from Paris could be picked up and rebroadcast over local stations.[3]

World War II necessitated new international broadcasting priorities. The United States broadcast some Arabic programming and in 1943 Russia formally started an Arabic service (Stepanova 1975). However, world interest in Arabic broadcasts is a post-World War II phenomenon and the dramatic increase in Arabic broadcast hours did not come until the 1960s and 1970s. The discussion that follows organizes Arabic-language broadcasters geographically, under the headings of Western Europe, Eastern Europe, Asia and the Middle East, the Americas, and Sub-Saharan Africa, as well as under the heading Christian Religious Broadcasters (and see Table 16).

5.3 Western Europe

A fashionable building on the Avenue Raymond Poincaré in Paris, between Place du Trocadero and Place Victor Hugo houses what may be the most popular foreign radio station in the Arab world. As of 1981, eight countries

---

[3]Some BBC programs were rebroadcast from Jerusalem over the Palestine Broadcasting Service. Italy used local facilities in Libya, as did France in Algeria and Tunisia.

Table 16. Hours of Broadcasting in Arabic to the Middle East, 1981

Country	Hours per Week
Western Europe	
France	119.0
Great Britain	63.0
Greece	8.0
Holland	22.1
Italy	14.0
Spain	31.5
Switzerland	3.5
West Germany	32.0
Total	293.1
Eastern Europe	
Albania	21.0
Bulgaria	21.0
Czechoslovakia	14.0
East Germany	38.0
Poland	17.5
Romania	14.0
Soviet Union	
Radio Moscow	49.0
Radio Peace and Progress	3.5
Yugoslavia	7.0
Total	185.0
Asia and the Middle East	
Afghanistan	3.5
Bangladesh	3.5
China	
People's Republic	14.0
Republic	14.0
India	17.5
Indonesia	7.0
Iran	10.5
Japan	3.5
Korea	
North	42.0
South	3.5
Malaysia	10.5
Pakistan	28.0
Sri Lanka	0.5
Turkey	7.0
Total	165.0
The Americas	
Chile	14.0
Cuba	14.0
U.S.A.	52.5
Venezuela	7.0
Total	87.5

Table 16. (continued)

Country	Hours per Week
The Americas (continued)	
Sub-Saharan Africa	
Ethiopia	7.0
Nigeria	10.5
Senegal	1.75
Somalia	7.0
Total	26.25
Christian Religious Broadcasters	
ELWA	13.5
FEBA	14.0
Trans World Radio	8.25
Vatican Radio	3.5
WYFR	3.5
Total	42.75

SOURCE: Notes compiled by Boyd.

of Western Europe broadcast 293.1 hours per week to the Arab world; of the eight countries, Radio Monte Carlo (RMC) Middle East accounts for almost half of the region's total transmission time. From its studios and offices in Paris, RMC sends 17 hours of programming per day by microwave links and undersea cable to a 600-kilowatt medium-wave transmitter on the island of Cyprus. The basic idea for a French commercial radio service to serve the Arab world originated with President Charles de Gaulle, who wanted to have a popular French voice in the Middle East to compete with services such as the BBC and the Voice of America ("Analysis/Radio Monte Carlo" 1979, p. 11; Regnier 1980). RMC is organized under the administrative control of SOMERA—a corporation owned by the French broadcasting organizations that succeeded ORTF—and Radio Monte Carlo (Monaco). Now SOMERA is owned half by SOFIRAD and the parent government corporation of Radio Monte Carlo (Monaco) and half by Radio Monte Carlo (Monaco) itself. Hence, this rather intricate organization is mainly owned by the French government. In December 1970, SOMERA completed an agreement with Cyprus for the location of the medium-wave transmitter. During the early 1970s, the studios were located in Monaco and the signal was sent by radio link to Cyprus. The completion of an undersea cable between Marseilles and Cyprus allowed a more reliable high-quality signal to reach the transmitter. In 1975, the programming and production departments started moving to Paris and, by 1978, the entire organization was in Paris (Bolbois 1975; Regnier 1980).

News is an important staple of the daily program and some observers date the popularity of RMC from the October 1973 Middle East War, when the station's newscasts were believed to be somewhat pro-Arab. RMC has an extensive network of correspondents throughout the Arab world who phone live reports to Paris regularly. Where this is not possible, bulletins are sent by telex by those correspondents with whom RMC has agreements. The impact of the news can possibly be illustrated by Saudi Arabia's reaction to the station's handling of the Mecca Mosque takeover in late 1979. The Saudi government jammed the station for three weeks; and in January 1980, when a French newspaper broke the news that French commandos had helped plan the retaking of the Mosque, the Saudi Arabian Embassy in Paris called the station and asked that it not broadcast the story—a request that the station honored (Regnier 1980). Arab listeners appear to tune in because of the programming, which features specific programs for women, some drama, interviews, French lessons, and regularly scheduled newscasts (Grille des Programmes 1980, pp. 2–3). However, the main ingredient in the schedule is popular music presented by skilled announcers in an American Top-40 format. Although announcers speak mostly Arabic, they occasionally use French and English expressions to introduce music in a style not unlike that which Arab MCs use in nightclubs catering to Egyptians, western-oriented Lebanese, and foreigners.

Programming is heavily commercial and the list of clients—80% of whom are represented by international advertising agencies—include most known multinational producers of food, automobiles, beer, cosmetics, and cigarettes. Of course, these advertisers are attracted to RMC because they believe that the service is popular and that it sells their products. RMC compares itself with other commercial stations in the Arab world, and the 1979 McCann survey gives it top popularity in Kuwait, Saudi Arabia and UAE/Oman, and second place in Jordan.[4] A 1978 PACC survey showed preferential listening across sex, age, and occupation groups in Saudi Arabia ("Extracts from Pan Arab Media Survey" 1978, pp. 1–6). Surveys done for the United States International Communication Agency in 1975 and 1977 indicates that RMC is more regularly listened to by urban populations than is the BBC (USICA 1978a, p. 2). Radio France International, the French state international service, does not now have an Arabic service.

The BBC transmits nine hours per day in Arabic on several short-wave and two medium-wave frequencies. London's Arabic schedule probably has the best coverage in the Arab world due to its powerful medium-wave East Mediterranean (Cyprus) and Eastern Relay (Masirah Island, Oman) trans-

---

[4] "Audience, Penetration and Listenership of Pan Arab Commercial Radio Stations in Jordan, Saudi Arabia, Kuwait, UAE/OMAN" 1979. Survey data on Arab foreign-radio listening can be unreliable and are open to a variety of interpretations. Also, the relative popularity of a station's music and entertainment programming is affected by factors such as availability of a clear, reliable short- and medium-wave signal, international and internal events at the time of the survey, and the relations between the receiving and transmitting countries. Survey data herein are not intended to be comprehensive, but rather are provided to give the reader a general picture of a service's popularity.

mitters. The initial Arabic Service in 1938 transmitted for three hours per week. This had expanded to seven hours by 31 August 1939, and by 1944 was at 21 hours per week. By the time of the Suez War in 1956, 28 hours per week were being programmed and were increasing in stages to 84 hours per week in 1959 and stabilizing to 70 hours per week by the June 1967 Six-Day War. During this conflict, the service peaked at 120 hours per week but by 1970 had returned to 70 hours per week (Mansell 1975). In April 1976, the economic situation in Great Britain necessitated a cutback of seven hours per week, bringing the 1980 weekly transmission time to 63 hours (Mansell 1979).

The Arabic Service has always originated from Bush House, London, but the BBC has occasionally produced recorded programs in the Arab world. Cairo was the production center prior to the 1956 war, after which the organization was located in Beirut until the 1975 civil war. The BBC has been a leader in innovative Arabic programming and has always been able to attract superior radio talent from the Arab world. Many of the early announcers and translators were instrumental in creating what would later become the modern form of broadcast Arabic (Mansell 1979: enclosure, "The Arabic Service Over Forty Years," p. 5). Some personnel were innovators and some were stars such as Issa Sabbagh, who broadcast throughout World War II. Sabbagh, a Palestinian, served as the Allies' answer to Yunis al-Bahri, who broadcast for Hitler. Sabbagh became an American citizen and a senior foreign service officer with the United States Information Agency.

Surveys by the International Communication Agency and commercial marketing firms as well as research done by this writer indicate that the BBC's Arabic Service is preferred to other foreign broadcasts. In addition, the BBC's Arabic news is perceived by respondents as being more reliable in terms of reporting world affairs. A 1974 VOA-CAAP survey in Kuwait concluded that 22.3% of respondents listened to the BBC Arabic Service at least once per week, and that 44.4% of households headed by professionals and technicians were regular listeners; only 18.1% were Voice of America listeners (USIA 1975, p. 3). A 1973 Bahrain survey produced similar results (USIA 1974). A 1977 survey in Jordan estimated that the BBC Arabic Service audience was three times the size of the Voice of America audience (USICA 1978b, p. 11). Survey data from the Sudan suggest that both of these services have similar audience sizes (USICA 1978a), but in Egypt the Voice of America tends to be more popular (USICA 1978c).

Deutsche Welle began in 1953 and is the oldest non-German language department in the Voice of Germany. Post war West German Arabic programs started in 1956 (Reichard 1979) and have gradually increased to where they can be heard 32 hours per week on both medium- and short-wave frequencies. Deutsche Welle's signal strength to the Middle East is helped by its Malta transmitter location that provides Arabic listeners with the DW program on mediumwave, although its signal is not as strong as the VOA or BBC because the latter's transmitter location in the Mediterranean is more advantageous. Surveys indicate that the West German Arabic Service is not as popular. This fact, however, has not discouraged Germany from broadcasting to an area of the world where it does substantial business.

Spain significantly increased its Arabic Service from 6 hours per week in 1975 to 31 hours per week by 1979. In fact, Radio Exterior de España uses Arabic as one of only two foreign languages; the other is English (Wood 1979, p. 118). The Spanish have a historical tie with the Arab world and increased trade and tourism between these areas apparently account for the importance that the Spanish external service attaches to its Arabic Service.

Holland was the first European country to inaugurate an Arabic service after World War II. In 1948, the Radio Nederland Board of Governors decided to start an Arabic service because of the interest that the Netherlands had in the Arab world, because of advice from a broad spectrum of the population including professors and the Foreign Ministry, and because other international broadcasters were interested in starting Arabic-language programming (Helbach 1979). By 1979, there were four transmissions per day for a weekly total of 22 hours. Radio Nederland has several relay stations outside Holland, but none is ideally suited for medium-wave transmission to the Middle East. Their relay station on Madagascar does, however, serve as a transmission site for short-wave relays in Arabic.

As for Italy, RAI's Arabic Service has had a history similar to that of Deutsche Welle. As noted earlier, the Italians were apparently the first to transmit in Arabic to the Middle East; Germany followed in the 1930s; and then there occurred after World War II a period of rebuilding facilities. RAI transmits 14 hours per week to the Arab world in Arabic—a two-hour per week increase since 1975 (Radiotelevisione Italiana). All programs are by shortwave and are primarily intended for North Africa, the area where Italy has traditionally had the most influence. Political and economic priorities have kept the Italian service small and no attempt has been made to reach the Arab world with a medium-wave signal. Preferences for the RAI service do not even appear on most surveys. Possibly, this is because of the nature of the broadcast schedule: the longest daily program is one hour, while the others occur for only 20 minutes at three separate times per day.

Swiss Radio International (SRI) started Arabic programming in 1964 and its current three and one-half hours per week in Arabic is only a slight decrease since 1975. The Swiss believe that their Arabic service is important because of traditional Swiss–Arab world ties, and the fact that many international organizations that have contacts with the Middle East are located in Switzerland. Because of the increasing volume of mail from that area, SRI believes that the service is both popular and respected in the Arab world (Fankhauser 1979). However, since 1978 a change in financing that involved the elimination of government support has prevented expansion of the service. Greece is the remaining European country to broadcast in Arabic and its two daily short-wave programs total only about four hours per week. Although there was a substantial Greek community in Egypt prior to Nasser, Greece has not had a close relationship with the Arab world. Contact with the Middle East increased after 1975 because many companies moved to Athens from Beirut after the Lebanese Civil War.

Radio Sweden has asked for government funding to start Arabic broadcasts, but thus far the money has not been provided (Gustafsson 1979).

Because of historical ties between some European countries (e.g., France and Great Britain) and the Arab world, and because of the continuing importance of Arab oil to Europe, it is likely that European-Arabic broadcasts will continue. Since 1975, transmission hours from Europe to the Middle East have increased by 32 hours per week.

5.4 Eastern Europe

The eight East European countries and the Soviet Union broadcast 185 hours per week in Arabic to the Middle East. This is a reduction of about 40 hours per week from 1975. Decreased transmissions have occurred in Albania, East Germany, and the Soviet Union. On the other hand, Radio Moscow increased transmission strength by the addition of medium-wave transmitters to serve the Arab world. Hungary is the only East European country that does not have an Arabic service. The remaining countries initiated transmission in the 1950s and 1960s after the Third World leaders such as Egypt's Nasser began turning to the Soviet Union and Eastern Europe for military and economic assistance.

Radio Moscow started sporadic Arabic broadcasts in 1943, followed by regular programming in 1944 (Stepanova 1979). Hours of programming have increased as the Soviet Union's interest in the Arab countries has grown. Conservative Islamic countries such as Saudi Arabia and the United Arab Emirates do not have diplomatic relations with the Soviet Union because of the alleged incompatibility between Islam and communism. On the other hand, some countries such as Libya, Syria, Iraq, and South Yemen have close ties with the Soviet Union. Both Egypt and the Sudan at one time welcomed Soviet aid and arms, but the relationship grew hostile when Egypt's Sadat moved closer to the west. Weekly transmission time of 49 hours is a decrease from 1975, but the Radio Moscow Arabic service is now available on mediumwave and can be quite clearly heard in countries such as Iraq, Kuwait, Syria, and Jordan. Available surveys undertaken by commercial research firms often show no respondents mentioning Radio Moscow as a station to which they tune. Only those specifically interested in Moscow's point of view select this service. Another Soviet station, "Radio Peace and Progress," broadcasts to the Arab world. The service started in February 1974 (Radio Station Peace and Progress 1975) and still broadcasts only one-half hour per day. This radio service, also called the "Voice of Soviet Public Opinion," attempts to separate itself from the Soviet state broadcasting bureaucracy, but the listed "sponsors"—various state organizations including the Soviet Writers' Union and the Soviet Peace Committee—do not provide it with transmitters and studios separate from Radio Moscow. Its intended goal is "to disseminate truthful information about the Soviet Union and about the life of people to foreign countries" (*Radio Station Peace and Progress* n.d., p. 2). Listeners appear to be few.

The East German Arabic service started in 1959 (Rummelsburg 1975) and, since 1975, has decreased its 49 hours per week by about 10 hours. Bulgaria started an Arabic service shortly after the 1956 Suez War; it has increased slightly its transmission time since 1975 to 21 hours per week. Albania transmits to the Arab world on both medium and shortwave for 21 hours per week. This is a slight decrease since 1975, which may be due to the break in close relations with the People's Republic of China (PRC). When relations between the countries were good, the Albanian transmitters relayed some of the PRC's Arabic service. Poland, a relatively recent Arabic broadcaster with a service that dates from 1968 (Frackiewicz 1979), presently broadcasts for 17½ hours per week.

Czechoslovakia and Romania each broadcast in Arabic for 14 hours per week, the former having started a service after the 1956 Suez War (Adrian 1975). Czechoslovakia, at that time, had close ties with Egypt because of an arms agreement and has since supplied several Arab countries—the Sudan, Egypt, and Syria—with broadcast transmitters, including high-powered medium-wave facilities. Yugoslavia's seven hours per week in Arabic is the smallest number of transmitted hours of any country in this region. The broadcasts were an outgrowth of the close friendship that Tito had with Egypt's Nasser in the 1950s and 1960s. Yugoslavia's nonaligned posture has made its relations with many Arab states quite good and trade has continued to be strong. Yet the Arabic service has not increased markedly despite continued Yugoslav interest in the Arab world. The broadcasting authorities in Yugoslavia realize that an increased number of programming hours would not bring favorable results considering the availability of competing services.

5.5 Asia and the Middle East

The 14 countries broadcasting in Arabic from Asia and the Middle East span a broad geographical area. With 165 hours per week, this region is second to Eastern Europe in terms of Arabic broadcasting.

Asian Arabic Services are among the newest and they tend to fall into three groups: those promoting a specific ideology; those broadcasting for religious reasons; and those programming for reasons of trade and related economic purposes.

North Korea is the most energetic Arabic-language programmer in this region, providing 42 hours of service per week. Since 1975, this country has tripled its broadcast hours to an area where it has close relations with some socialist governments; it has also provided aid and military training for members of various liberation movements, including the Palestine Liberation Organization.

The 14 hours per week in Arabic from the People's Republic of China are the same as in 1975. During the 1960s and 1970s, China was active diplomatically in the Arab world. Although the two hours per day have not changed since Mao's death, the Chinese are still competing with the Soviets for influence in this area of the world.

Religion provides a strong incentive for broadcasting to an area that is the homeland of Islam. Most predominantly non-Arab Moslem countries have close relations with the Arab world—specifically with Saudi Arabia—because cooperation is needed for travel to Mecca for the pilgrimage. In addition, several Asian Moslem countries receive economic aid from the wealthy Arab states (see *Aramco World Magazine* 1979) and believe that a broadcasting presence is important. Afghanistan's Arabic service transmits for three and one-half hours per week. After the December 1979 Soviet invasion, the service naturally underwent changes. The invasion caused sharp adverse reaction from many Arab countries and it seems likely that transmission time increased at the urging of Soviet advisors in Kabul.

Both India and Pakistan broadcast in Arabic; in fact India's British-influenced All India Radio (AIR) was the area's first Arabic broadcaster in 1941 (Srivastava 1979). AIR transmits 17½ hours per week to the Middle East in Arabic. Its motivations for doing so include the fact that India, although not Moslem, has a substantial Moslem population. Also, Indian nationals work in various capacities in the Arab countries and broadcasts strive for greater cultural understanding between Arabs and Indians. Pakistan started Arabic programming after independence in 1948 (Butt 1975; Kazmi 1979). It has more than doubled its broadcast time since 1975 to 28 hours per week. Pakistan is a Moslem country that provides a large work force for the wealthy Arabian Gulf states—an important source of hard currency for Pakistan.

Iran's international service in Arabic has decreased since 1975. Because of the country's proximity to the Arab world, it is difficult to calculate the number of hours of Arabic broadcasts specifically intended for Arabic speakers outside of Iran. Ten and one-half hours per week are sent by shortwave to the Arab world. However, some local programming in Arabic for the areas where the language is spoken reaches other countries. Also, Iran provided medium-wave broadcasts to Arabian Gulf countries during the period when the Shah's government assumed the role of protector of the Gulf shipping lanes. Shifting broadcast priorities and unstable internal political conditions since the Shah's departure have increased the religious content of Iranian Arabic transmissions. During the initial stages of the war with Iraq, the Arabic service increased its hours of transmission in an effort to win support from the Arab world.

Bangladesh, Indonesia, and Sri Lanka have started Arabic broadcasts since 1975. Moslem Bangladesh and Indonesia transmit three and one-half and seven hours per week respectively. Sri Lanka's service is modest, at best, with only five minutes of Arabic programming per day. Sri Lanka has a regional commercial service that can be received in some parts of the Middle East and that is occasionally mentioned in surveys. However, the commercial service is not in Arabic.

The two remaining Moslem countries with Arabic services are Turkey and Malaysia. Turkey is content to program one hour per week to the Arab Middle East. Malaysia started Arabic programming in 1972 for the purpose of "strengthen[ing] relations between the peoples of Malaysia and all our Arab brothers" (Shaw 1975). Transmission time has increased from 7 hours per week in 1975 to 10½.

Japanese presence in the Middle East has increased significantly since the 1960s. The Middle East is an important source of oil for Japan, which imports almost all its petroleum products. The Japanese have oil concessions in the Arabian Gulf and are important suppliers of automobiles, electronic equipment, and machinery to the Arab countries. Japan's Arabic service is transmitted three and one-half hours per week and is clearly intended to provide a broadcasting presence. It began in 1954 and maintains this level of service, possibly because of a belief that increased hours will not bring measurable benefits. Surveys indicate that the programs are not popular.

The Republics of South Korea and China (Taiwan) have economic ties with the Arabian Gulf states. These two anticommunist states have increased trade dramatically with Arab countries. Korean construction companies now do most of the work in the Gulf states formerly undertaken by western firms. It is estimated that at least 50,000 South Korean workers are employed in Saudi Arabia. The Korean Broadcasting Service's Arabic programming started in September 1975 with a 15-minute daily program that has been expanded to one and one-half hours per day. Cultural contact between South Korea and Arab countries is the stated goal of the service (Choi 1979). Taiwan's Arabic service is new, having been started since 1975. The country has close cultural and economic ties with the Gulf states, for it undertakes some security training for Saudi Arabia (see *Free China Weekly* 1979). Taiwan transmits 14 hours per week to the Arab World, the same number of hours broadcast by the People's Republic of China. The schedule is relatively ambitious for a small nation, but apparently the government believes that the service will help promote solid ties with the Arab world during a time when countries, including the United States, are normalizing diplomatic ties with the People's Republic of China.

During the early 1970s, Cyprus broadcast a commercial Arabic service on mediumwave. This service was discontinued when Radio Monte Carlo became popular and when Lebanese clandestine stations became commercially active after the 1975 civil war.

5.6 The Americas

Four countries in the Americas—the United States, Cuba, Chile, and Venezuela—broadcast 87½ hours per week in Arabic to the Middle East. Chile and Venezuela are new Arabic programmers, having started services in 1975. In the summer of 1980, Chile announced a temporary cessation of its Arabic service. Canada, an important international broadcaster, does not transmit Arabic and does not plan to do so (Ramsay 1979).

Limited Arabic broadcasting, reportedly funded by British Intelligence, was done over WRUL, a privately owned short-wave station with studios in New York City. In 1948, the VOA started some Arabic programming, but the service did not become regular until 1950 (Hopkins 1975). During the early years of the service, a daily half-hour program was beamed by short-wave to the Arab world from studios in New York City. In 1954, the service was moved to Washington, D.C., when the VOA was consolidated there.

From its inception, the VOA Arabic service has expanded transmission time, personnel, and facilities to provide a level of service to the Arab world commensurate with the growing United States interest in the area. In February 1963, the Arabic service began originating from a studio on the island of Rhodes. The Middle East studios were built there to eliminate the short-wave "hop" between U.S.-based short-wave transmitters and the Middle East. In 1964, a powerful medium-wave transmitter was completed on Rhodes to broadcast programs in Arabic, and occasionally in other languages, to the Middle East. Prior to the completion of the new transmitter, the United States outfitted a U.S. Coast Guard cutter, *Courier*, with a medium-wave transmitter to broadcast Arabic programming to the Arab world. The floating facility was originally intended to minimize the effects of the Soviet Union's jamming of VOA broadcasts to Russia. In September 1977, when satellite circuits became available to feed the Rhodes transmitters a high-quality signal, the Rhodes studios were phased out and the staff returned to Washington (Tuch, 1979). Program hours have gradually increased and have generally expanded during times of armed conflict such as the 1967 Middle East war, when VOA broadcasts in Arabic were temporarily lengthened to 14 hours per day. The VOA broadcasts 7½ hours per day in Arabic (Tuch 1979)—a 30-minute per day increase since 1975.

Surveys indicate that the VOA Arabic broadcasts are frequently heard on both short and mediumwave, although the BBC has better medium-wave coverage because of transmitters located on Cyprus and off the coast of

Oman in the Arabian Sea. As noted earlier, surveys suggest that the BBC is preferred in areas where Great Britain has had historical and political ties, such as in the Arabian Gulf area (USIA 1975a; USIA 1974; USICA 1978b). Preferences for both stations tend to be similar in countries that have become politically close to the United States—the Sudan, Egypt, and Saudi Arabia (USICA 1978a; USICA 1978c). There is a natural tendency for listeners, Arab broadcasting officials, and western Arabic-language programmers to compare the BBC with the VOA. Recent research tends to confirm that Middle East listeners prefer the BBC for news and public affairs programs. They perceive the service to be impartial in that it is not owned and operated by a government. Arab listeners know the VOA is a government service, like those in the Arab Middle East; but it is nevertheless thought to be a reliable source of news and information about the United States (Boyd and Kushner 1979, pp. 106–13).

Radio Habana Cuba started Arabic short-wave programming in 1963 and the service still broadcasts two hours per day. According to a Cuban broadcasting official, the country broadcasts to Third World countries to "spread the truth about different world affairs and to offer to far away peoples full information on [Cuba] and Latin America" (Triana 1979). Since its inception in 1963, the Cuban Arabic program has become somewhat more pragmatic in order to facilitate Cuba's attempts to achieve Angola-type successes in the Arab world. Occasional reports note Cuban advisors in South Yemen; also, Castro has supported various Palestinian resistance movements. Cuban Arabic broadcasts, which are occasionally relayed from the Soviet Union, are motivated by a desire to establish a broadcast presence in the area. Respondents to available surveys do not mention the Cuban service.

The entrance of Chile's and Venezuela's respective 14- and 7-hour per week Arabic programs may indicate a trend in closer Latin American–Arab world relations. The motivations for these two new services are unclear despite the fact that some countries in South America—notably Brazil—have large numbers of Arab immigrants. Venezuela has had close ties with many Arab countries since the formation of the Organization of Petroleum Exporting Countries (OPEC), to which it belongs.

5.7 Sub-Saharan Africa

Arabic broadcasting from Sub-Saharan Africa is continually changing due to political instability in some countries in this region. African countries broadcast 26¼ hours per week in Arabic.

Egypt's Gamal Abdel Nasser greatly enhanced Arab-African relations during the 1950s when Radio Cairo began transmitting African vernacular programs to those countries that had achieved or were attempting to gain independence. Nasser believed that his radio support for various liberation movements would help rid the continent of imperialists and raise his status as a Third World leader (see Nasser 1955, pp. 85–111).

Only four countries—Nigeria, Somalia, Senegal, and Ethiopia—broadcast to Arab countries in Arabic. Nigeria's Arabic service dates from 1964 (Okesanya 1975); this large and relatively prosperous country transmits 10½ hours per week to the Arab world. Since 1975, Somalia has doubled its hours per week to seven. Senegal's Arabic service is limited, transmitting only one and three-quarter hours per week. Ethiopia's Arabic programs are a post-1975 activity. After the overthrow of the former leader Haile Selassie, Radio Voice of the Gospel (RVOG) (see following section) was nationalized and government Arabic broadcasts started. The service operates for one hour per day. These four countries share a common interest in and/or dedication to Islam, or have nationals who follow that religion.

Ghana, one of the first Arabic broadcasters in Sub-Saharan Africa, has discontinued transmissions for economic reasons. One of the main motivations for the beginning of Ghana's 1961 service—to bring African nations together (Amoako 1975) and therefore to realize Nkrumah's ambition to enhance the stature of the country—is apparently no longer considered important by political leaders. Uganda started Arabic programs in 1975, but when Idi Amin was forced to leave the country the service was stopped and has not been resumed (Warugaba 1979). Surprisingly, South Africa's external services do not include Arabic. The country has frequently been attacked in Arabic broadcasts from Egypt and other countries, but Radio South Africa does not plan to counter these attacks with its own Arabic service.

5.8 Christian Religious Broadcasters

Five Christian religious broadcasting organizations provide 42¾ hours of Arabic programming per week to the Middle East. The quality and availability of the broadcasts vary, but they share a goal of seeking to maintain contact with Christians or to convert non-Christians in the Arab world. New Jersey-based Trans World Radio (TWR) owns and leases studios and transmitters around the world. Arabic broadcasts started in 1954 from the Voice of Tangier, TWR's predecessor. TWR broadcasts its Christian message in many languages, but Arabic has special meaning to the station's founder, Ralph Freed, who learned Arabic as a missionary in Palestine in the 1920s (R. Freed 1972; for a history of TRW see P. Freed 1979). Eight and one-quarter hours of TWR Arabic broadcasts reach the Middle East each week by way of Radio Monte Carlo short- and medium-wave transmitters in Monte Carlo and the Radio Monte Carlo Middle East medium-wave facility on Cyprus. ELWA (Eternal Love Winning Africa) has been broadcasting from Monrovia, Liberia, since 1954 and its 13½ hours per week (Edwards

1979) of Arabic make it a leading religious broadcaster. The Far East Broadcasting Association, transmitting from the Seychelles, is a relatively new Christian religious programmer but its two hours per day of Arabic make it the service with the largest number of hours in Arabic transmitted by a religious broadcaster. Radio Vaticana started Arabic broadcasts in 1950 and was using two hours per week in transmitting Masses in Arabic by 1975. The three and one-half hours per week (Radio Vaticana 1979) reached Arab countries only by shortwave. Finally, an American station—WYFR, owned by Family Stations of Oakland, California—is the only religious programmer that does not have studios and transmitters in proximity to the Arab world. The station, started during the 1930s as W1XAL in New York, operated during the 1960s as a privately owned commercial station with transmitters in Massachusetts. After Family Stations purchased the facilities in 1974, new transmitters were built in Florida, and Arabic programming started. The Arabic schedule of WYFR (as it became) is three and one-half hours per week (*WYFR International Program Schedule* 1979).

Since 1975, a major African-based Arabic religious broadcaster was forced to stop broadcasting. Radio Voice of the Gospel (RVOG) was operated by the Lutheran World Federation Broadcasting Service from 1963 until Ethiopia's revolutionary government nationalized the service. Addis Ababa-based RVOG had broadcast to Africa and the Middle East in several languages and was generally respected for the quality of its news and public affairs programming. A 1977 survey done in the Sudan indicated that RVOG was second to Radio Cairo and ahead of the BBC as a preferred foreign broadcaster (USICA 1978a, pp. 2, 11).

6 International Radio Broadcasting among Arab Countries

6.1 Introduction

There appear to be three factors that determine whether an Arab country broadcasts to listeners outside its own borders. Hardware—sophisticated and expensive equipment such as a directional antennas and powerful medium- and short-wave transmitters—is, for one, essential; and not all countries can or will invest sufficient time, personnel, and financial resources. Countries such as Egypt and Saudi Arabia, which differ vastly in their political and cultural orientations, have built impressive medium- and short-wave transmitters and studios. Saudi Arabia can well afford this kind of undertaking. Egypt saw fit after its revolution in 1952 to devote relatively large amounts of its development funds to the construction of a radio system that could reach other countries. Those countries that have built extensive facilities and powerful transmitters have tended to continue using them to reach other Arab countries.

Determination to export political and/or religious philosophies is another important factor that affects whether a country is willing to invest in the effort necessary to reach other Arab countries with a radio service. Egypt, under Nasser, was interested in spreading the message of Pan-Arabism; and there is some evidence that this effort was at least partially effective. Saudi Arabia believes that its conservative religious (Wahhabi) tradition and the presence of the holy cities of Mecca and Medina within its borders obligate it to reach other countries with a reliable radio service. The kingdom, moreover, has a strong political motivation for its regional broadcasting effort. Iraq's Arab Ba'ath Socialist Party seeks to unite all Arab countries into one nation and broadcasts radio programs that attempt to win listeners to this belief. South Yemen also has devoted some of its national resources to a radio service that incites Omanis to overthrow the national government in Oman.

The third factor is affluence, for affluence determines whether one country broadcasts to another. Quite apart from the funds required to acquire the hardware and personnel necessary for such an undertaking, the poorer countries—many of which depend on trade, loans, or grants from the wealthier—feel restrained in this kind of broadcasting and tend to be un-aggressive. Examples include the Sudan, Oman, Bahrain, and Tunisia, which have tried to steer a middle course and concentrate on economic development rather than on the export of a particular religious or political philosophy. Conversely, countries that are relatively secure financially, mostly because of a steady income from petroleum exports, have tended to use radio to disseminate their messages, with no fear that economic retaliation will take place. Examples include Libya, Iraq, and, to some extent, Algeria.

Countries that do not meet at least two of these requirements have not become active in broadcasting to other Arab countries. Examples include pre-1975 Lebanon, Jordan, and North Yemen.

Radio remains an important medium of communication within the Arab world. It is true that the penetration of television is high in the wealthy Arab countries, but the majority of people in the Arab world still depend on radio as a source of entertainment and information. Although the number of illiterate Arabs is decreasing, the overall rate of illiteracy is very high; Egypt's 70–75% illiteracy rate is not unusual.

There have been a series of on-going as well as short-term radio propaganda campaigns by various Arab governments since the 1950s. Non-Arab observers have often been amazed at the strong rhetoric that is involved in these radio battles. Those who have had some experience with Arab culture and have studied the radio exchanges have observed the apparent inconsistency in people who are so polite in interpersonal situations yet so hostile and vindictive on the radio. Arabs tend to use their language as a substitute for action—particularly physical action. This aspect of Arab culture was much discussed following the 1967 Six-Day War. The Arabs themselves have become particularly sensitive to and increasingly cognizant of this characteristic, because the subject has been so widely studied and discussed in the west. In the spring of 1972, a Kuwaiti newspaper printed a cartoon that accurately described thinking at the time. The cartoon showed a large radio receiver made to look like a military tank. The caption, referring to those who threaten war in their radio broadcasts, said "We will fight you every word of the way."

One of the most important aspects of Arab radio broadcasting is the Arabic language itself—particularly when the subject is politically motivated propaganda. Traditionally, there have been two types of Arabic, classical and colloquial. Classical Arabic is the language of the Koran and is rich in both religious and historical connotations. Colloquial Arabic differs from one country to another and often from one area of a country to another. The spoken dialects are so different that North African Arabic speakers must converse with peninsular Arabs in classical Arabic or another language. The growth in Arab mass media since the 1950s, however, has greatly enhanced the wider use of yet a third form—neo-classical (or modern standard) Arabic. This is the language of newspapers and the electronic media and is generally understood by the population of the Arab world. There are certain characteristics of Arabic speakers and of Arabic itself that tend to make this language ideally suited for those who wish to make effective persuasive use of radio for propaganda purposes. In the west, it is generally agreed that it is difficult to change public opinion through radio broadcasts; an extensive mass media campaign can only hope to alter the opinion of a small, albeit sometimes important, segment of the population. On the other hand, there remains a general belief in the Arab world that the Arabic language, creatively employed and strongly delivered, will produce the intended reaction among listeners. Of course, the recipient of radio broadcasts from other Arab countries must be receptive to efforts to change existing attitudes; but Arabic itself is viewed as an important element in the effectiveness of a propaganda effort. Laffin makes the following observations about Arabic and its effect on speakers:

1. To the Arab there may be several truths about the one situation, depending on the type of language he is using.
2. Language is not used to reason, but to persuade.
3. The Arab means what he says at the moment he is saying it. He is neither a vicious nor, usually, a calculating liar but a natural one.
4. The value of words is often assessed by quantity.
5. Words can justify or rationalize anything. [1975, pp. 81–82]

Arabic is not an exact language and much of the responsibility for interpretation is left to the listener. Sharabi observes:

In political life Arabic is a most effective instrument of influence and persuasion. . . . In public speeches effect is created not so much by reasoning and explication as by repetition and intonation. Indeed, a speaker trying to sway an audience seldom expresses his ideas directly or succinctly; meaning is conveyed rather than directly or precisely expressed, and is always couched in terminology that evokes emotional rather than rational responses. [1966, p. 93]

Shouby discusses the general vagueness of Arabic words and sentences; several circumstances, in his view, may cause this ambiguity of words.

1. They perhaps were never sharply defined when they first came into use, and have been retained without much change.
2. They have gradually been used to denote meanings which were later introduced into Arabic culture, with the result that they now represent not only the original vague and global meaning but also the numerous usages which have accreted to them throughout the centuries.

3. The recent sudden and rapid influx of Western culture into the Arab World has forced writers and thinkers independently to use old words to denote new meanings. The same word may be used to denote one thing by one writer and another by another.
4. A further factor contributing to the vagueness of the Arabic language is the rigidity of Arabic grammar—an extra-complex conglomeration of intricate rules and regulations which certainly restricts the freedom of the Arab thinker. The matter-of-fact acceptance of the vagueness of meaning on the one hand, and the strict insistence on the observance of the rigid grammatical and formal aspects of the language on the other, naturally heightens the only too human tendency to be lax and tolerant. [1951, pp. 292–93]

Arabic, then, is in many ways ideally suited to radio broadcasts specifically designed to influence others because of its rich grammar, repetitive style, and vagueness. The Arabic speaker who seeks to persuade others uses appeals that are more emotional than logical.

6.2 Voice of the Arabs[1]

The radio service whose name would literally become a household phrase in the Middle East was started on 4 July 1953 ("The A.R.E. Broadcasting in Brief" n.d., p. 3), less than one year after the Egyptian revolution. There is a difference of opinion among Egyptian media observers as to who started the Voice of the Arabs. Although Ahmed Said would become well known as its director and chief announcer, he was not in a position at the time to authorize its beginning. The real power behind the Voice of the Arabs lay with Gamal Abdel Nasser and Mohammed Abdel-Kader Hatem (Annis 1974; Sharf 1974). Dr. Hatem, who would serve Egypt in several information-related capacities including the post of Minister of Information, probably initiated the idea for the service, and Nasser provided enthusiastic support.

Following its half-hour daily beginning, the service grew at a steady pace, eventually becoming a 24-hour-a-day service. The particular geographical target areas and major subjects for discussion were constantly changing, but it is possible to note trends or general phases. For the first three years, the Voice of the Arabs tended to concentrate its efforts on the various political struggles occurring in the Maghreb. The radio was used to support the cause of French-exiled Sultan Mohammed V in Morocco, as well as for Habib Bourguiba's Neo-Destour party in Tunisia. It gave support also to the Algerian revolution, putting a heavy strain on Egyptian-French relations, and allowed its facilities to be used by Algerian revolutionary leaders who

---

[1]Portions of the following were first published in *Journalism Quarterly*, and appear here re-edited. See Boyd 1975a, pp. 645–53.

maintained an office in Cairo (Hatem 1974, p. 167; see also Fanon 1965, pp. 69–97). From the mid-1950s, Cairo would embrace resident representatives of liberation movements in Africa and the Middle East and would allow—in fact, would encourage—their use of its radio services.

During this early period, the service experimented with various program formats, many of which were eventually utilized in some form as the demand for programs expanded with increased transmission time. The Voice maintained a broad appeal, but it also became regionally oriented during certain periods of the day. Programs were designed for the Gulf states, Lebanon and Syria, and the southern peninsula, Yemen and Aden. Programming consisted of news and commentary, the two often indistinguishable; press reviews from Egyptian papers; speeches; talks by and interviews with various Arab politicians; and dramas with political themes and music. Songs praising Nasser and his accomplishments, performed by popular artists such as Abdel Wahhab and the late Um-Kalthoum (Loya 1962, p. 105), were used both as a propaganda vehicle and as an attraction for "serious" programs scheduled adjacent to the musical programs.

It was the circumstances surrounding Egypt's campaign against the participation of Jordan and Iraq in the Baghdad Pact as well as the events leading to the nationalization of the Suez Canal and the 1956 Suez War that first gave the Voice of the Arabs its rather infamous reputation.[2]

6.2.1 Revolutionary Propagandist

After testing its effectiveness to the west of Egypt during the first three years of broadcasting, the service became increasingly bold in supporting President Nasser's Middle East political aspirations. One reason for the shift in regional emphasis was that Egyptian broadcasts had been significantly strengthened during the three years following the revolution. Although it is impossible to determine the exact amount of power that the Voice used at any one time as the service could be shifted to any number of transmitters by master control, Egypt's total short- and medium-wave transmission power grew from 72 kilowatts at the beginning of the revolution in 1952 to more than 500 kilowatts by 1956.[3]

---

[2]The Voice was not the sole Egyptian radio service that could be heard in the Middle East. Radio Cairo, which is sometimes confused with the Voice by expert and casual listeners alike, is the main Egyptian domestic service, and also can be heard in most other Arab countries. The confusion stems partially from the fact that Cairo is the city origin for all of Egypt's national and international radio services. Although Radio Cairo's medium-wave signal is powerful, it was not originally intended for international consumption, as was the Voice's, and each service has always had a separate programming staff. But Radio Cairo's news and commentary, in fact its entire programming tone, have not been inconsistent with those of the Voice of the Arabs.

[3]*Arab Broadcasts* 1971, p. 76. In the early part of 1956, some western powers became concerned about the reach of Egyptian broadcasts, and in that year the American Central Intelligence Agency sponsored a survey that concluded that Cairo's broadcasts were heard from Morocco to Iraq. Copeland 1969, p. 247.

It was during the second half of the 1950s that the Voice of the Arabs established itself as an enthusiastic medium for revolutionary propaganda. Under Nasser, Egypt adopted an anti-colonialist, anti-imperialist position, and although anti-Zionist themes were ever present, Egypt turned her attention to other Arab countries. Nasser's stature in the Middle East and Africa increased greatly as the result of a 1954 agreement that he negotiated with Great Britain for the removal of British military forces from the Suez Canal Zone. With this accomplished, he set out to rid the rest of the Arab world of western influence and turned his attention to Iraq and Jordan, respectively a member and a potential member of the Baghdad Pact.[4] For the next three years until the 1958 Iraqi revolution, the Voice of the Arabs waged a propaganda war with varying degrees of intensity against Nuri as-Said, Iraq's pro-west prime minister. The service was also involved with events surrounding the 1958 Lebanese crisis. But it was radio propaganda against western efforts to include Jordan in the Baghdad Pact that brought to the forefront the effectiveness of Egypt's radio efforts.

What follows is a discussion of radio broadcasts as they relate to specific events in the Middle East. It would be misleading to imply that radio was solely responsible for those events; yet the broadcasts by the Voice of the Arabs did constitute a major part of the entire Egyptian propaganda effort, and there is reason to believe that the radio broadcasts were the most important and influential part of the propaganda campaign. Egyptian newspapers could be banned or censored, activities of Egyptian citizens in other countries could be restricted, but at the time there was no effective deterrent to Egypt's powerful radio transmitters. A deterrent that might have been effective—viable domestic and international radio services—did not exist in any Arab country outside of Egypt until well into the next decade.

Jordan had long been closely associated with Great Britain. British subjects exercised considerable influence over Jordan's Arab Legion in the persons of General John Glubb, a veteran soldier/arabist who had been in Jordan for more than 25 years, and other British military officers. Through a series of particularly vehement radio broadcasts that started in late 1955, Nasser appealed directly to Jordanian citizens to campaign against their country's participation in the Baghdad Pact. The demonstrations that resulted from this campaign gave observers one of the first indications of the broadcasts' effectiveness. The responsibility for demonstrations in remote Jordanian villages was laid directly to the Voice's urgings, as they occurred simultaneously with those in the capital (Carruthers 1956, p. 5). A specific target of the broadcasts from the Voice of the Arabs was General Glubb himself. It was relatively easy to point to Glubb as a foreigner who by nature of his position influenced Jordan's young King Hussein. Although the exact

reason for Glubb's dismissal by Hussein on 1 March 1956 is open to specula-
tion, Egyptian radio broadcasts seem to have played a significant part. As
one observer noted, "a foreigner [Glubb] is never fully accepted by the
Arabs, but the Jordanians had to be reminded of that by the Voice of
[Ahmed] Said" (Ellis 1961, p. 58). General Glubb himself believed that the
Voice of the Arabs was partly responsible for Hussein's action: "I think we
may say without hesitation that my dismissal was really entirely due to
Egyptian propaganda. . . . The radio played a leading part" (Glubb 1973).

The result of the radio broadcasts and Glubb's subsequent dismissal may
well have been far-reaching. According to Anthony Nutting, "after the
news [of Hussein's action against Glubb] reached London, the Prime Minister [Anthony Eden] declared a personal war on the man whom he held
responsible for Glubb's dismissal—Gamal Abdel Nasser" (Nutting 1967,
p. 17). After Nasser nationalized the Suez Canal Company, this personal
war probably influenced Britain's decision to join France and Israel in an
attack on Egypt that would result in the 1956 Suez War.

By the time that Nasser nationalized the Suez Canal Company in the
summer of 1956, he was widely known in the Arab world as a leader to be
reckoned with; daily broadcasts from Egypt's increasingly powerful radio
transmitters seldom failed to note the stance that Egypt was taking as a
"progressive" Arab state. Nasser's accomplishments had been broadcast to
every corner of the Arab world, and village peasants—including the hereto-
fore ignored women—found themselves sought after as important members
of the listening audience. The Czechoslovakia arms deal, the agreement for
the departure of British forces from Egypt, and the Suez Canal nationalization caused some worry among western powers who were concerned about
communist influence and about their own waning prestige in the Middle
East. Britain, for one, hoped that its participation with France and Israel in
the Suez attack would result in the political end of Gamal Abdel Nasser. Just
the opposite happened.

All of these events drew western attention to Egypt's radio expansion and
the monitoring of Egyptian broadcasts was intensified. Great Britain and
France drew up plans that proposed ways to counter these broadcasts. The
British took the most drastic measures when, during preinvasion raids on
Egyptian military installations, radio transmitters at the Abu Zabal site near
Cairo were bombed. They hoped to silence the Voice of the Arabs as well as
to make way for their own station on the island of Cyprus that would
propose Nasser's ouster. The British tactics failed for two reasons. The
bombing attack was only partly successful: antennae and towers were
knocked down, but damage to the equipment was not extensive and engineers soon had other transmitters on the air (El-Kashlan 1974). The
British began broadcasting from Cyprus by way of the Near East Broadcasting Station; although owned by a private company, it reportedly had links
with British Intelligence. The station, renamed "The Voice of Britain,"

came on a vacant Egyptian frequency calling on Egyptians to support those who had come to free them from their "mad" leader.[5] The British station was not successful with what it hoped would be a propaganda coup, largely because the station's Arab staff resigned *en masse* when they realized the new direction the programming had taken.[6]

In addition to raising President Nasser's prestige in the Arab world, the Suez War had a significant effect on Egypt's radio transmission planning. Those responsible saw the need for more transmitters and an emphasis on decentralization of transmitter sites (El-Kashlan 1974).

The three-year radio war against Iraq's Nuri es-Said government, which lasted from 1955 until the summer of 1958, is a further example of Egypt's efforts to promote revolution in another Arab country. When Iraq became a member of the Baghdad Pact, Nasser sought to bring about a reversal of what he saw as a western attempt to influence Middle Eastern affairs. The main target of the Voice of the Arabs broadcasts was Prime Minister Nuri as-Said. After diplomatic attempts failed to halt the radio attacks, Iraq decided that an offensive strategy would be the best defense; but it was inadequately equipped either to jam or to match Egyptian transmission power. In this connection, Iraq's Prime Minister personally appealed to the American Ambassador in Baghdad for assistance in securing 100-kilowatt medium- and short-wave transmitters that he wished air-shipped in a matter of weeks. Because of bureaucratic inefficiency in Washington, Iraq never got the equipment that it had requested, and instead British transmitters were eventually supplied (Gallman 1964, pp. 50–57; Eilts 1974). Even with the increased transmission strength and attempts to jam Egyptian broadcasts, the Iraqis clearly remained the underdogs in the radio contest. As Glubb notes, the radio war "illustrated the extraordinary efficacy of Egyptian methods in this form of radio demagogy. Broadcasting indeed appears to be a weapon ideally suited to the Egyptian mentality, with its eloquence, excitability and emotional appeal."[7]

The events surrounding the Suez War brought a brief respite from the radio attacks on Iraq, but by 1957 the Voice of the Arabs was openly calling for the assassination of Prime Minister as-Said and the royal family. "The

---

[5]Nutting 1972, p. 174. There were other clandestine radio stations that broadcast to Egypt during this period. Although most were located in other Middle Eastern countries, one operated by an exiled Egyptian transmitted from France.

[6]The BBC was concerned about the Cyprus station because it was feared that the station, which also relayed the BBC Arabic service, would damage the BBC's credibility.

[7]John Bagot Glubb, *Britain and the Arabs* 1959, p. 330. One of the techniques that the Voice of the Arabs employed was the derogatory reference to Arab leaders to whom Egypt was opposed. For example, Nuri es-Said was "Traitor Nuri"; King Faisal of Saudi Arabia was the "Bearded Bigot"; and King Hussein of Jordan was "Son of Zain"—a good example of how Egyptians effectively use Arabic to convey subtle meanings. "Son of Zain" is a derogatory phrase that implies that Hussein's mother was not married.

hearts of the people in Iraq are full of vindictive feelings against the rule of Nuri es-Said and British colonialism. . . . The extermination of the agents of imperialism is the first step towards the extermination of imperialism itself (BBC, *Summary* 1958a, p. 2). On 14 July 1958, a military coup overthrew the government and a republic was proclaimed. The bodies of Prime Minister as-Said and King Faisal were dragged through the streets of Baghdad in a particularly gruesome display of antiwestern feeling. After the revolution, Ahmed Said, the chief announcer and director of the Voice of the Arabs, received a letter in which was enclosed a piece of Nuri as-Said's finger: it had been sent in appreciation of the support that the Egyptian radio service had given to the revolution (Ellis 1961, p. 56).

The union of Egypt and Syria in February 1958 into the United Arab Republic brought an expansion in Egypt's radio transmission facilities. Those in Damascus could be added to those in Cairo, resulting in a more powerful Voice of the Arabs. Although the attacks on Iraq temporarily stopped after the July revolution, the attacks turned with renewed enthusiasm against Jordan and Lebanon as well as against the British and American military forces that landed in these countries at the request of the respective governments.

Today America is intervening in the affairs of the Lebanon. America is aggressing against the Lebanon. America is hurling its soldiers into the Lebanon. America is killing free Lebanese. . . . American imperialism has forgotten the utter defeat which was inflicted by Arab nationalism and the whole world against British and French imperialism. [BBC, *Summary* 1958b, p. 2]

The British and American governments in addition to the United Nations began diplomatic moves intended to cool down the Egyptian radio offensive. U.N. Secretary General Hammarskjold himself attempted to persuade Egyptian officials to tone down the radio broadcasts (Urquhart 1972, p. 265), but these moves were ineffective in bringing about a change in Egypt's radio attacks. Hammarskjold then decided to appeal directly to Nasser, who, by 1958, brought Egyptian radio more directly under his control when it was shifted from the Ministry of National Guidance to the office of the President (*Arab Broadcasts* 1970a). The British and Americans had hinted that their respective withdrawals from Jordan and Lebanon might be stepped up if the Voice of the Arabs would stop the hostile broadcasts. In a meeting with Nasser in Cairo in September 1958, Hammerskjold asked Nasser, "Can we disarm the radio?" Nasser's emphatic refusal to stop the broadcasts provided some insight into his feelings about his radio service: "How can I reach my power base? My power lies with the Arab masses. The only way I can reach my people is by radio. If you ask me for radio disarmament, it means that you are asking me for complete disarmament" (Heikal 1973, p. 173).

6.2.2 Decline of Impact

After 1958, although the Voice of the Arabs attacks on various Arab leaders continued, relative stability replaced the stormy period that marked Egypt's 1954–58 consolidation as the leading Pan-Arabic power. Nasser believed that the union with Syria was but the first step to a united Arab world, the center of which would be Cairo. The radio broadcasts of the Voice of the Arabs continued to play an important role in Egyptian efforts to promote President Nasser's call for Arab unity. In this connection, Egypt's transmitter power continued to grow to the point that by 1960 the total medium- and short-wave power was over 1300 kilowatts, or more than double what it had been four years earlier (*Arab Broadcasts* 1971, p. 76). Some of this new transmitter power was being used to broadcast to African countries south of the Sahara for the specific purpose of supporting liberation struggles.

During the period 1958–67 there were no spectacular successes such as those that had marked the Voice's previous development. There are several reasons for the Voice's loss of impact. First, audiences of the 1960s were more sophisticated than those of the 1950s; radio was a relatively new phenomenon when the Voice of the Arabs scored its Jordanian and Iraqi successes. As time passed, however, it is likely that listeners became accustomed to Cairo's namecalling, exaggerations, and outright untruths. Other Arab countries also had increased their domestic media services during the 1960s, adding television, for example, thereby providing competition for the Voice's broadcasts.

Another reason for the Voice's loss of impact was the lack of research by Egyptian media managers. Apparently the only sources of feedback were listener letters and reports from Egyptian diplomatic missions, the latter usually dealing with comments on signal strength rather than listener reactions (H. Shaban 1974; M. Shaban 1974). Those in management positions at the Voice may well have been lulled into a sense of success after 1958, and they appear to have become increasingly out of touch with Arab audiences.

The Voice looked for new targets. British forces in the Suez Canal Zone, the Baghdad Pact, General Glubb, and western intervention in Arab countries had been vulnerable targets; and, once these were eliminated, the propaganda turned with increasing vehemence against those countries that were termed to be less "progressive" than Egypt, notably Jordan, Saudi Arabia, and the Gulf states. King Faisal of Saudi Arabia was a particularly formidable target as it was he who supported the Royalists in the Yemen War—Nasser's Vietnam.

There had been a period when Saudi Arabia both diplomatically and financially had supported some of Nasser's Middle Eastern policies. The situation changed after King Saud (son of the kingdom's founder) was, in effect, made a figurehead when his brother Faisal became crown prince in 1958 and king in 1964. Saudi Arabia became an example of a "reactionary" regime; and because of its enormous oil wealth, its unevenly distributed revenues, and its close ties with the United States, it was a ready-made target for radio attack from Egypt. A conservative Islamic society that to this day does not allow nightclubs or public cinemas, Saudi Arabia did not have a domestic radio service that could serve the entire country until the mid-1960s. With visits to family and friends being the major social diversion, and with the growing availability of the transistor radio, the Voice of the Arabs was a popular radio service. The Voice took the obvious approach in its campaign against Saudi Arabia: it told the Saudis that their government was tied to the United States and to its oil company, ARAMCO; that the royal family squandered most of the oil revenue; and that Saudi workers were being exploited by imperialist sympathizers.

The Saudi government acted slowly to counter Egypt's radio propaganda. During the early 1960s plans were initiated that would give the kingdom a powerful domestic as well as an international radio service. The country started its own version of the Voice of the Arabs, stressing Saudi Arabia's importance as an Islamic country and as the home of the holy cities of Mecca and Medina. Saudi Arabia was not alone in pointing out that Nasser's army in Yemen was killing Arabs, that Nasser's radio service was meddling in the internal affairs of an independent country, and that perhaps the most important goals should be national development and the Palestine question. The Saudis also took another step that they hoped would, among other things, help divert their citizens' attention from Egyptian radio broadcasts—they started a television system.[8]

While the Voice was popular in Saudi Arabia,[9] the incessant attacks against the kingdom were greeted by some as entertainment rather than as something that was to be taken seriously. The Voice of the Arabs attacks on King Faisal and ranking officials were particularly vicious:

Arabs, is Faysal an Arab or a British King? Arabs, is Faysal a King of the Muslims' Holy Land, or a King of the Jews and the Saxons? Arabs, by God, Arabs: what is the people's verdict, what is God's verdict on such an agent King? We know the verdict and wait for the execution. For the people always convict agents; and always inflict the traitor's destiny on all agents. [BBC, *Summary* 1967, A6]

However, the broadcasts did not produce the reaction that similar broadcasts had produced in Jordan and Iraq. There were no discernible effects of the radio propaganda on the kingdom's population; but Saudi government

---

[8]The author was an employee of both the Saudi Arabian and the U.S. governments during the planning and construction of the television system.
[9]Associated Business Consultants n.d., pp. 8–10. The survey indicated that the Voice of the Arabs was the third most popular radio service (following the local service and the BBC) among those listeners surveyed. But when combined, the Voice of the Arabs, Radio Cairo, and Middle East Radio—the three Egyptian radio services that could be received in Riyadh—ranked second in popularity.

officials were concerned about Egyptian media. A facility for jamming Egyptian television broadcasts was built in Jidda in order to interfere with Cairo television signals that travel long distances during the summer months and are regularly received in Jordan, Lebanon, and Syria.

Much of the Voice of the Arabs propaganda directed toward the Arabian peninsula concerned the Yemen War that pitted Egyptian troops—50,000 at one point—against Saudi-supported Yemeni Royalist forces. In this relatively remote and inaccessible country, radio proved to be an efficient means of reaching the people. Ahmed Said, the popular Voice of the Arabs announcer, was given in Yemen the status of President Nasser and Abdul Hakim Amer, the Egyptian Army commander, when his picture was included with Nasser's and Amer's on the cover of student writing tablets.[10] The Yemen propaganda campaign also provides an example of the importance that Nasser placed on reaching the masses directly by radio. Heikal notes, "Following several setbacks [in Yemen] he [Nasser] ordered the distribution of 100,000 transistor radios to the tribes. That connected them to the Voice of the Arabs and it had more effect than a whole division" (1973, p. 173). Voice broadcasts incited revolution in Yemen and probably speeded the withdrawal of British troops from Aden. However, the broadcasts did not acheive their intended effect on all of the Arabian peninsula, as they brought neither victory to Egypt in Yemen nor an end to the Saudi monarchy.

6.2.3 Loss of Credibility

Although the Voice of the Arabs gradually lost its impact during the 1960s, it was its broadcasts during the early days of the 1967 Middle East War that seriously undermined the Voice's credibility. Ahmed Said repeatedly told the Egyptians and others in reach of the Voice's signal that Egypt was winning the war. These claims, which were widely broadcast by other radio stations in the Arab world, only built up the hopes of those who wanted victory. When the reality of defeat became known, the letdown was more complete than it would have been had battle reports been more truthful.

One casualty of the June 1967 war was Ahmed Said, who had personally made many of the victory claims and had thus put himself in a vulnerable position. Said had become the brunt of jokes in Cairo as he had become the symbol of Egypt's self-deception, and his eventual dismissal was necessary in order to remove that symbol.[11] Although he undoubtedly had a hand in

[10]Kandil 1974. It was apparently in Yemen that the now famous story about a man who wanted to purchase a "Voice of the Arabs radio" originated. The customer entered a radio shop asking for such a radio and the clever merchant told him that he would have one for him if he returned at 7 P.M., a time when he knew the Voice would be broadcasting. The man returned at the appointed time to find the radio he had requested.

[11]Reportedly, Saudi Arabia's late King Faisal demanded Said's ouster during the Khartoum Summit following the 1967 war, making it a precondition to the granting of financial aid to Egypt. What more likely happened was that Said was sacrificed by Nasser—like the lamb before the arrival of the honored guest.

shaping the Voice's programming, Said did not make the policy decisions; these were made by Nasser himself. Journalist Mustapha Amin states that Nasser even hand-wrote instructions to Said on a day-to-day basis and that the service was a reflection of Nasser's personality (1974).

6.2.4 Conclusion

The Voice had not entirely given up its revolutionary radio propaganda, as evidenced by broadcasts during the late 1960s and early 1970s that encouraged liberation movements in Muscat and Oman;[12] but the 1967 war and the government change after Nasser's death clearly affected the Voice of the Arabs. In an obvious reference to past practices, the service lists as one of its goals the "adher[ence] to the scientific interpretation of language [and] purif[ication of] that language from repetition, exaggeration, superficiality, and unpreparedness" (*Arab Broadcasts* 1971, p. 69). Missing during the October 1973 war were the Voice's widely distorted claims of victory—even when the Egyptians moved across the Suez Canal during the first days of the conflict. The Voice's calm tone seemed to have a stabilizing effect on the Arabs and instilled in them a sense of pride in Arab accomplishment.

Charles Issawi perhaps best characterized the Voice of the Arabs' pre-1967 period when he observed that it had "to be heard to be believed: for sheer venom, vulgarity and indifference to truth it [had] few equals in the world" (1963, p. 217). In contrast, it is not unusual now to hear Middle Eastern media observers refer to the Voice's broadcasts as "tame" or even "almost unexciting." Given the confidence and economic strength that the Arabs have acquired since October 1973, the Egyptian government is likely to maintain the present programming philosophy rather than return to the pre-1967 days when Nasser personally called the shots.

Although Egypt did not return to the approach taken before 1967 by the Voice of the Arabs, this service as well as others operated by the Egyptian government have worked since 1975 to counter radio attacks from Libya, Iraq, and other Arab countries that oppose the Sadat-inspired peace agreement with Israel.

It is unlikely that any other Arab radio service can match the attention given to or the alleged successes of the pre-1967 Voice. During the 1970s, there appeared many imitators on Arab radio frequencies who called for revolution or promoted their political philosophy. Listeners became increasingly subjected to a kind of radio service that no longer held their attention. Yet, while there are obvious exceptions, such as Iraq and Libya, emotional appeals to support a particular political party, religious sect, or national leader are heard from the recognized government radio services less often on the whole than in the 1960s. The rise of domestic radio services that cater to the needs of the local populations has made it unnecessary for

---

[12]These broadcasts may have been motivated in part by a desire to show the competition—a revolutionary-oriented station near or in Aden—that it still retained some revolutionary zeal.

nationals to tune to radio services of other countries to obtain news and entertainment programming. Television has apparently decreased radio listening—particularly at night. Also, home video recorders among residents of the Gulf area have allowed a further diversion from radio. So many powerful transmitters have become operational in the Arab countries since the late 1960s that finding a clear medium-wave signal at night can be challenging for the most dedicated radio-listening enthusiast. Yet, this situation has not discouraged the continued proliferation of radio services officially identified as operated by Arab governments; nor has it altered what appears to be a continued interest in unofficial or clandestine radio broadcasting.

6.3 Clandestine Radio in the Arab World

There is no clear definition of clandestine radio broadcasting in the Arab world. Many kinds of unofficial stations operate for various purposes and under different conditions. Some stations operate from within a country or from a neighboring country to support revolutionary activities. Others appear for short periods during armed conflicts. Still others operate intermittently to support a particular political movement. Very few are clandestine in the sense that their location and affiliation are unknown. This is due in part to the fact that even casual listeners know that the stations operate on frequencies that are associated with a country. Each Arab country monitors the official and clandestine radio broadcasts of other Arab countries, and when an unofficial station is identified as hostile to a regime, the government publicizes the supposed location and purpose behind the station. Some countries jam clandestine broadcasts.

Some clandestine broadcasting took place during World War II. Prior to that time, the signals from Italy and Germany, for example, were clearly identified with those countries as the radio programs were intended to promote favorable reactions among Arab listeners toward those countries. One of the first documented users of secret radio transmissions in the Arab world was the United States. A 10-kilowatt transmitter aboard the battleship *Texas*, stationed off the coast of North Africa, broadcast programming on the frequency adjacent to Radio Morocco's, so that the Allied point of view could be heard (Carroll 1948, p. 37).

There was considerable clandestine radio broadcasting from both the Arab and Jewish sides prior to and during the 1948 Palestine War. The Jews were more organized in this respect and did most of the broadcasting. Hebrew and Arabic broadcasts were featured by both sides. From the Jewish side, three major clandestine services were active during the 1948 Palestine War. The Hagana station started broadcasting in the 1930s when there were disturbances by those who opposed Jewish immigration to Palestine. Hagana Radio, named after the illegal Jewish military organization, appears to have been the oldest and most well-organized of the Jewish clandestine services. Between 1945 and 1948, its Arabic broadcasts increased and, at one time, were headed by Shaul Bar-Haim, an Iraqi Jew who had immigrated to Palestine (Bar-Haim 1980). The Hagana Radio was most active during the months immediately prior to May 1948, when the British officially left the area, thus triggering the first Arab-Israeli war. On 12 May 1948, Hagana Radio announced that it would later become the Voice of Israel, Kol Israel (Foreign Broadcast Information Service 1948a)—the official name of the Israeli national broadcasting service after independence was declared. Another service was operated by the Irgun Zevai Leumi, a terrorist group headed by Menachem Begin. This station used the name Voice of Fighting Zion to broadcast its own philosophy in the British mandated area (Begin 1951, pp. 332–35). Finally the Lohame Herut Yisrael, or Stern Gang, operated a clandestine service that it called Fighters for the Freedom of Israel (Foreign Broadcast Information Service 1948b). When the various factions of Jews decided to cooperate after the state of Israel was declared in May 1948, the stations amalgamated and became the official government station. It would, however, be inaccurate to leave the reader with the impression that these stations were operated only to propagandize Arabic speakers. It is true that Arabic broadcasting increased in 1948, but the initial motivation for the stations was to provide Jewish residents with information that each faction believed most helpful to its cause.

The Palestinian Arabs did not need clandestine stations as much as the Jews did because the radio services of the neighboring countries served as advocates for the Arab side. Although transmitter power was limited, Egypt and Syria appear to have been most involved with Arabic broadcasting to Palestine. One Arab station, Inqza Radio, was operated by the Arab Liberation Army from an undisclosed location. First identified on 25 March 1948 (Foreign Broadcast Information Service 1948b), broadcasts were lengthened as the May 1948 fighting intensified. Two other Arab stations were active prior to and during the 1948 war. "Saut al-Sawra" (Voice of the Revolution) and "The Secret Jihad" (Holy War) clandestine operations broadcast in several languages, including Hebrew, in support of the Arab side (BBC, *Summary* 1948, p. 56; BBC, "Monitoring" 1947).

6.4 Sharq al-Adna

The beginnings of Sharq al-Adna (The Near East Arab Broadcasting Station) remain unknown. The station started broadcasting from Palestine just prior to the 1948 War. As the British left the country, Sharq al-Adna moved to Cyprus. At first, the station transmitted its commercial Arabic programs from four short-wave transmitters near Limassol.[13] By 1955 a 100-kilowatt medium-wave transmitter broadcasting on 635 kHz had been added (*World Radio Handbook* 1957, p. 88). After the British left Palestine, the station was criticized by the various Jewish political factions as being pro-Arab, specifically pro-King Abdullah of Jordan. Following the peace agreement establishing the boundaries of the State of Israel, the station turned its attention to building what appears to have been an audience big enough to attract advertisers. In many respects, Sharq al-Adna was an early Radio Monte Carlo (Middle East). Most of the production and announcing staff were Palestinians. The British association with the station was no secret and Hale in *Radio Power* notes that the Lebanese referred to the station as the "Cavalry of St. George," after a British coin then in circulation that featured the patron saint's image (1975, p. 121). The exact relationship between the station and the British government until the 1956 Suez War is not clear. Barbara Castle, a prominent British politician, remarks that the station "kept in touch with the Foreign Office and had helped to 'sell' British policy, as well as British exports, in Arab countries—all the more successfully because it was not tied to official directives" (1956, p. 832).

As part of the preparations for the British-French-Israeli invasion of Egypt, the British government decided to take over the station and provide its own alternative to the Voice of the Arabs, which the British military had failed to eliminate by destroying its transmitters. The commandeering of the studios and transmission facilities of Sharq al-Adna was made easy by the fact that they were adjacent to a military facility near Limassol, Cyprus (Zada 1979b). Under the direction of an officer attached to the Psychological Warfare Unit of the invasion forces, preparations to broadcast calls to overthrow President Nasser were made. However, the British did not anticipate that the Arab staff would resist such moves and on 30 October 1956, only hours after the station became the "Voice of Britain," the Arab staff resigned *en masse*. In support of the Arab staff, the British station director resigned too (Zada 1979b). BBC Arabic Service employees who were rushed to the station in an attempt to keep programming going were not able to gain audience respect. Gradually the attacks against Nasser diminished and by March 1957 the station went off the air. The BBC used the frequencies assigned to Sharq al-Adna, but suffered some loss of credibility following the "Voice of Britain" fiasco. After the invasion, the British Foreign Office assumed responsibility for programming the station. Some material supplied by the BBC was relayed over the "Voice of Britain" frequencies along with the obviously pro-British material supplied by the

---

[13]Early station program schedules and transmission frequencies supplied by the BBC External Broadcasting Audience Research Office. See BBC Monitoring Service reports entitled *Cyprus Station: Sharq al-Adna*, dated 28 June 1948; 20 March 1952; and 1 April 1954.

Foreign Office. At times there appeared to be rather obvious inconsistencies between the two different sources of news about events in the Middle East. Attempts after 1957 by non-Arab governments to influence broadcasting in the Arab world have been covert and apparently better organized and executed than the attempt by the British in October 1956.

6.5 Clandestine Broadcasting, 1960 to 1980

The following excludes the unofficial stations operating from Lebanon since 1975 that were discussed in section 2.3.3. It also excludes those stations that appear to be clandestine, but that use frequencies of Arab countries.

Voice of Arab Syria, first heard on 26 October 1976, the voice of Arab Syria originated from Iraq (BBC, *Clandestine . . . Middle East,* p. 2). Syria has consistently jammed the station because of its attacks against Syrian President Assad. When the station first appeared, it devoted considerable time to attacking the Syrian Army's role in the efforts to bring peace to Lebanon. Iraq became the country most active in this kind of broadcasting activity during the 1970s, replacing Egypt as the Arab world's foremost disseminator of virulent radio propaganda. John Cooley observed:

In tone some of these [Voice of Arab Syria] broadcasts remind some observers of the years before the 1967 Arab-Israeli war when the late Egyptian President Nasser's radio station in Cairo, Voice of the Arabs, broadcast a program called Enemies of God by commentator Ahmed Said. It included attacks on Israel, the United States, and the reactionary Arab regimes like Saudi Arabia, now the target of some rather similar, though less vituperous language from Radio Baghdad. [1977, p. 11]

Voice of the Arabian Peninsula People. Started on 10 May 1973, and last heard on 25 March 1975 (BBC, *Clandestine . . . Middle East,* p. 2), the Voice of the Arabian Peninsula People was located in Iraq and promoted anti-Saudi Arabian feelings in the Middle East.

Voice of Iraqi Kurdistan. The Voice of Iraqi Kurdistan started transmitting on 10 September 1965, and was last heard on 16 March 1975 (BBC, *Clandestine . . . Middle East,* p. 3). It broadcast in Arabic and other languages in support of the Kurdish cause.

Mutawakallite Royal Radio. The exact location of Mutawakallite Royal Radio, a Saudi Arabia-sponsored clandestine service, was never learned. It started on 5 October 1962, at the beginning of the civil war in Yemen, and was last heard on 30 May 1970 (BBC, *Clandestine . . . Middle East,* p. 3).

Free Yemeni South Radio. Free Yemeni South Radio was another broadcasting operation backed by the Saudi Arabian government. The service used Mutawakallite facilities and concentrated on broadcasts against South Yemen. First heard on 16 December 1970, the broadcasts ceased prior to April 1976 (BBC, *Clandestine . . . Middle East,* p. 3).

Radio Freedom from South Yemen. Radio Freedom from South Yemen began transmitting anti-South Yemen government material in mid-1978 on the same frequencies as Free Yemeni South Radio.

Aden Voice of Oman Revolution. Aden Voice of Oman Revolution uses the radio facilities of South Yemen to broadcast propaganda attacking Oman's Sultan Qaboos. Started in November 1973 as the Voice of the Popular Front for the Liberation of the Arabian Gulf, the station's name was later changed to reflect the aims of the Popular Front for the Liberation of Oman. On 19 November 1976, Aden Radio announced that the program was being discontinued, but it did not stop (BBC, *Clandestine . . . Middle East*, p. 3). PFLO broadcasting activity intensified after the Iranian Revolution as efforts were increased to prevent British and United States military forces from helping Oman protect the Straits of Hormuz. The following is an example of PFLO broadcasting style:

Brothers, of late the secrets of the game being played by Qabus and some of his advisers have started to come out into the open, especially after most of the Omani citizens in Muscat have noted the intensive visits by the American Ambassador to the regime of Qabus. . . .

While Britain, because of certain exigencies, had to abandon its role in the Gulf region for the benefit of American imperialism, Qabus for his part revealed some months back a letter written in his own hand to the American President, Jimmy Carter, in which he included a tempting offer to the U.S. Qabus promised in the letter to compensate America for its losses in Iran by offering extensive facilities and privileges for an American presence in Oman and its territorial waters.

All this is in harmony with what Qabus said some years ago; that he would enter into an alliance with even the Devil if that would protect his regime. [BBC, "Aden Voice of Oman Revolution" 1979]

Voice of Palestine. Voice of Palestine is apparently the only radio service under the complete control of the Palestine Liberation Organization. Almost all Arab countries allow broadcasting time to Palestinians for cultural, educational, and information programs. However, the host country usually maintains some control, and when broadcasts are not in accordance with the policy of the country whose studios and transmitters are being used, they have been suspended. The Voice of Palestine started in September 1973 from Syrian territory under the title "Voice of Fatah, Voice of Asifah [The Storm]." On 13 July 1975, the station discontinued broadcasting, but resumed again on 21 September 1975 from somewhere in Lebanon. The loss of Lebanese government authority during the civil war allowed the move to be made. However, according to the BBC Monitoring Service, the station reportedly suspended transmissions on 20 February 1977 (*Clandestine . . . Palestine*, p. 1) because of the presence of the Syrian Army in Lebanon. Although the PLO lost its only independent means of radio programming, it still has the use of radio facilities in many other Arab countries.

Voice of the Eritrea Revolution. Another clandestine service financed and equipped by Iraq, the Voice of the Eritrea Revolution started daily broadcasts in August 1976, on four short-wave frequencies. The programs, in Arabic and Tigrigna, feature newscasts and information about military operations supported by Iraq against Ethiopian troops (BBC, "Monitoring" 1979a).

Gafsa Radio. Gafsa Radio broadcasts in Arabic and occasionally in French. Programs last for several hours per day on mediumwave and allow the service, also known as the Voice of the Revolutionary Movement for the Liberation of Tunisia, an opportunity to program material that is hostile to the Tunisian government (BBC, "Gafsa Radio" 1980).

National Radio of the Saharan Arab Democratic Republic. National Radio of the Saharan Arab Democratic Republic, first heard in 1980, broadcasts in Arabic and Spanish on mediumwave material hostile to the Moroccan government (BBC, "National Radio" 1980).

Voice of the Egyptian People. The Voice of the Egyptian People, an unofficial Libyan service, uses one short-wave frequency to disseminate material hostile to the Sadat government in Egypt. The station was first heard during the summer of 1979, following the formalization of the Egyptian peace treaty with Israel (BBC, "Monitoring" 1979b).

It is difficult to forecast the future of international broadcasting to and within the Arab world. The 1980s are quite different from the 1960s. All frequencies are very crowded and even the most dedicated and determined listener may have trouble finding a clear signal. The occasional as well as the sophisticated listener in the 1980s is more aware that Arabic's vagueness tends to breed exaggeration. Also, the focus of international broadcasting within the Arab world has changed since the 1960s. Egypt no longer has the most powerful transmitters in the Arab world nor the dynamic radio personalities that it had under Nasser. The fact that Egypt has become somewhat isolated has caused Egypt's stature in the Middle East to change. It is too early yet to determine whether Iraq will replace Egypt as a leading Arab country, but Iraq has increased its radio broadcasts to other Arab countries with the aim of achieving this goal. Another change since the 1960s is that with the increase of government services in many countries—specifically in the Gulf states—Arab listeners no longer need to tune to the transmissions of other Arab countries for news and entertainment. Television has decreased interest in radio broadcasts from other countries during evening hours. The growing affluence in some countries has promoted the purchase of high-quality home sound systems. Local FM stereo music has become an attraction for those with sophisticated systems and for owners of portable radios with FM bands.

For those countries and organizations that transmit in Arabic to the Middle East the above observations have some relevance. One important technical advantage that a non-Arab country can have is a strong medium-wave signal to the area. However, more than a technical advantage is needed to attract Arab listeners. Services such as Radio Monte Carlo, the BBC, and VOA all find an audience because listeners are attracted to broadcasts that fill some need not satisfied by local or regional services. It is true that there are some important countries, such as Canada, that have not started an Arabic service, but most others that have political or economic ties with the Arab world will not want to find themselves in this position. They will continue to broadcast in Arabic to Arabs.

Part 4   Conclusion

7   Arab Broadcasting: Problems

The preceding chapters of this study have explored various aspects of Arab world broadcasting. They have focused on the problems of individual Arab countries, as well as on more broadly defined concerns such as transmitter construction, broadcast rhetoric, and programming: they have sought to delineate the major problems that Arab countries will face in the 1980s and 1990s, as changes occur in the Arab systems of broadcasting that will, in turn, affect the communication patterns of the Arab culture. These concluding pages discuss the major problem areas under the headings of cooperation, training, financing, and technology.

Cooperation. Those who have read much about the Arab world already know that the concept of Arab unity and cooperation is largely a myth. Despite religious, linguistic, and other cultural similarities, each nation state in the area has a unique character; often this character is defined and promoted by the mass media. Yet, while it is recognized that differences do exist from country to country and region to region, there have been numerous attempts to bring the Arab countries together in order to promote interests common to all. A good deal of this cooperation has been undertaken under the framework of the Arab League, an organization chartered in Egypt following World War II. The League has been successful in promoting agreements among Arab countries in a range of fields, among them civil aviation, health, education, postal services, and broadcasting. With the League's help (and after several false starts), the Arab States Broadcasting Union (ASBU) was officially formed in 1969, with headquarters in Egypt: full alliance was achieved when Saudi Arabia agreed to join in 1974 (Boyd 1975b, p. 313). The Arab States Broadcasting Union meets annually in a member country; the head of the organization, then elected, serves for one year.

ASBU has been successful in varying degrees in promoting news exchanges and cooperative audience research, training, and technical efforts.

Perhaps the area of cooperation that held the greatest promise was the first, and the Arab world was divided into areas within which both radio and, more importantly, television news were to be exchanged. But after an initial enthusiastic response among member countries generally, the regional exchanges prospered only in the Gulf states: financial, technical, and political matters undermined the experiment. A more successful outcome of the interest in news among Arab countries was an agreement negotiated between ASBU and the European Broadcasting Union (EBU) for daily satellite relay to the Middle East of important North American and European television news stories: this has become an important source of news for those Arab countries that have the capability of receiving the transmissions. Through the ASBU some of the wealthier countries have subsidized the service so that poorer countries are able to take it at little or no cost.

ASBU has been an almost prototypical victim of shifting political priorities in the Arab world. The Arab League headquarters had been located in Egypt since that organization's creation; like most of the other specialized agencies of the League, ASBU was also located in Cairo and was staffed mainly by Egyptian nationals. When Egyptian President Sadat signed the peace agreement with Israel in 1979, there was an immediate reaction among other Arab countries, headed by Iraq, to isolate Egypt. While it is too soon to tell how effective the various calls for a boycott of Egyptian products and services will be, one action that the "rejectionist" countries were able to promote was the move of the Arab League headquarters from Cairo to Tunis—and the headquarters of the ASBU were shifted with it, the non-Egyptian staff being permanently moved there. Other Arab League agencies were likewise moved from Cairo to other countries. Egypt responded by freezing all financial assets to League agencies in Cairo and mandating that Egyptians remain in Cairo—continuing work as before, still receiving salary and benefits. Although the Tunis ASBU headquarters under their new Secretary General—Abdallah Chakroun, a Moroccan—is recognized as the legitimate one by Arab League supporters, the original ASBU Secretary General, Salah Abdel Kader, has kept the Cairo office operating: many publications are still produced there. After the office officially moved to Tunis, some associate members continued to pay annual dues to the Cairo office, thus adding more hard currency, in this case American dollars, to the several million that that office has in the bank (Kader 1979). Before the 1979 dislocation, in an attempt to decentralize the administrative functions of ASBU, offices were created in various Arab countries to promote training, technical research and monitoring, and audience research: there arose questions among the Khartoum (Sudan) Technical Center, the Baghdad (Iraq) Research Office, and the Damascus (Syria) Training Center staffs regarding to whom they should report. Indeed, overall confusion and the associated financial problems have stymied the development of the Training Center and brought about the closing of the

Technical Center, in the wake of its frustrated director's resignation (Yousef 1979). The result of all this has been an erosion of the effectiveness and credibility of the organization that had the greatest immediate potential to promote Arab electronic media—and that in a period when such cooperation in the broadcasting field as it fostered seemed most to be needed.

Yet the events surrounding the fragmentation of ASBU since 1979 may ultimately be beneficial. The organization itself has attempted to promote regional and binational cooperation; and with the weakening of the umbrella organization promoting Arab radio and television interests, efforts have increased among smaller groups of Arab countries. Probably the best example of this is the continuing effort among Gulf states to cooperate in many facets of broadcasting. This region has achieved what no other area has been able to do: undertake joint television production projects. Even if ASBU again becomes a strong, respected organization, the future of cooperation in broadcasting apparently rests with those countries in the Levant, North Africa, and the Gulf that believe it to be in their best interests to cooperate in limited ways in certain areas.

Training. Broadcasting executives in Arab countries usually state that personnel matters rank high among major concerns. Almost every Arab country has shortages of adequately trained research, production, and technical personnel: though several schools, institutes, and specialized training centers in the Arab world provide education in the field of mass communication, training continues to be largely on-the-job. Egypt has tended to be a leader in several respects. The Egyptian Radio-Television Federation operates both radio and television training centers that attract nationals from other Arab countries, especially for advanced training. The courses through which students progress are very specialized: a student may concentrate on either production or engineering. Common criticisms of the Federation operation are that it is underfunded, and that the training is often done in an informal and unstructured manner.[1] Several Egyptian universities also offer courses in mass communication. The courses, unlike those offered by the radio and television institute, are usually theory and policy oriented. The largest communication school in the Arab world is the Faculty of Information at Cairo University, which offers undergraduate, M.A., and Ph.D. degrees in broadcasting, print journalism, and public relations. Thousands of students attend the large lecture sections there, many of them graduate students who are already employed in some field of mass communication and hope that a graduate degree will benefit their careers. The American University in Cairo offers undergraduate and M.S. degrees in mass communication. The mass communication unit is housed within a Department of Political Science, Economics, and Mass Communication; instruction is by both Egyptian and American professors and is

---

[1]This writer lectured at the institute in 1977.

generally practical in nature, courses in radio and television news, script writing, and research methods being offered. The instruction at the American University is in English, although graduates often find employment in the Arab-language press and radio and television stations.[2] Egypt, and indeed Jordan, train adequate numbers of students *for themselves* in all facets of broadcasting—but then have difficulty retaining them. Many people from those countries are lured by high salaries to wealthier countries, mostly in the Gulf states, which have to import most of their production and technical staffs.

The most ambitious effort by the Arab broadcasters to help train technical and production personnel was promoted under the auspices of ASBU. Recognizing that ASBU could play an important role in the training of broadcasters, the organization decided in the mid-1970s to build a training center where nationals of all Arab countries could be sent for basic as well as advanced study. Originally, the location for the ASBU center was to have been in Amman, Jordan; however, the Jordanian government was unable to provide the necessary land for the facility (Shaar 1979). The Syrian government did provide the needed land, in Damascus, and that city became the location of the ASBU Training Center under the leadership of Khudr Shaar, a former Syrian broadcasting official. Construction on the facility, which includes a dormitory, started in 1977, and in 1980 the building was completed. But—and it is another result of Middle East political tension—the Training Center lacks essential equipment. The original funding for the building was gained through ASBU with the hopes that funds for equipment would be contributed by the Gulf states, those countries that would most benefit from the Center's instruction. However, the Gulf states are hesitant to contribute to the undertaking, primarily because of its location. Gulf broadcasting officials have many reservations about Syria: they cite the political instability of the country, the continuing Syrian friendship with the Soviet Union—with whom many of the conservative Gulf states do not have diplomatic relations—and, finally, their fear that students will be given political instruction along with their broadcast training. ASBU officials deny that these fears will be realized, but nonetheless the fears persist; and the 1980 war between Iraq and Iran served to exacerbate them, Syria supporting Iran while the Gulf states gave tacit support to Iraq. At one point, the Gulf states considered the possibility of building their own training facility, which, it was reasoned, would mesh well with the other non-ASBU efforts at cooperation that those states had fostered in the broadcasting field. But until a decision is made about the location of a facility, training will continue in the Gulf states, as elsewhere, to be on an informal basis. The expertise of some Egyptian-, Jordanian-, and western-trained personnel notwithstanding, one of the most pressing problems of Arab broadcasters remains unsolved.

[2]This writer taught at both Cairo University and the American University, during the 1976–77 academic year, under the sponsorship of the Fulbright Program.

Financing. Except for those Arab countries that have become wealthy from petroleum exports, the financing of radio and television broadcasting will continue to be a serious problem. Though many of the less wealthy Arab countries discussed in this study, such as Jordan and the Sudan, realize how important the electronic media have become to the internal and external political process, funds to continue the dissemination of their services have become increasingly scarce in light of national military, education, and health needs. The less financially fortunate countries will have to continue to struggle and to compromise to find funds needed to continue national broadcasting services. Those Arab broadcasting organizations that would rather not accept advertising are likely to continue to accept it: it yields income, in some cases in hard currency. However, more innovative attempts to finance both radio and television services may be found. Several Arab countries, Jordan and Tunisia for example, have adopted the system of financial help for radio and television pioneered by Egypt: it being reasoned that every citizen benefits from broadcasting, a surcharge that goes to the broadcasting authority is added to all electricity bills. But of course in that case, in a developing country where many lower-income people do not own television sets, those who have sets pay an unfairly low share of the burden and those who do not own sets pay an unfairly high one. And as color television equipment ages and must be replaced, and as the demand for more high-quality local programming increases, additional funds will be even more necessary: the difficulties in raising them both reliably and fairly will remain a major problem for many Arab countries.

Technology. Satellite communications probably has been the technical advance of greatest benefit to Arab broadcasters. During the 1970s, most Arab countries constructed ground stations in order to help provide faster and more reliable telephone and telex communication, and the satellite circuits leased from INTELSAT also brought television signals from Asia, Europe, and North America. Perhaps the most used satellite service is the daily European Broadcasting Union (EBU) news exchange sponsored by ASBU. International sporting events are also popular in Arab countries and some soccer events are taped from the satellite or televised directly. Leased satellite circuits, moreover, make possible an internal distribution of television signals that would otherwise have been almost impossible in those Arab countries with large land masses—Saudi Arabia, Oman, the Sudan, and Algeria. Long distances, rough terrain, and difficult weather conditions make microwave or cable distribution of television programming difficult and extremely expensive therein: satellites have pushed some of them as much as ten years ahead of schedule for television signal distribution. Enthusiasm for satellite technology has prompted a group of Arab states to contract with a French consortium to build and launch, by 1985, a satellite for their exclusive use: the organization, ARABSAT, is headquartered in Riyadh, Saudi Arabia. Yet—predictably—nationalist jealousies and the move of the Arab League from Cairo to Tunis have tended to slow the

ARABSAT project. The wealthier countries such as Saudi Arabia that have supported the projects have become less enthusiastic: they know that while they will benefit from an Arab satellite, they will also provide most of the funding. The interest that Saudi Arabia is showing in launching a satellite for its exclusive use may be a sign that in fact ARABSAT will never come to fruition.

But earthbound broadcasting technologies also present Arab countries with difficulties and with grounds for confrontation. The rapid growth of superpower medium-wave transmissions has made clear daytime and evening medium-wave reception more difficult—and each new superpower transmitter tends to motivate its neighbors to purchase additional high-power facilities of their own that only make matters worse. The scarcity of medium-wave frequencies is also a serious problem, and even relatively friendly countries—Jordan and Saudi Arabia—have argued over frequency ownership. These problems and the growth in sales of high-quality home sound equipment, especially in the Gulf states, have increased interest in FM transmission. If for no other reason than lack of medium-wave frequencies, the FM spectrum will be the area of important development in the 1980s and 1990s.

But, in the end, such problems as those here summarized are only challenges: they will not deter further development of radio and television systems in the Arab world. The electronic media have become an established part of the political and cultural process. Whatever political and cultural changes occur, then, in the 1980s and 1990s—and however rapidly and dramatically they occur—Arab broadcasting will continue to be an integral part of the busy scene.

Bibliography

Printed Sources

Abderahim, Mohamed. 1978. "L'Information audiovisuelle au Moroc: Aspects et politique de développement." M.A. thesis, Paris. Institut français de presse.

Abu-Lughod, Ibrahim. 1963. "The Mass Media and Egyptian Village Life." *Social Forces*, pp. 97–104.

Abu-Nasr. 1971. *A History of the Maghrib*. Cambridge: Cambridge University Press.

Adams, John B. 1964. "Problems of Communication in the Arab World." *Arab Journal* (Spring-Summer): 83-8.

"Advertising Rates and General Conditions Effective April 1, 1980." N.d. Doha, Qatar: Ministry of Information.

Adwan, Nawaf. M.A. thesis, Université de Droit, d'Economie et de Sciences Sociales de Paris II. In Arabic. Translated in Cairo, Egypt, by Sami Aziz.

Agha, Olfat Hassan. 1978. "The Role of Mass Communication in Interstate Conflict: The Arab Israeli War of October 6, 1973." *Gazette* 24, no. 3: 181–95.

Akol, Jacob. 1979. Interview with Ahmed Abdel Rahman. *Sudanow,* October.

Akrout, Hassan. 1966. "Television service inaugurated in Tunisia." *EBU Review* 100B (November).

Alexander, Yonah. 1973. *The Role of Communications in the Middle East Conflict: Ideological and Religious Aspects*. New York: Praeger.

Al-Ghassani, Anwar. 1974. "The Necessity of Establishing the National Democratic Mass Media in the Arab Countries of the Non-Capitalist Way of Development." In *The Contribution of the Development of Consciousness in a Changing World*. Leipzig, East Germany.

Al-Lawzi, Salim. 1980. Interview with Amir Fahd. *Al Hawadith,* 11 January. Translated by Foreign Broadcast Information Service, London.

Allebeck, S. S., Errahmani, A. B., and Ouldali, B. 1971. "Radio-Télévision Educative en Tunésie." Mission Report ED/FT/o13 Rev. (January). Paris: UNESCO.

Allen, Edward. *Report on the Establishment of Television Broadcast Service in Saudi Arabia.* 30 April 1963.

Almaney, Adnan. 1972. "Government Control of the Press in the United Arab Republic." *Journalism Quarterly,* 49, no. 2 (Summer): 340–48.

Al-Mu'ti, Abd al-Basit. 1980. "Egyptian Broadcasting: Content Analysis." *The Jerusalem Quarterly,* Fall, pp. 110–14.

Al-Soze, Abdul Amir. 1963. "Factors Influencing Public Opinion Formation in Iraq." M.S. thesis, University of Wisconsin.

"Analysis/Radio Monte Carlo: How to Reach the Arabs from a Station in France." 1979. *Campaign Mid-East,* June-August.

Arab Broadcasts. 1970a. "The History of the U.A.R. Radio Since Its Establishment in 1934 Until Now." Translated by Fatima Barrada. August, p. 63.

———. 1970b. "Text of the Presidential Decree on the Law Concerning the Establishment of the Egyptian Radio-Television Federation." Translated by Fatima Barrada. August, pp. 50–51.

———. 1971. "What Do You Know About Egyptian Broadcasting?" Translated by Fathi Yousef. July, p. 63.

Arab States Broadcasting Union. 1969. "The United Arab Republic: TV." 22 July. Cairo, Egypt: ASBU. Mimeographed.

"Arab World to Get First Commercial TV." 1959. *Broadcasting,* 29 June, p. 84.

"Arabic Broadcasts from London." 1938. *Great Britain and the East,* 13 January.

Aramco World Magazine. 1963. "Aramco TV on the Air." 14, no. 5 (May): p.p. 3–7.

———. 1979. November-December.

"The A.R.E. Broadcasting in Brief." Cairo: Egyptian Radio-TV Federation. Mimeographed.

ASBU Review. 1975. "Recommendations of the Eighth Meeting of the Permanent Program Committee." April, pp. 16–28.

———. 1979. "News." January, pp. 34–35.

Associated Business Consultants, Ltd. 1972. "A T.V. and Radio Survey in Jordan." February.

———. *Extracts of a Media Audience Survey, May-June 1978.* Beirut, Lebanon.

———. "A Seven-Day Media Effectiveness Survey Conducted of Behalf of the Hashemite Broadcasting Service in the City of Riyadh." Beirut, Lebanon.

Associated Business Consultants/RTV International. "Recent RTV Contracts." Beirut, Lebanon. Mimeographed.

"Audience, Penetration and Listenership of Pan Arab Commercial Radio Stations in Jordan—Saudi Arabia—Kuwait—UAE/Oman." Table no. 1 only, supplied by SOMERA MMEMS 1979.

Baker, Raymond William. 1974. "Egypt in Shadows." *American Behavioral Scientist* 17 (January-February): 393–423.

Barbour, Neville. 1951. "Broadcasting to the Arab World." *Middle East Journal* 5 (Winter): 60.

Barghouti, Shawki M. 1974. "The Role of Communication in Jordan's Rural Development." *Journalism Quarterly* 51, no. 3 (Autumn): 418–24.

Batson, Lawrence D. 1930. *Radio Markets of the World.* U.S. Department of Commerce Trade Promotional Series No. 109. Washington, D.C.: Government Printing Office.

Begin, Menachem. 1951. *The Revolt.* New York: Nash Publishing Company.

Benoist-Mechin, Jacques. 1958. *Arabian Destiny,* trans. by Denis Weaver. Fairlawn, N. J.: Essential Books, Inc.

Binder, David. 1980. "U.S. Concedes It Is Behind Anti-Khomeini Broadcasts." *New York Times,* 29 June, p. 3.

Boyd, Douglas A. 1975a. "The Arab States Broadcasting Union." *Journal of Broadcasting* 19, no. 3 (Summer): 311–20.

———. 1975b. "Development of Egypt's Radio: 'Voice of the Arabs' Under Nasser." *Journalism Quarterly* 52, no. 4 (Winter): 645–53.

———. 1977. "Egyptian Radio: Tool of Political and National Development." *Journalism Monographs* 48 (February).

———. 1972. "An Historical and Descriptive Analysis of the Evolution and Development of Saudi Arabian Television: 1963–1972." Ph. D. dissertation, University of Minnesota.

———. 1976. "International Broadcasting in Arabic to the Middle East and North Africa." *Gazette* 22, no. 3: 183–96.

———. 1978. "A Q-Analysis of Mass Media Usage by Egyptian Elites." *Journalism Quarterly* 55, no. 3 (Autumn): 501–7, 539.

———. 1980. "Saudi Arabian Broadcasting: Radio and Television in a Wealthy Islamic State." *Middle East Review* 12, no. 4 (Summer) and 13, no. 1 (Fall): 20–27.

———. 1970–71. "Saudi Arabian Television." *Journal of Broadcasting* 15 no. 1 (Winter): 73–78.

———. 1973. "The Story of Radio in Saudi Arabia." *Public Telecommunications Review* 1, no. 2 (October): 53–60.

———, and Kushner, Jim. 1979. "Media Habits of Egyptian Gatekeepers." *Gazette* 25, no. 2: 106–13.

Brewer, Sam Pope. 1958. "Lebanese Rebels Close Radios: Business in the Capital Improves." *New York Times,* 6 September, pp. 1, 2.

Briggs, Asa. 1965. *The Golden Age of Wireless*. London: Oxford University Press.

British Broadcasting Corporation. 1979. "Aden Voice of Oman Revolution." 1545 GMT, 25 August.

———. 1979. *BBC Handbook 1980*. London: British Broadcasting Corporation.

———. *Clandestine and Unofficial Broadcasts*. Reference WBI/5 and 7.

———. *Clandestine and Unofficial Broadcasts*. Reference WBI/5 and 6.

———. *Clandestine and Unofficial Broadcasts*. Reference ME/5520/A/2 and WBI/21.

———. *Clandestine and Unofficial Broadcasts*. Reference ME/5515/A/1 and WBI/20.

———. *Clandestine and Unofficial Broadcasts,* Part 4, Middle East. Reference ME/5158/i; ME/5388/i; WBI/51.

———. *Clandestine and Unofficial Broadcasts: Middle East*. Caversham Park, Reading, England.

———. *Clandestine and Unofficial Broadcasts: Palestine*. Caversham Park, Reading, England.

———. 1948, 1952, 1954. *Cyprus Station: Sharq al-Adna*. 28 June, 20 March, and 1 April.

———. 1980. "Gafsa Radio." February.

———. N.d. Monitoring Service Report no. 129/78.

———. 1979a. Monitoring Service Report no. 92/79, July.

———. 1979b. Monitoring Service Report no. 121/79, September.

———. 1980. "National Radio of the Saharan Arab Democratic Republic." February.

———. 1969. *Summary of World Broadcasts,* ME/W527/B/1, July.

———. 1947. *Summary of World Broadcasts*. Monitoring Report. 7 December.

———. 1948. *Summary of World Broadcasts,* no. 36, Part 3, 5 February.

———. 1958a. *Summary of World Broadcasts,* no. 539, 2 May.

———. 1958b. *Summary of World Broadcasts,* no. 603, 17 July.

———. 1967. *Summary of World Broadcasts,* no. 2460, 9 May.

British Colonial Office. 1960. Sound and Television Broadcasting in the Overseas Territories. The Information Department, Colonial Office, July.

Browne, Donald R. 1980. "The Media of the Arab World and Matters of Style." *Middle East Review* 12, no. 4 (Summer) and 13, no. 1 (Fall): 11–19.

———. 1975a. "Television and National Stabilization: The Lebanese Experience." *Journalism Quarterly* 52: 692–98.

———. 1975b. "The Voices of Palestine: A Broadcasting House Divided." *The Middle East Journal* 29 (Spring): 133–50.

Brunner, Edmund deS. 1953. "Rural Communications Behavior and Attitudes in the Middle East." *Rural Sociology* 18 (March): 149–55.

Business Week. 1957. "Battling Radios Vie for Arabs' Ears." 16 March, p. 48.

Carroll, Wallace. 1948. *Persuade or Perish.* Boston: Houghton Mifflin Company.

Carruthers, Osgood. 1956. " 'Voice of Arabs' Stirs Mideast." *New York Times*, 15 January, p. 5.

Cassirer, Henry R. 1975. "Les Moyens de communication au Service d'une nouvelle orientation de l'éducation au Maroc." Ref. ED-75/WS/28. UNESCO. Mimeographed.

Castle, Barbara. 1956. "The Fiasco of Sharq al-Adna." *The New Statesman and Nation*, 29 December, p. 832.

Cawston, Richard. 1963. "Television—a World Picture." In *The Eighth Art: Twenty-Five Views of TV Today.* New York: Holt Rinehart and Winston.

Celarie, André. 1962. "La Radiodiffusion Harmonisée au Service du Développement." *Les Cahiers Africains* 6.

Cento. 1971. *Cento Seminar on Management and Training in Television and Radio Broadcasting.* Tehran, 4–8 November. Ankara: Cento, 1971.

Chakroun, Abdallah. 1975. "Broadcasting Cooperation Between Moslem Countries." *EBU Review* 26 (November): 14–17.

———. 1979. "Cinquante années de radiodiffusion au Maroc." *Revue de l'UER*, July, pp. 12–20.

———. 1972. "Educational Television in Morocco." *ASBU Review*, January, pp. 46–47.

Cheriet, Abderrahmane. 1970. *Circulaire No. 2/DG.* RTA. 25 September.

The Christian Science Monitor. 1976. "Arabs Try to Tone Down News-Agency Furore." 5 February.

Clark, Bearsford. 1959. "The B.B.C.'s External Service." *International Affairs* 35, no. 2 (April): 170–80.

CLT Program Schedule. 1972. Supplied by CLT, Beirut, Lebanon. 1 April.

Codding, George. 1959. *Broadcasting Without Barriers.* New York: UNESCO.

Continental Electronics. 1979. "Broadcast Transmitter Customer List, January, 1979."

Cooley, John K. 1977. "A Propaganda War Rages on Mideast Radio." *Christian Science Monitor*, 11 January.

Copeland, Miles. 1969. *The Game of Nations.* New York: Simon and Schuster.

Crane, Rhonda J. 1979. *The Politics of International Standards: France and the Color TV War.* Norwood, New Jersey: Ablex Publishing Corporation. 10 April.

Dajani, Karen Finlon. 1980. "Egypt: Film Center of the Arab World." *Middle East Review* 12, no. 4 (Summer) and 13, no. 1 (Fall): 28–33.

————. 1979. "Egypt's Role as a Major Media Producer, Supplier and Distributor to the Arab World: A Historical-Descriptive Study." Ph.D. dissertation, Temple University.

Dajani, Nabil H. 1979. *Lebanon*. London: International Institute of Communications.

————. 1975. "Media Exposure and Mobility in Lebanon." *Journalism Quarterly*, Summer, pp. 297–305.

————. 1971. "The Press in Lebanon." *Gazette* 17: 152–74.

Dakhakhni, Mamdough. 1976. "Television: Three for the Dustbin." *The Egyptian Gazette,* 3 October, p. 2.

De-Borchgrave, Arnaud. 1974. "Egypt's Anti-Nasser Campaign." *Newsweek,* 1 April, pp. 42–43.

Delcourt, Xavier. 1978. "Le transistor des veillées paysannes." *Le Monde*, 9–10 July, p. 42.

de Onis, Juan. 1975. "Saudis Bury Faisal and Hail Khalid." *New York Times*, 27 March, pp. 1, 3.

Dizard, Wilson P. 1966. *Television: A World View*. Syracuse, N.Y.: Syracuse University Press.

Dodd, Peter. 1968. "Youth and Women's Emancipation in the United Arab Republic." *Middle East Journal* 22 (Spring): 159–72.

"Dubai Radio and Colour Television Program Schedule." 1980. 1 January–31 March.

Duvignaud, Jean. 1970. *Charge at Shebika*. New York: Vintage Books.

EBU Review. 1980. 31, no. 2 (March): 45.

The Economist. 1965. "Faisal the fabian." 13 November, p. 742.

Eddy, William. 1963. "King ibn Sa'ud: 'Our Faith and Your Iron.' " *Middle East Journal* 17, no. 3 (Summer): 257–63.

Egly, Max. 1974. "Etude de la Réception Transnationale d'Emissions de Télévision Educative." Paris: Agence de Coopération Culturelle et Technique.

The Egyptian Gazette. 1974. "LE 1.45 m Modern TV Studio Opened." 7 August, p. 1.

————. 1976. "TV Employees Banned from Private Work." 29 November, p. 1.

————. 1977. "Television's 12,000." 7 April, p. 2.

————. 1980. "Knowing the Job." 29 January, p. 2.

Egyptian Radio-Television Federation. Rate Card for 1979. Cairo, Egypt.

Eilts, Hermann. 1971. "Social Revolution in Saudi Arabia, Part II." *Parameters,* Summer, pp. 22–33.

El Fathaly, Omar I., Palmer, Monte, and Chackerian, Richard. 1977. *Political Development and Bureaucracy in Libya*. Lexington, Mass.: Lexington Books.

Elgabri, Ali Z. 1974a. "The Maghreb." In *Broadcasting in Africa: A Continental Survey of Radio and Television,* edited by Sydney W. Head. Philadelphia: Temple University Press.

————. 1972. "Maghrebvision. Aims and Present State of Television Cooperation Between Tunisia, Algeria, and Morocco." *EBU Review,* November, pp. 39–42.

————. 1974b. "Morocco." In *Broadcasting in Africa: A Continental Survey of Radio and Television,* edited by Sydney W. Head. Philadelphia: Temple University Press.

El-Harouni, Youssef. 1973. "Mass Media in Egypt and Their Role in Simplifying Sciences." *ASBU Review,* April, pp. 10–22.

El-Khatib, M. Fathalla, and Hirabayashi, Gordon K. 1958. "Communication and Political Awareness in the Villages of Egypt." *Public Opinion Quarterly* 22 (Fall): 357–63.

Ellis, William S. 1961. "Nasser's Other Voice." *Harper's Magazine,* June, p. 58.

El Shafei, el Mungi. 1974. "Maghreb-Vision: An experiment in TV cooperation between Tunisia, Algeria and Morocco." *ASBU Review,* January, pp. 26–30.

El-Shaked, Mahmoud. 1973. "Qatar Radio enters its sixth year." *ASBU Review,* October, pp. 18–22.

El-Shenaway, Wagih. 1970. "An Educational Television Pilot Project in Cairo." *Educational Broadcasting International* 4 (December): 301–4.

El-Sherif, Mahmoud. 1980. "The Arab Attitude to Mass Media." *InterMedia* 8, no. 2 (March): 28–29.

"Extracts from Pan Arab Media Survey, 1978: Saudi Arabia." 1978. Pan Arab Computer Center Information Systems.

"Facts about Iftah Ya Simsim." Furnished by the Arabian Gulf States Joint Program Production Institution. Kuwait.

Fanon, Franz. 1965. *A Dying Colonialism,* trans. by Haakon Chevalier. New York: Grove Press.

Farley, Rawle. 1971. *Planning for Development in Libya.* New York: Praeger Publishers.

Farrag, Mohamed Youssef. 1965. "The Postrevolutionary Development of International Broadcasts in the United Arab Republic." M.A. thesis, Stanford University.

First, Ruth. 1974. *Libya: The Elusive Revolution.* Middlesex: Penguin Books.

Foreign Broadcast Information Service. 1979. Monitoring Report.

Foreign Broadcast Information Service, European Section. 1948a. Report 311.

————. 1948b. Report 314.

"Fourth Cycle JTV3." Supplied by Jordan Television Commercial Department.

Free China Weekly. 1979. "Taipei, Riyadh Pledge Cooperation." 20, no. 27 (15 July).

Freed, Paul E. 1979. *Towers to Eternity: Reaching the Unreached*. Nashville, Tennessee: Sceptre Books.

Freed, Ralph. 1972. *Reaching Arabs for Christ*. Chatham, N.J.: Trans World Radio.

Gallman, Waldemar J. 1964. *Iraq Under General Nuri*. Baltimore: The Johns Hopkins Press.

Garrett, Steve. 1978. "Three Million Viewers in Morocco." *The Media Reporter* (U.K.) 2, no. 2: 46–8.

Gartley, John. 1980. "Broadcasting in Libya." *Middle East Review* 12, no. 4 (Summer) and 13, no. 1 (Fall): 34–39.

Gavin, R. J. 1975. *Aden Under British Rule*. New York: Harper and Row, Publishers.

Geertz, C. 1975. *The Interpretation of Cultures*. New York: Basic Books.

Glubb, John Bagot. 1959. *Britain and the Arabs*. London: Hodder and Stoughton.

Grandin, Thomas. 1939. "The Political Use of Radio." *Geneva Studies* 10, no. 3 (August): 50–55.

Green, Timothy. 1974. "Egypt." In *Broadcasting in Africa: A Continental Survey of Radio and Television*, edited by Sydney W. Head. Philadelphia: Temple University Press.

Gress, Lina. 1973. "Jordan Television: The First 5 Years." *EBU Review,* September, pp. 30–31.

Grille des Programmes. 1980. Radio Monte Carlo Moyen Orient. SOMERA. January.

Guide to Broadcasting Stations. 1970. London: Iliffe Books.

Gulf Daily News. 1979. 4 December, p. 6.

Gulf Mirror. 1980a. "TV and Tape May Blank Out Screens." (Kuwait) 12–18 January, p. 3.

———. 1980b. 12–18 January, pp. 16, 17.

Hale, Julian. 1975. *Radio Power: Propaganda and International Broadcasting*. Philadelphia: Temple University Press.

Harik, I. F. 1971. "Opinion Leaders and the Mass Media in Rural Egypt: A Reconsideration of the Two-Step Flow of Communications Hypothesis." *American Political Science Review*. 65: 731–40.

"Harris Wins $5.2 Million Egyptian Radio Contract." 1979. Melbourne, Fl.: Harris Corporation Public Relations Department, 19 March.

Hashemite Broadcasting Service. *History of the Hashemite Broadcasting Service*.

Hatem, M. Abdel-Kader. 1974. *Information and the Arab Cause*. London: Longmans Group.

Head, Sydney W. 1974. *Broadcasting in Africa: A Continental Survey of Radio and Television*. Philadelphia: Temple University Press.

————. 1962. "The NAEB Goes to the Sudan." *The NAEB Journal* 21, no. 2 (March/April): 48–53.

Heikal, Mohamed. 1973. *The Cairo Documents*. New York: Doubleday and Company.

Hilleson, S. 1941. "Broadcasting to the Near East." *Royal Central Asian Journal* 27, part III (July): 340–48.

Hirabayashi, Gordon K., and El Khatib, M. Fathalla. 1958. "Communication and Political Awareness in the Villages of Egypt." *Public Opinion Quarterly* 22, no 3 (Fall): 357–63.

Hirsch, Michel-Leon. 1968. "Professional solidarity expressed in concrete terms." *EBU Review* 107B (January).

Holden, David. 1966. *Farewell to Arabia*. London: Faber and Faber.

Hussein, Saddam. 1977. *Democracy Is a Comprehensive View of Life*, Republic of Iraq Documentary Series No. 61. Baghdad, Iraq: Ministry of Information.

International Press Institute. 1954. *The News from the Middle East*. Zurich: IPI. Reprinted by Arno Press, 1972.

Interstages. 1979. "L'Enjeu socio-culturel du Cinéma en Tunésie." 107 (October).

Issawi, Charles. 1963. *Egypt in Revolution: An Economic Analysis*. London: Oxford University Press.

Jarrar, Farouk A. 1970. *Television in Jordan*. Amman, Jordan: Jordan Television Corporation.

Jibril, Mohamed. 1977. "Le marasme télévisé." *Lamalif* 87 (April): 26–34.

Jordan Television Engineering Department. 1979. "Television Transmitter Locations and Power." October.

"Jordan Television Foreign Program, JTV 6." Fourth Cycle Television Schedule. Supplied by Jordan Television Commercial Department.

Journal Officiel. 1963. Décret No. 63.684. 1 August.

————. 1964. 150: Loi no. 64-621. 27 June.

Kader, Salah Abdel. 1976. "Role of Radio and Television in Strengthening Afro-Arab Ties." *ASBU Review*, January, pp. 5–12.

Kahn, Rais Ahmed. 1967. "Radio Cairo and Egyptian Foreign Policy, 1956–1959." Ph.D. dissertation, University of Michigan.

Kallati, Idriss. 1973. *La politique marocaine de l'information face au développement*. Paris: Institut français de presse.

Katz, Elihu. 1971. "Television Comes to the Middle East." *Trans-Action* 8 (June): 42–50.

————, and Wedell, George. 1977. *Broadcasting in the Third World*. Cambridge, Massachusetts: Harvard University Press.

Keesing's Contemporary Archives. 1980. 23 May.

Keith, Agnes Newton. 1965. *Children of Allah*. Boston: Little, Brown and Company.

Khadduri, Majid. 1969. *Republican Iraq*. London: Oxford University Press.

Khaldun, Basir. 1973. "Educational Programmes in the Algerian Radio and TV." *ASBU Review*, April, pp. 5–9.

Khoury, Claude. 1976. "The Lebanese Radio and Television Stations Present: The Reluctant Partisans." *Monday Morning,* 28 March, pp. 40–44.

Kingdom of Saudi Arabia Central Planning Organization. 1970. "Development Plan 1390 A.H. (1970)."

Knapp, Wilfrid. 1970. *Tunisia: Land and People.* New York: Walker and Company.

Koppes, Clayton R. 1976. "Captain Mahan, General Gordon and the Origins of the Term 'Middle East.' " *Middle Eastern Studies* 12, no. 1 (January): 95–98.

Kuwait Television Schedule for first quarter. 1980. Supplied by Ministry of Information.

Labib, Saad. 1972. "TV in the Culture Struggle." *ASBU Review*, July, pp. 43–52.

Laffin, John. 1975. *The Arab Mind Considered.* New York: Taplinger Publishing Company.

Lamalif. 1977. 87 (April).

———. 1979a. 103 (January).

———. 1979b. 104 (February).

Lamrhili, Ahmed El K. 1980. "Information ou débilisation." *Al Asas* 20 (June).

Lapham, Robert J. 1970. "Family Planning and Fertility in Tunisia." *Demography* 7, no. 2 (May): 241–53.

Lerner, Daniel. 1958. *The Passing of Traditional Society: Modernizing the Middle East.* New York: The Free Press.

Lichty, Lawrence W. 1970 *World and International Broadcasting: A Bibliography.* Washington: Association for Professional Broadcasting Education.

Lorimor, E. S., and Dunn, S. W. 1968–69. "Use of the Mass Media in Egypt." *Public Opinion Quarterly* 32 (Winter): 680–87.

Loya, A. 1962. "Radio Propaganda of the United Arab Republic—An Analysis." *Middle Eastern Affairs.* 13, no. 4 (April).

MacDonald, Callum A. 1977. "Radio Bari: Italian Wireless Propaganda in the Middle East and British Countermeasures 1934–38." *Middle Eastern Studies* 13 (May): 195–205.

Mackenzie, A. J. 1938. *Propaganda Boom.* London: John Gifford.

Macro, Eric. 1968. *Yemen and the Western World.* New York: Praeger.

Madanat, Nasim. 1976. *The Story of Jordan Television.* Amman, Jordan, 8 August. Mimeographed.

Mahjoub, Elizabeth Miller. 1976. "The Role of the Change Agent." In *Change in Tunisia.* Albany: State University of New York Press.

Le Matin (du Sahara). 1980a. 2 June.

———. 1980b. 27 July.

McDaniel, Drew. 1980. "Some Notes on Political Broadcasting in the Arab World." *Middle East Review* 12, no. 4 (Summer) and 13, no. 1 (Fall): 5–10.

McKenzie, Vernon. 1940. *Here Lies Goebbels*. London: Michael Joseph.

Metwally, Ezz Al-Dine. *Historical Survey of the Egyptian Broadcast with Background of Pre-revolution Period*. Cairo: Egyptian Radio-Television Federation. Mimeographed.

Middle East and North Africa. 1980. London: Europa Publications.

Middle East Economic Digest. 1976. 20, no. 5 (30 January).

Ministry of Information and Culture. 1979. "Sudan Refutes Libyan and Syrian Distorted News Reporting." *Newsletter* 2 (17 March): 4.

Ministry of Information and Culture. 1971. *Sudan Today*. Nairobi, Kenya: University Press of Africa.

Mirshak, Myra. 1972. "Mother Hen Government: Farid Salman's Campaign for Press Freedom." *The Daily Star*, 13 April, p. 7.

Mohamed, Safia Khalid. 1965. "A Plan for the Alleviation of Illiteracy Through the Use of Television in the United Arab Republic." M.S. thesis, Boston University.

Le Monde Economique. 1956. "Tunisia Faces the Future." Special Issue, June, p. 196.

Mowlana, Hamid. 1974. "Mass Communication, Elites and National Systems in the Middle East." *The Contribution of the Mass Media to the Development of Consciousness in a Changing World*. Leipzig, East Germany.

———. 1976. "Trends in Middle Eastern Societies." *Mass Communication Policies in Changing Cultures*. New York: John Wiley.

———. 1971. "Mass Media Systems and Communication Behavior." *The Middle East: A Handbook*. London: Anthony Blond.

Nadir, Muhammed J. Minister Plenipotentiary, Embassy of Saudi Arabia. 1971. "The Modernization of Saudi Arabia." Talk given at Morgan State College, Baltimore, 2 March.

Nallino, Carlo Alfonso. 1939. *Raccolta di Scritti, Vol. I: L'Arabia Sa'udiana*. Rome: Instituto per l'Oriente.

Nasser, Gamal Abdul. 1955. *Egypt's Liberation: The Philosophy of Revolution*. Washington: Public Affairs Press.

Nasser, Munir K. 1979. *Press, Politics and Power: Egypt's Heikal and Al-Ahram*. Ames, Iowa: Iowa State University Press.

Nassr, Bahie E. 1963. "TV in Egypt." *Broadcasting*, 10 June, pp. 86–7.

Nelson, Harold, D., *et al.* 1979. *Libya: A Country Study*. Washington, D.C.: Govenment Printing Office.

"New Hours of Overseas Transmission on Shortwave by Radio Lebanon." 1972. Supplied by Radio Lebanon Department of International Programs. 1 April.

New York Times. 1958. "Lebanese Rebels Close Radios: Business in the Capital Improves." 6 September.
———. 1962. "Arab ETV." 5 August.
———. 1968. 28 December, p. 38.
———. 1973a. "Peace Ship Broadcasts to Arab and the Israelis." 24 May.
———. 1973b. 4 June.
Newsweek. 1972. "The Peacemaker." 26 June, pp. 6–7.
———. 1975. "The Murder of King Faisal." 7 April, pp. 21–3.
———. 1976. "Nimeiry's Justice." 16 August, pp. 36–7.
———. 1978. "Peace Crusader." 2 January, p. 5.
1978 Yearbook of International Trade Statistics. 1979. New York: United Nations.
Novotay, J. 1976. "Sudan Rural Television Project." Pictorial brief. Rome: FAO.
Nutting, Anthony. 1967. *No End of a Lesson.* New York: Clarkson N. Potter.
———. 1972. *Nasser.* New York: E. P. Dutton & Company.
Nyrop, Richard F., *et al.* 1977. *Area Handbook for the Yemens.* Washington, D.C.: Government Printing Office.
"Oman Colour Television: TV Transmitters in Operation." Supplied by Ministry of Information, Muscat, Oman.
"Oman Television Schedule: January 1 to March 31, 1980." Supplied by Ministry of Information. In English and Arabic.
ORTF '73. 1973. Paris: Presses Pocket.
Osterhaus, William E. 1979. *Tele-Liban 1979: An Evaluation with Some Recommendations.* October. Photocopy.
Ottaway, David, and Ottaway, Marina. 1970. *Algeria: The Politics of a Socialist Revolution.* Berkeley, Calif.: University of California Press.
Palestine Department of Posts and Telegraphs Annual Report, 1935. 1935. Jerusalem.
Palestine Department of Posts and Telegraphs Annual Report, 1936. 1936. Jerusalem.
Pan Arab Computer Center. 1978. "Extracts from Pan Arab Media Survey 1978: Saudi Arabia." December.
Peled, Tsiyona, and Katz, Elihu. 1974. "Media Functions in Wartime: The Israel Home Front in October 1973." In *The Uses of Mass Communications,* edited by Jay G. Blumler and Elihu Katz. Beverly Hills, Calif.: Sage Publications.
Penrose, Edith and E. F. 1978. *Iraq: International Relations and National Development.* London: Ernest Benn Boulder Westview Press.
Philby, H. St. John. 1952. *Arabian Jubilee.* London: Robert Hale.
———. 1955. *Sa'udi Arabia.* London: Ernest Benn.
Phipps, Kathleen. 1972. "The Stranglehold of Radio Lebanon." *The Daily Star,* 10 April, pp. 4, 5.

Pigé, François. 1966. *Radiodiffusion et Télévision Au Maghreb*. Paris: Fondation National Des Sciences Politiques.

Present-Day Iraqi Culture. 1970. Baghdad, Iraq: Ministry of Culture and Information.

La Presse. 1962. "Les projects gouvernmentaux." Tunis, 16 October, p. 2.

Qadhafi, Mu'ammar. n.d. *The Green Book*.

Rachty, Gehan, and Sabat, Khalil. *Importation of Films for Cinema and Television in Egypt*. Paris: UNESCO.

Radio Bahrain Commerical Rate Card Number 5. Provided by Radio Bahrain.

"Radio and Colour Television Advertising Rates Effective January, 1980." Dubai.

Radio Corporation of America. 1969. *Summary Report of Propagation and Coverage as Related to Dammam, Saudi Arabia TV Station*. 27 June. Livorno, Italy.

"Radio Jordan English Service." 1979. Schedule for July, August, September.

Radio Jordan Frequency Schedule. 1979. Supplied by Hashemite Broadcasting Service, Engineering Services Department. 1 June.

Radio Station Peace and Progress. n.d.

Ragheb, Mousa Eid, and Haddad, Yehya. 1979. *A Pilot Study on the Opinions of Certain Categories of Citizens of the Establishment of a Second Television Channel (1978)*. Kuwait: Ministry of Information.

Rand McNally Illustrated World Atlas. 1975. New York: Rand McNally.

Rawya, Ammar. 1965. "A Historical and Cultural Analysis of Broadcasting in the United Arab Republic 1932–1962." M.A. thesis, San Francisco State College.

Report on the Near East Farm Broadcasting Seminar. 1963. Cairo, 2 March–5 April. Rome: FAO.

Republic of Algeria. 1970, 1974, 1978. *Plan Quadrennial 1970–1973; Plan Quadrennial 1974–1977; Plan Quadrennial 1978–1981*. Algiers: Secretariat d'Etat au Plan.

Republic of Tunisia: A Communications Factbook. 1964. Report R-87-64, June. Washington, D.C.: United States Information Agency.

Revue de l'UER. 1979. July.

Richardson, David R. 1979. "Malta: The Rock That May Trip Qadhafi." *U.S. News and World Report*. 87, no. 4. (23 July): 40–41.

Rolo, Charles J. 1941. *Radio Goes to War*. New York: G. P. Putnam's Sons.

Rubin, Barry. 1975–76. "The Media and the Middle East." *Middle East Review*, Winter, pp. 28–32.

Rubin, Ronald. 1973. "Israel's Foreign Information Program." *Gazette* 19: 65–78.

Rugh, William A. 1975. "Arab Media and Politics During the October War." *The Middle East Journal* 29 (Summer): 310–28.

————. 1979. *The Arab Press: News Media and Political Process in the Arab World.* Syracuse, N.Y.: Syracuse University Press.

————. 1980. "Saudi Mass Media and Society in the Faisal Era." In *King Faisal and the Modernisation of Saudi Arabia,* edited by Willard A. Beling. Boulder, Col.: Westview Press.

Said, Ebtisam. "Qatar Broadcasting Service: 1980/1981." Qatar: Ministry of Information.

"Saudi Arabian Broadcasting: A Synopsis." 1980. Supplied by the Office of the Assistant Deputy Minister for Radio and TV, Riyadh, Saudi Arabia.

"Saudi Arabian Television: A Synopsis." Supplied by the Office of the Assistant Deputy Minister for Radio and Television. Riyadh, Saudi Arabia.

Schmidt, Dana Adams. 1961. "Kassim Dedicates Radio Station, First of Soviet's Iraqi Projects." *New York Times,* 17 July, p. 7.

Shalaby, Ahmed A. 1979. "The Arab World: An Eligible Case for Collective Self-Reliance." In *International Foundation for Developmental Alternatives, Dossier 10,* pp. 3–11.

Sharabi, Hisham. 1966. *Nationalism and Revolution in the Arab World.* Princeton, N.J.: D. Van Nostrand Company.

Shobaili, Abdulrahman S. 1971. "A Historical and Analytical Study of Broadcasting and Press in Saudi Arabia." Ph.D. dissertation, Ohio State University.

Shouby, E. 1951. "The Influence of the Arabic Language on the Psychology of the Arabs." *Middle East Journal* 5, no. 3 (Summer).

Shummo, Ali. 1977. "Communication Delivery Services in Developing Nations." Paper delivered at international Institute of Communications Conference, Washington, D.C. September.

Smith, Anthony. 1973. *The Shadow in the Cave: The Broadcaster, the Audience and the State.* London: Allen and Unwin.

Smith, Richard M. 1974. "Censorship in the Middle East." *Columbia Journalism Review,* January-February, pp. 43–49.

Sound on Television Broadcasting in the Overseas Territories, Handbook 1960. 1960. London, England: Information Department, Colonial Office.

Souriau, Christiane. 1975. "La Libye Moderne." In *La Libye Nouvelle: Rupture et Continuité.* Paris: Centre de Recherches et d'Etudes sur les Sociétés Méditerranéennes.

Special Committee for the UN/Libyan Institute for Radio and Wire and Wireless Communications. 1971. Operational plan (draft). In Arabic.

"State of Qatar: Qatar T.V." Doha, Qatar: Ministry of Information.

Sudan Echo. 1965. "Radio and Television Advertising in the Sudan." 6 July.

Sudan Television. "Extension of Television Service—Sudan Centralized Regional Rural TV Programmes Project, 1978–1980." Khartoum, Sudan.

————. "The First Survey of Television: 1968–1969." In Arabic. Translated portions provided by United States Information Agency, Khartoum Office.

Sudanow. 1979a. "Radio." October, p. 70.

————. 1979b. "Television." October, pp. 69–70.

SUNA-Daily Bulletin. 1979. "On the Iraqi News Agency Allegations." 3180, 10 October, p. 7.

Syrian Television Schedule. 1979. Supplied by Syrian Television.

Tanner, Harry. 1975. "Egyptian Take-Over of Voice of Palestine Broadcasts Is Indicated." *New York Times,* 12 September, p. 3.

Tawffik, Tomader. 1980a. "Television in Egypt." Paper delivered at Annenberg School of Communications World Communication Conference, Philadelphia, Pa. 12 May.

"Telecommunications—MEED Special Report." 1977 *Middle East Economic Digest.*

Télé-Orient Program Schedule. 1972. Supplied by Télé-Orient, Beirut, Lebanon. 3–9 April.

Thomas, Ruth. 1972. *Broadcasting and Democracy in France.* London: Bradford University Press.

Time. 1958. "Voice of Venom." 3 March, pp. 28–30.

Tracy, William. 1979. "Sesame Opens." *Aramco World Magazine.* September-October, pp. 9–17.

Tunisia: A Country Study. 1979. Washington, D.C.: U.S. Government Printing Office.

T.V. in the Gulf States. 1979. Riyadh, Saudi Arabia: Gulfvision.

UNESCO. 1975. *Arab States Media Innovation System.* Paris: UNESCO.

————. 1973. *Management and Planning of New Systems of Communication: Conclusions Drawn from an Inventory of Communication Resources in Tunisia.* Paris: UNESCO.

————. 1949. *Press, Film, Radio.* Paris: UNESCO.

————. 1951. *Press, Film, Radio.* Paris: UNESCO.

————. 1965. *World Radio and Television.* Paris: UNESCO.

UNESCO Statistical Yearbook 1977. 1978. Paris: UNESCO.

United Nations Statistical Yearbook 1978. 1979. New York: United Nations.

United States Department of State. 1964. "Saudi Arabia, Establishment of Television System in Saudi Arabia." *United States Treaties and Other International Agreements.* Washington, D.C.: U.S. Government Printing Office.

United States Information Agency (USIA). 1960. "International Radio Broadcasting in the United Arab Republic." Research Note 32-60. 1 July.

————. 1961b. "UAR Reorganizes and Increases its International Radio Broadcasting Services." Research Note 21–61. 10 August.

————. 1975b. "VOA Audience Estimate for Israel 1974." E-15-75. 16 December.

United States Information Agency, Office of Research. 1973. "Media Habits of Priority Groups in Saudi Arabia—Part II Appendix." Research Report R-20-73A, 30 August. Washington, D.C.

———. 1975a. "VOA-CAAP Audience Estimate for Kuwait 1974." Research Report E-7-75, 16 June.

United States Information Agency, Office of Research and Analysis. 1961a. "UAR Broadcasting." Research Note 19-61, 8 August.

United States Information Agency, Office of Research and Assessment. 1974. "Media Habits and VOA Listening among Priority Audiences in Bahrain." Research Report R-1-74, 27 March.

United States International Communication Agency (USICA), Office of Research and Evaluation. 1978a. "Listening to International Radio Stations, Including VOA, and Perceptions and Interests of Radio Listeners in Urban Sudan." Research Report E-17-78, 16 August.

———. 1978b. Listening to International Radio Stations, Including VOA, and Perceptions and Interests of Radio Audiences in Urban Jordan." Research Report E-20-78, 12 September.

———. 1978c. "Listening to International Radio Stations, Including VOA, and Listener Reactions and Program Interests in Urban Egypt (1977)." Research Report E-23-78, 6 October.

Urquhart, Brian. 1972. *Hammarskjold.* New York: Alfred A. Knopf.

USAFE Television Story. 1955. From the files of the Office of Information for the Armed Forces, OASD (M&RA). 13 December. Washington, D.C.: Department of Defense.

VHF Television Assignments obtained for Aden at the African VHF/UHF Broadcasting Conference, Geneva, 1963. Document written by British authorities.

Voss, Harald. 1962. *Rundfunk und Fernsehen in Afrika.* Koln: Verlag/Deutscher Wirtschaftsdienst, GmbH.

Walpole, Norman C., *et al.* 1971. *Area Handbook for Saudi Arabia.* Washington, D.C.: U.S. Government Printing Office.

Watson, Paul S. 1965. *Operation Report.* Jidda, Saudi Arabia: NBCI.

Wilbur, Donald N. 1969. *United Arab Republic: Egypt.* New Haven, Conn.: Hraf Press.

Williams, Kenneth. 1933. *Ibn Sa'ud: The Puritan King of Arabia.* London: Jonathan Cape.

Wireless World. 1934. "Broadcasting from Jerusalem." 17 August, p. 128.

———. 1935. "England in Egypt." 4 January, p. 15.

———. 1936. "Palestine Calling." 1 May, p. 424.

Wood, Richard E. 1979. "Language Choice in Transnational Radio Broadcasting." *Journal of Communication* 29, no. 2 (Spring): 112–23.

World Bank Atlas, 1978. 1978. Washington, D.C.: World Bank.

World Radio Handbook. 1957. Copenhagen, Denmark: Lindorffsalle Hellerup.

WRTH (World Radio-TV Handbook). 1955. Edited by O. Lund Johansen. Copenhagen: Johansen.

WRTH (World Radio-TV Handbook). 1970. Edited by J. M. Frost. New York: Billboard Publications.

————. 1980.

WYFR International Program Schedule. 1979. 2 September–3 November.

Ysami, Shibli-L-A'. 1977. *The Ba'th Party: The Period of its Foundation (1940–49)*. Baghdad, Iraq: Ministry of Information and Culture.

Zakya, Daoud. 1979. "Le véritable débat sur l'information." *Lamalif* 104 (February).

Zimmerman, John. 1973–74. "Radio Propaganda in the Arab-Israeli War 1948." *Wiener Library Bulletin* 30–31: 2–8.

Personal Communications

Abdu, Mohammed. Acting Chief Radio and Television Engineer, Egyptian Radio-Television Federation. Personal interview. Cairo, Egypt. 29 October 1979.

Abdullah, Tawffik. Controller, Commercial Section, Egyptian Radio-Television Federation. Personal interview. Cairo, Egypt. 26 October 1979.

Adrian, Otto. Head, English Language Broadcasts, Radio Prague. Personal communication. Prague, Czechoslovakia. 29 August 1975.

Adwan, Nawaf. Director, Arab States Broadcasting Union Center for Radio and Television Research. Personal interview. Baghdad, Iraq. 17 January 1980.

Ahmed, Hassan. Radio Controller General, Radio Dubai. Personal interview. Dubai, U.A.E. 7 January 1980.

Al-Fieli, Rida. Director, Kuwait Television. Personal interview. Kuwait City, Kuwait. 16 January 1980.

Ali, Jawad. Director, Iraqi Radio Broadcasting. Personal interview. Baghdad, Iraq. 19 January 1980.

Al-Mowaled, Fawzia. Director, People's Program. Personal interview. Cairo, Egypt. 10 August 1974.

Al-Sharif, Essam. Director, Commercial Sector, Syrian Television. Personal interview. Damascus, Syria. 7 November 1979.

Al-Warthan, Othman M. Manager, Dammam Television Station. Personal interview. Dammam, Saudi Arabia. 29 December 1979.

Al Yusuf, Ibrahim. Director General, The Arabian Gulf States Joint Program Production Institution. Personal interview. Kuwait City, Kuwait. 15 January 1980.

Amin, Mustapha. Editor, *Al-Akbar Al-Youm*. Personal interview. Cairo, Egypt. 12 August 1974.

Amoako, Ayo. Head of Management Services, Nigerian Broadcasting Corporation. Personal communication. Lagos, Nigeria. 24 April 1975.

Annis, Ahmed. Under Secretary for External Information and Official Egyptian Government Spokesman. Personal interview. Cairo, Egypt. 12 August 1974.

Ashfoura, Osama. Director of Engineering, Hashemite Broadcasting Service. Personal interview. Amman, Jordan. 4 November 1979.

Ashworth, Anthony. Advisor to Minister of Information. Personal interview. Muscat, Oman. 9 January 1980.

Bang, Hans. Agency for International Development. Personal interview. Cairo, Egypt. 29 October 1979.

Bar-Haim, Shaul. Advisor, Israeli Broadcasting Authority, Former Director of Arabic Broadcasts, Voice of Israel. Personal interview. Jerusalem. 26 January 1980.

Bellatt, Fouad. Director General, Syrian Radio and Television. Personal interview. Damascus, Syria. 8 November 1979.

Bolbois, Henri. Office of the Director General, Radio Monte Carlo. Personal communication, transmitting "Note sur la 'Société Monégasque d'Exploitation et d'Etudes de Radiodiffusion.' " Monte Carlo, Monaco. 17 April 1975.

Butt, Shamsuddin. Controller, External Services, Pakistan Broadcasting Corporation. Personal communication. Rawalpindi, Pakistan. 1 August 1975.

Choi, Chang Hoon. Chief, Overseas English Broadcasting Division, Radio Korea. Personal communication. Seoul, Korea. 30 June 1979.

Corcoran, Marilyn. International Business Associates. Personal interview. Cairo, Egypt. 27 January 1980.

Edison, Edward. Hammett and Edison, Incorporated. Personal communication. San Francisco, California. 28 August 1979.

Edwards, Jim. Public Information Office, ELWA. Personal communication. Monrovia, Liberia. 22 August 1979.

Eilts, Herman Frederick. Former United States Ambassador to Egypt. Personal interview. Cairo, Egypt. 27 July 1974.

El-Kashlan, El-Garhi. Chairman, Broadcast Engineering Section, Egyptian Radio-Television Federation. Personal interview. Cairo, Egypt. 10 August 1974.

El Sheki, Saleh Ahmed. Director of Public Affairs, PRBC. Personal interviews. Tripoli, Libya. June, July 1975.

El Shweikh, Rashid Tawfik. PRBC Staff member. Personal interviews. Athens, Ohio. May, June, July, August 1980.

Fakery, Mohammed. Chief of Planning and Projects, Ministry of Information. Personal interview. Baghdad, Iraq. 24 January 1980.

Fankhauser, W. Press Officer, Swiss Radio International. Personal communication. Berne, Switzerland. 3 August 1979.

Frackiewicz, Zdzislaw. Editor, Polskie Radio. Personal communication. Warsaw, Poland. 12 October 1979.

Glubb, Lieut. General Sir John. Personal communication. Sussex, England. 17 April 1973.

Gustafsson, Bengt. Director, Radio Sweden. Personal communication. Stockholm, Sweden. 17 September 1979.

Haffar, Awater. Director, Public Relations, Syrian Radio and Television. Personal interview. Damascus, Syria. 7 November 1979.

Hamilton, George. Vice President, RTV International. Personal interview. Beirut, Lebanon. 24 May 1972.

Hart, Parker T. President, Middle East Institute. Personal communication. Washington, D.C. 23 December 1970.

Helbach, J. C. Weltcamp. External Relations Department, Radio Nederland. Personal communication. Hilversum, Holland. 8 September 1979.

Hellyer, Peter. Advisor, Foreign Language Broadcasting, U.A.E. Radio. Personal interviews. Abu Dhabi. 9, 10 January 1980.

Helwani, Ahmed. Director General, Syrian Radio and Television. Personal interview. Damascus, Syria. 3 March 1977.

Hijab, Abdul Salam. News Director, Syrian Television. Personal interview. Damascus, Syria. 7 November 1979.

Hopkins, Arthur H. Voice of America Public Information Officer. Personal communication. Washington, D.C. 15 April 1975.

Ibrahim, Mohammad. Acting Director, Qatar Television. Personal communication. Doha, Qatar. 16 October 1980.

Ismail, Salal. Assistant Director Kuwait Radio and Director of Foreign Programs. Personal interview. Kuwait City, Kuwait. 16 January 1980.

Jarrar, Farouk. Program Director, Jordan Television. Personal interview. Amman, Jordan. 5 November 1979.

Kader, Salah Abdel. Secretary General, Arab States Broadcasting Union. Personal interview. Cairo, Egypt. 27 October 1979.

Kandil, Hamdy. Radio-TV Expert, UNESCO. Personal interview. Cairo, Egypt. 14 August 1974.

Karkoush, Antone. Deputy Chief Engineer, Syrian Radio and Television. Personal interview. Damascus, Syria. 8 November 1979.

Kazmi, M. A. Controller, External Services, Pakistan Broadcasting Corporation. Personal communication. Islamabad, Pakistan. 17 July 1979.

Khoury, Ibrahim. Program Director, "The Voice of Lebanon." Personal interview. Ashrafieh, Beirut, Lebanon. 13 November 1979.

King, Everett L., Jr. Manager, International Marketing, Continental Electronics. Personal communication. Dallas, Texas. 18 July 1979.

Kouhakja, Mickel. Director Arabic Service, Syrian Radio. Personal interview. Damascus, Syria. 7 November 1979.

Mahrns, Abdel Moez A. General Controller of Research and Statistics, Egyptian Radio-Television Federation. Personal interview. Cairo, Egypt. 11 August 1974.

Mansell, G. E. H. Managing Director, BBC External Broadcasting. Personal communication with attachments. London, England. 1 May 1975.
————. Deputy Director-General and Managing Director, External Broadcasting, British Broadcasting Corporation. Personal communication, with "The Arabic Service Over Forty Years." London, England. 16 July 1979.

Megri, Abdullah. Director of Programming, PRBC. Personal interviews. Tripoli, Libya. June, July 1975.

Monsour, Abdul Aziz. Director, Kuwait Radio. Personal interview. Kuwait City, Kuwait. 16 January 1980.

Mubarak, Abdul Hadi. Director of Radio Programs, U.A.E. Radio. Personal interview. Abu Dhabi. 8 January 1980.

Nasser, Salah Bin. Assistant Deputy Minister for Radio and Television, Ministry of Information. Personal interview. Riyadh, Saudi Arabia. 3 January 1980.

Nawwab, Ismail. Director ARAMCO Public Relations Department. Personal interview. Dhahran, Saudi Arabia. 29 December 1979.

Odeh, Adnan Abu. Minister of Information. Personal interview. Amman, Jordan. 9 March 1977.
————. Personal interview. Amman, Jordan. 5 November 1979.

Okesanya, Ayo. Head of Management Services, Nigerian Broadcasting Corporation. Personal communication. Lagos, Nigeria. 24 April 1975.

Oun, Amer Salem. Director of Planning and Training, PRBC. Personal interviews. Tripoli, Libya. June, July 1975. Athens, Ohio. December 1976.

Patel, Adi. Instructional Resources Center, University of Delaware. Personal interview. Newark, Delaware. 14 October 1980. (Mr. Patel was employed by Aden television prior to independence.)

Radio Station Peace and Progress. Personal communication. Moscow, U.S.S.R. 22 December 1975.

Radio Vaticana. Propaganda Office. Personal communication. Città del Vaticano. 13 July 1979.

Radiotelevisione Italiana. Il Segretario di Radazione, Direzione Servizi Giornalistici e Programmi per l'Estero. Personal communication. Rome, Italy. 19 October 1979.

Rahman, Hassan Ahmed Abdel. Director General, Sudan Television. Personal interview. Khartoum, Sudan. 21 October 1979a.
————. Personal interview. Khartoum, Sudan. 22 October 1979b.

Rahman, Samiha Abdul. Director of Television Programming, Egyptian Radio-Television Federation. Personal interview. Cairo, Egypt. 7 August 1974.

Ramsay, John M. Operations Manager, Radio Canada International. Personal communication. Montreal, Canada. 12 September 1979.

Regnier, Jean Pierre. Commercial and Marketing Manager, Radio Monte Carlo Middle East. Personal interview. Paris, France. 1 February 1980.

Reichard, Herbert. Chief of Near and Middle East Department, Deutsche Welle. Personal communications. Koln, West Germany. 13 August, 11 September 1979.

Rizk, Charles. President, Télé-Liban. Personal interview. Beirut, Lebanon. 12 November 1979.

Robertson, Lewis. General Manager, Dubai Television. Personal interview. Dubai, U.A.E. 7 January 1980.

Rugh, Andrea B. Personal interview. Cairo, Egypt. 28 January 1980.

Rummelsburg, David. Radio Berlin International. Personal communication. Berlin, East Germany. 10 April 1975.

Rushty, Ali. Director of International and Foreign Language Broadcasting, Egyptian Radio-Television Federation. Personal interview. Cairo, Egypt. 29 October 1979.

Salheen, Mohammed. Director General of Radio Broadcasting, Ministry of Information. Personal interview. Khartoum, Sudan. 2 February 1977.

Shaar, Khudr. Director, Arab States Broadcasting Union Training Center. Personal interview. Damascus, Syria. 7 November 1979.

Shaban, Hassan. Director General for Planning and Research, Radio-TV Federation. Personal interview. Cairo, Egypt. 8 August 1974.

Shaban, Mohammed. Chairman, Egyptian Radio Broadcasting, Egyptian Radio-Television Federation. Personal interview. Cairo, Egypt. 14 August 1974.

Sharf, Mohammed. Director General for Foreign-Language Programming, Egyptian Radio-Television Federation. Personal interview. Cairo, Egypt. 6 August 1974.

Shaw, Indris Ahmad. Head, Overseas Service, Radio Television Malaysia. Personal communication. Kuala Lumpur, Malaysia. 16 April 1975.

Shobaili, Abdulrahman S. Director General of Television. Personal interview. Riyadh, Saudi Arabia. 20 May 1972.

Shummo, Ali. Minister of State for Youth and Sports, former Minister of Information. Personal interview. Khartoum, Sudan. 21 October 1979.

Siyabi, Salam. Director General of Radio and Television Broadcasting. Personal interview. Muscat, Oman. 9 January 1980.

Skowrowski, Michael B. Chief Engineer, ARAMCO Radio and Television. Personal interview. Dhahran, Saudi Arabia. 29 December 1979.

Sobh, Massoud. Télé-Orient. Personal interview. Beirut, Lebanon. 3 April 1971.

Srivastava, G. P. L. External Services Division, All India Radio. Personal communication. New Delhi, India. 28 June 1979.

Stepanova, Eugenia. North American Service Radio Moscow. Personal communication. Moscow, U.S.S.R. 29 May 1975.

————. Personal communication. Moscow, U.S.S.R. 19 July 1979.

Suliman, Ahmed. Manager, Radio Bahrain. Personal interview. Manama, Bahrain. 13 January 1980.

Sweiden, Mohamed Saleh. Director, Overseas Broadcasting, The Voice of Friendship and Solidarity. Personal communication. Tripoli, Libya. 2 January 1980.

Tawffik, Tomader. Director, Egyptian Television. Personal interview. Philadelphia, Pennsylvania. 13 May 1980b.

Thiik, Ambrose Riny. Regional Minister of Information, Southern Region, Sudan. Personal interview. London, England. 12 September 1979.

Triana, Maria Montero. Head of Correspondence Department, Radio Habana Cuba. Personal communication. Habana, Cuba. 24 October 1979.

Tuch, Hans. Acting Director, Voice of America. Personal communication. Washington, D.C. 27 July 1979.

Warugaba, Cosma. Deputy Director of Broadcasting and Television. Personal communication. Kampala, Uganda. 30 August 1979.

West, Harold. Chief of Construction Division, United States Army Corps of Engineers. Personal interview. Livorno, Italy. 28 March 1972.

Yasmie, Walid. Manager, Télé-Management. Personal interview. Beirut, Lebanon. 12 November 1979.

Yousef, Abdul Amir. Director, Iraqi Television. Personal interview. Baghdad, Iraq. 19 January 1980.

Yousef, Ahmed. Director, Arab States Broadcasting Union Technical Center. Personal interview. Khartoum, Sudan. 24 October 1979.

Zada, Jawad. Director, Radio Jordan, English Service. Personal interview. Amman, Jordan. 4 November 1979a.

————. Personal interview. Amman, Jordan. 5 November 1979b.

Index

Aden Voice of the Oman Revolution, 102, 267

Agency for International Development (AID): loans to Egyptian Radio-Television Federation, 32 (Table 4); loan to Egypt, 31; in the Sudan, 53

AJL-TV, 126

al-Bahri, Yunus, 236, 240

Algeria, 170–83; financing of broadcasting in, 180

Algeria, radio in: establishment of national service (RTA), 173; first broadcasts of, by the French, 172; foreign-language services, English/Spanish, 181; International Service, 179; western programming and, 182

Algeria, television in: first broadcasts of, 172; western programming and, 182

American Broadcasting Company (ABC), 69

Arabian Gulf States. *See* Gulf States

Arabian Gulf States Joint Program Production Institution, 168

Arab League Boycott Office: RCA, 38, 81, 131; Saudi Arabian circumvention, 131

ARABSAT: headquarters, 277–78; in Saudi Arabia, 133

Arab States Broadcasting Union (ASBU), 167, 181, 210, 273–76

ARAMCO: broadcasting in Eastern province of Saudi Arabia, 122; dual language broadcasts of, 141; early television station, 33, 127; program subtitling in Lebanon, 37; radio services of, 141; television program censorship and, 141

Associated Business Consultants (ABC). *See* RTV International

Audience research, 9; in Egypt, 39; in Jordan, 90; in Kuwait, 116; in Morocco, 211; in Saudi Arabia, 86, 143–44; in the Sudan, 57; on BBC programs, 240; on RMC programs, 239; on VOA programs, 57, 240

AVCO, 132

Bahrain, 146–51; importance of Saudi Arabian market to broadcasting in, 148

Bahrain, radio in: first broadcasts of, 147

British Broadcasting Corporation (BBC), 5; Arabic Service, 239–40; first broadcast of, 235; relay from Masirah Island (Oman), 163; relay from South Yemen, 100; use of personnel in Aden, 101

Broadcasting in Arabic from non-Arab countries, 30 (Table 2), 237–38 (Table 16)

Broadcasting, educational/instructional: in Algeria, 182 (Figure 5); in Egypt, 22, 45; in the Gulf States, 168; in Iraq, 113; in Morocco, 207–9; in Saudi Arabia, 138; in the Sudan, 55 (Table 8); in Tunisia, 225–27

Broadcasting equipment suppliers:

—Belin (Algeria), 181

—Britain (Egypt), 15

—Continental Electric: Egypt, 31; Jordan, 89; Saudi Arabia, 124

—Fernsehen (Algeria), 181

—Harris Corporation (Egypt), 31

—ITT (Saudi Arabia), 121

—Marconi: Jordan, 91; Kuwait, 117; Saudi Arabia, 120

—Phillips (the Sudan), 53

—Pye: Algeria, 181; Iraq, 111